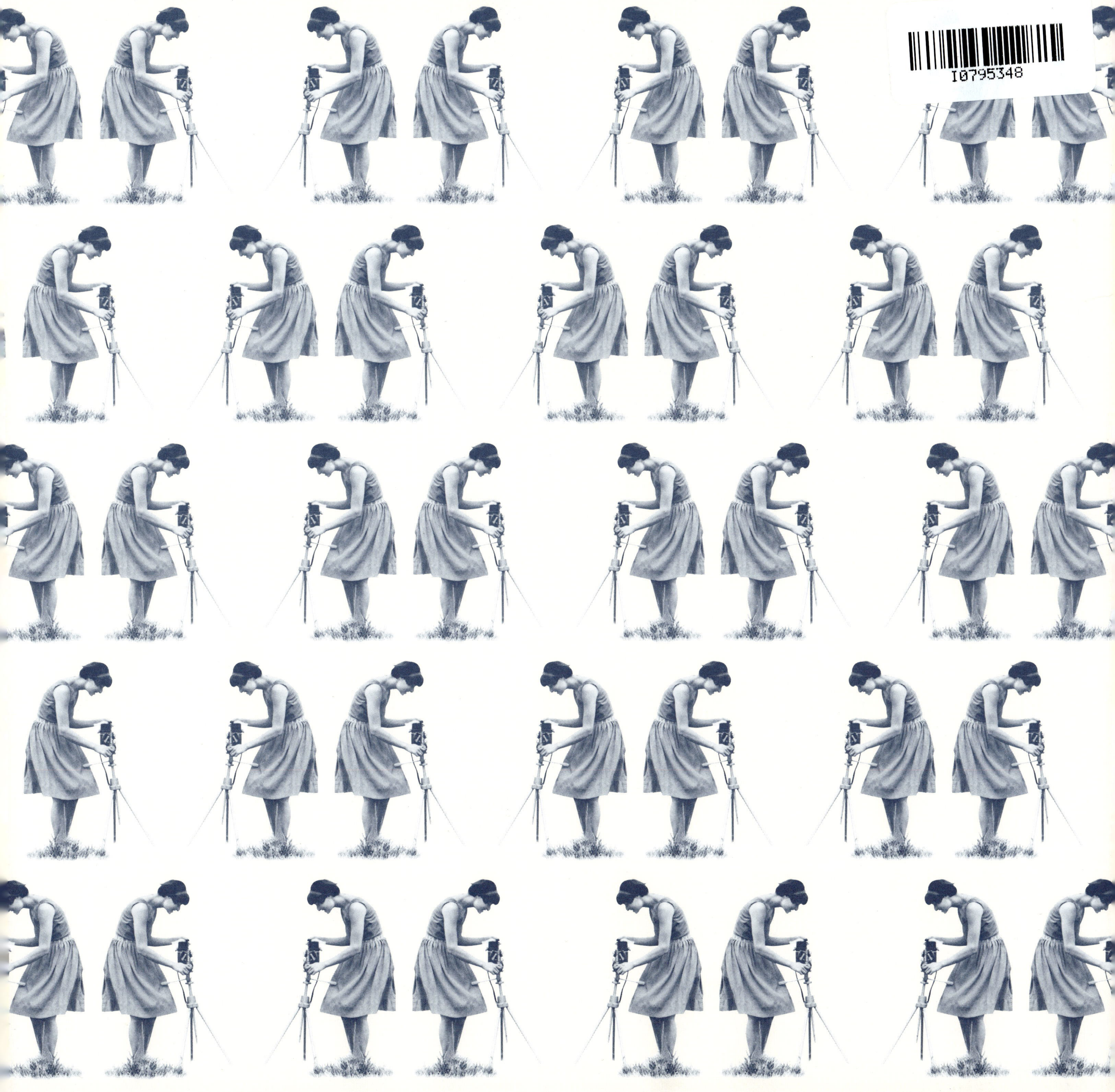

Being in Pictures

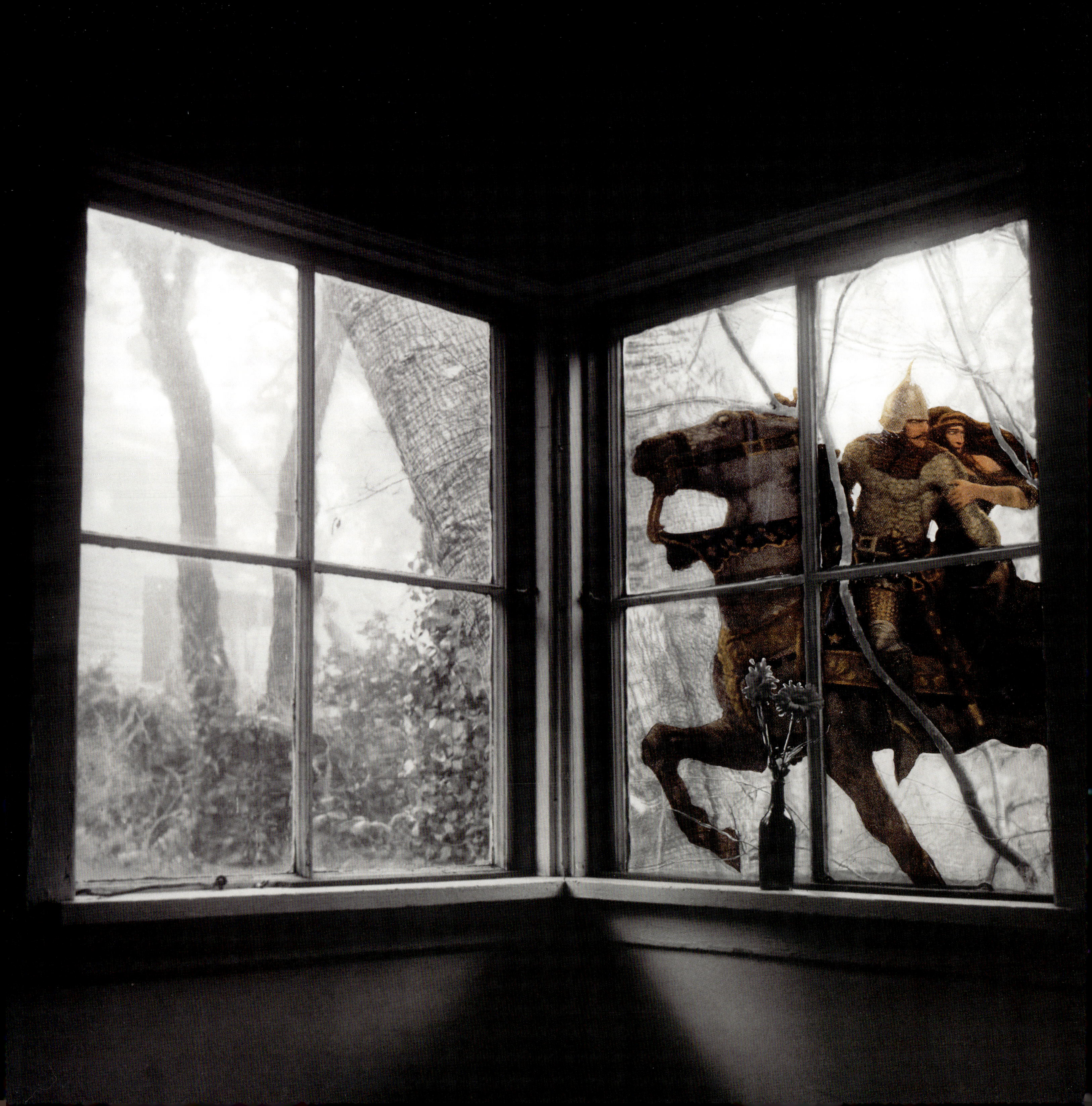

Joanne Leonard **Being in Pictures** An Intimate Photo Memoir

Foreword by Lucy R. Lippard

The University of Michigan Press • Ann Arbor

Published in the United States of America by
The University of Michigan Press
Manufactured in China
∞ Printed on acid-free paper

2011 2010 2009 2008 4 3 2 1

A CIP catalog record for this book is available from the British Library.
Library of Congress Cataloging-in-Publication Data

Leonard, Joanne.
Being in pictures : An intimate photo memoir / Joanne Leonard.
p. cm.
ISBN-13: 978-0-472-11402-3 (cloth : alk. paper)
ISBN-10: 0-472-11402-6 (cloth : alk. paper) 1. Portrait photography. 2. Photography, Artistic. 3. Leonard, Joanne. 4. Women photographers—United States—Biography. I. Title.
TR680.L3824 2007
779.092--dc22

[B] 2006036429

Design by Savitski Design

Endpapers: Photograph of Joanne Leonard by Dr. Palmer Beasley, 1967

To Julia Marjorie Leonard,

my beloved and dazzling daughter

Foreword

Doubling Back

This book is a visual/textual autobiography that expands and enriches almost forty years of Joanne Leonard's life in photography by putting it all in context. Those of us who have followed her work for much of that time are now given a chance to see it all together—a whole, though hardly completed, life. This is the story of a woman with two great loves—her art and her family—and how she has performed the balancing act so many of us have confronted, wondering, like all of us, where the successes and the failures really lay.

Leonard's art is an undisputed success. Within the framework she calls "intimate documentary," she has proved that it is possible to move from "the smallest picture in the show" to a twenty-two-foot collage, missing very few beats in between. Along with technical challenges and discoveries, she tells a family story (made up of family stories) by braiding the lives of four generations of women—her grandmother; her mother; herself and her two sisters (one of them her twin); and her beloved daughter, whom she bore and raised as a deliberately single mother. The Jewish element in the story comes late but resoundingly with the *Reel Family* scroll (2000), inspired by a wallet of anti-Semitic clippings, which fills the empty nest left when Leonard loses her accomplished mother to dementia and death and her daughter to her own life.

It is a story with its share of personal pain in which creative joys triumph, in which youthful romantic expectations go unmet and artistic achievements exceed expectations. It is a feminist story par excellence, and its guardian angel is the spirit of collage, which hovers over so much art by women. By allowing for a "both/and" rather than an "either/or" approach—especially appropriate to Leonard's fusion of the stark and the lyrical—collage nourishes the layering, veiling, and contradictions that inform her work. The 1973 miscarriage collages, though still not well enough known, were a feminist landmark. Her striking Vietnam collages, in which the war intrudes into domestic life, also deserve to be more visible. From the "committed documentarian" of the 1960s in Oakland to the adventurous photo-collagist of the 1970s on, Leonard has reached into the cosmos that so often figures in her imagery.

Constantly resurfacing throughout this book is the notion of doubling and bonding, connections and separations. The 2001 destruction of the "twin towers"—one falling as the other still stands; the second falling to join the first—offers a broader context for personal musings on these themes, as collage again comes to the rescue, reconnecting the fragments. As we watch Leonard's oeuvre unfold sequentially, we can trace the images—mothers and babies, mothers and daughters, sleepers and dreamers, children and memories, the teapot and one or two teacups, loneliness and companionship. The power of these images lies not merely in personal honesty and expressive talent but in the artist's clear-eyed acknowledgment of multiple truths. *— Lucy R. Lippard*

Contents

Prologue

One's whole notion of what art is all about can change in the process of examining women artists. . . . Feminism is like a key that unlocks many of the closed compartments in the mind, compartments created by one's "natural" expectations which now have to be revised, cast aside, sorted out again. — Linda Nochlin

Toward the end of my mother's life, her memory began to fail. My sister took her to doctors for possible diagnosis. A neurologist's report begins with a humorously incongruous list of female family traits: "There is a family history of allergies, twinning, prematurely gray hair, uterine fibroids . . . and artistic talent." I can't think of a better way to suggest the dual nature of this book: as personal as medical histories yet with a public in mind of those who might be both intrigued and captured, as I am, by the prospect of exploring women's lives through pictures and stories.

Through my work as an artist, I've discovered that the realms of the personal and the public are rarely as separate as I once imagined. Writing this book clearly revealed to me how things in the public sphere such as the women's movement have stimulated, provoked, and even enabled my work. On the other hand, my personal photographs showing the highs and lows of daily life have made their way into the public realm through publications, exhibitions, and teaching. My most well-known work, *Romanticism Is Ultimately Fatal,* is an image I made at one of the lowest moments of my life, but this image transformed from private to public when it appeared in a major art history textbook.

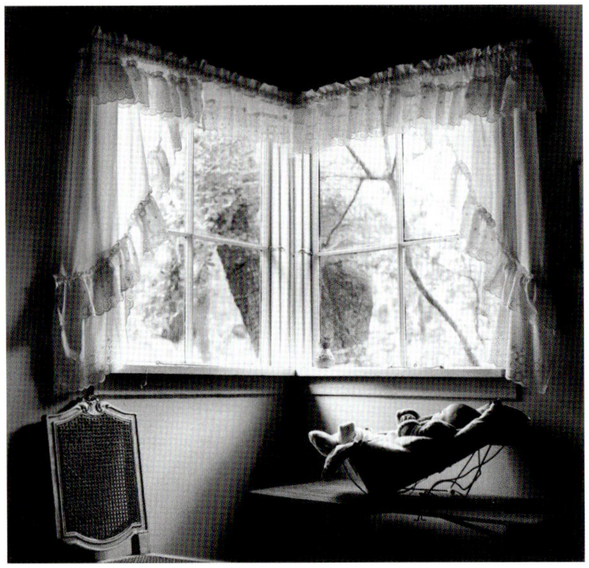

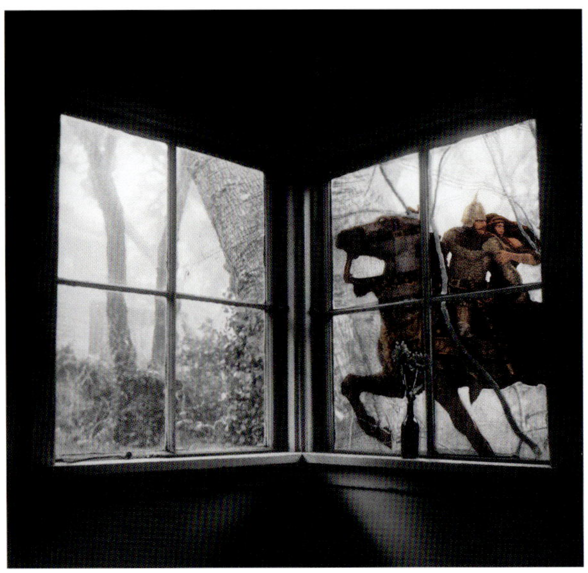

I didn't start out to become a photographer. My path led me from upper-middle-class Los Angeles, where I was born, to the impoverished streets of West Oakland, where I first took up my camera with conviction. This outcome was nothing I'd imagined as the twin daughter of an aristocratic and artistic Jewish mother and a musical, erudite European father who was a refugee from the Nazis.When I entered college, I had pictured a liberal education followed by romance, marriage with children, and maybe a job on the side. I never imagined becoming a photographer, professor, and feminist or inventing my own visual forms of "intimate documentary." The tensions between realism and idealization, photography and fantasy, have been present throughout my adult life, as they are in this book.

Top: *Julia's Morning,* silver print, 1975

Bottom: *Romanticism Is Ultimately Fatal,* fine grain positive transparency, selectively opaqued, over collage, 10 inches × 12 inches, 1972

Opposite: Joanne in mirror (self-portrait), silver print, 1960s

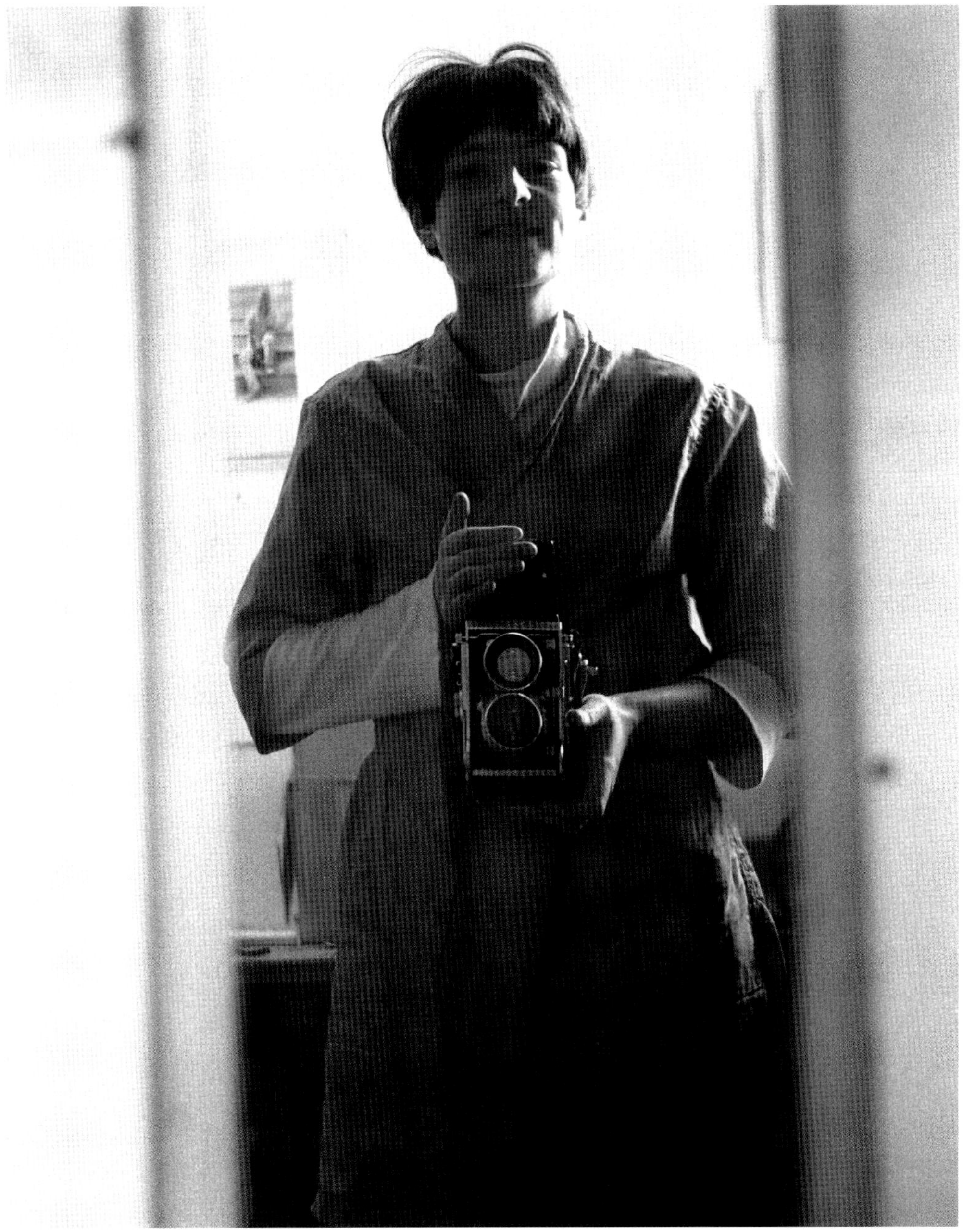

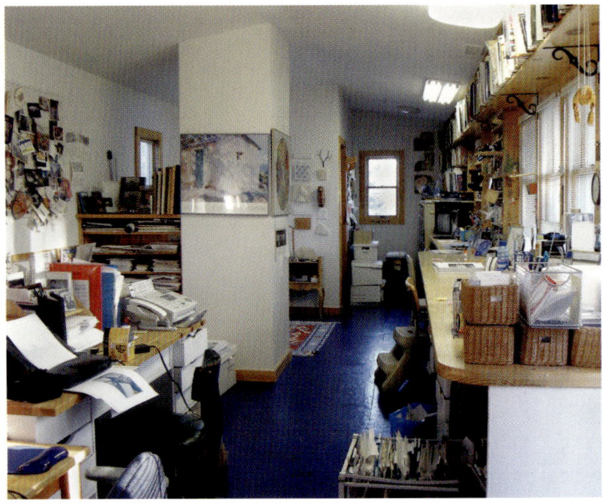

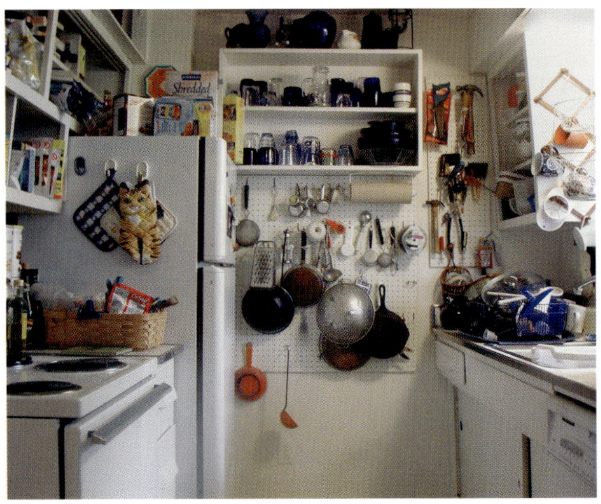

It's not easy for anyone to mark the moment of realization: "*Now!* I've become an artist." Especially in a case like mine (I never majored in art or got a degree in it), becoming an artist might seem to have happened by accident. A colleague at the University of Michigan once told me that it wasn't for him (or me) to say whether either of us was an artist—that the definition/designation of who is an artist comes from outside oneself, from the recognition by art historians, critics, and the like. I thought that's all very well for *him* to say; men are expected to dedicate themselves to vocations and avocations, but even as a young woman, I had to take myself seriously as an artist in order to allow myself the time, money, and space for my art. In fact, looking back, I think it was that very "allowing" more than anything else that defined me as an artist; I built a darkroom and, later, a studio when I could have fixed up a kitchen.

I have taken time for my art even when that took time away from activities traditionally considered the province of women: friendships, housekeeping, maternal roles, activities for social good. Even before I knew her writings, I somehow understood Virginia Woolf's concept of a "room of her own" and that the designation "artist" is not in the first place an honor one earns after years of work; it's an attitude and a goal one takes on in order to get where one is going.

Top: Joanne's studio view, digital photograph, 1990s

Bottom: Joanne's kitchen view, digital photograph, 2004

Opposite: Lupe's kitchen, silver print, 20 inches × 24 inches, 1970s

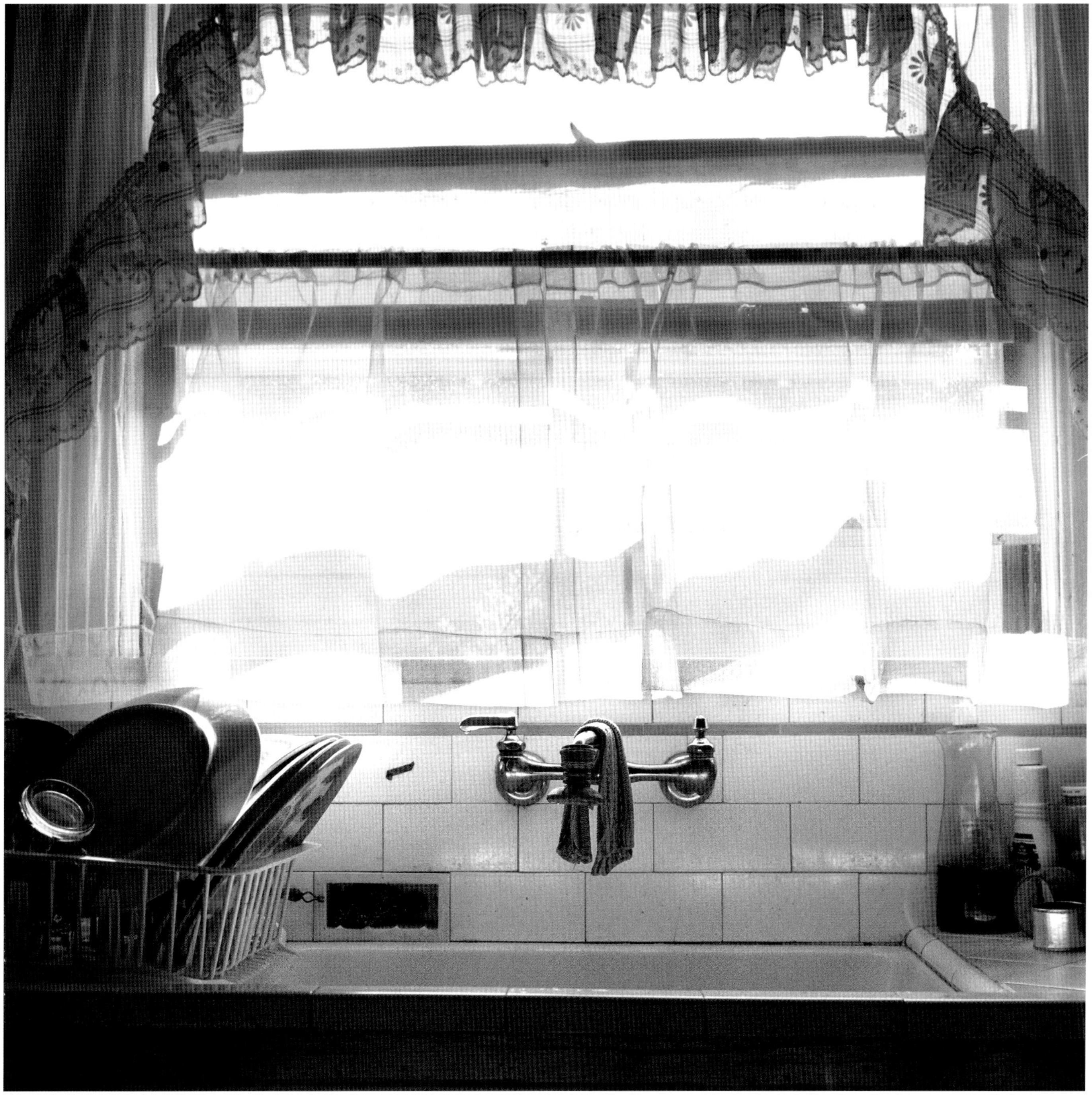

I think of this photo as my "first" photograph. The camera I had at the time was an inexpensive point-and-shoot, a Kodak Brownie camera. Serious as I was about photography, I had no early thoughts about fancy cameras. In fact, most cameras were very intimidating to me. It didn't seem to occur to me that it might be hard to take good pictures with a primitive camera.

I share credit for this photo with my friend Judy. When we noticed these children at play, I hesitated to approach them, but she eagerly ran across the street to make the picture, and this gave me the courage to follow. My life as an artist and photographer is full of such moments of indebtedness to others.

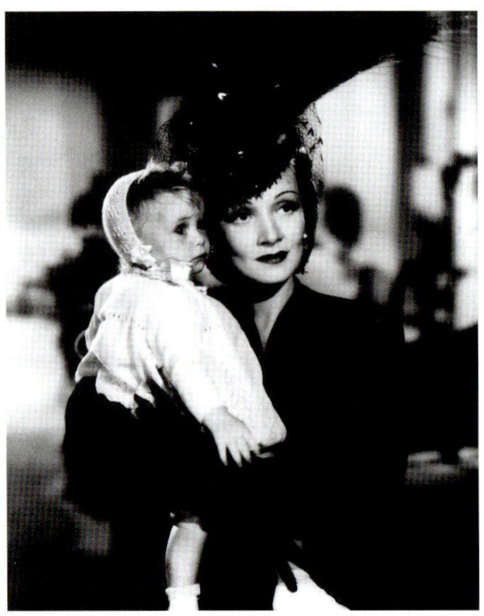

In one sense, I began "being in pictures" as an infant in front of the camera. My twin sister, Elly, and I, at the age of eleven months, alternated in playing the part of one baby in a Hollywood comedy, The Lady Is Willing, *starring Marlene Dietrich. We don't know which one of us is the baby in this photo. Ultimately we appeared in only a few scenes, and a baby boy was credited with the role. Marlene fell and broke her ankle while carrying one of us on the set, and, our mother reported, we were too traumatized and tearful on the set after that to continue our screen life.*

Above: Marlene Dietrich on the set of *The Lady Is Willing* (Columbia Pictures, 1942) with Joanne or Elly Leonard, 1940

Opposite: Two children and lily, by Joanne Leonard and Judith Fuss Adell, silver print, ca. 1960

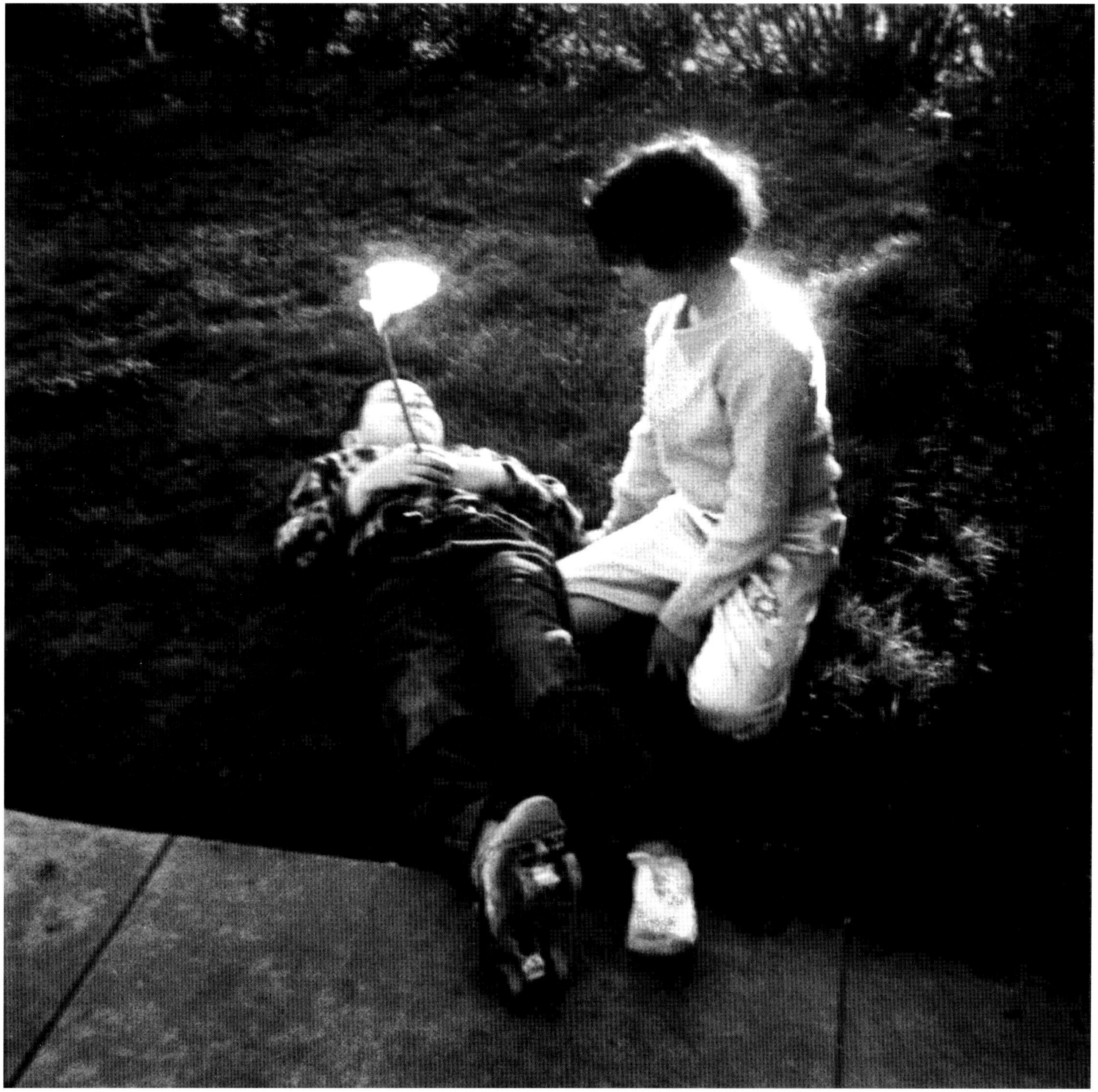

Is there an almost inevitable link between picturing others and having concern for one's own image in the world? I'd love to be immune to feeling the pain that images of women's bodies inflict on women, but I have to admit I dread pictures of myself. Without this childhood note that my mother saved, I would never have realized how early I first encountered the problem of weight and self-image.

To Momma:

i am getting Fatter
and
my Piano playing
Worse
Won't you plese Help me

Joanne

(ca. 1950, age ten)

What does it mean that I knew and wrote so early about the anxiety surrounding weight gain? That I even connected it with diminished "ability" (to play the piano) and that I rarely if ever wrote again so succinctly or clearly about something that was to be a lifelong preoccupation for my sisters and me? What did I do with those thoughts and feelings?

Perhaps I saw them mirrored everywhere, particularly in magazines with airbrushed photographs of impossibly perfect models. Eventually, turning my camera to face moments in my own and other women's lives became a vehicle for asking questions about women's lives in more nuanced ways.

Opposite: Picture taking and posing, silver prints

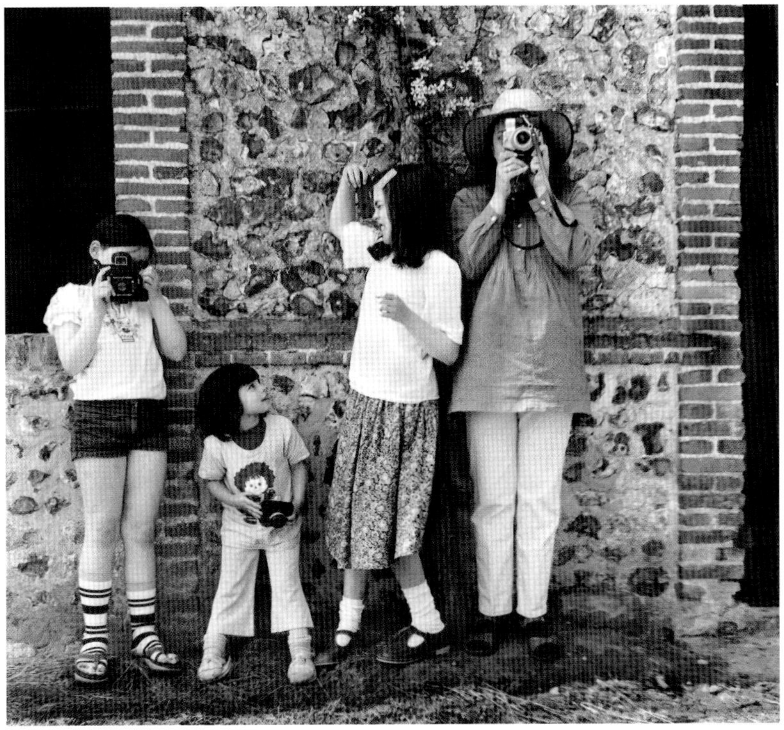
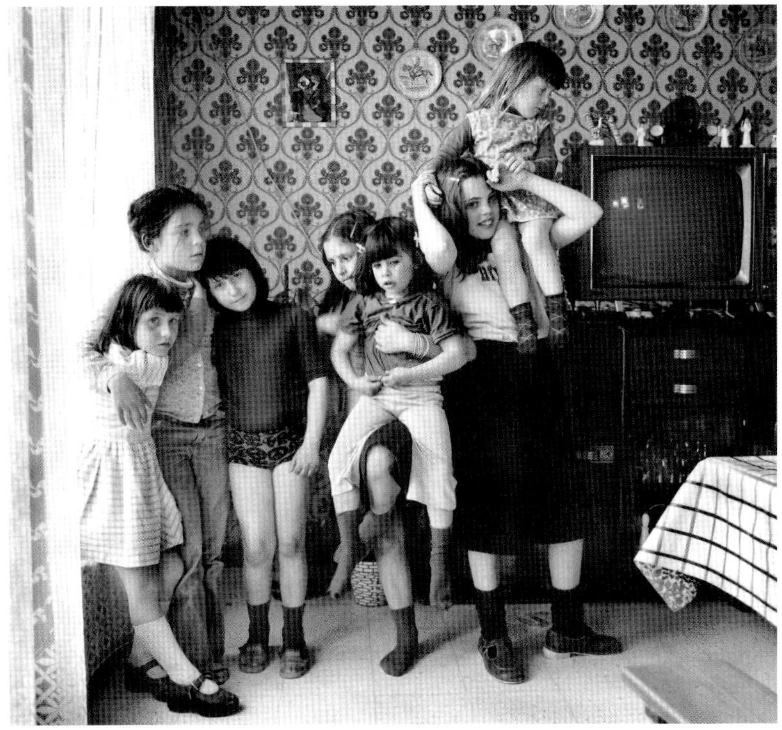
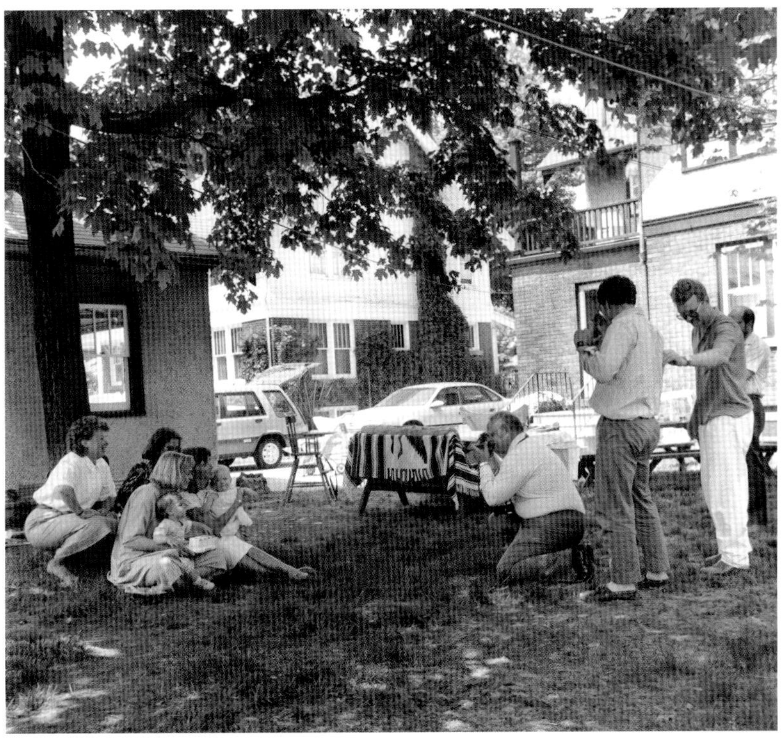
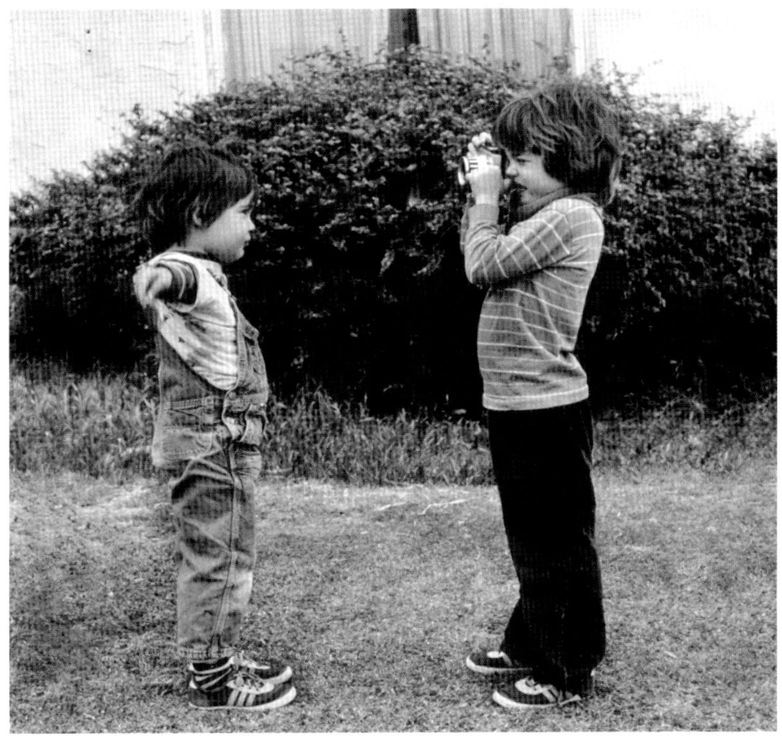

The Latent Image

At what age did I begin to think about my mother as a person in her own right and not just as "my mom"?

In 1928 she left home for Berlin, where she studied for four years at the Berlin Psychoanalytic Institute and the University of Berlin with such leading analysts as Sandor Rado and Kurt Lewin. It was as an American student studying abroad that she met my father.

I was proud of her and also pleased because she was interested in my sisters and me and our friends. Her interest extended from the lizards we found (she had studied zoology as an undergraduate and loved animals of all sorts) to our thoughts and feelings at the end of a school day. I knew she wasn't a typical mom of the 1950s. She was not as available as other moms were for leading the Girl Scout troop and carpooling, though I couldn't fully understand at the time that she was becoming an accomplished professional. She headed the Child Study Center in Los Angeles, wrote articles for professional journals, and eventually joined the psychiatry faculty at the Albert Einstein Medical School in New York. We sometimes competed for her attention with her professional interests, but she was hugely warm and affectionate, and we knew she loved us.

My earliest encouragement to pursue art came from my mother, who herself had longed to be an artist. My sisters, Elly and Barbara, and I remember well how, as kids, we adored the ceramic animals we saw her fashion and the drawings she made for our family holiday cards. In her later years she took sculpture lessons and carved soapstone, crafting fine creatures and figures.

My sense that I could become a professional who was vitally involved with a serious, intellectual, and nondomestic endeavor came from my mom. Toward the end of her life she became the center of my art and writing, as I explored themes of female family history and memory.

My mother was a third-generation American from a well-to-do family whose German Jewish members, upon arriving in the United States in the 1850s, quickly put aside anything that might mark them as overtly Jewish. This quick shedding of outward Jewishness was apparently quite typical of German Jews who immigrated to the United States during this era. That no Jewish family themes and stories appeared in my visual work until the late 1990s is perhaps not surprising, given this bent toward submerging Jewish identity that I received from my mother and that was also reflected in my dad's reluctance to talk about his traumatic past as a Jew in Germany.

I took this photograph of my mother in 1968, when she was exactly the same age that I was as I began this book. She had flown out to some psychoanalytic meetings in San Francisco, and I had driven across the bay from Oakland, where I was living, to meet her in her hotel room. While it's a rather formal portrait, I've always felt this photograph captures her. When she began to decline from Alzheimer's, I often looked at this photograph to remind me of the person behind the strange blank face I saw more and more as she declined.

Opposite: Marjorie Rosenfeld Leonard, San Francisco, silver print, 1968

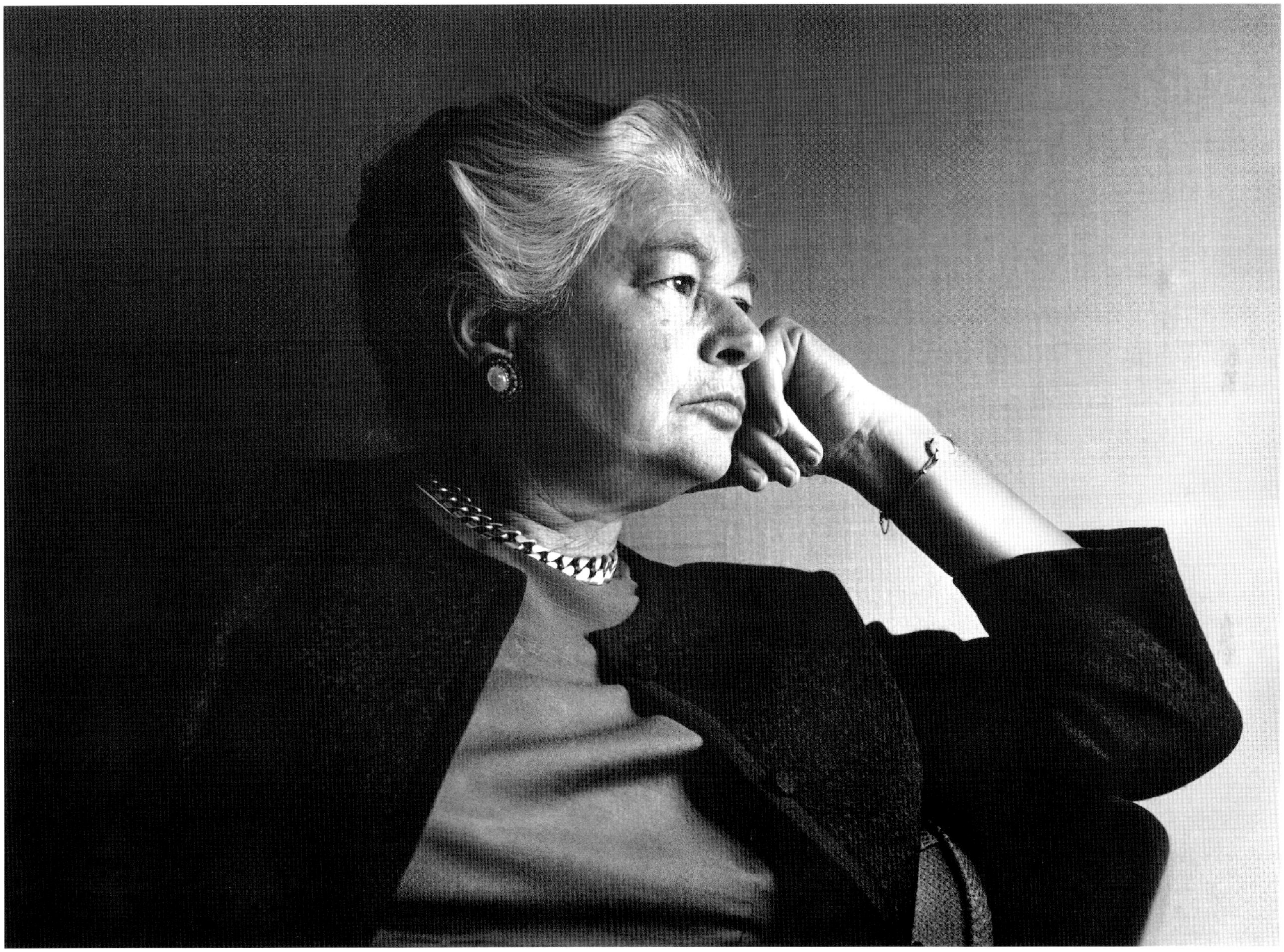

I made this photograph of my dad on his sixtieth birthday. He was amazingly fond of and deferential to this dog. When I'd travel to visit my parents (perhaps once a year) with my little daughter, Julia, in tow, he was far more likely to go on about Mike, the dog, than about his granddaughter. "Look how he puts his head on my foot when he's resting. Isn't that something?" And it was. They had a great rapport. When Mike suffered joint pain as he aged, the vet prescribed medications that damaged the dog's internal organs. On one of my visits Mike was miserable with bleeding ulcers. He did something I'd only read about in books but never seen. He took himself off to die—went down to the basement, where he had hardly ever gone. My dad looked for the dog, and when he found his dying Mike, he carried him upstairs and laid him gently on the floor. I watched my dad kneel and bend tenderly over his dog. Shortly, Mike expired, and my dad began to weep. I had never seen Dad cry. Later it was my mother who took the dog to the vet's office for cremation. My dad couldn't face it.

My father was born in Mannheim, Germany. When he met my mother in Berlin, he was a young German Jewish lawyer who had dedicated his career to opposing the rise of fascism and anti-Semitism. He was on one of the earliest arrest lists when the Nazis came to power. My mother helped him escape to America in 1933, and they were married in Los Angeles that same year. After his mother died, my parents managed to bring Dad's father and brother to the United States as well. In Los Angeles my father began to work in the fledgling field of recorded classical music, eventually opening a classical music record store, managing a chamber music concert series, and conducting weekly broadcasts of classical music. When his Los Angeles record store failed in the late 1950s and he went to work for RCA in Manhattan, my parents moved their home to Connecticut and my dad commuted to work. They lived out their lives together on the East Coast.

Opposite: Alfred Leonard and dog Mike, Connecticut, silver print, 1969

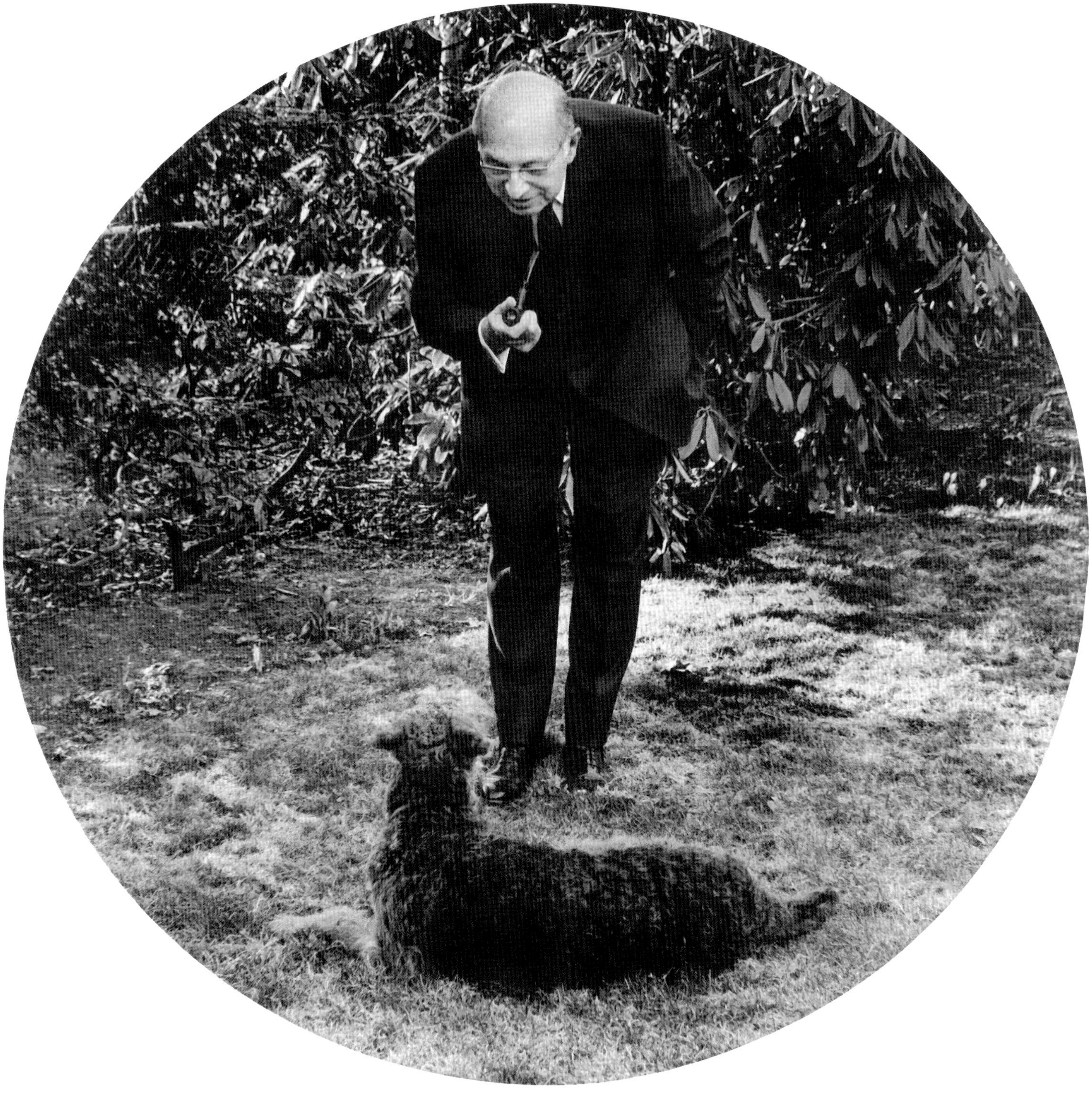

My dad was often exhausted. He was something of a workaholic, using work, I now suspect, to avoid family. As a result of his reluctance to talk about his past and his distance from us, we, his three daughters, knew him very little. We also knew remarkably little about World War II beyond what we learned from the story of Anne Frank.

In 1957, when Elly and I were seventeen, we applied to go to Germany with a summer exchange program. Our choice of Germany had at its heart our desire to know our father, to know the country where our parents had met, and to learn the German language they sometimes used to keep secrets from us. At some level our parents must have been enthusiastic about the prospect of our having our own experience of Germany. Perhaps, too, they were satisfied that we'd be in good hands on our trip because it was arranged in part by the American Field Service, a peace organization founded by ambulance drivers during the war.

Opposite: Alfred Leonard sleeping, Connecticut, silver print, 1970s

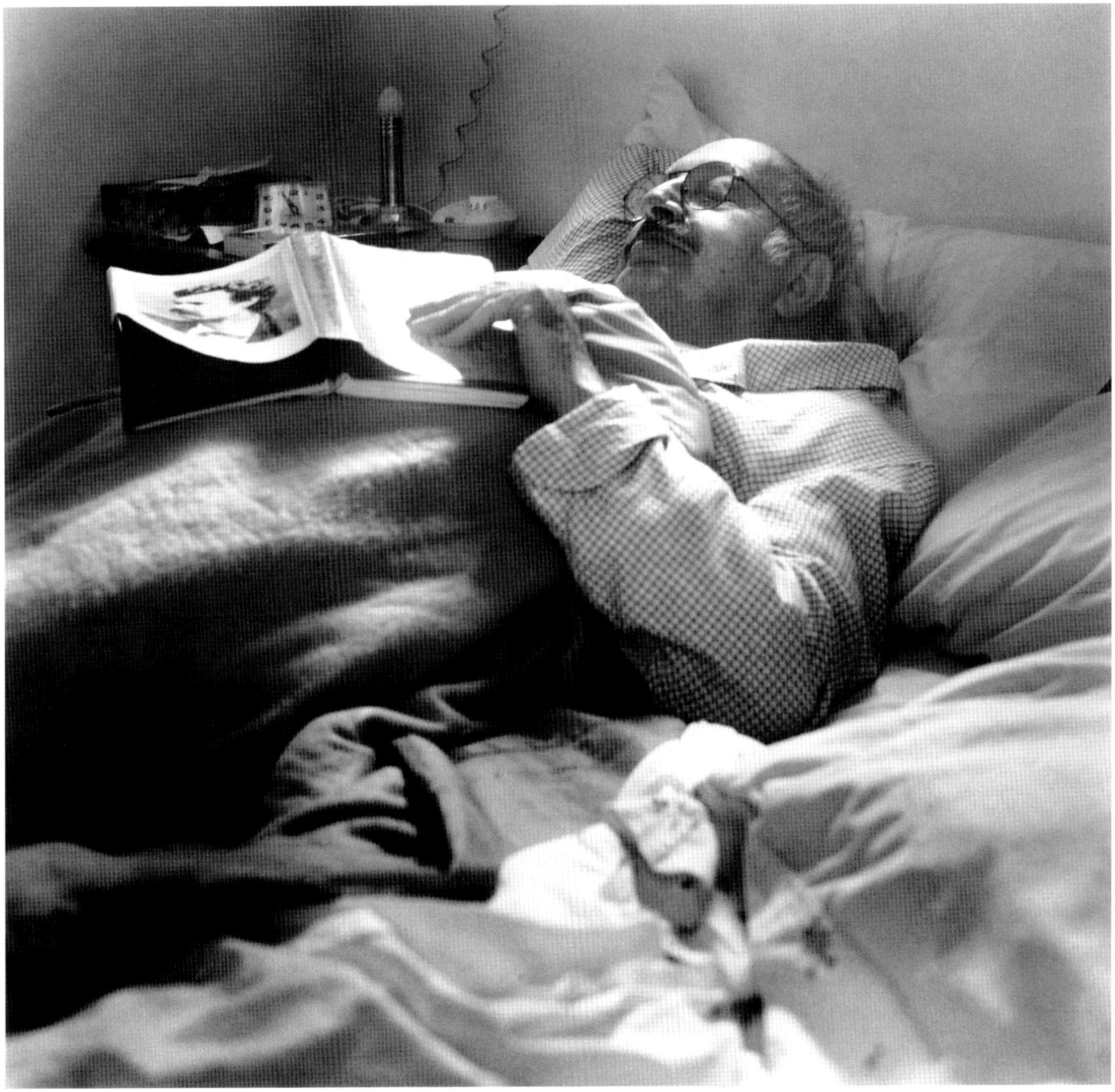

Yet the letter my father sent to our ship's dock to reach us on board our ship revealed a depth of feeling. After opening the letter with a few fatherly words, he quickly moved on to how he felt about Germany.

> There is something I want to tell you. You are going to Germany, the country where my family lived for as many generations as we can trace back, where I grew up with many wonderful experiences of friendship and learning . . . met and fell in love with the girl who became my wife and your mother. On the other hand, this is also the country which caused so much suffering, not only to me and my family, but to every Jew and to millions of others. . . .
>
> Could anyone blame me, or even fail to understand if I had nothing but bitterness in my heart for Germany and its people? For a long time I actually felt a deep hatred against Germany and its people; I hated them not only for what they did to me and to so many others, but for their betrayal of a great heritage. Just think of what Germany contributed to the world—in art, music, philosophy, in everything that makes life richer and more worthwhile. Names like Dürer, Kant, Heine, Beethoven, Goethe, Schiller, Schopenhauer will mean much more to you once you have lived in Germany, even for a short while. How can a country which produced such men also be the country of such Hitler-Barbarism? The answer is, or at least I hope and want to believe the answer to be that neither the great men nor the barbarians should be identified with a country, merely because they were born there. . . . another point . . . What about being a Jew? . . . I was born into a Jewish family, just as I was born in Germany. Neither has any value, merit or even meaning when taken by itself. One can be good or bad as a German, good or bad as a Jew.

He concluded by assuring us that his thoughts and love would be with us on this journey and always.

Even as teenagers, I think we sensed, if only a little, his anxiety for us and understood, though not fully, the balance to our enthusiasm that he was trying to provide without dampening our excitement. I read the letter over now and find myself wishing he'd been able to say more, then or ever.

He'd said so little before, that I never knew, until my sister's twins were thirteen, my dad had had his own bar mitzvah and knew Hebrew. Our entire family life had adopted my mother's Jewish family's highly assimilated practice of celebrating Christmas. Once or twice in our lives we'd been to temple, but only because my uncle Joseph, my dad's brother, played the organ there. We'd had one Seder in our home, when I was perhaps eleven or twelve. The one detail I remember of this event was not what I learned about being Jewish but that I found the afikomen (hidden matzo) and was thrilled to win the prize my father had provided—a recording of a piano concerto performed by Robert Casadesus.

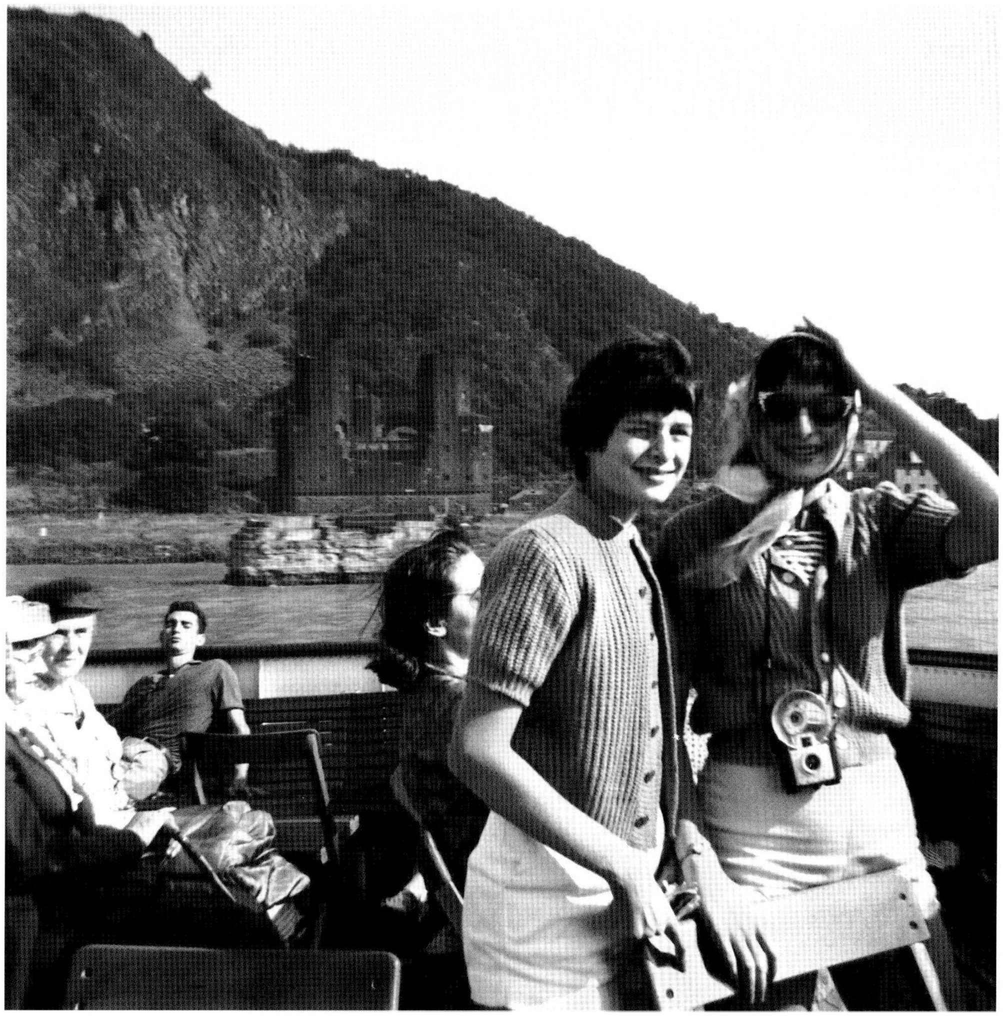

We each had a Brownie Star Flash camera with us, but we took only a few pictures on the trip, and very few have survived. Someone took a picture of Elly and me on a cruise down the Rhine, where I (prophetically?) am the one with the Brownie hanging from a neck strap.

We stopped in Connecticut before returning to my parents in Los Angeles. It took the shocked questions of an East Coast relative and her friends to awaken us to how unusual my parents' decision to let us go to Germany could seem. These reactions helped us begin to understand all that we'd carry forward from our trip.

My uncle Joseph was blind, and my closeness to him clearly had an effect on my becoming a visual artist. I read to him. I tried to understand what his sightless world was like ("Can you see lights?"). My sisters and I described our world to him, and he sometimes "saw" the action on TV through our voiced narrations. He was an artist himself—a composer and a pianist. He could not see my photograph of him that sat on the piano in its silver frame, but he loved to hear it described. He was also very proud of me and welcomed guests' compliments about the photograph as a chance to talk about his niece. My sisters and I basked in the praise that came more readily from him than from our father. I was not very old when Joseph (who had no children of his own) began to treat me as a young adult he could rely upon, especially after my parents and sisters moved to the East Coast while I started college in California. I feel terribly sad now when I remember that he turned to me, thinking I might help him get some of his choral music (particularly a work he based on a poem I wrote) performed at the university where I was an undergraduate; I hadn't a clue how to be helpful—was too unsure of myself in general and especially in relation to my own poem—and turned away from his inquiries.

Opposite: Piano with portrait of Joseph Leonard, silver print, mid-1960s

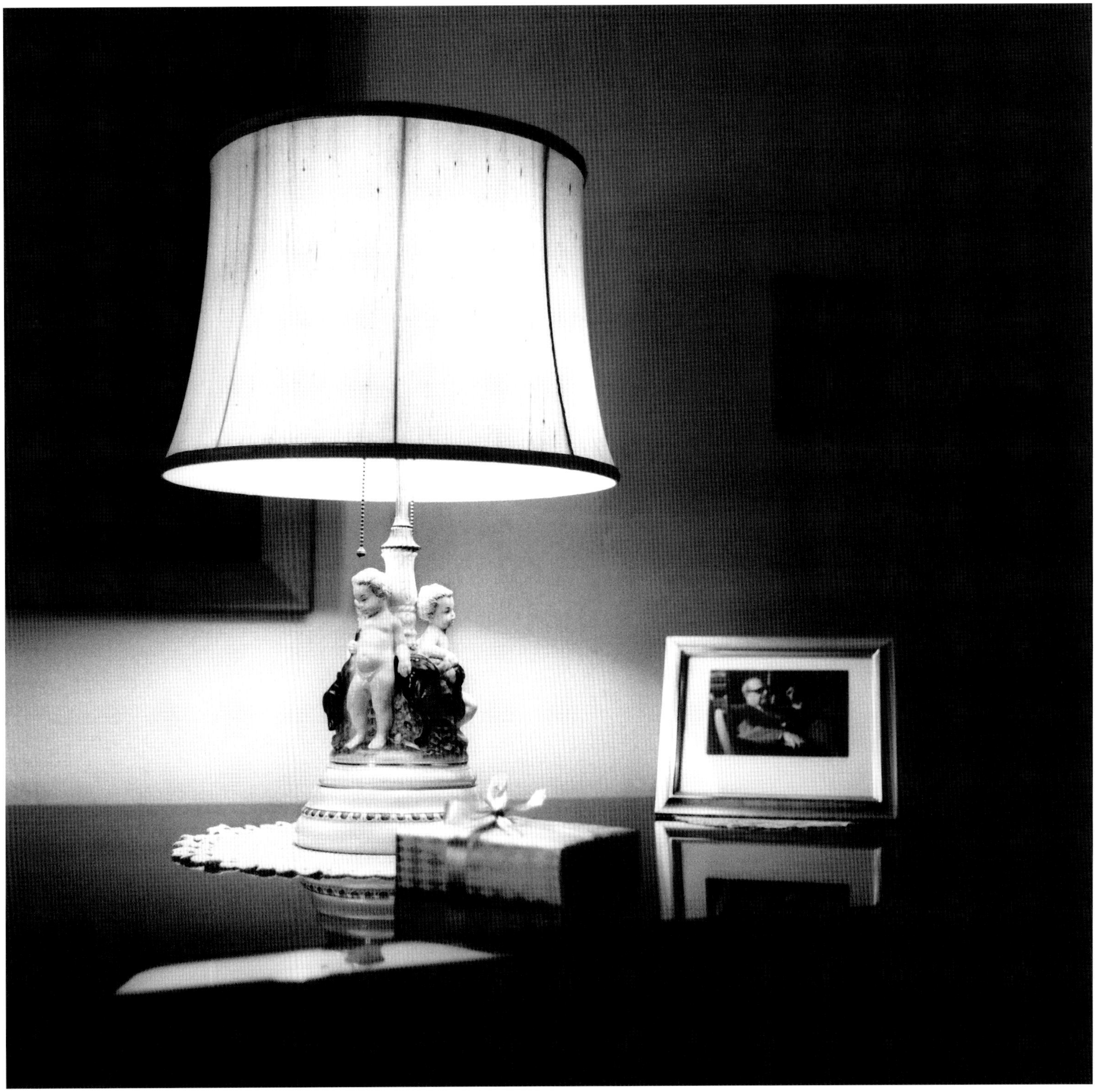

Double Exposures/Multiple Exposures

As an identical twin I often encountered people's fascination. "How do you know who is who?" "What if your mother got you mixed up? Then you might be the other one!" "Do you have mental telepathy with your twin?" When you are young and a twin, it's fun to realize that people consider you special and even envy you. But being compared isn't always fun. Other children (and, later, adults) make comparisons and sometimes say right out whom they judge smarter, more fun or talented, prettier, bigger. Such assessments continue into adulthood and can be painful.

Elly (Eleanor Rubin) is an artist, too. The differences in our artistic work have been important to both of us. She's a printmaker, and I'm a photographer. By and large, her work is more fanciful—she has created a repertoire of invented creatures—and abstract, in ideas as well as imagery, than mine. Yet there are similarities too. We both deal in pictures that are often black and white, yet we both introduce color. She makes monoprints (one-of-a-kind prints), and I make collages (one-of-a-kind photographs).

Outside of the arts, our differences play out in various ways. Sometimes it seems we are two sides of a coin. If she is generally sweet and cooperative, I'm often a bit more assertive and oppositional. Both Elly and I have careers and families. But she has had more on the family side, and I've had more on the career side.

Coping with the challenges of being a single parent might have been miserable or even impossible without Elly in my corner. She has never flaunted one thing she had that I didn't or failed to be really glad for me about something I had that she didn't. She's invited me to join her family on vacations. We attend each other's exhibitions, cheer each other's publications and awards. We write or talk every day. In fact we write *and* talk almost every day. Through almost everything. When she is away, I hold conversations with her in my mind, and we have to catch up the minute she returns. When I was recently in Rome, she made a project of postcard-sized drawings, mailing me one almost every day for a month. We have collaborated artistically a number of times. I've written this book about me, but Elly is in every phrase and page of it.

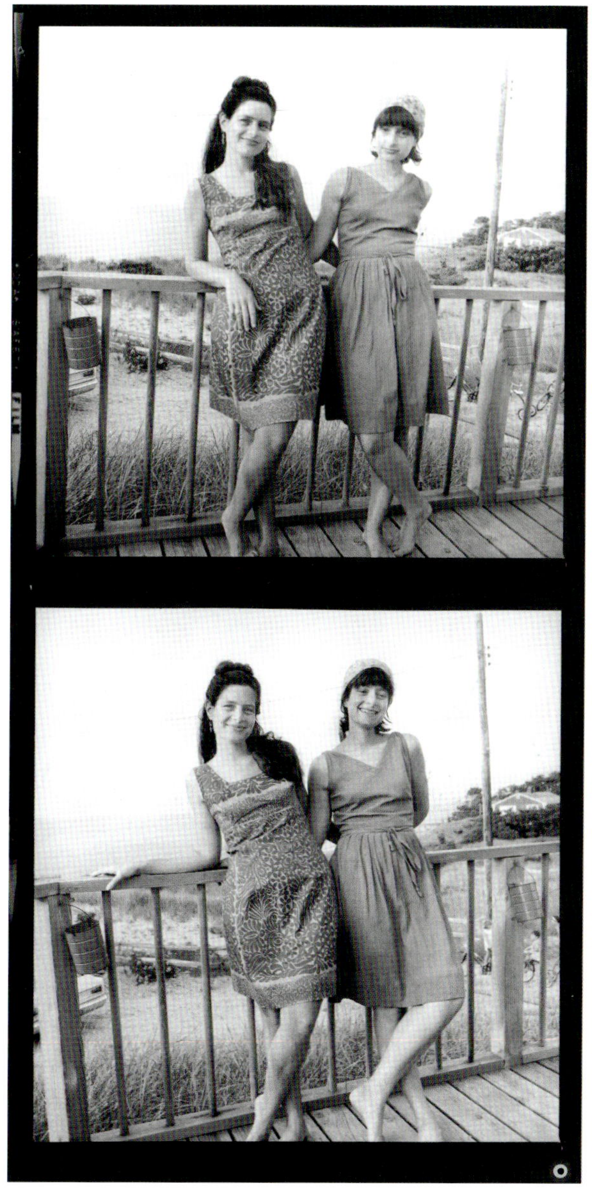

Above: Joanne Leonard and Elly (Leonard) Rubin, Cape Cod, 1968, by David Rubin

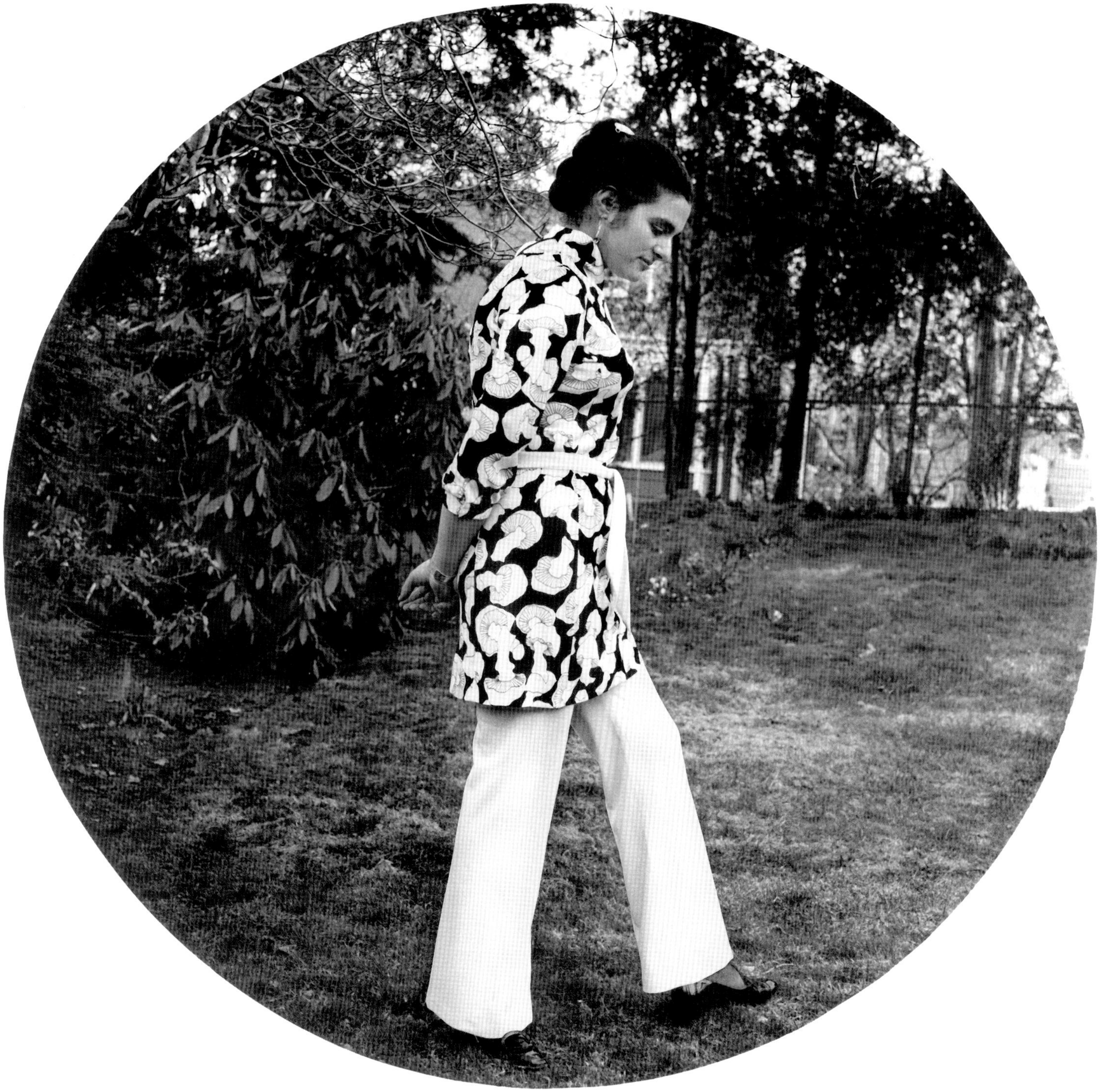

Barbara, our "baby" sister (she is four years younger), eventually grew much taller than either of us, and, though I know it is probably not possible to grow by wanting to, I've always imagined that she grew taller in order, as the little sister, to best her double dose of big sisters. As twins Elly and I were always a special and rather exclusive pair. Barb, too, has involved herself in the arts in many ways, including photography, but, as she reflected in an e-mail recently, "your 'artist's bond' seems always just beyond my reach."

That "artist's bond" naturally makes Elly a larger part of this book's story, but Barb, with her love of animals and her quick take on all things digital, tells her own story. As a result of illness, Barb has become disabled. She uses a wheelchair and is now an expert in training dogs to meet the needs of disabled people. The print and digital teaching materials she creates under her professional name (Barbara Handelman) tell of her own experiences and serve at the same time as instructional tools. She and her husband have a private practice as family counselors and together have raised their own twins, who are now in college.

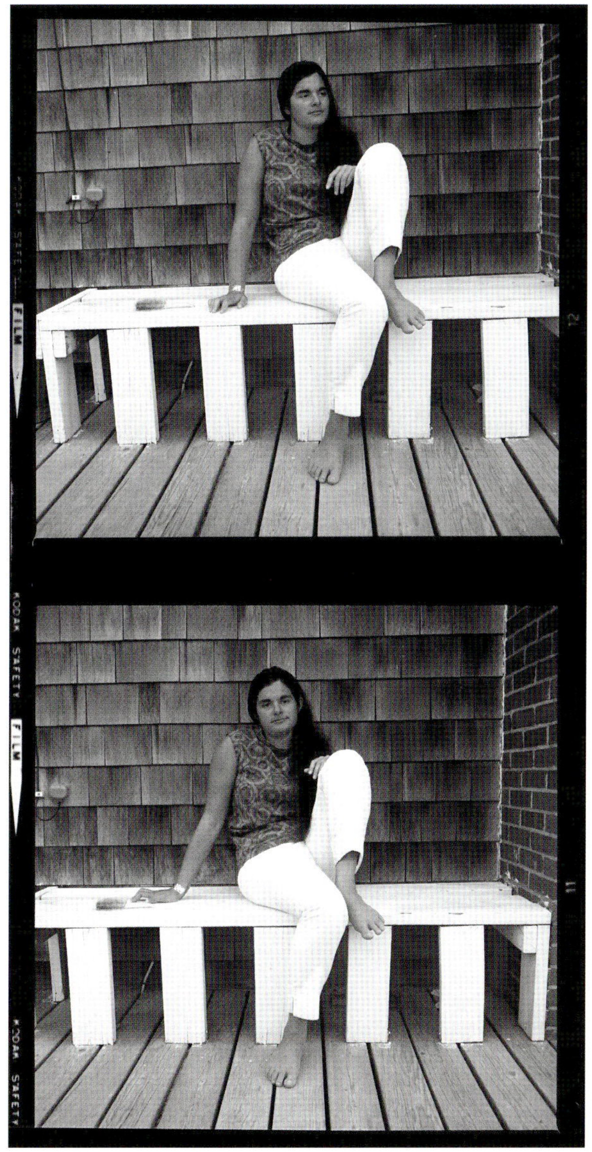

Opposite: Barbara (Leonard) Handelman, Stamford, Connecticut, silver print, 1969

Above: Barbara, Cape Cod, Contact strip, silver print, ca. 1967

Pictures of twins are like playful jokes. Seeing double. Double trouble. This photograph shows my father holding Elly's twins, Anna and Joe, when they were babies. It appeared in *Dads*, a lovely photo anthology published in 1994, and in a *People* magazine review of that book. Dad would have been so pleased, but publication came nearly twenty years after I took the picture, and he had already died.

Did I wait until age thirty-four before I had my daughter partly due to what I observed when I visited my sister with her twin babies? Her small family's means were slim. Her husband was still in graduate school. The diapers were freezing on the clothesline. I had the freedom to travel and to work on my art that Elly did not, at least then. The private reminders hidden below the surface of this picture may have helped me be happy in postponing motherhood.

Opposite: Dad with Elly's twins, Waltham, Massachusetts, silver print, 1966

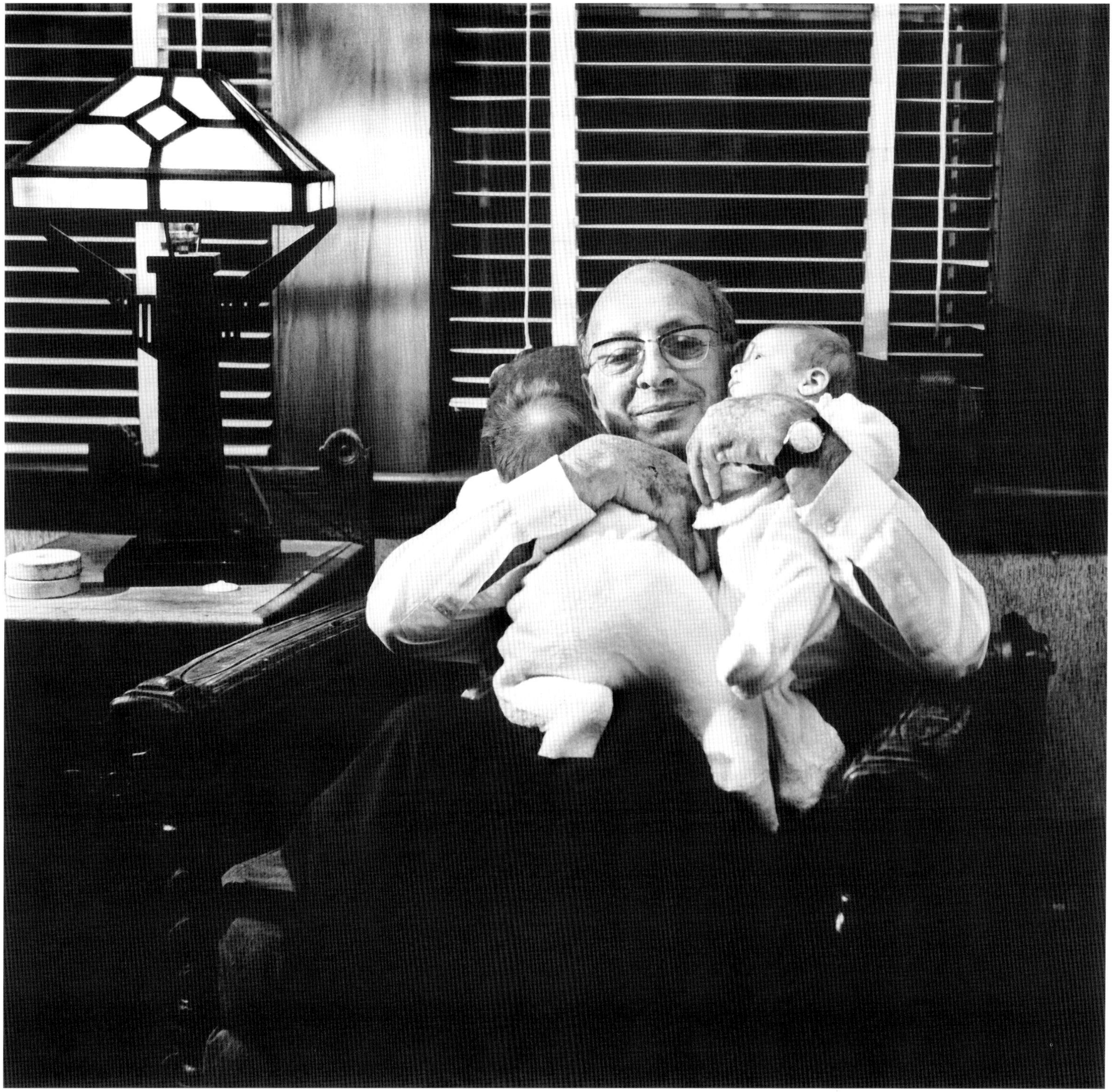

How pleased I am to have captured the rippling out of twin themes—the plaster head mirroring Elly's profile, the chicks and hen of the sculpture in the window repeating the cluster of Elly's twins circling her.

I would forever fail to live up to the idealizations of motherhood and family I created in many of my photographs. Where do accidental pregnancy, abortion, miscarriage, or single parenthood fit in this beautiful world I continued to create and re-create in my images? A perceptive viewer of these photographs may see through them to a more difficult reality, a more complex notion of motherhood that lurks at the edges of the image on the page. Susan Sontag wrote:

> For photographers there is, finally, no difference—no greater aesthetic advantage—between the effort to embellish the world and the counter-effort to rip off its mask.

Opposite: Elly with twins, Joe and Anna, West Newton, Massachusetts, silver print, 1969

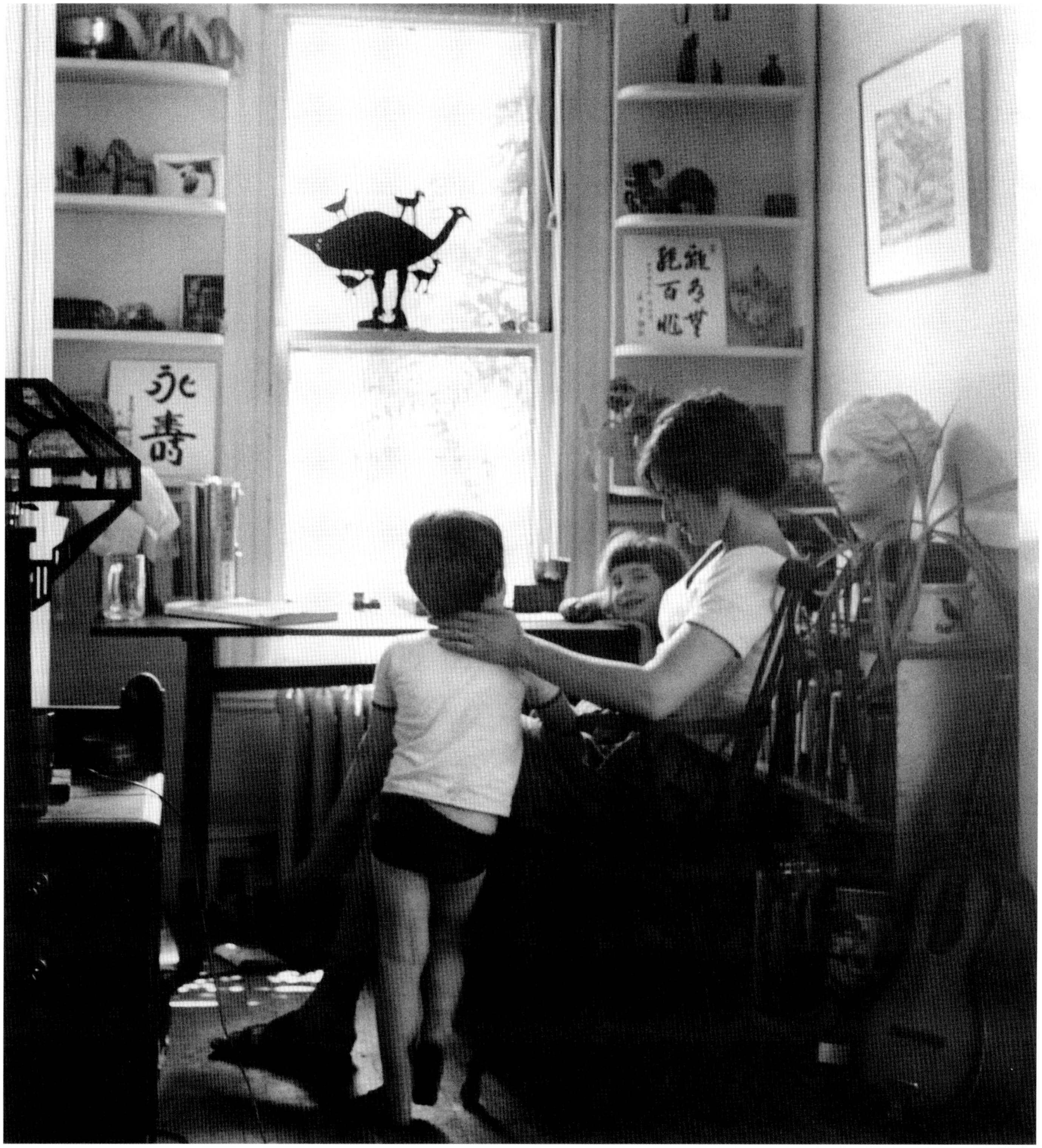
永壽

I've always loved this photograph because it is such a wonderful contradiction to the idealized mothers-and-babies photos typically taken by portrait studios, where the desired image is one of composure—peaceful babies, smiling mothers. Today I read this photo also for the histories of the women in the picture. One woman is an artist now, another a college administrator. One is a pathology lab tech who brings health care to poor women in Central America and unionizes health care workers in the United States. All the children in the photo are now adults with complex lives of their own.

Jeannie, on the far right, wrote this about the photograph: "The entire afternoon was bathed in the warmth of sitting in the sunshine with our oldest friends watching the next generation playing. I also remember the warm summer California dust, smelling of sagebrush and eucalyptus."

Opposite: Four old friends with babies, Los Angeles, silver print, 1967

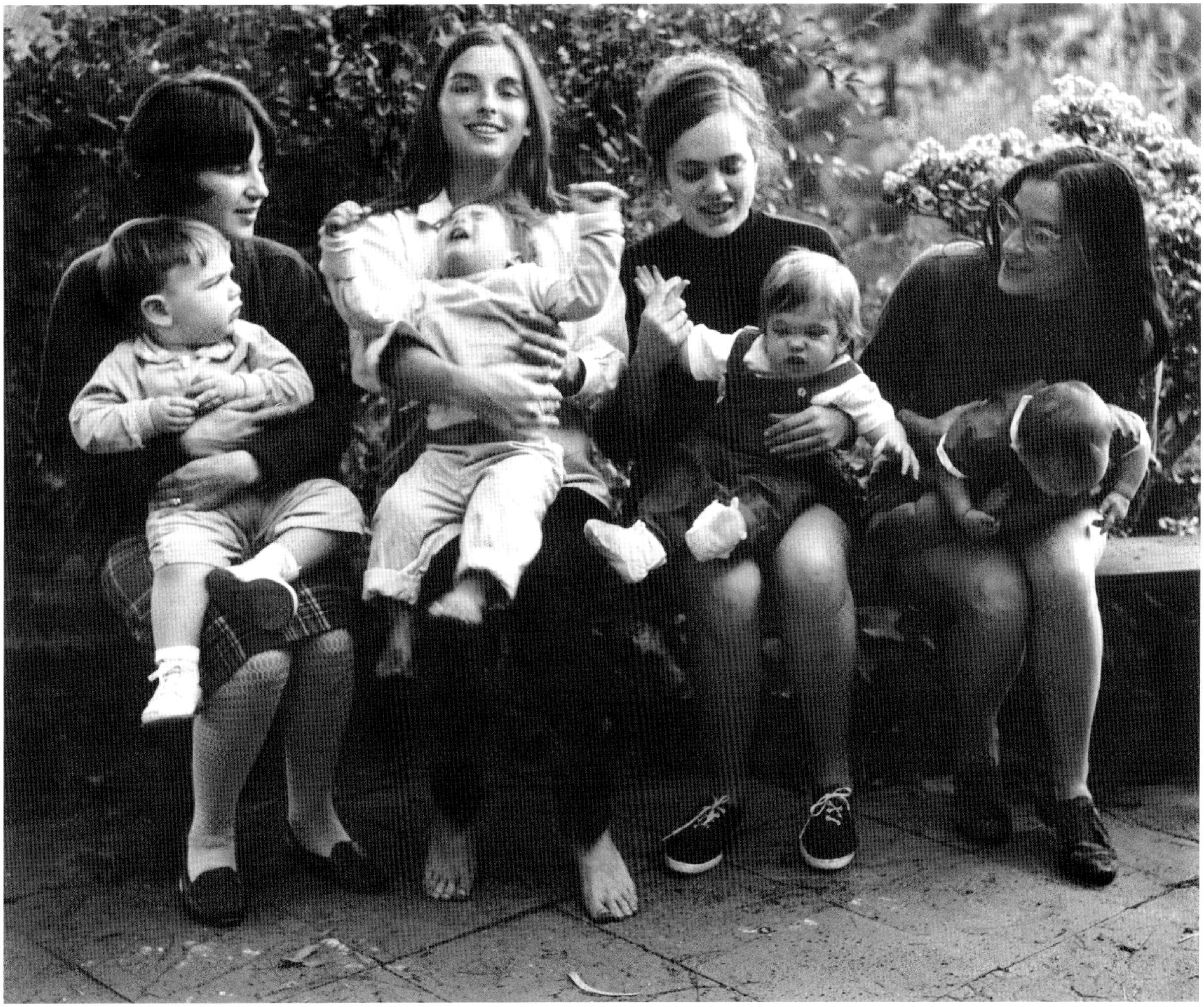

I'm the fourth friend here, out of sight—the photographer. It's 1968. We've known one another since grade school in Los Angeles. What you see is something of a reunion because Elly is visiting Los Angeles (where Harriet and Judith live) from the Boston area and I'm visiting from the Bay Area. It's now forty years later, and we are all still friends.

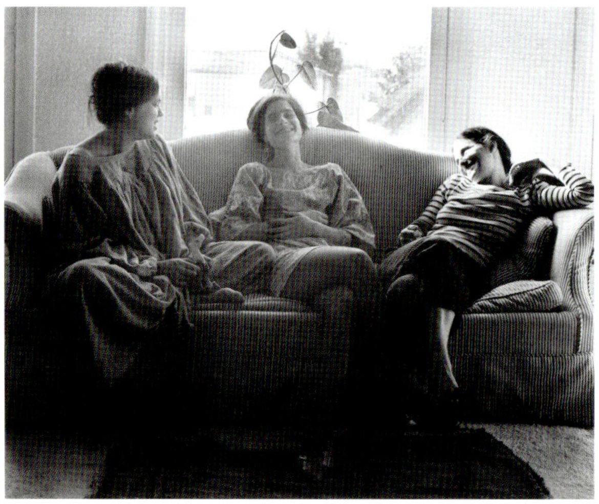

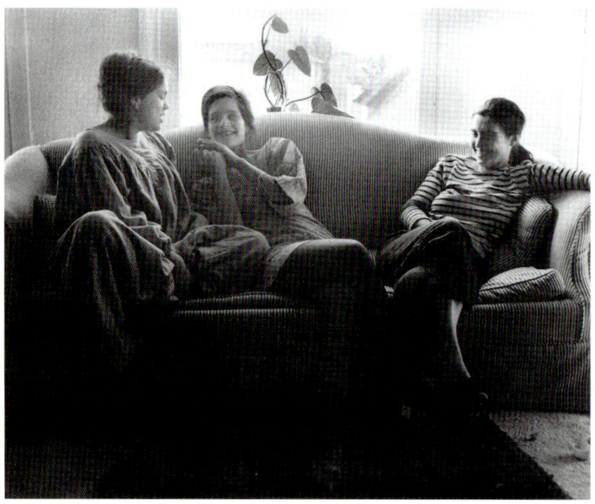

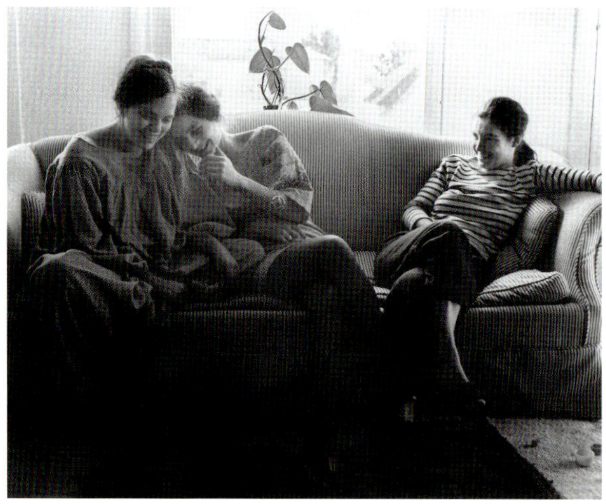

Above/Opposite: Reunion of lifelong friends, Los Angeles, silver prints, 1968

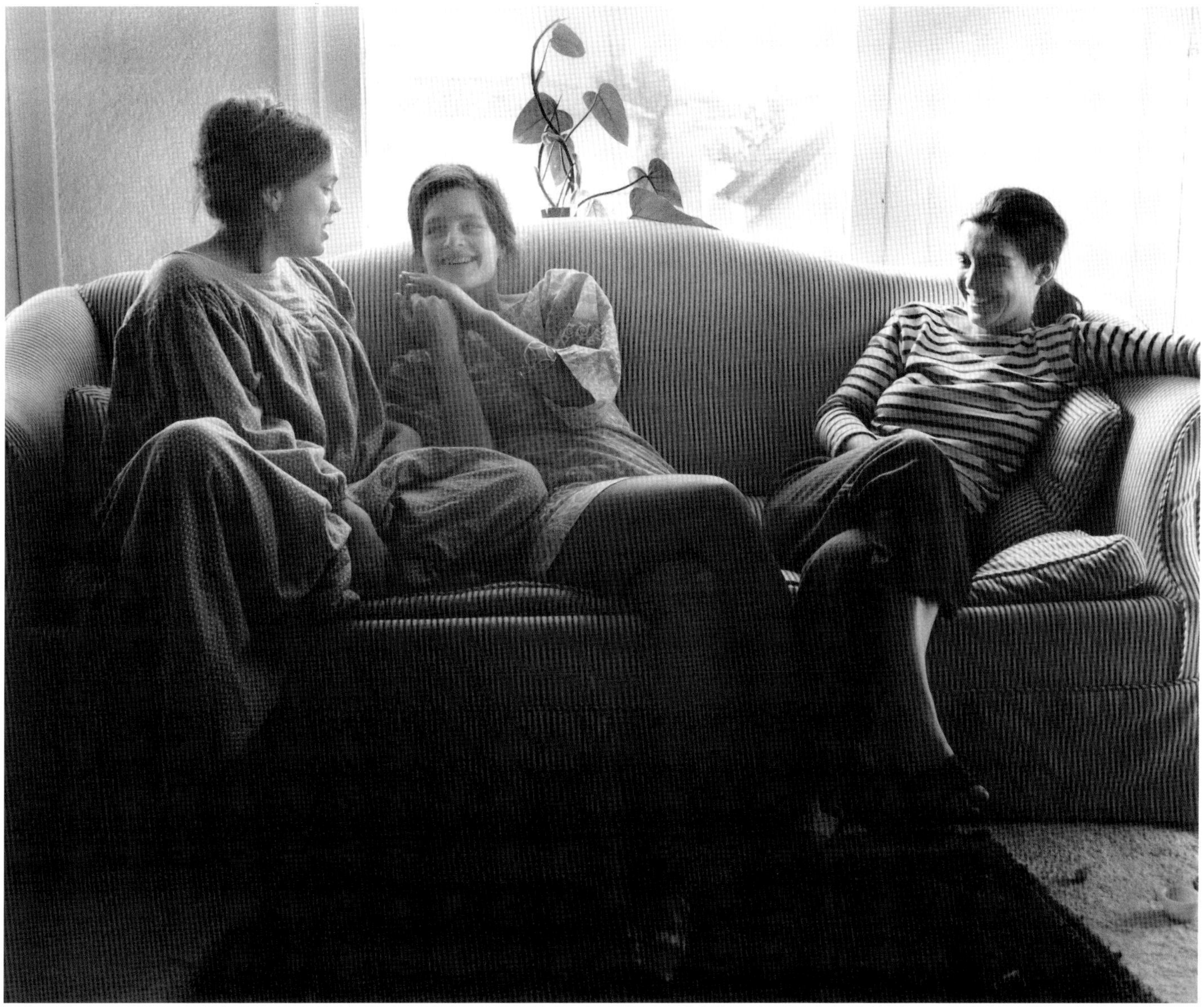

Decisive Moments

I couldn't study photography in college because when I was there, Cal (as we called the University of California's Berkeley campus) didn't yet have courses in photography. I went to an evening high school class in photography and printed photographs for the first time. After I graduated from Cal in 1962, I stayed in the Bay Area long enough to take a photography class at a local junior college. But somehow, even with so little learning or experience with photography, I had vaguely begun to think of myself as a photographer.

When I was in high school, I had always imagined going to college, but I had made no mental space for the time between college graduation and the fabled "ever after" of getting married and having children. During this time, I had to forge ahead and silence my fears that I'd already taken a wrong turn and would never enter the realms of my Hollywood-inspired notions of happiness. I lived (and worked, took classes) in Berkeley, New York, Boston, San Francisco, and Berkeley again, then moved to West Oakland, all within a few years. During that time my skills in photography and sense of myself as a committed photographer grew.

I'd been proud of myself and elated when I used my first paycheck (from my first after-graduation job shelving books at Harvard's zoology library) to buy a photo enlarger. Within the next two years, I would make three darkrooms for myself: the first one that winter in a cold-water flat in the North End of Boston near Elly and her new husband, David; then, under the stairs in a house in the Haight Ashbury district of San Francisco, where I rented a room when I returned to California that January to take some photo classes at San Francisco State; and, later, in the closet of a tiny first-floor garden apartment in Berkeley, where I was living when I met Bruce Beasley, a sculptor, just before the summer of 1964. My "professional" work in photography (the first substantial body of work I exhibited) began in West Oakland, living with Bruce.

Bruce and I had mutual friends, and when we met, he told me he'd admired a photograph of mine that he'd seen at someone's home. I had heard about Bruce and his work and was impressed by the recognition he'd already had as an artist; among other successes, his sculpture had been part of an American exhibit at the Paris Biennale. I enjoyed that first conversation with him, and that encounter grew into a romance.

The first time he invited me for dinner, he cooked but asked me to wash the dishes. I should have taken note, maybe even fled (he turned out to have strict ideas of traditional gender roles), but I didn't. I was far too taken with him and his makeshift home in a tin warehouse that doubled as a bronze-casting foundry. Inside the warehouse was an unconventional living space where heat came from a stove, fueled with wood scraps from a nearby forklift pallet manufacturer. I look back now with amazement at how undaunted I was by Bruce's quarters: during the first night I stayed there, I woke to realize a rat had just run across the bed! Bruce soon invited me to move in, and we joined households.

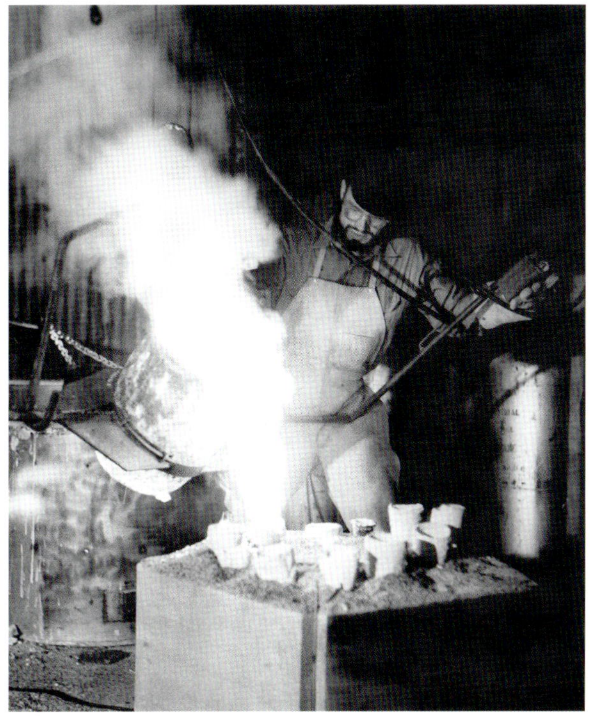

Above: Bruce Beasley casting bronze at 343 Cypress Street, West Oakland, silver print, ca. 1963

Our tin warehouse was in West Oakland, near the railroad tracks of the poorest section of Oakland, California's fifth largest city. Southern Pacific Railroad had once owned land there and eventually sold off some of the land to its workers. While many residents in West Oakland owned their own homes and kept them up beautifully, some were so poor that the houses were horribly run-down and substandard. During World War II, Kaiser Industries brought African Americans up from the South to work as cheap labor in war-related jobs, and Oakland's black population grew from then on, concentrated in the sections of the city known as East and West Oakland.

Bruce and I were in a sense part of a 1960s counterculture—a group of youth with enough privilege to be able to reject material comfort in exchange for the adventure and challenge of living as artists, political activists, even dropouts and street people. Both in our early twenties, we were our own variation on these 1960s themes. We were ambitious for ourselves, working long, hard hours in our studios, and were quite willing to live with our shabby used furniture, little heating, and only a dollar a day for groceries. Bruce's father was a banker, but since Bruce was not going into banking or, like his brother, becoming a doctor, his family was testing his commitment by not allowing him to draw on family funds.

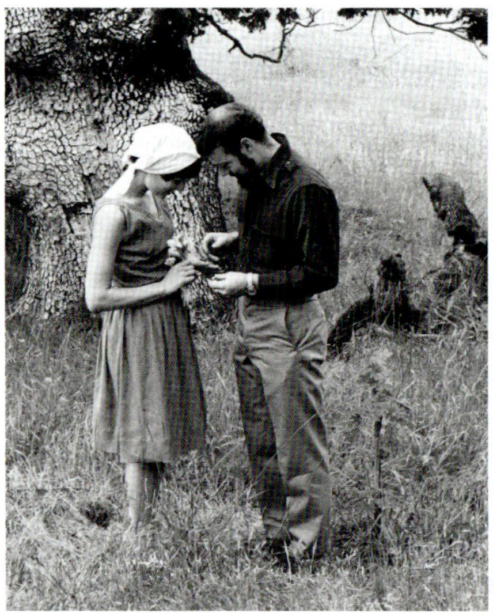

Even when we married, we did so in a counterculture fashion, on a camping trip with a ceremony we wrote. When I joined my life with Bruce's, I was determined not to need money from my parents or from Bruce and paid many of my own expenses with earnings I made as a darkroom lab assistant and wedding and portrait photographer. The very block where I lived in this gritty, semi-industrial neighborhood had homes dotted among yards where workers salvaged lumber and bricks. There were no curbs and gutters, and, in addition to rats, there were packs of homeless dogs. Sometimes I photographed neighbors on my own block. Eventually, I also made photographs for families I came to know who invited me into their warm and comfortable homes a few blocks away.

Above: Joanne and Bruce's wedding, Mendocino, 1967, by Dr. Palmer Beasley

Opposite: Interior and exterior views of house at 343 Cypress Street, West Oakland, silver prints, ca. 1963; Oakland Museum of California

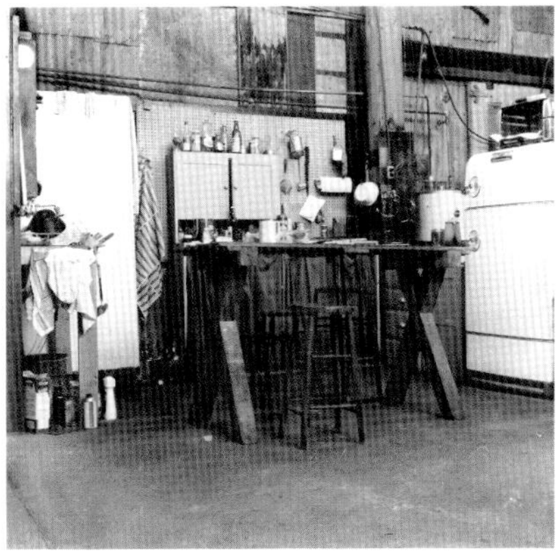

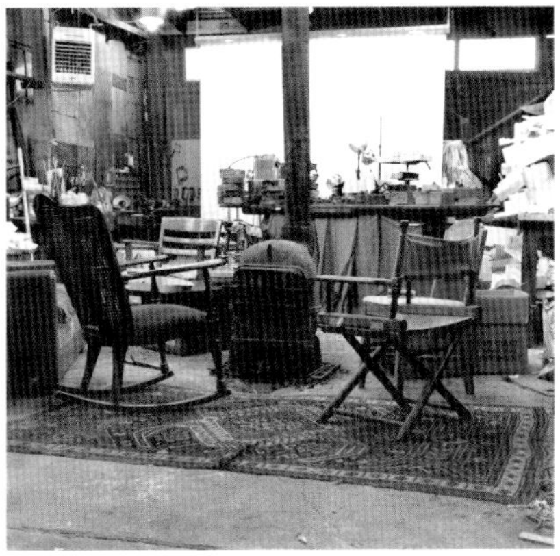

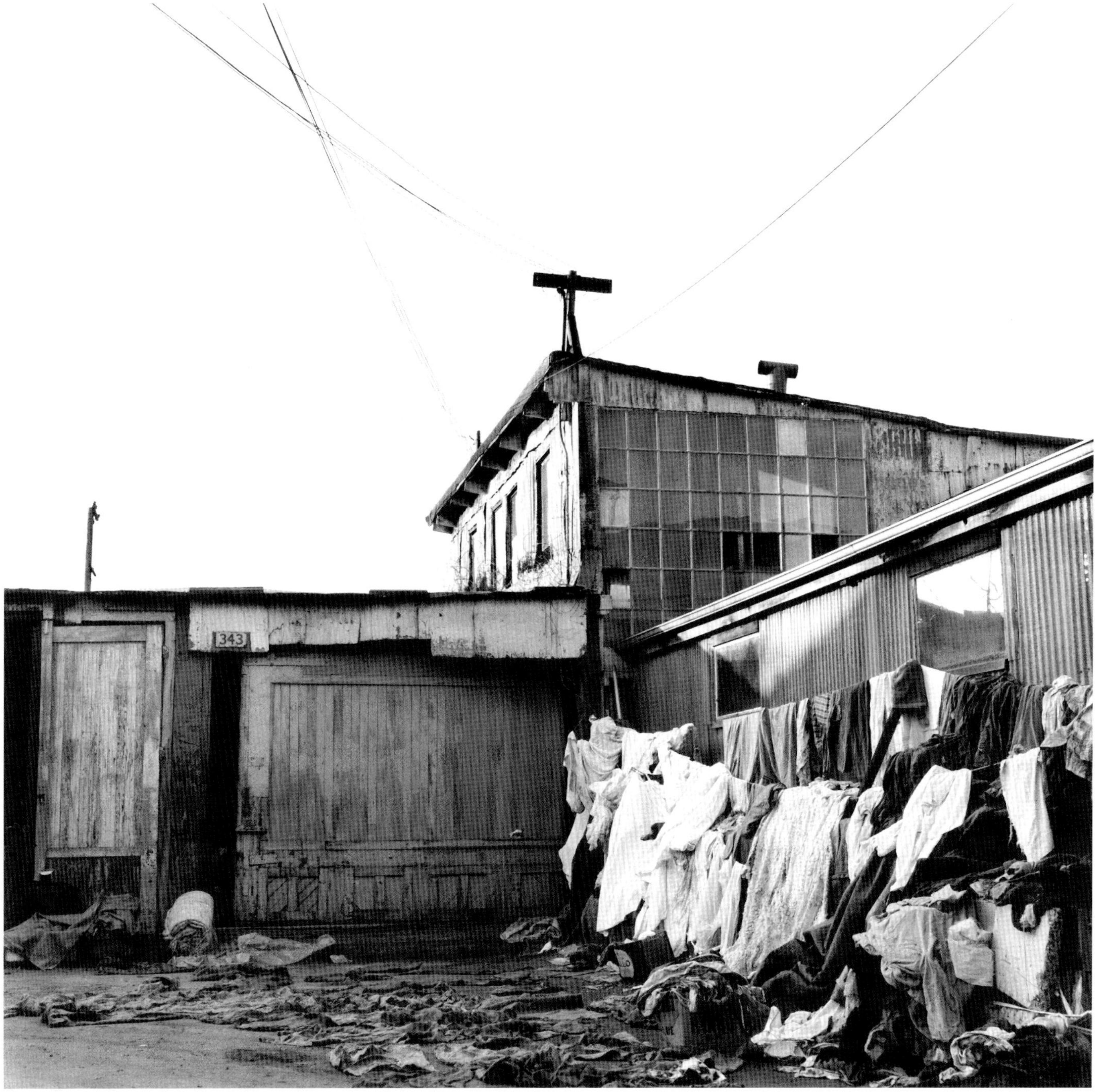
343

I made friends in West Oakland. By taking part in neighborhood improvement efforts that were launched as part of Lyndon Johnson's War on Poverty, I met two wonderful women, Everlee Tyler and Bea Slider, and their families. For a time, Bruce and I were regularly invited to Thanksgiving dinners at the Sliders' home. Later I photographed Everlee and Bea's daughters and many family events, including graduations, the weddings, and the arrival of a grandchild.

Opposite: Ruth Esther Tyler Austin's wedding, West Oakland, silver print, 1970; Oakland Museum of California

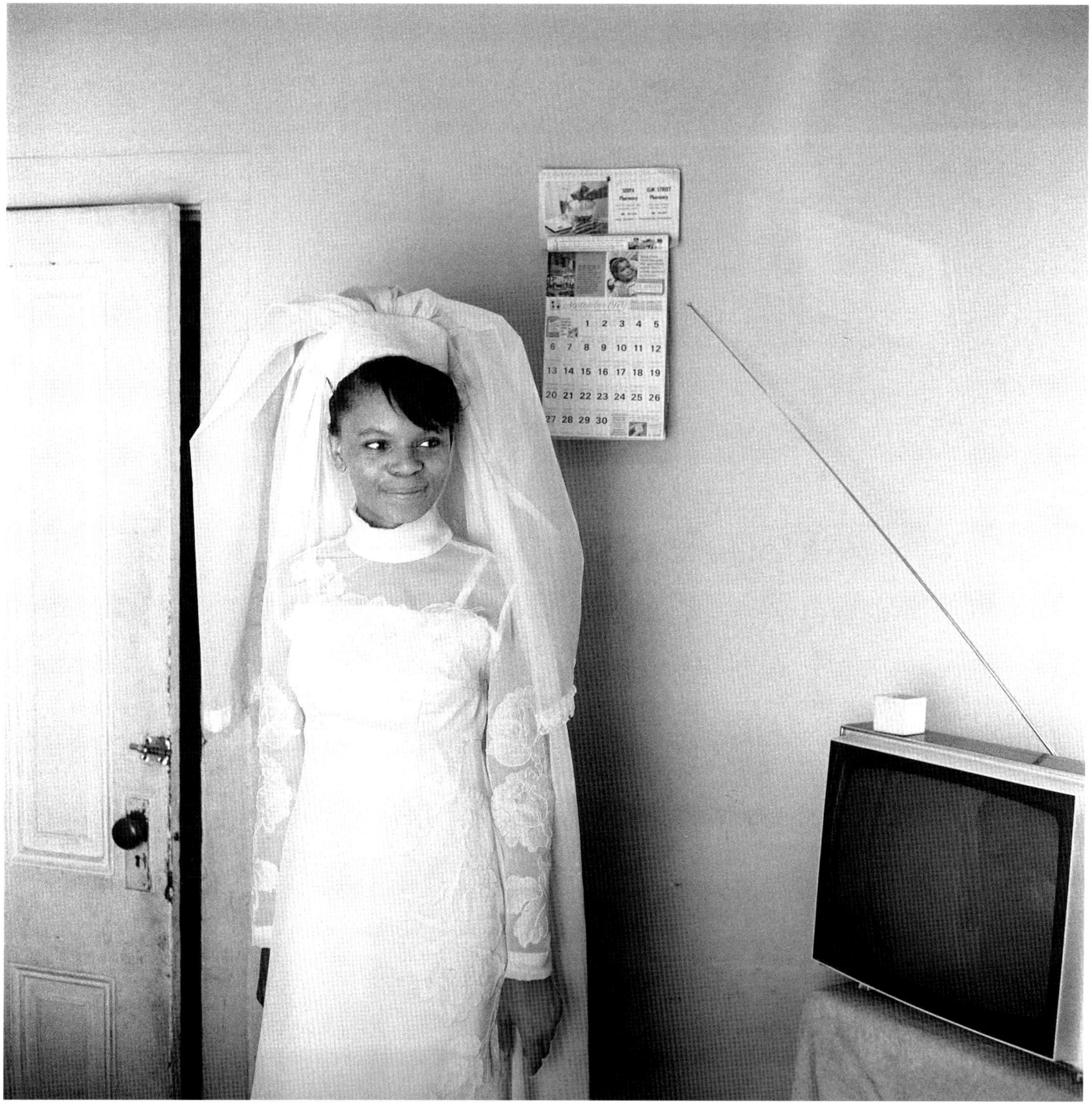
1 2 3 4 5
6 7 8 9 10 11 12
13 14 15 16 17 18 19
20 21 22 23 24 25 26
27 28 29 30

When Ruth Esther got married, I had a great time photographing her preparing for her wedding and putting on her wedding dress. As a guest at this wedding, I had to be careful not to get in the way of the photographer hired by the Tylers for the occasion, so I stood behind him. I like having that arm-in-a-cast photographer there in the foreground of my picture. It's almost as if his presence erases my own and gives this photograph the perspective of the proverbial fly on the wall.

Opposite: Bride throws bouquet, West Oakland, silver print, 1970; Oakland Museum of California

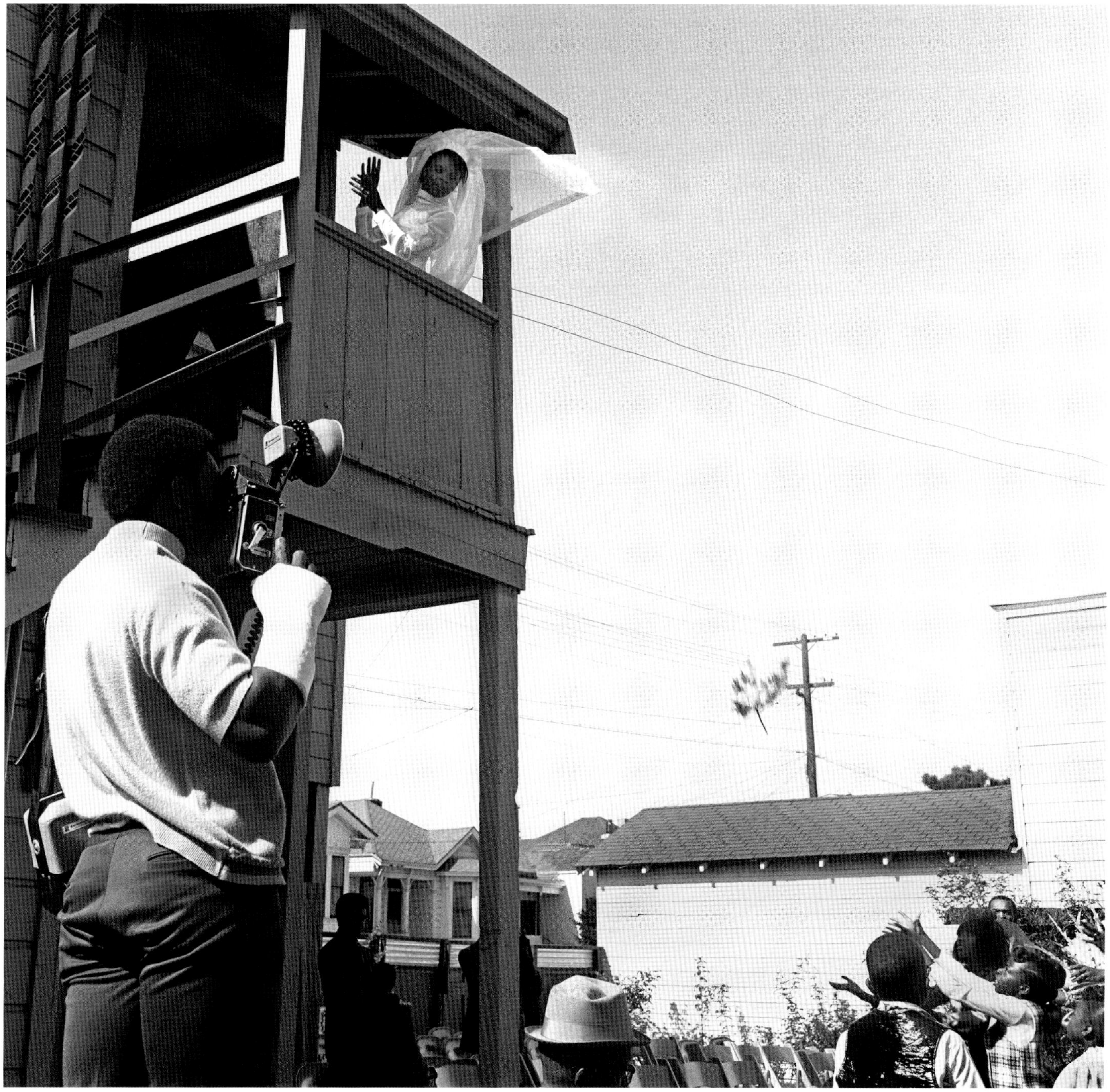

One summer in the early 1980s I taught photography in the architecture program building at the University of California, Berkeley, and was invited to put up a display of my photographs from West Oakland. Ingrid King, who was coauthoring a book to be titled *A Pattern Language*, noticed these photographs. As a result of her visit, King and Christopher Alexander, the principal author, chose a photograph of mine for publication in their book.

The book turns out to have become important to twentieth-century architecture and is said to be the first complete book ever written in hypertext fashion. The people pictured in the photograph of my elderly neighbors on the front porch are poor, and the house is run-down, but the book suggests that this house is a model of some things to *desire* in housing. "Common areas of the heart, sequence of sitting places"—wonderful reminders of what is so often destroyed by urban renewal or gentrification.

I was pressed in those years for time and funds to make prints of my own photographs. I worked in some commercial darkrooms and once in a while managed to make a few prints from my own negatives during my work hours in those labs. I printed these pictures small so as not to attract too much attention to this personal work on company time. In this way, I made a nearly square print, only four inches across, of my sister-in-law Sonia hanging laundry and submitted it to a competitive exhibition at the San Francisco Museum of Art (now the San Francisco Museum of Modern Art, or SFMOMA). It was my first photograph ever shown in a museum and the smallest print in the show!

Emboldened by the success of my little print, I made an appointment to show my first large body of work, my four years of photography from West Oakland, to the director of photography at the de Young Museum in the middle of San Francisco's Golden Gate Park. The director said he liked my photographs but, unfortunately, the calendar for photo shows was already filled for at least a year. I was almost certain I'd just been given a brush-off but ventured that I'd be glad to wait a year or more. He wrote me onto the calendar for 1968—my first solo show, and in a major museum.

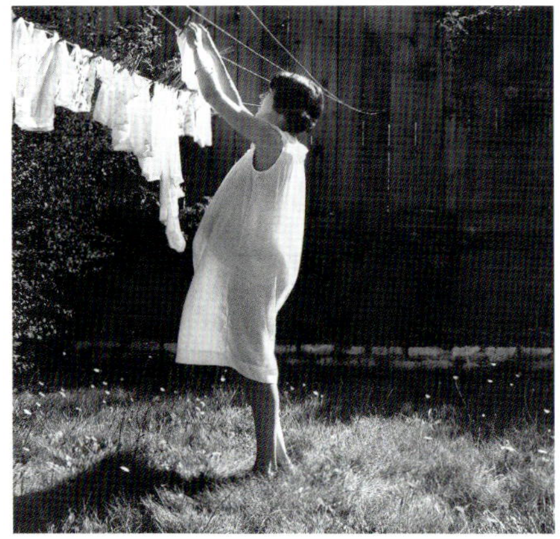

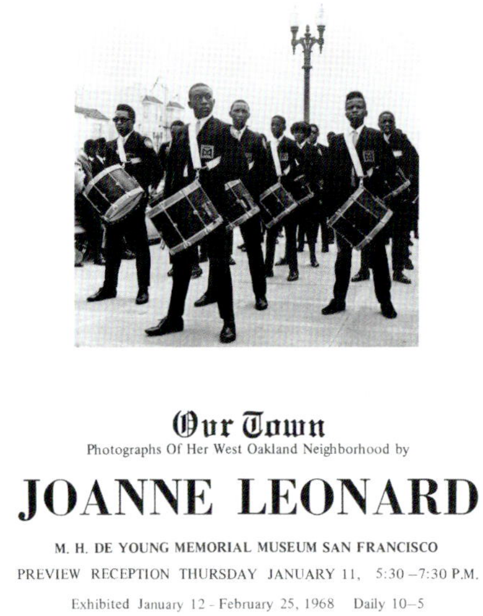

Opposite: Couple on front porch, West Oakland, silver print, mid-1960s; Oakland Museum of California

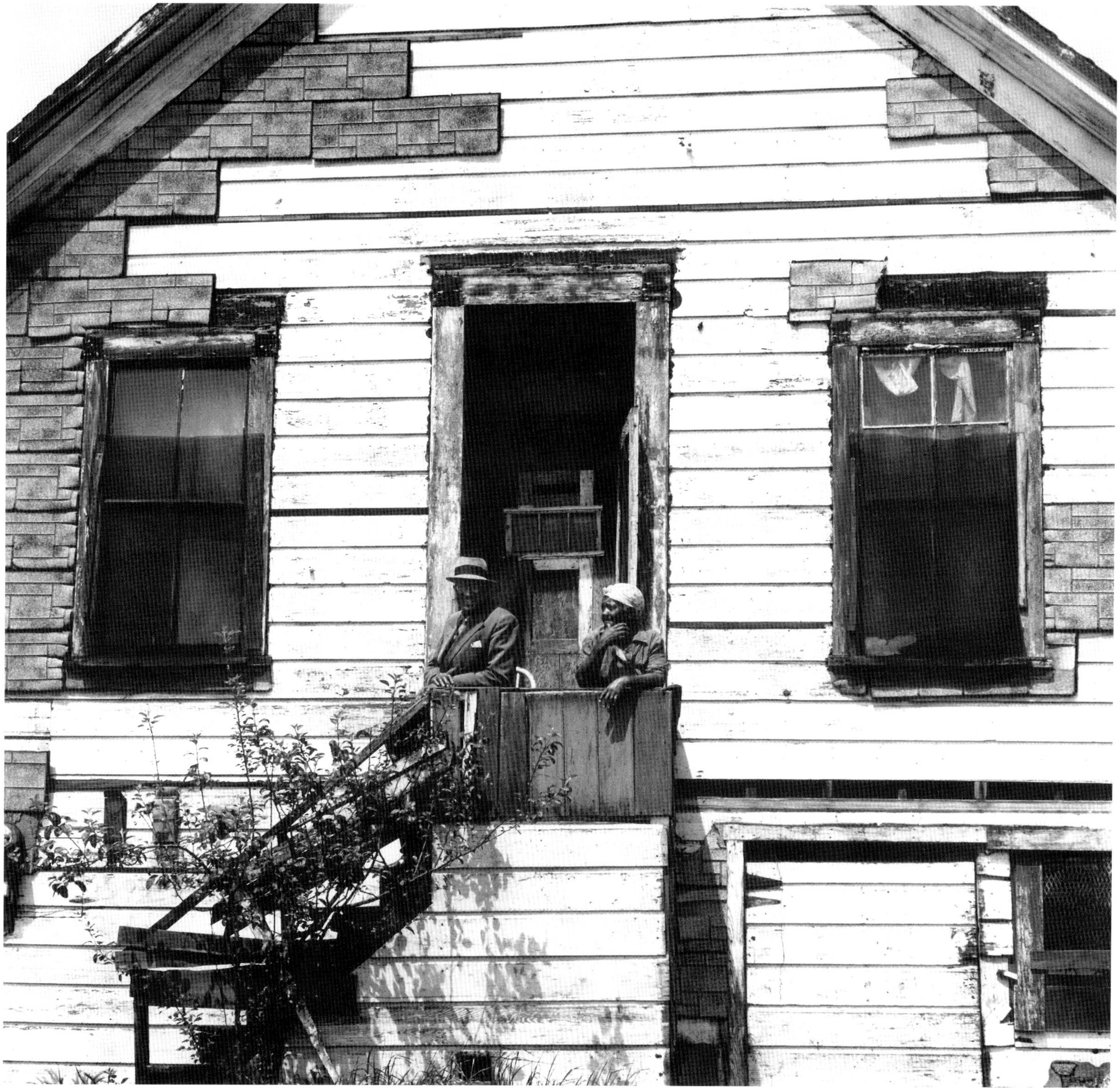

The work I exhibited as Our Town at the de Young Museum was based on the teachings of John Collier Jr., with whom I'd studied at San Francisco State. He urged his photo students to give their photographs to their photo subjects. He taught that photo subjects tell you things about your photographs that you might well have no other way to know. For example, your training as an artist might lead you to think of the people in your photographs in formal terms. You might say about one picture, "The shape of the man in the corner anchors the composition." But your neighbor might point to the same photograph and say, "Oh, I see my cousin who lives down the block." Inspired by Collier's teaching, I had given my photographs to neighbors whom I came to know and talked with them about the photographs. As a result, I had been invited to photograph family members, invited to come inside homes, invited to photograph events like graduations and weddings. After a while, I realized that photographing my own family and close friends with the same attention to intimacy, ceremony (graduation, weddings), place (rooms, home interiors), and daily life would be my way of continuing the work I began in West Oakland. This was when I began to work out the idea of the intimate documentary that continues as the heart of my work today.

Opposite: Pairs, silver prints; Oakland Museum of California

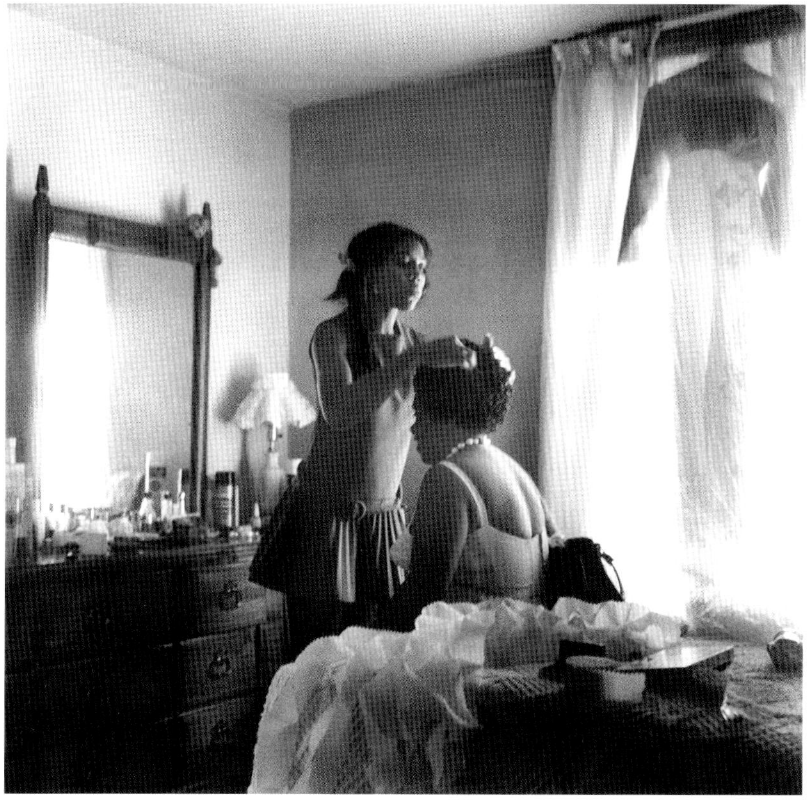

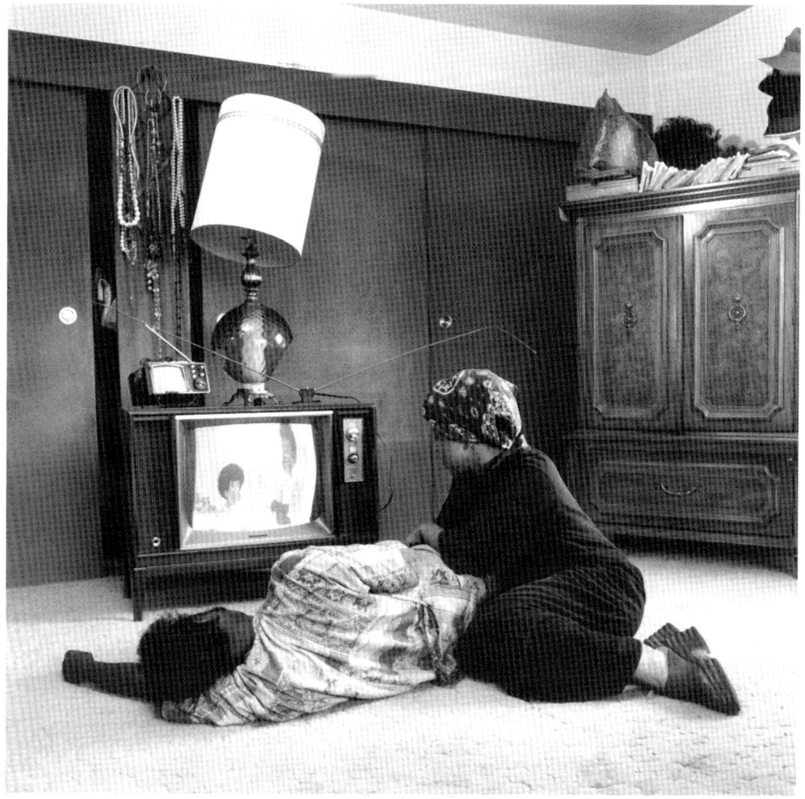

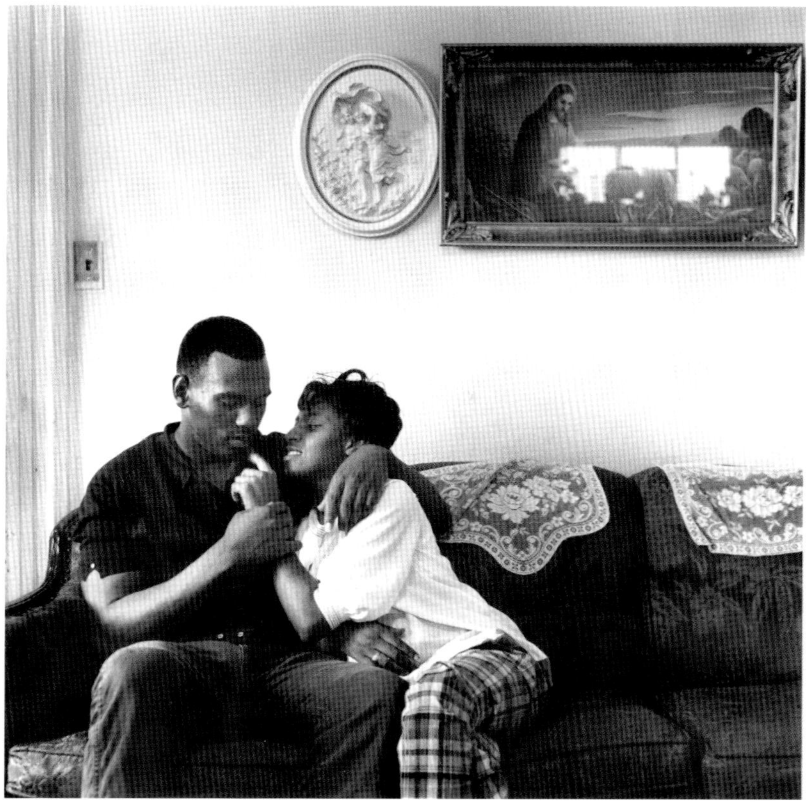

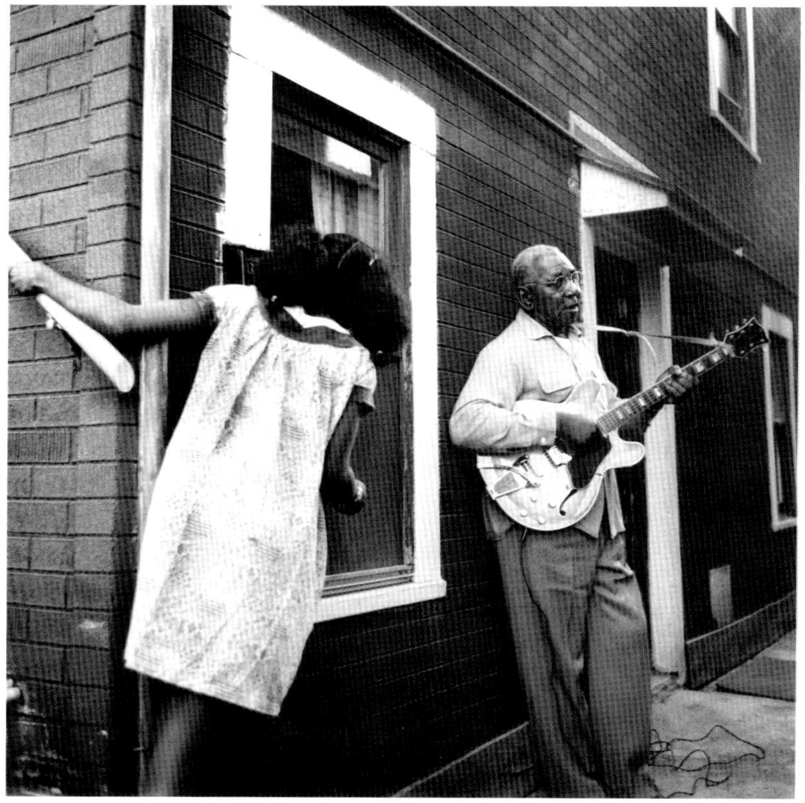

In 1971, on a visit to Manhattan, I was on a bus heading toward Greenwich Village when a woman got on. I noted right away that she was a serious photographer. She carried a very large soft-sided bag that (somehow it was obvious) was full of cameras. This was not a typical camera bag, and the cameras that pressed their outlines against the bag's interior were also large. She was dressed in a fashion I thought of as bohemian. She had on shoes with laces that crisscrossed up her leg like ballet slipper ties. I wondered—could this be Diane Arbus? Although this woman was older than the person in the only photo I'd seen of Arbus, taken when she was in her twenties, I felt I recognized her. I leaned over and asked. Yes, she said, not seeming startled at all. I suppose many people in New York recognized her.

I told her I admired her work. She was not at all unfriendly. I said I was from San Francisco, and she asked me about photography out there. While in New York I had been trying to interest galleries and publishers in my work and had with me a copy of *Life* magazine featuring my photograph as a winner in the *Life* international photo competition. I'd taken the daring—for so early in my career—step of entering the professional part of the competition, when only a year or so before I surely would have submitted as an amateur. I proudly showed the magazine to Arbus but was immediately worried that she would find this photograph of Bruce's brother and his wife with their first baby far too sweet. It lacked the edge, the emphasis on things startling or unexpected, that I so admired in her work. The only photograph that I knew of hers with babies made a drooling baby look rather monstrous and unappealing. I don't recall her exact words but remember that she was gracious about my photograph despite my apprehensions. After a short while, we came to her stop, and she was gone. Arbus died later that year, a suicide.

Opposite: Fletcher, Palmer, and Sonia Beasley, silver print, 1967

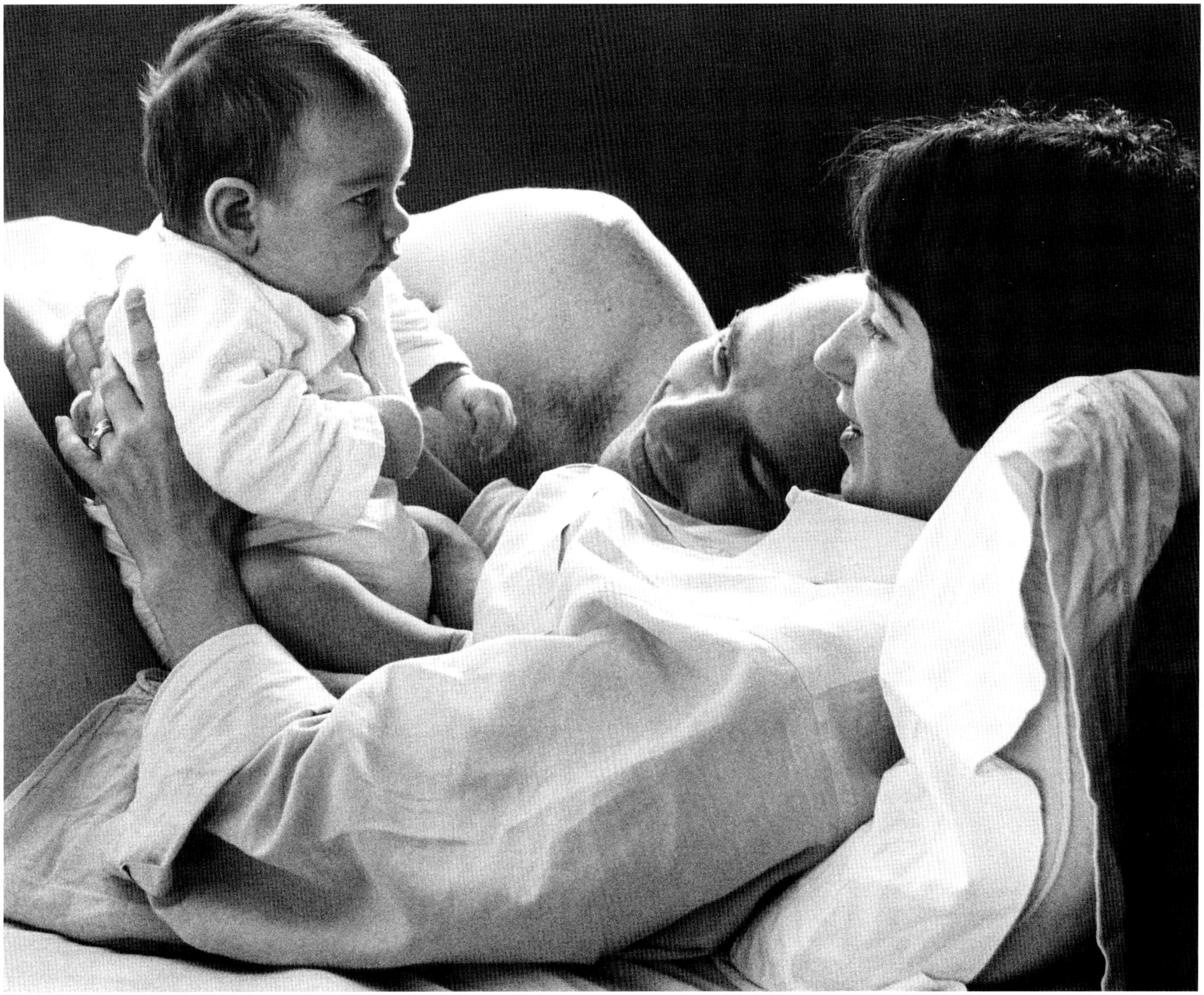

While I continued to photograph in West Oakland, I was struggling to reconcile the largely sunny worldview of my family photographs, like the one I had shown Arbus, with the daily experiences of West Oakland poverty I saw, as well as the anger and energy of the political actions in which I took part. These included marches for more construction site jobs in the community during the construction of the Bay Area Rapid Transit system, or BART. The "JOBART" sign in my photograph means "Jobs for BART." I joined the protest march with some neighbors who had made the signs they carried in my photographs.

Opposite: West Oakland protest march for jobs: Bay Area Rapid Transit (JOBART protest) and McClymonds High School band, West Oakland, silver prints, mid-1960s; Oakland Museum of California

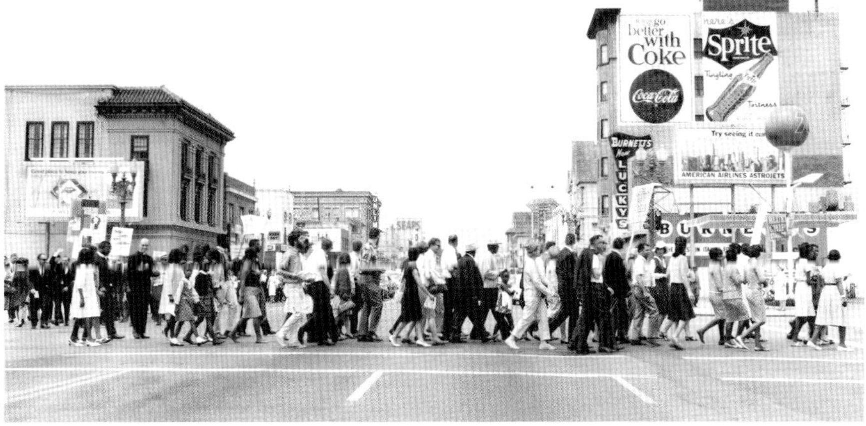
better with Coke
Coca-Cola
Sprite

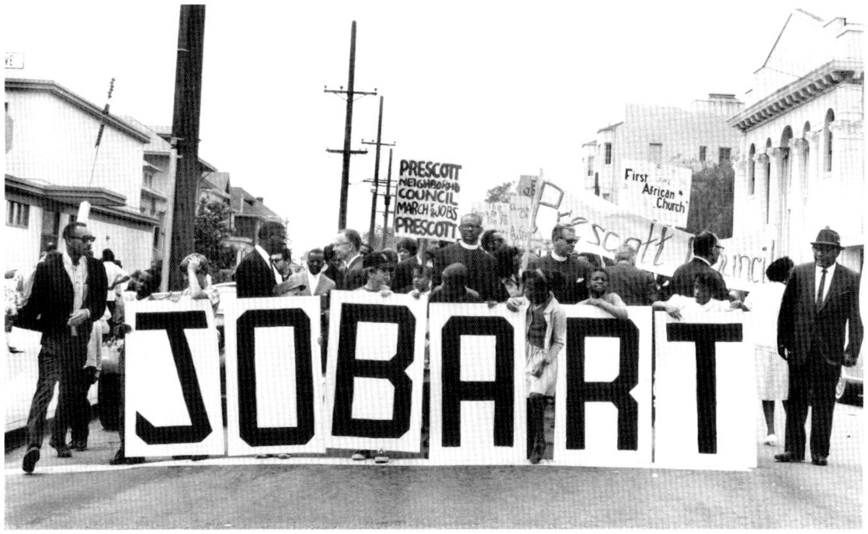
PRESCOTT
NEIGHBORHOOD
COUNCIL
MARCH for JOBS
PRESCOTT
First African Church
JOBART

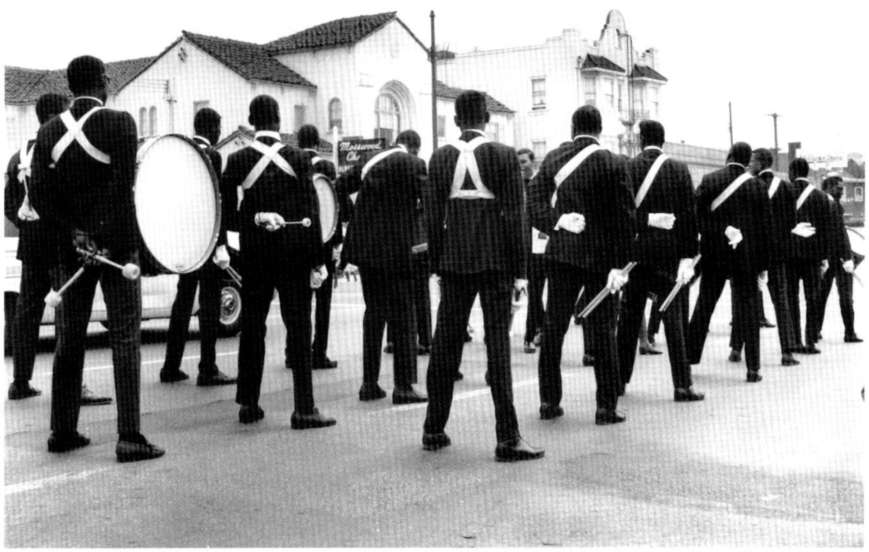

This photograph of Sonia and her baby, taken on a camping trip, is another of the family photographs that were important to my work at the time I lived and photographed in West Oakland. This image figures in one of the earliest collage works (the *Red Triptych*) that I began to make as a way to pull together ideas about the politicization and activism I was a part of in West Oakland and photographs from the daily press, particularly of the deeply troubling war in Vietnam.

Opposite: Sonia and Fletcher Beasley, Mendocino, silver print (round), ca. 1967

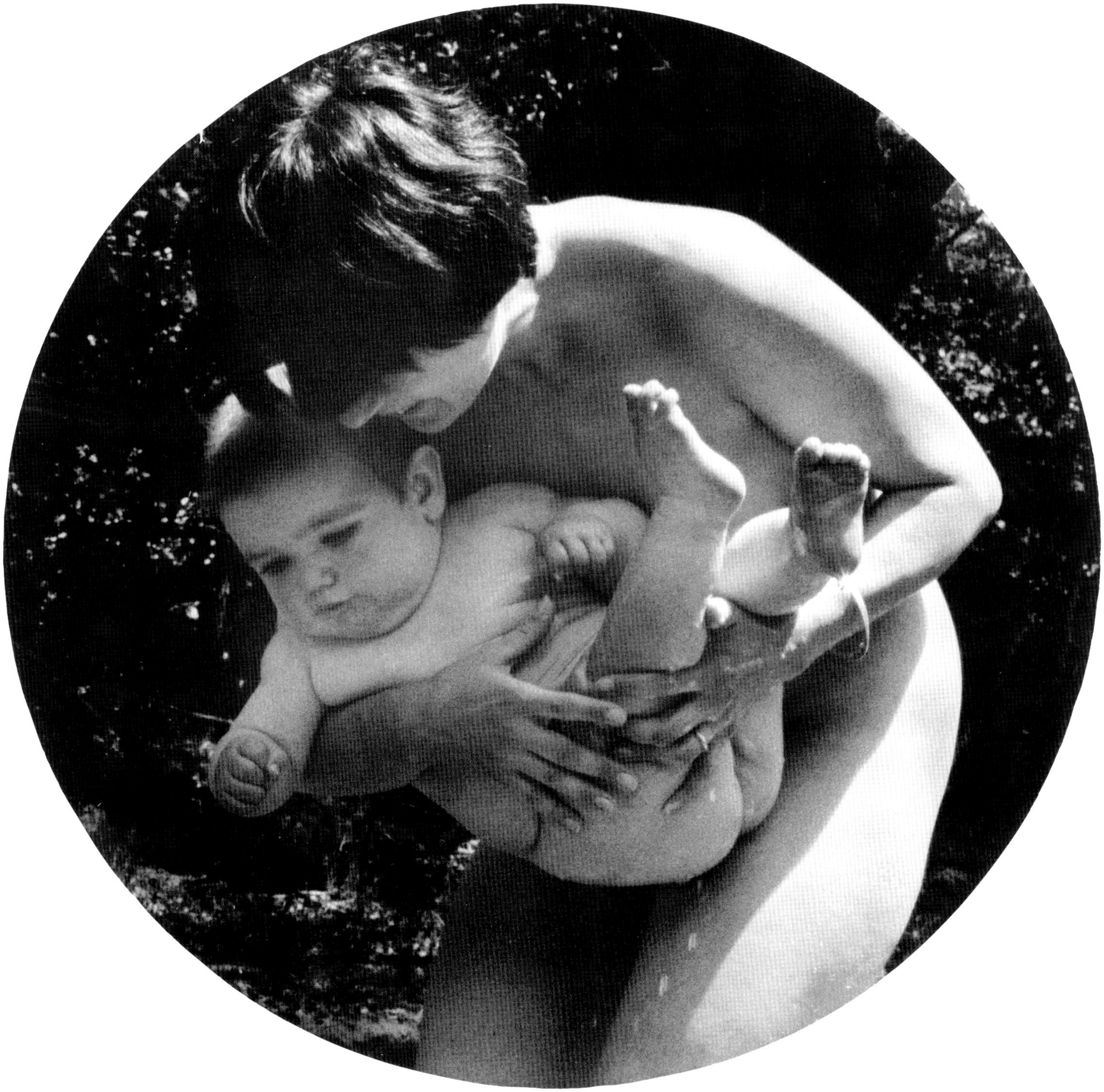

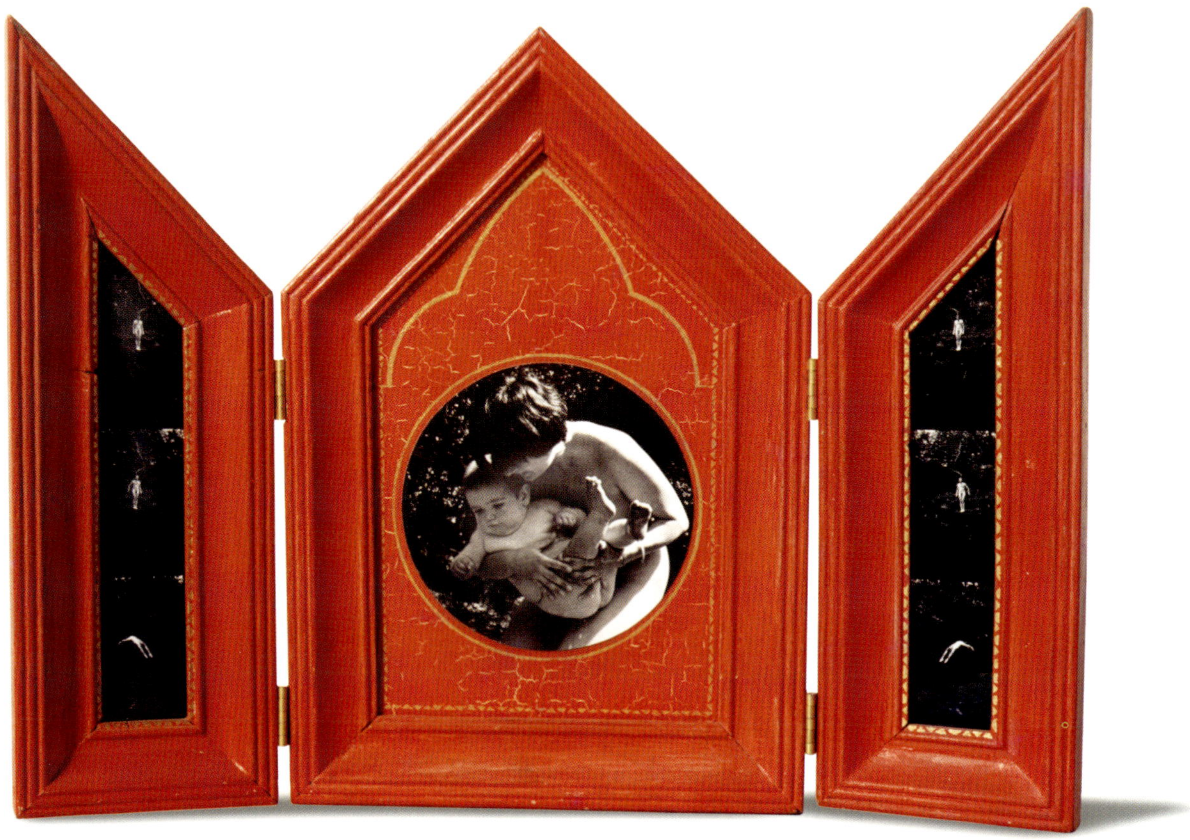

How could I remain content recording intimate moments like Sonia's with her baby in the face of war news, especially when some of the carnage and misery was the result of actions by my own country? I was determined to find ways of contrasting idyllic scenes on one side of a triptych with reality such as the daily news on the reverse side.

Above: *Red Triptych* (front), Wood, red and gold paint, silver print photographs, 13 inches × 18 inches × ¾ inches, opened, ca. 1969

I clipped a photograph of a wounded baby and anguished mother from the news for the back of the triptych in order to contrast them with my mother and child and diving man on the front. I placed bits of headline copy taken directly from the newspapers—all that could be seen when the doors were closed but evident from the back when the doors were open.

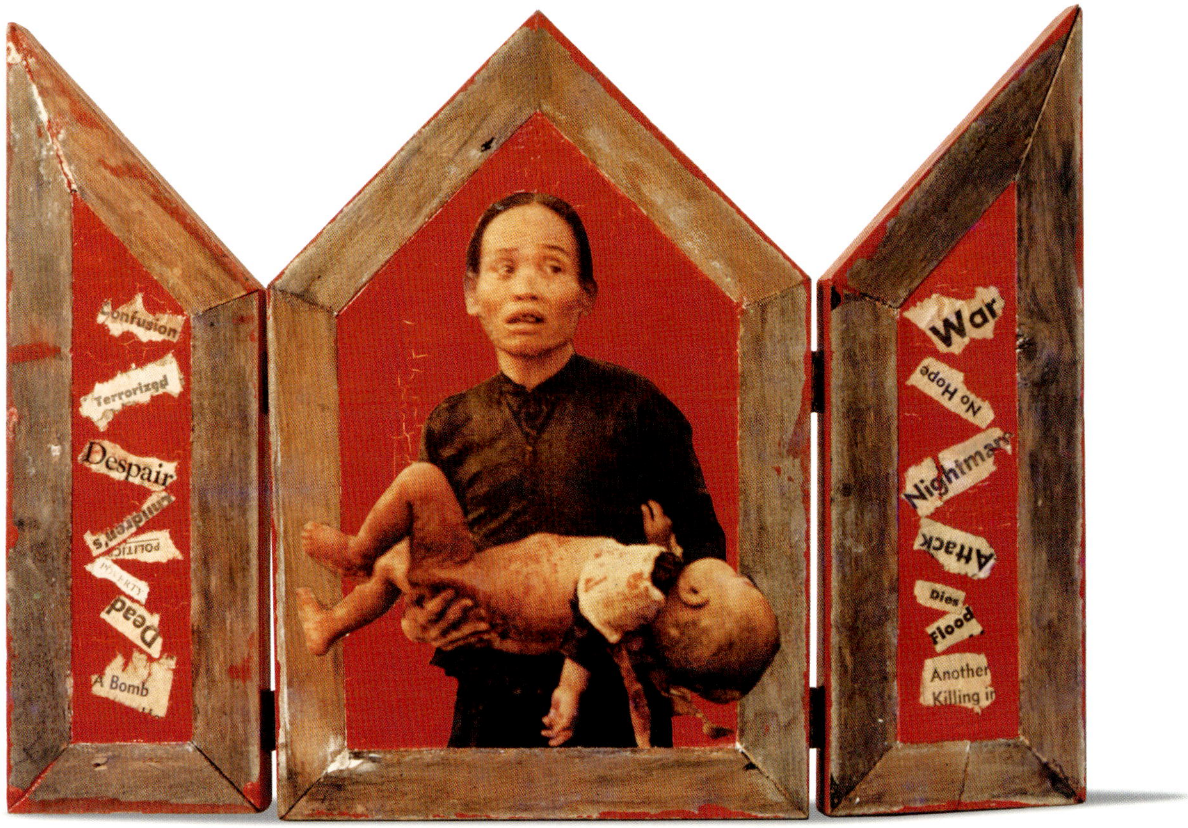

Above: *Red Triptych* (back)

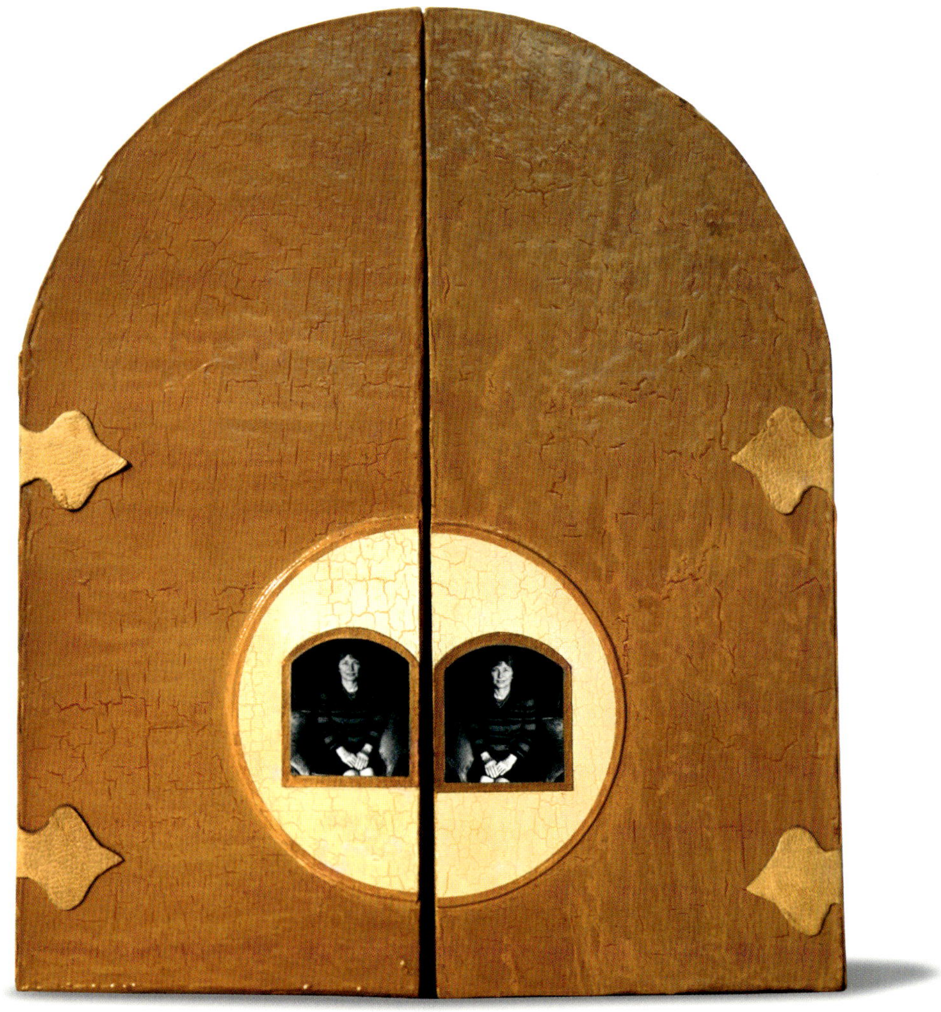

The triptych on these pages (called simply *Yellow Triptych*) drew on moments of loss and grief that I witnessed: a friend (at center of triptych) grieves for her mother who had just died. In the side panels I added images from the news, combined with reproductions of medieval religious views. Thus I began here and in other work to juxtapose occasional anguish at home with the horrors of war.

To me photographs are precious, important, often gripping or disturbing, yet they are also so ubiquitous that they can seem completely mundane. How, visually, to give them the appearance of the weighty treasures they really are? The forms I've borrowed, such as triptychs, help suggest the gravity I've wanted the pieces to have. The triptych form is also something like a book: it opens. Inside, in medieval altarpieces, the imagery often can be read as the lines of a story. Using strategies somewhat reminiscent of these medieval forms has not had religious meaning for me but has been a device for visually building separate still images into longer statements or stories.

Above: *Yellow Triptych* (closed), cardboard, paint, silver print, photographs, leather hinges, approximately 18 inches × 20 inches × 1 ½ inches, closed, ca. 1969

Opposite: *Yellow Triptych* (opened), approximately 20 inches × 36 inches × 1 ½ inches, opened

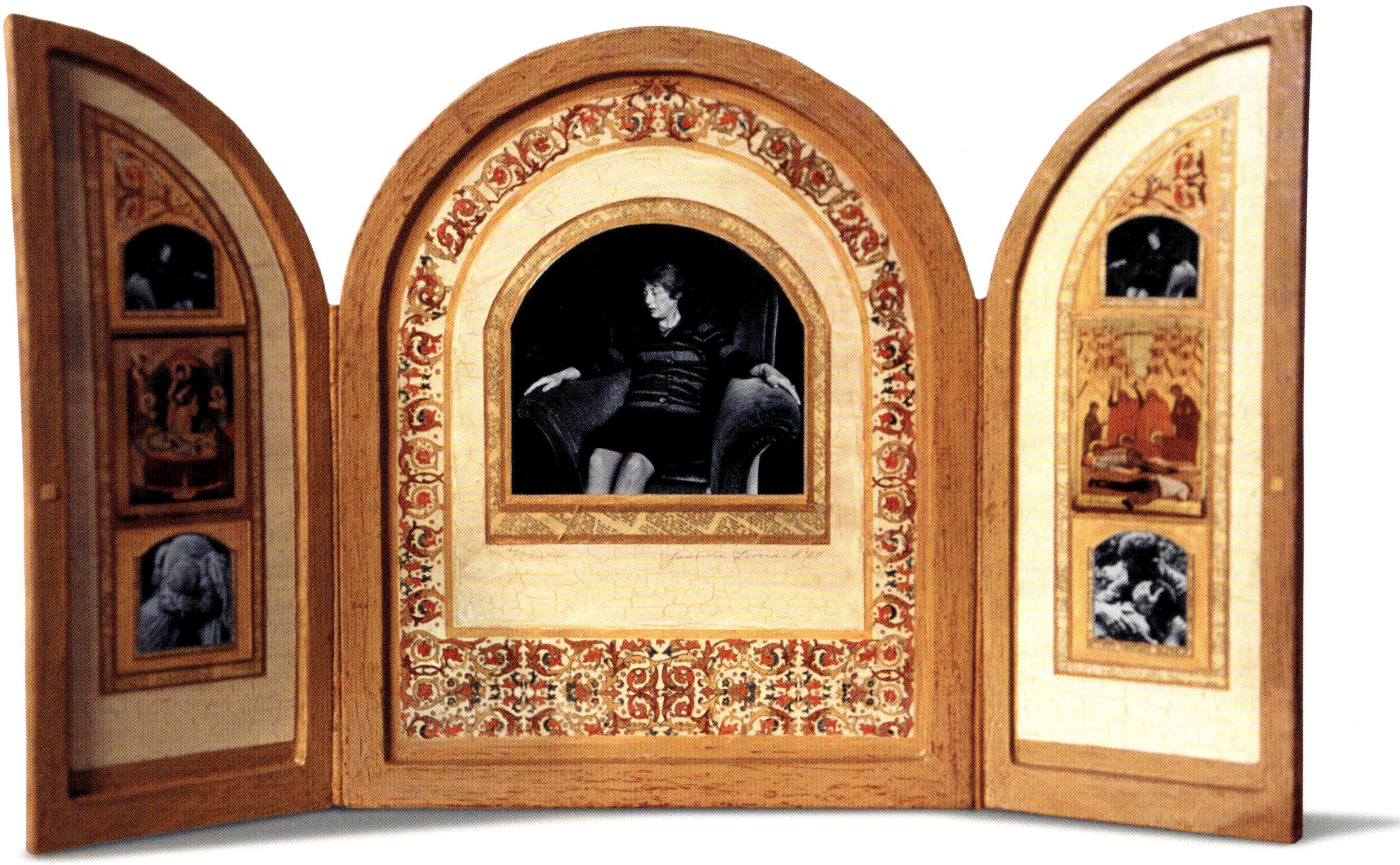

Putting one's work before the public opens it to contested meanings. In 1992, I commented about my piece *Of Things Masculine* in a book on sexuality:

> Above my photograph of the nude, sleeping figure of my husband, I placed a starry sky (actually sperm under a microscope) and below, war-wounded bodies. I understood that I was contrasting an intimate view in our bedroom with forces of life and death in the world beyond but only later realized the extent to which I had tried to describe my relation to power and vulnerability.

Later that same year, the critic Richard Mohr, assuming the man in my photograph was gay, lambasted me (among people who "consider themselves feminists") for creating "a photograph that managed to equate gay sexuality with mass murder":

> Joanne Leonard's late 1960s photo collage *Of Things Masculine* pictures a wholly naked, self-indulgently languorous, totally sensual man . . . (who) . . . dreams on high of cum. His heaven is a celestial river of spermatozoa, the actuality of which in the real world below his feet, however, is mass murder, massacred Vietnamese children.

When women's ideas comprise *more* of the published language and thinking about art, we will have the corrective to authors like Mohr, who apparently could not imagine a woman's point of view and was too quick to substitute his own.

Opposite: *Of Things Masculine,* magazine clippings (including images of Biafran war casualties), silver print, Plexiglas layers, approximately 10 ½ inches × 10 inches, ca. 1971

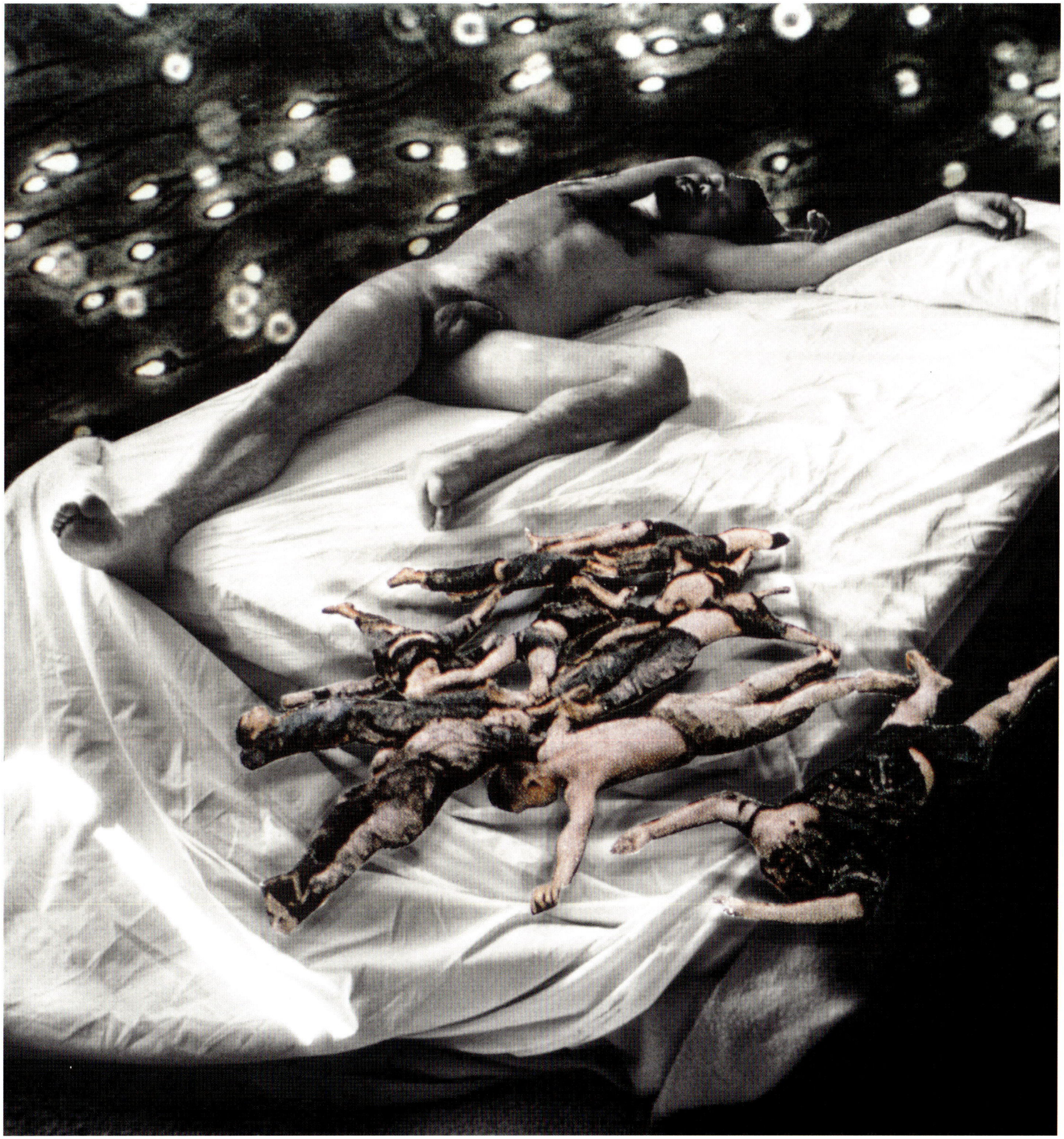

Night Photography

Sleeping figures have attracted me throughout my years in photography, particularly during moments of transition or when I felt driven by ideas and dormant feelings I could not yet identify. The early photographs of sleeping figures formed a bridge between my activist work in West Oakland and the personal documenting of family and friends that would come later. Carrying the sleeping series further over the years has allowed me to reflect on intimate relationships as well as the larger world.

Opposite: Sleeping series, silver prints, 1970s

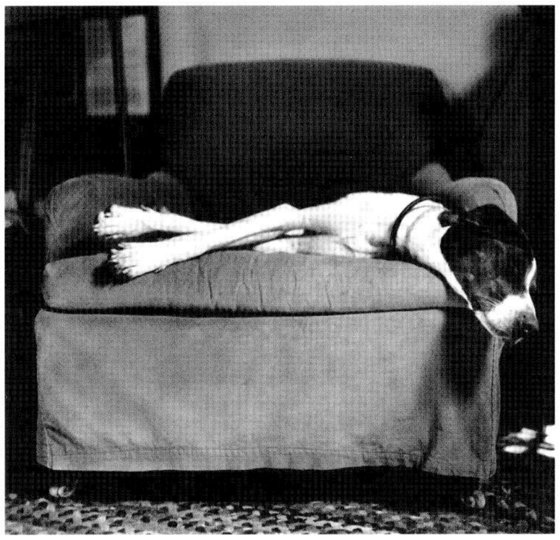
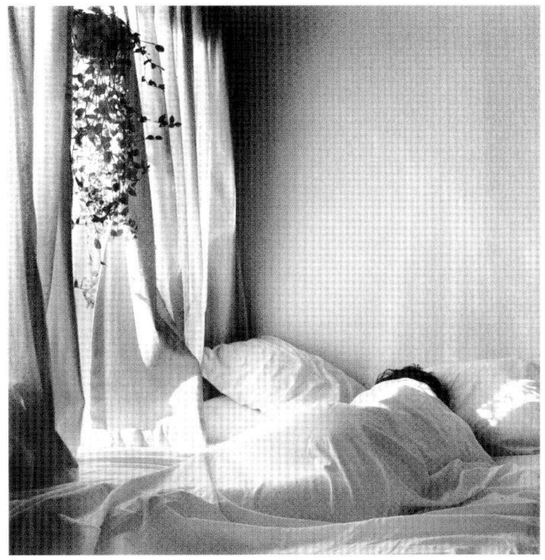
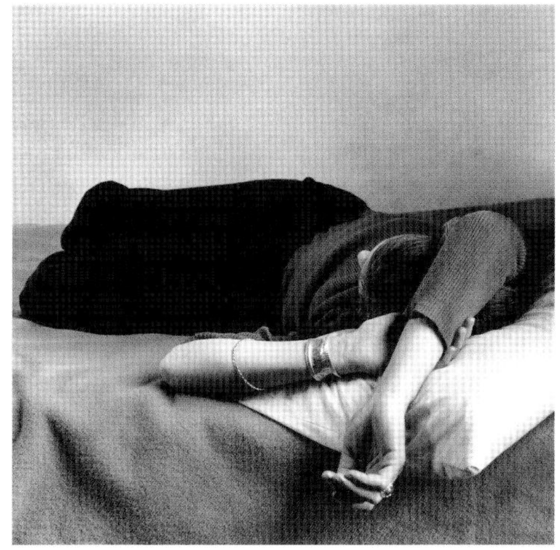
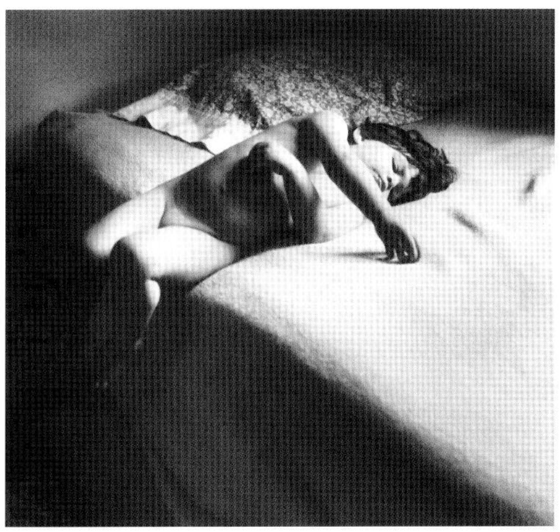
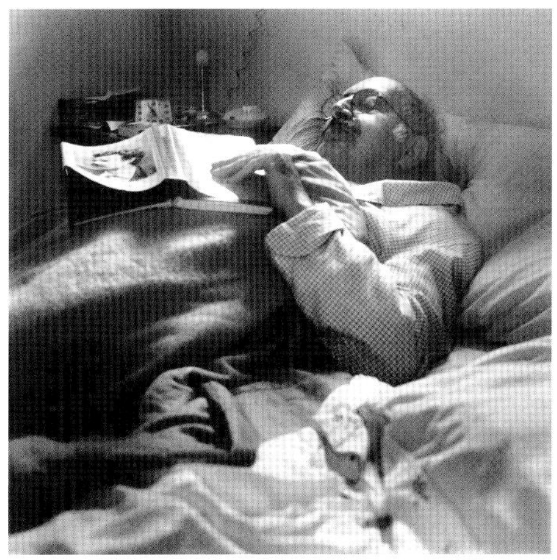
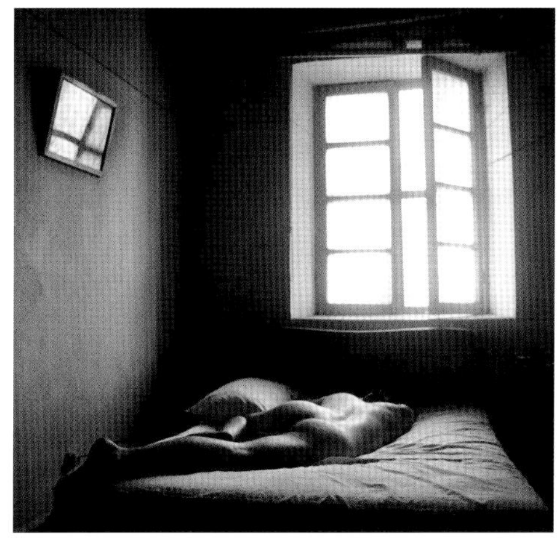
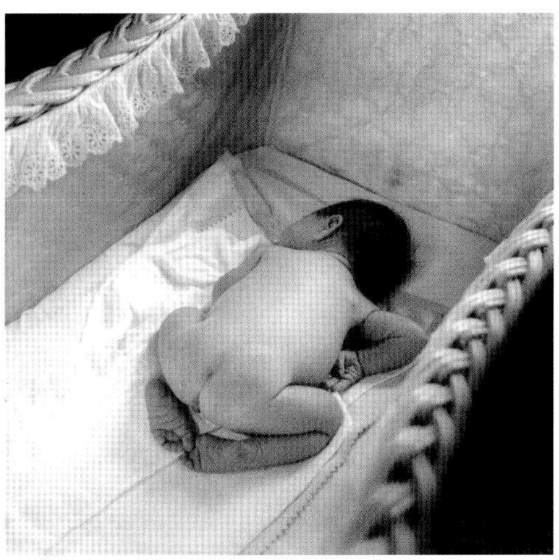
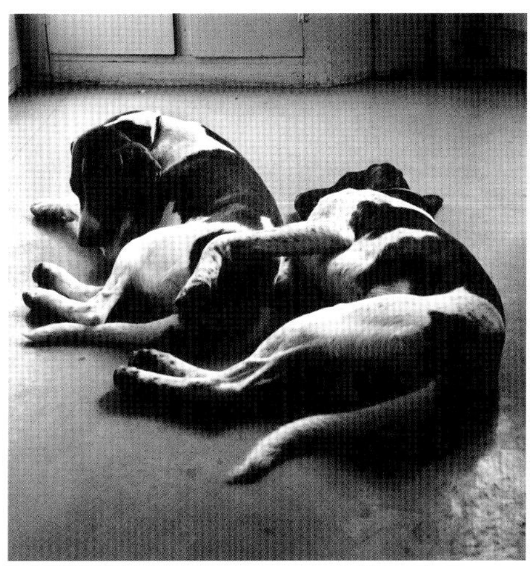
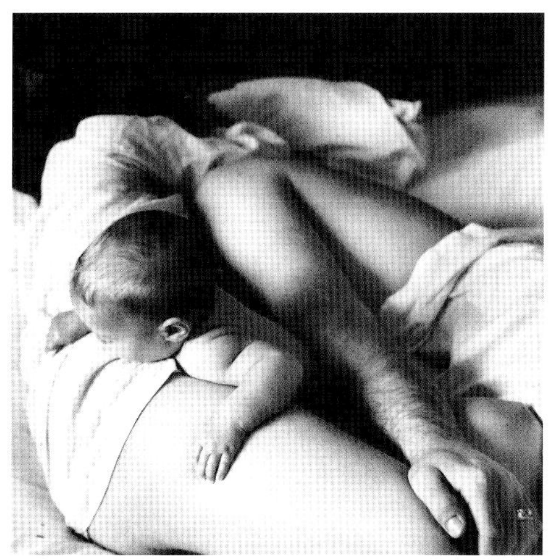

There is a sense of voyeurism in most photographs of sleepers, heightening, I think, the potential erotic possibilities of the image. My own photographs of sleepers have also served as a springboard to the dreams, fantasies, and commentary I often approach through collage.

Opposite: *Another Morning* (sleeping houseguest), silver print, ca. 1972; Stanford University Art Museum

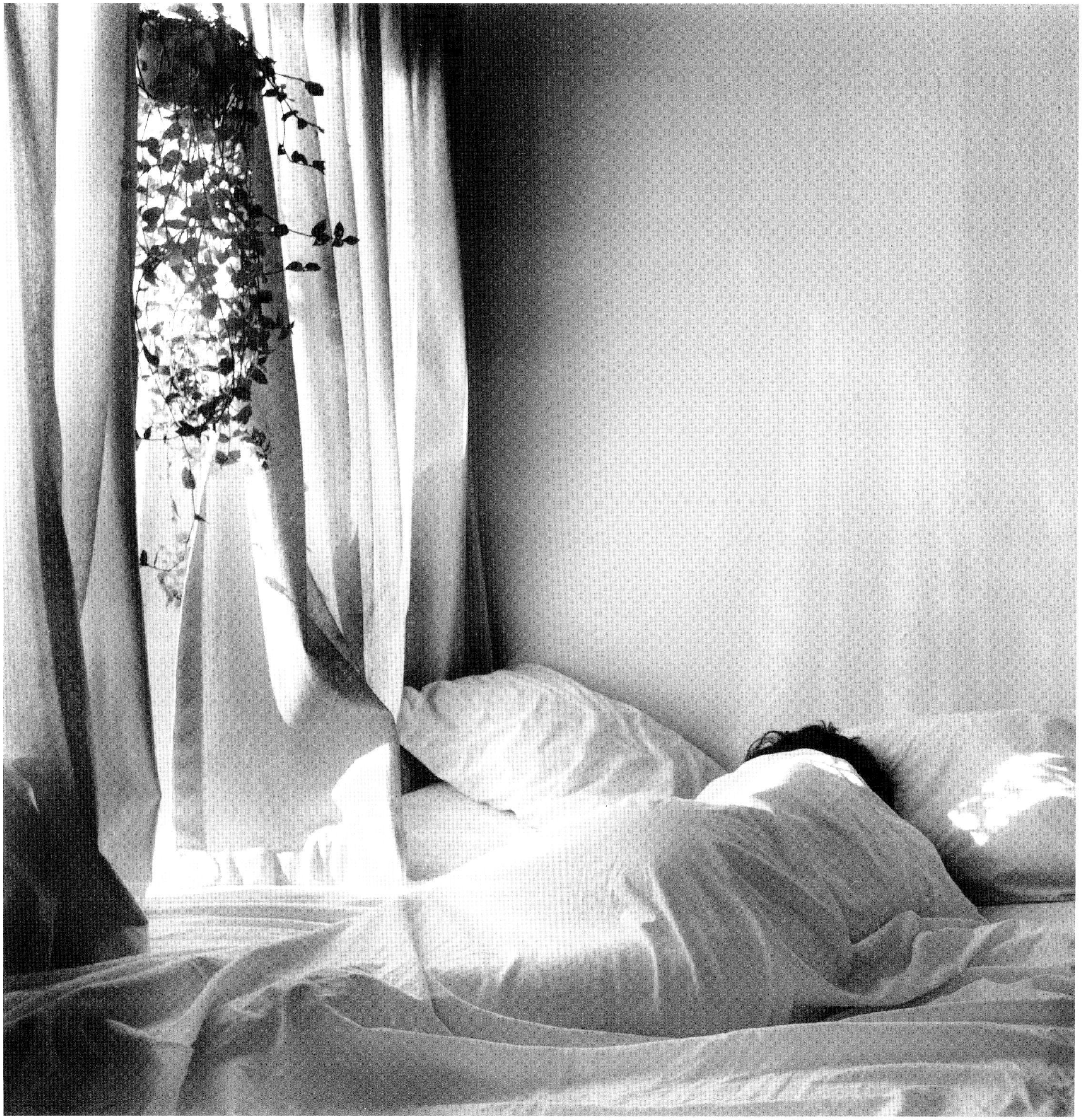

Many of my collages are based on photographs of ordinary moments from everyday life—like this one, which brings back for me the feelings of bodies and skin and warmth in the morning—tactile recollections that might be otherwise entirely lost these many years later.

Early on, I took pictures of Bruce casting bronze from a glowing crucible of molten metal. One might say I was swept into a blaze—or blinded by it. For the moment, Bruce was an art-world star, and I was very taken with him. Quite handsome and so self-assured that some considered him arrogant, he appealed to me for what I would have called then his contagious self-confidence. I felt energized and pleased when we were together. I was learning some of what it meant to "foster one's career" (work like mad, take good photographs of the artwork, attend friends' openings, and follow up all new art-world contacts with letters and phone calls).

I loved our daily routine of working away intensely in different corners of our building, and Bruce was an astute and appreciative critic of my work. My women friends and I sometimes joked about women who married doctors or lawyers, women who "married the men that they wanted to be." But the idea wasn't altogether a joke; by teaming with Bruce, I was choosing a man I admired, the artist I wanted to be. I didn't realize at first how little deep affection or partnering Bruce gave me. Everything was fine as long as the real center of attention was Bruce, his sculpture, his career. Yet even when everything fell apart and I was devastated by the loss of love I thought I'd had, the loss of the home we'd built, the dreams I'd dreamed and thought he'd shared, I realized there were things I'd gained. Unlike so many women of my generation with no blueprint for a career, I had come quite a way toward my own.

Opposite: Bruce Beasley in mirror, West Oakland, silver print, 1971

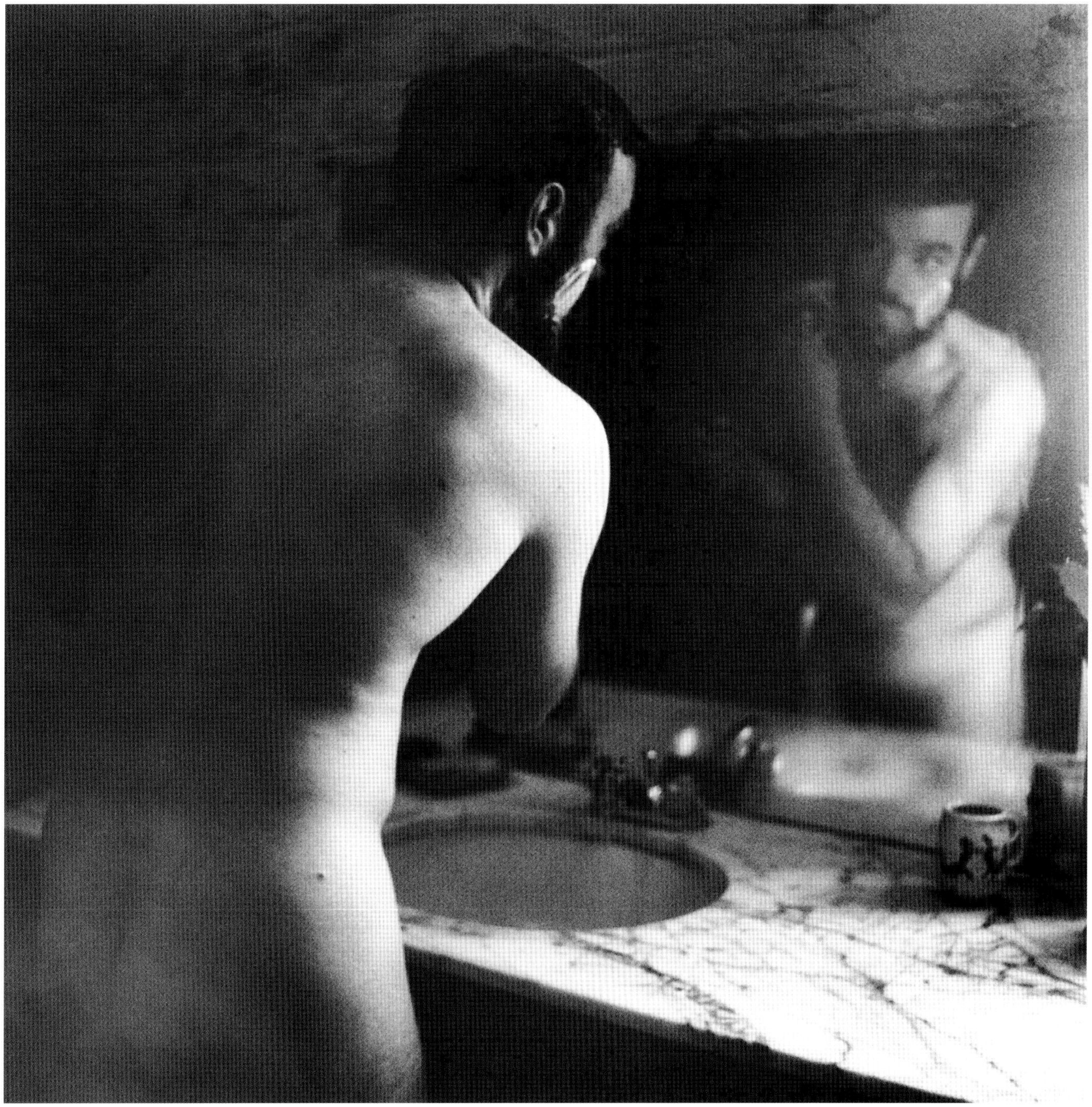

Nothing difficult has happened in my life for which I've been so unprepared as this: Bruce left and never turned back. He walked back into his life as if I'd never been there.

Perhaps it isn't surprising that the first of the events surrounding Bruce's departure was a significant professional accomplishment for me. I was photographing a story for *Life* magazine when Bruce decided to spend the weekend with the woman he'd met at most a month before. He returned from his weekend away, announced that he was leaving me, and departed just a few days later (on my birthday) for six months in France. Later we divorced, and he married his new love, settling down in what had been our home.

For a long time I was completely devastated. The depth of my distress surprised some of my friends, who said they could have predicted the breakup. In so many ways he had not been good for me, but I had not come to terms with that. As a twin, I was better suited to merging my identity with someone else than to hanging on to the person I was (or could be) alone.

He was very controlling, but I'd lived with his edicts: "Don't talk while I'm talking." "Don't ask where we're going when I'm driving." "We'll eat when I'm hungry." "Don't even think about having children—my career would be jeopardized." I'd put off my dreams of having a child but became sad and angry, feelings that would recur years later, when I had a miscarriage. Still, you could not have convinced me until then that we'd been headed toward separation. I'd carried with me a fantasy version of the life I was leading as part of an artistic duo, glad to be sharing a life I somehow thought I wanted.

Several weeks after Bruce's tumultuous departure I pulled myself together and left West Oakland. I found a house to share in the Oakland hills, taking with me almost nothing that belonged to both Bruce and me. Not taking things was a kind of conciliatory posture I maintained until I eventually was able to feel outrage.

Though I'd earned little money and had no savings, I had a certain degree of independence during our marriage. Having covered most of my own expenses while we were together, I was somewhat prepared to find the steady work that I'd be needing. But my independence hurt me too: Bruce's lawyers used it as an excuse to relieve him of almost any financial responsibility for my transition to life alone.

Opposite: Dreams and Nightmares series, layered works incorporating continuous-tone positive transparencies, selectively opaqued, and collage, 1972

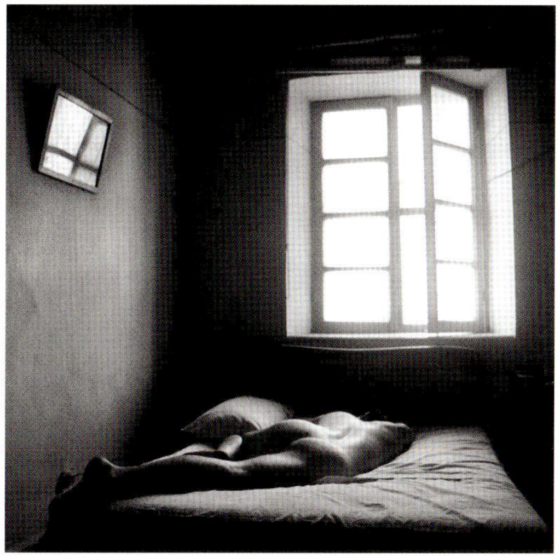

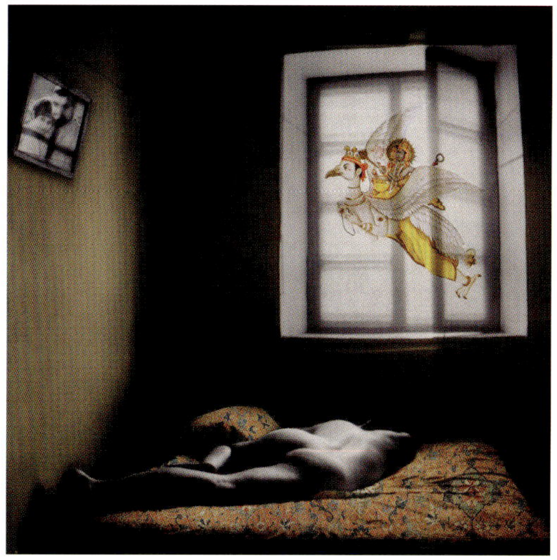

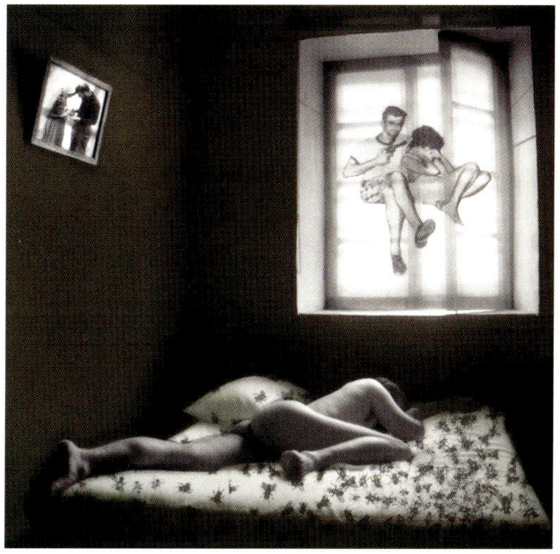

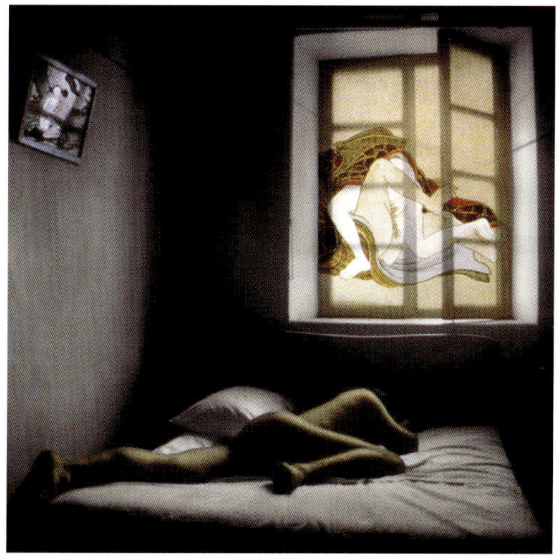

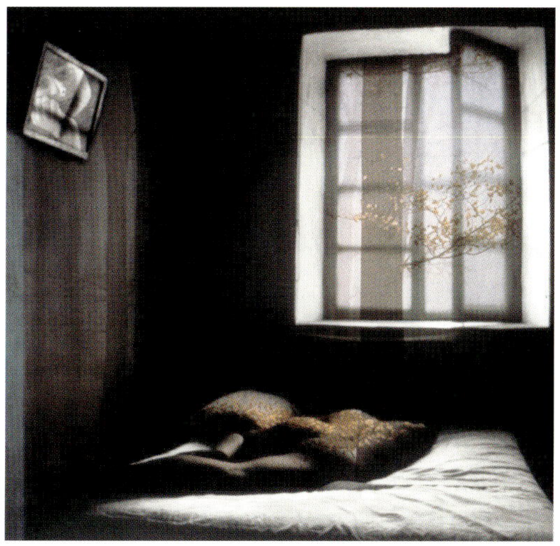

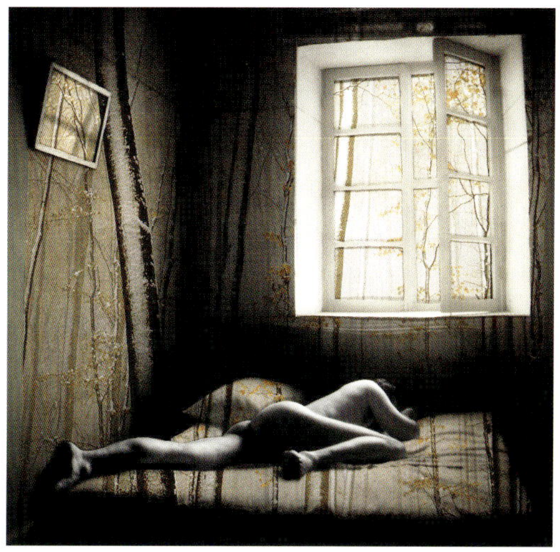

After I'd moved from West Oakland and had begun to deal with the likely permanence of our separation, but before the shock and hurt had dulled in the least, I began the series Dreams and Nightmares, based on a photograph I had made of Bruce sleeping in a hotel room in Mexico, where we'd traveled not long before the separation.

Opposite: *Merida Morning* (Bruce on bed), silver print, 1971

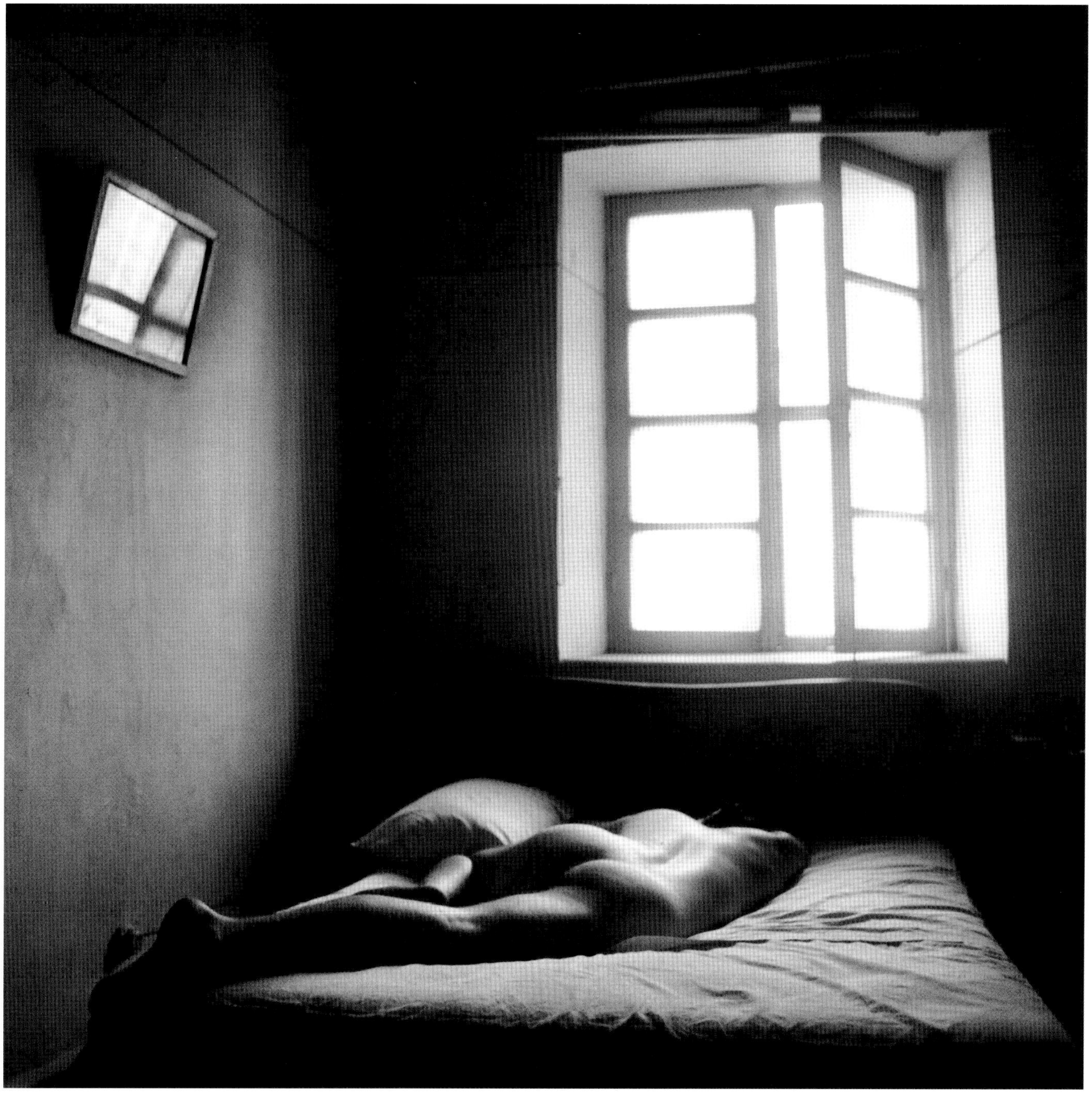

Lost Dreams is the first photo collage of the series made over a period of a few months titled Dreams and Nightmares. In *Lost Dreams,* in the space where a picture had hung on the wall in the hotel room, I substituted a picture of Bruce and me from earlier days. I made other small inclusions in the picture frame area of some other works of the series. The despairing tone of some of the work's titles—*Lost Dreams, Death for a Wife, Sad Dreams on Cold Mornings,* and *Romanticism Is Ultimately Fatal*—echoes the dark mood of the imagery and suggests the hopelessness, hurt, and anger that gripped me while I made the work.

Opposite: *Lost Dreams*, 10 inches × 10 inches, 1972; collection of Dr. Arlan Cohn

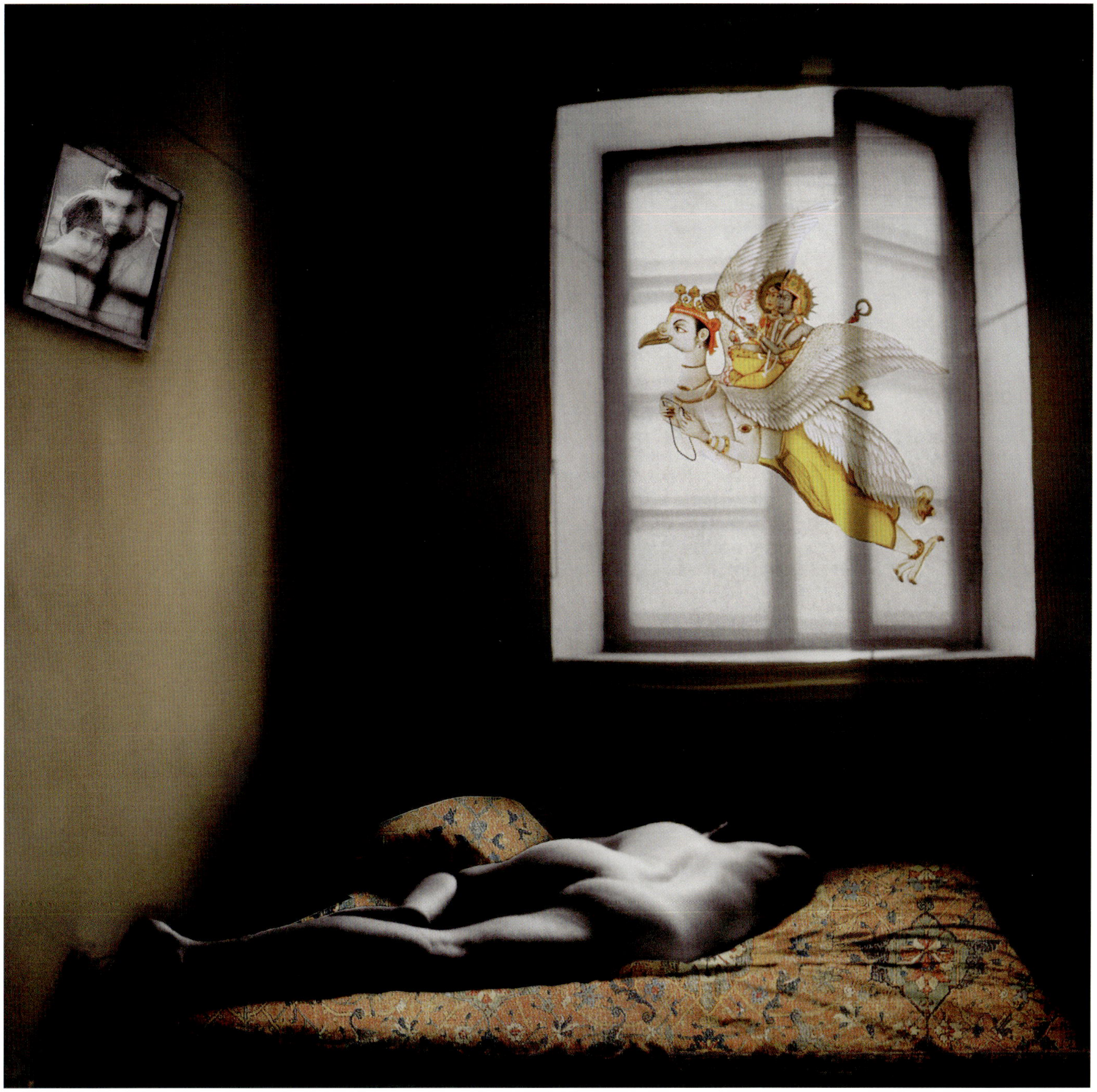

When I made *Death for a Wife,* I considered the picture illustrating a woman being shot in the head a metaphor for sudden, terrible pain inflicted by a husband on a wife. But real battering and murder were not part of my experience, and I had not stopped to think from what a safe place I'd made the experience of another woman into *my* metaphor. In the photo I had taken from a newspaper, a man had brought his wife onto the front porch, called the press, and actually shot her in front of the journalists who responded to the call.

Despite my naïveté and grandiosity in equating the horror in this image with my anguished psychological state, I intend that *Death for a Wife* speaks to the range of pain and violence women experience.

Opposite: *Death for a Wife,* 10 inches × 10 inches; private collection

Overleaf Left: *Erotic Dreams,* 10 inches × 10 inches; private collection

Overleaf Right: *Sad Dreams on Cold Mornings,* 10 inches × 10 inches; San Francisco Museum of Modern Art

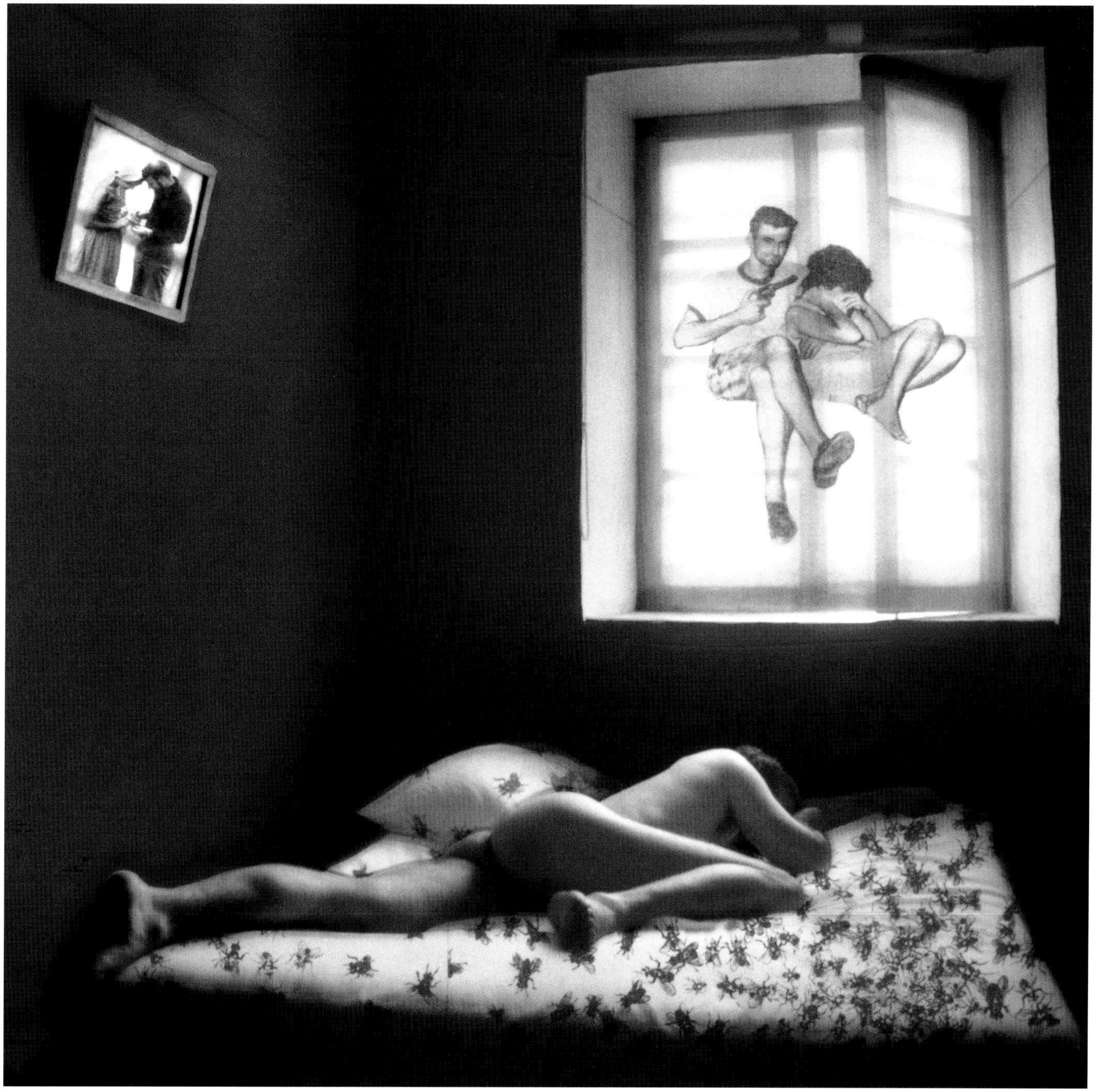

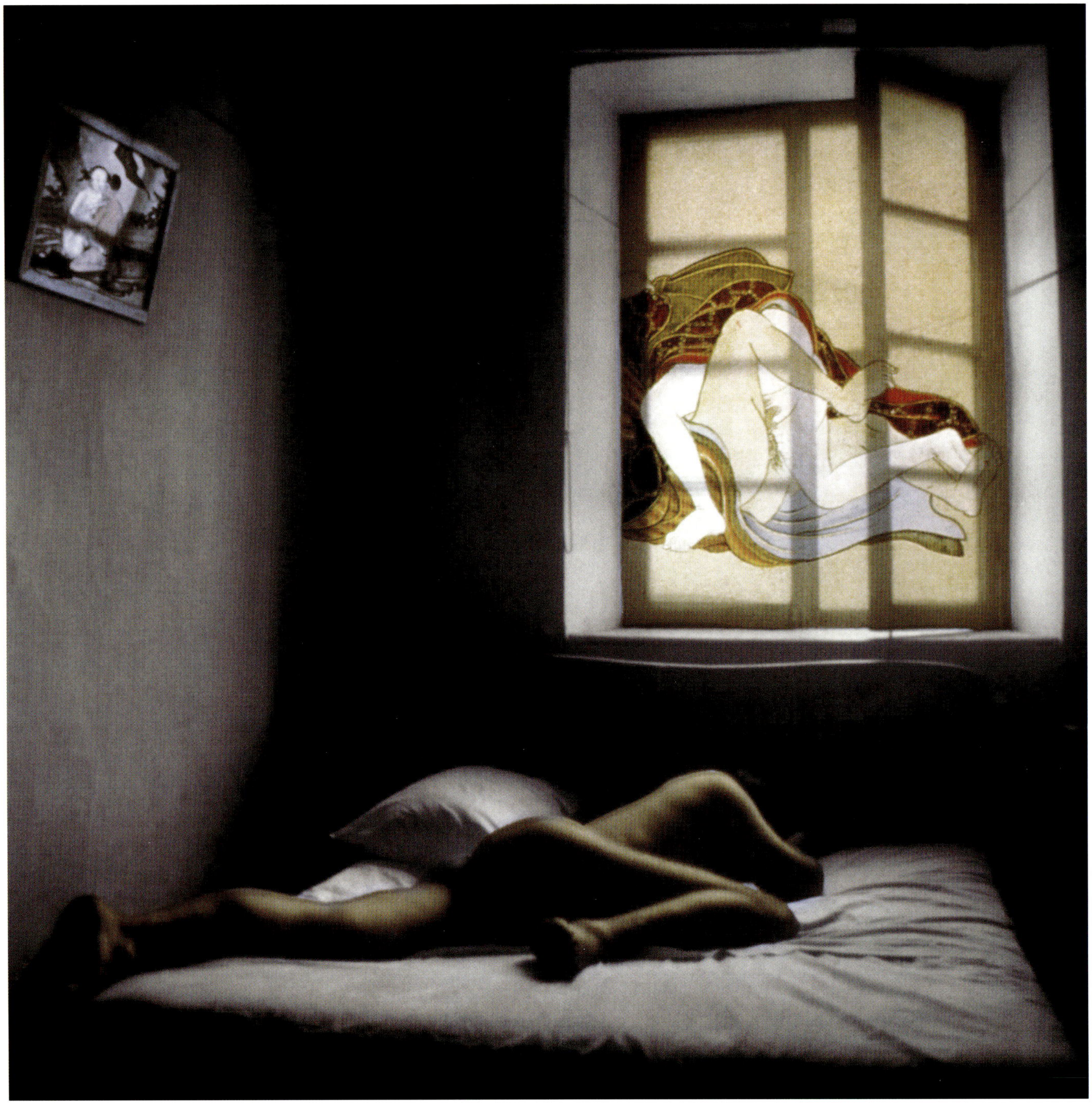

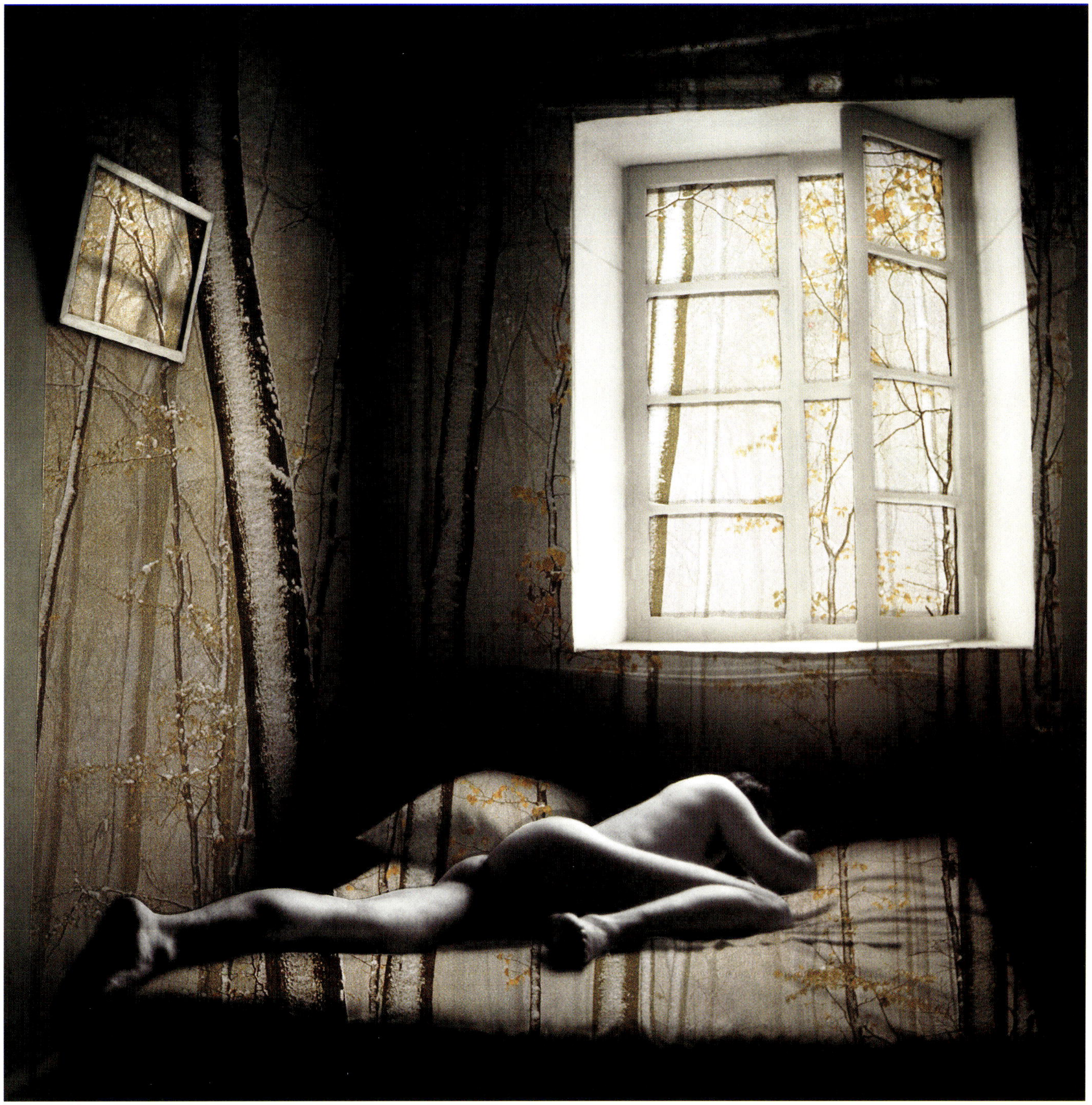

I found a book about the legend of King Arthur and cut from it the image of a knight on horseback a few weeks before I had any idea what I would do with it. I saw the image as one in which a woman was rescued by a knight in armor. I felt I had to work against the dream of rescue and find my own strength. A few years later, when *Ms. Magazine* published *Romanticism Is Ultimately Fatal,* I wrote:

> *My husband and I had just separated when I began the series that I call "Dreams and Nightmares." The difficulties of my marriage had been partly obscured by an overriding romanticism; the loss of some of my romantic dreams is the theme of these window collages. I have selected elements to recall feelings of longing, loneliness, the passing of time and anger.*

I'd felt I'd made this work and then titled it *Romanticism Is Ultimately Fatal* in order to purge sorrow over love lost. Later the women's movement helped me (and other women) understand one of the work's larger themes—that "romance" is a powerful cover often masking the very bad deal marriage can sometimes be, especially for women.

As has happened at other times in my life, I was at a point of discovery in my work just as I was enduring an emotional crisis. The charge of excitement I felt about the work I was creating and the darkroom strategies I was discovering made the loss of physical and emotional pleasure more bearable. In the Dreams and Nightmares series, I was exploring how to work with transparent photographs, placing collage behind the transparent photo image. This work was made twenty years before the availability of digital photo editing programs like Photoshop that would have provided a very different approach to the idea of a transparent, layered image. Many of my collages evolved without any use of digital tools.

In the 1970s, when I was discovering how to accomplish in the darkroom what I wanted to do with transparency, I found Kodak's fine grain positive film, which allowed me to print large (10 × 12 inch) black-and-white positive transparencies. I printed my photographs on the photo-transparency material and processed these film prints in darkroom trays, very much as one would do for a paper print. Later I painted on the back of the film to render the painted areas opaque, so collage would show through only in the areas where I wanted it to show. Then I laid the film over a separate layer that held my collage elements. To finish each of these collages, I gathered the layered segments together in a conventional picture frame. The pieces have been reproduced in books and on record album covers, but there is only one original of each of the images from the Dreams and Nightmares series.

Opposite: *Romanticism Is Ultimately Fatal,* 10 inches × 10 inches; collection of Manuel Neri

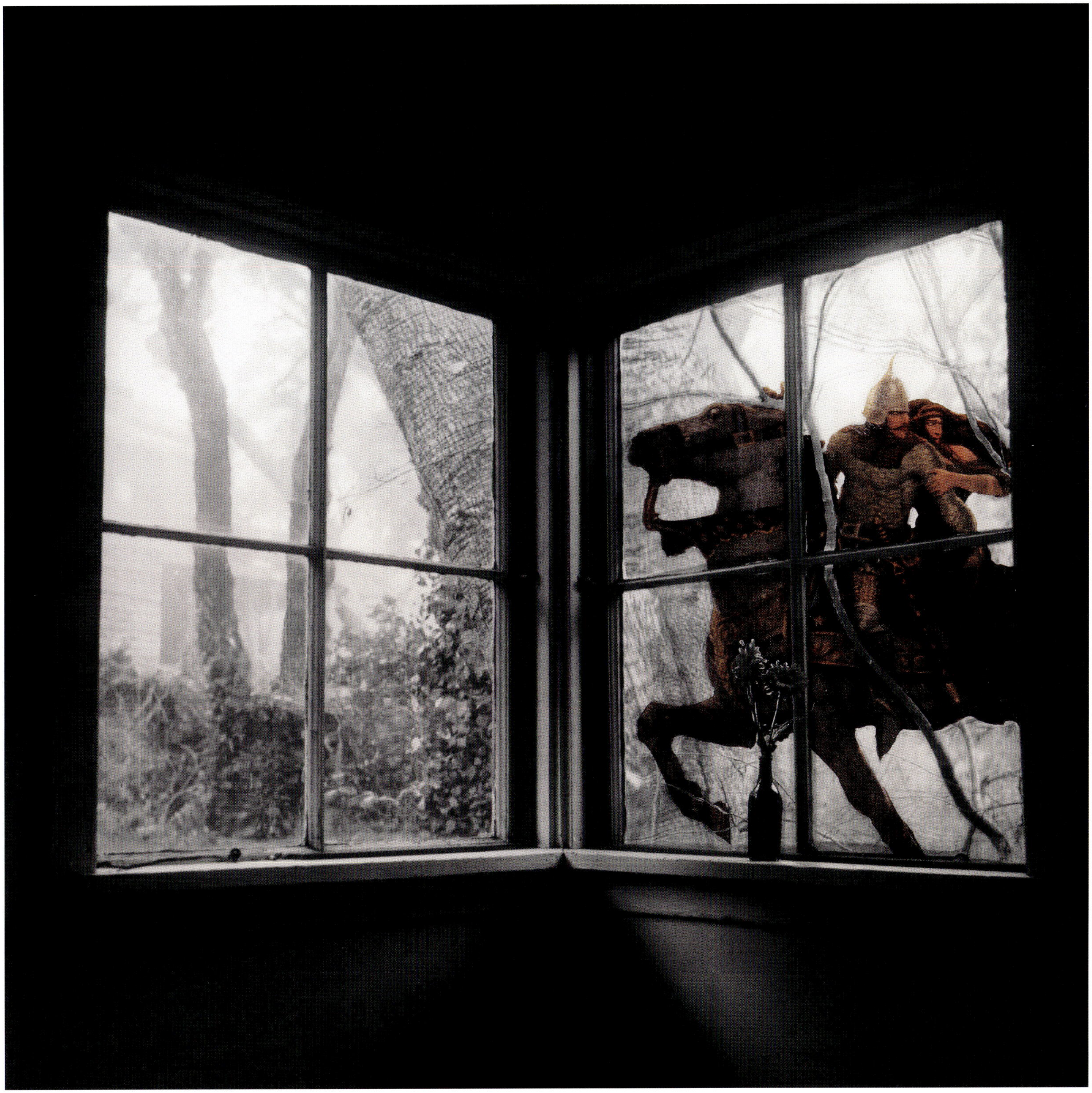

Travels with Camera

During my marriage, I earned some income by taking wedding photographs, working as a darkroom technician, and making studio photographs of other artists' work, and I also tried teaching. At first I taught in museum workshops for kids. When my exhibition history was sufficient to make me desirable as a lecturer in art schools and university programs, I taught all over the Bay Area. I had a new life as a single woman and new relationships. I'd had two museum exhibitions (at the de Young and the San Francisco Museum of Art), and I continued to exhibit. I was tremendously involved in my career, and in 1972 I was invited to fly to Japan to be one of two official photographers to the U.S. Olympic team.

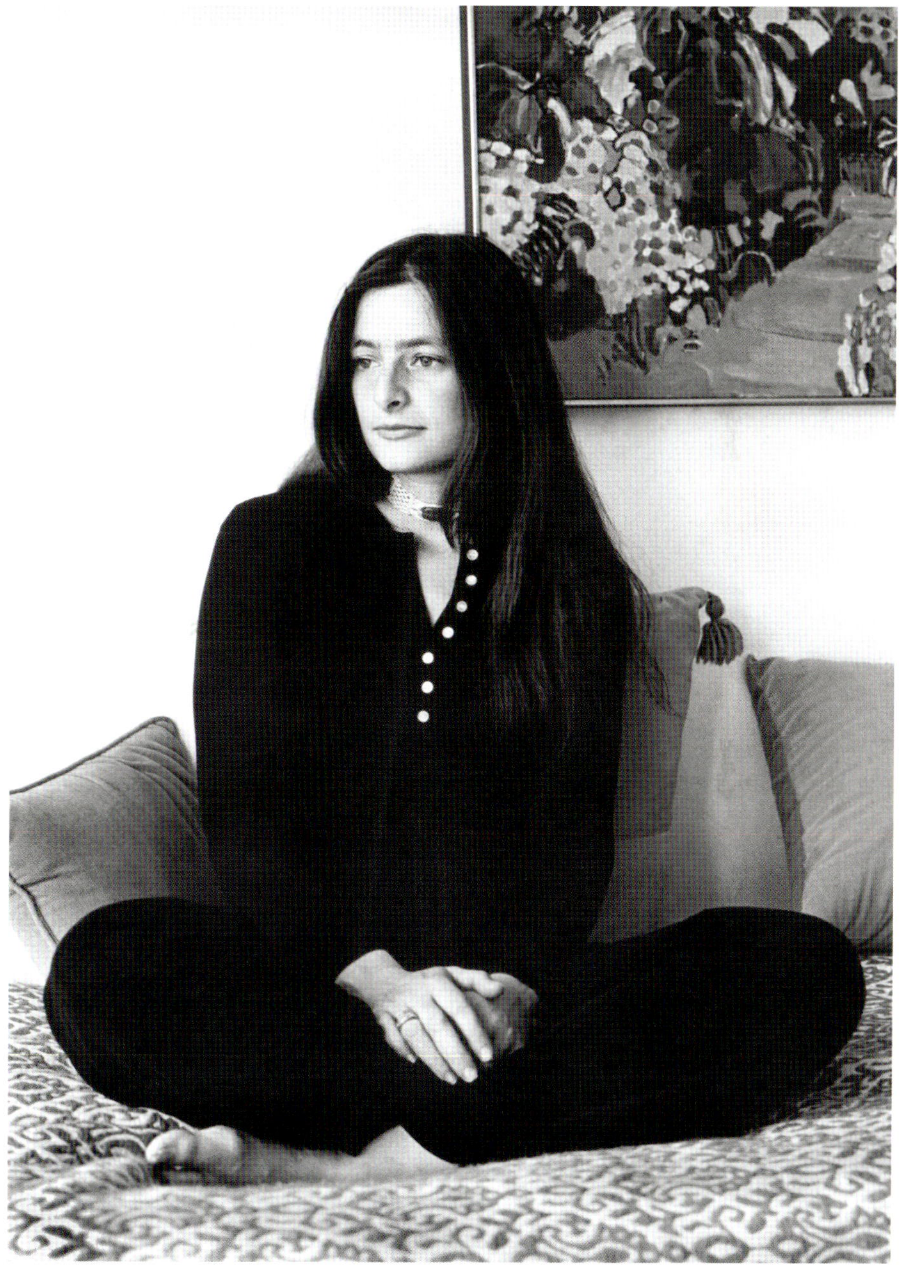

Above: Portrait of Joanne Leonard, by Joan Murray, 1972

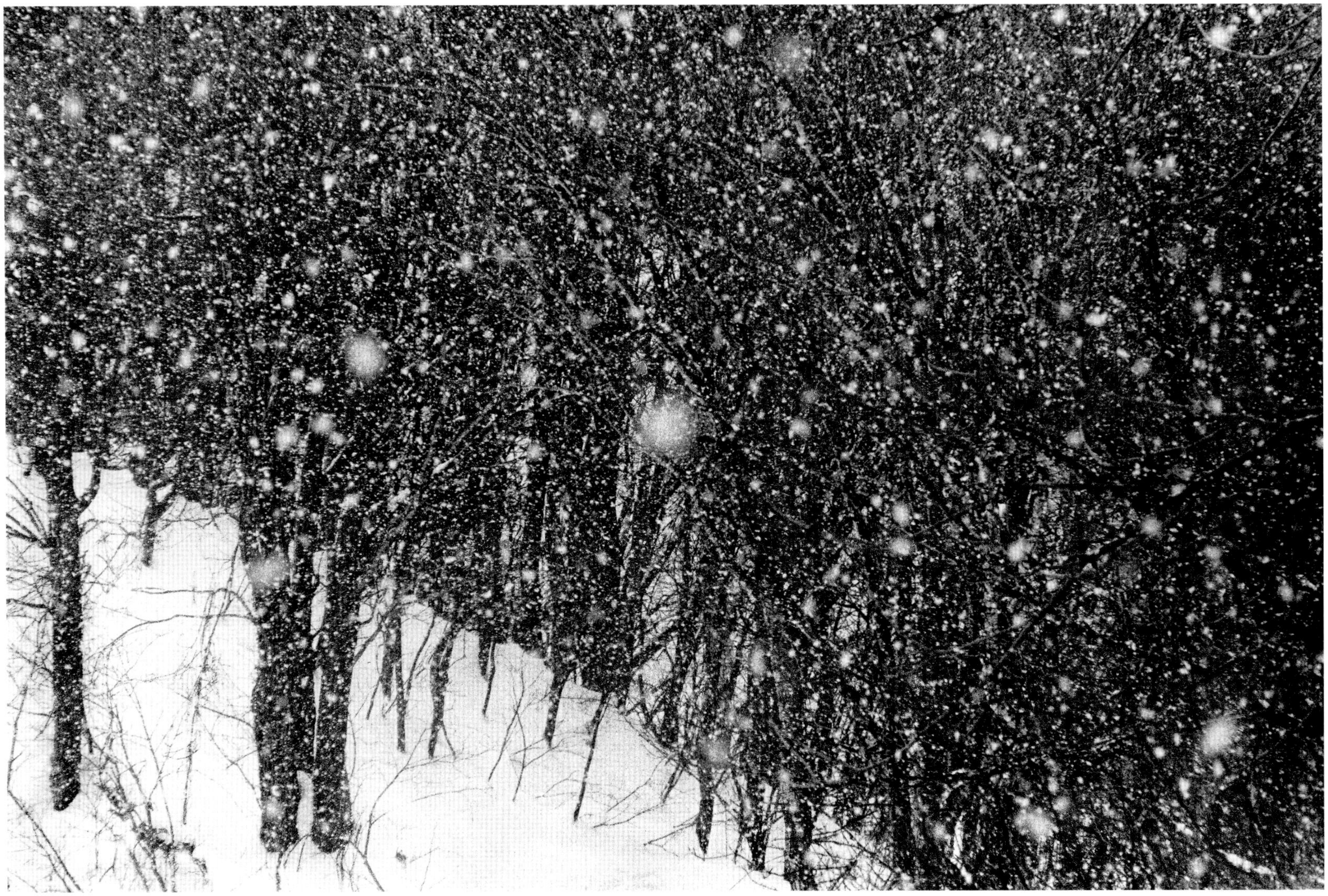

Fran Ortiz, a photographer for the *San Francisco Examiner,* admired my work and shortly after my marriage ended invited me to join him as one of the two official photographers for the U.S. team in the Winter Olympics of 1972. The invitation to photograph the Olympics lifted my spirits. I was to be paid a handsome stipend and was suddenly deemed worthy in a profession I'd not yet fully recognized as my own.

I was excited about the assignment, capturing Japan, sports, and snow on film; visually each was stunning. Winter landscapes and sports were worlds as new to me as Japan itself, as I had hardly ever experienced snow. (Snow later became a theme of some of my collages when I left California and was living through snowy winters in Michigan.) I'd never followed sports in the least. Fran and I returned from the Olympics with two hundred rolls of film, and from these Fran and I made a selection and the Bank of America, our sponsor, had huge enlargements made for exhibition in the bank's lobby gallery.

Some publicity followed—about the young woman who knew nothing of sports (a favorite angle for the writers) who took some beautiful photographs of the Olympics. This would have been an ideal moment to try to capitalize on the attention, to try for other traveling photo assignments, and to try to spin out a journalism career from this great start. But I recognized that such a life would be incompatible with the quieter pleasure I took in working out ideas in my studio and would be especially unlikely to accommodate my dream of having a child. I realized I was something of a stay-at-home person and would need to find another way to support myself with my photography. I did nothing to promote new assignments in journalism and instead continued to accept invitations to teach.

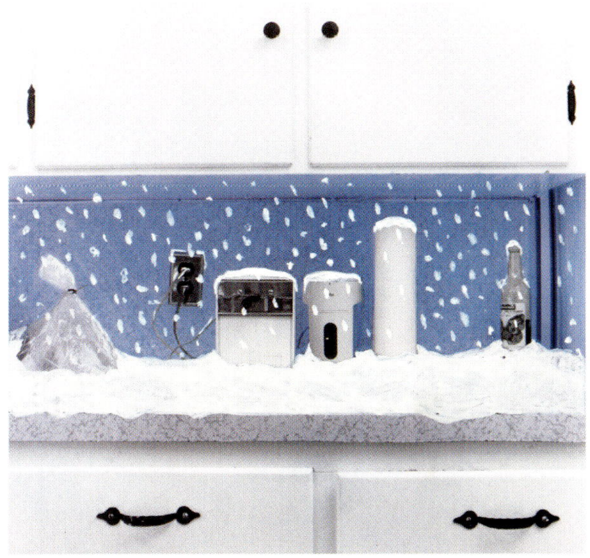

Opposite: Snow scene, Winter Olympics, Sapporo, Japan, silver print, 1972

Above: *Countertop Snowing,* silver print, water-soluble wax pastel and gouache, 6 ½ inches × 6 ¾ inches, 1980; private collection

Reproduction

I returned from the Olympics to face life after the end of my marriage. I had the cart before the horse, so to speak. The marriage ended at the point where my desire to have a child had become central, a desire that had not been shared. At this juncture, my heart was set on life with this child, even more than on my next adult relationship.

Pregnancy and parenthood had been motifs of my work since my first exhibited photograph, *Sonia, 1966*, and continued in my first book publication, *Women by Three*, published in 1969, a collection of about seventy-five photographs by two other photographers and me. In the section of the book featuring my work, half of my two dozen photographs were devoted to pregnant mothers and parents with children.

I have had three pregnancies—one that I terminated, one that ended in miscarriage, and the one that gave me my precious daughter, Julia. I kept a visual journal using collage during the miscarriage. But I cannot adequately describe this time of artistic innovation, intense desires, hopes, losses, and sorrows that brought the *Journal of a Miscarriage, 1973* into being without relating briefly a period that was its opposite, an earlier moment when, as a teenager and not yet an artist, I wanted desperately *not* to be pregnant.

Opposite: *Sonia, 1966*, silver print, 1966

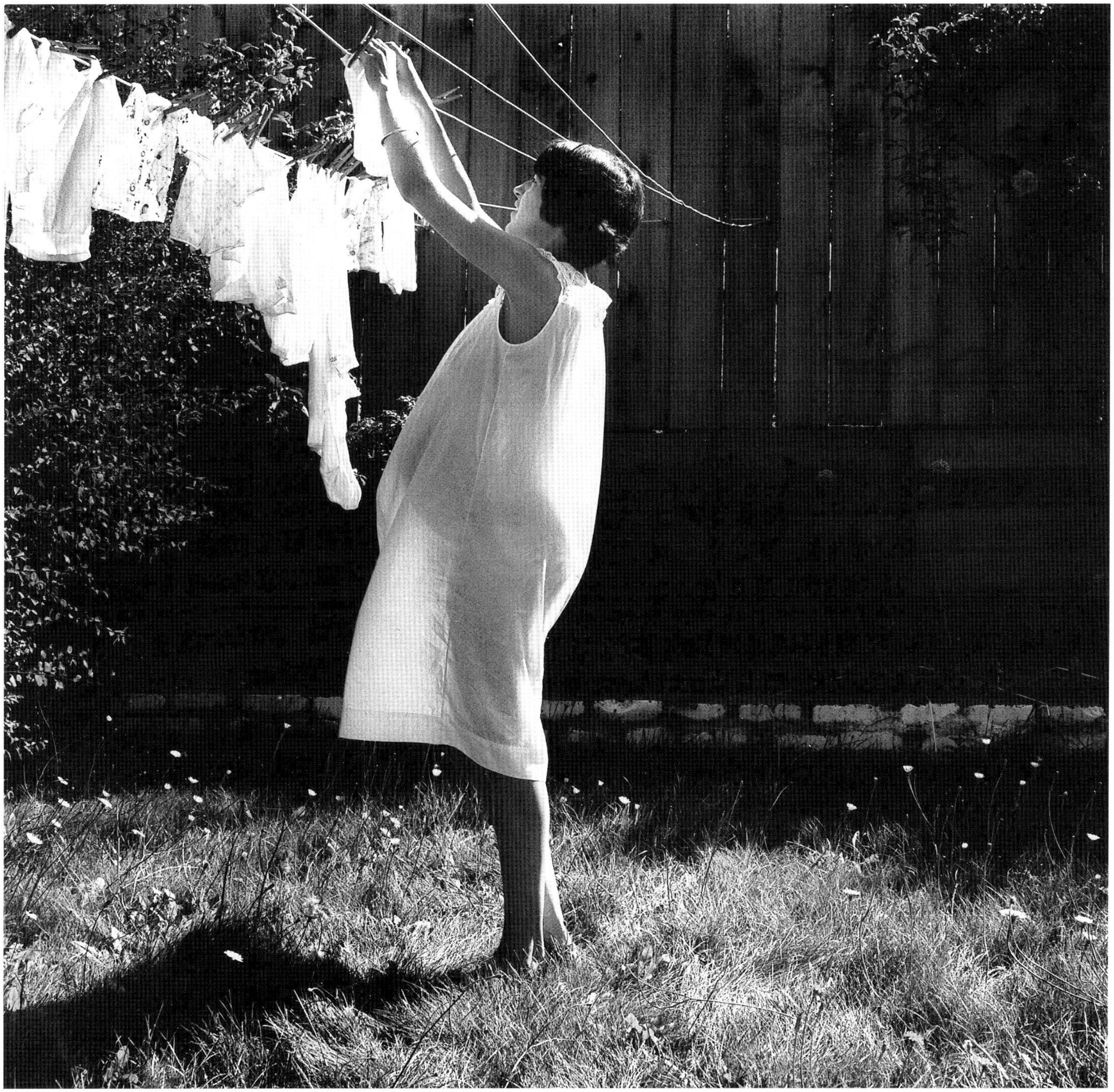

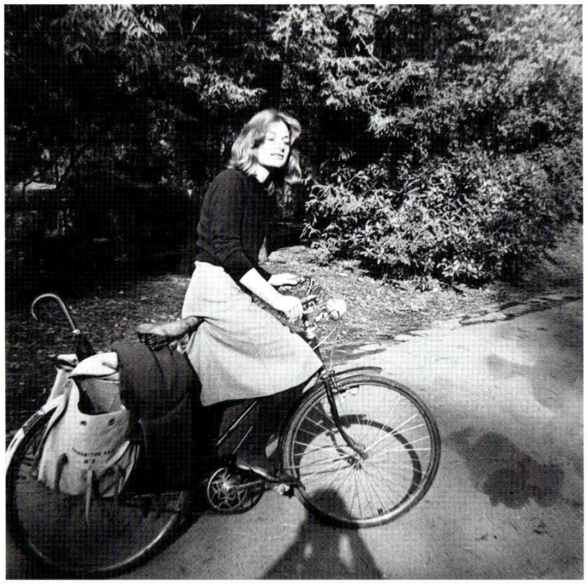

In 1958, my first year at college, I didn't know any peers who had had intercourse, however naive and unbelievable that may seem today. I had sought birth control from a doctor who refused because I was a virgin and who told me I wouldn't get pregnant the first time. But I did.

Abortion was illegal at this time. I didn't have to seek out a back-alley abortion, as many of my contemporaries did, because California law allowed abortion if the mother's life was in jeopardy. A psychiatrist could certify that a woman's emotional state was life threatening. Thanks to my mother's psychiatric connections, I had a legal abortion, but the doctor, a family friend, swore me to secrecy. I experienced the frightening blood clots and other aspects of the aftermath of the surgery but never spoke of this experience to my friends. When my boyfriend learned that I was pregnant, he feared he might have to marry me; he chose the time right after the abortion to enumerate my faults and make it clear he didn't love me.

Having gone through the trauma of unwanted pregnancy as a teenager, I became vigilant about using birth control and reached my thirties with a great longing for the *planned* pregnancy I would have one day.

Above: Joanne on bike by Judith Fuss Adell, ca. 1960

At age thirty-three, I had more confidence in my ability to be a good mother than I had in finding a partner I could count on for the long run. I began to tell myself that, were I to become pregnant now in a relationship that didn't last, I'd go it alone. This somewhat uncharacteristic sense of confidence and independence was new and gave me a feeling of power over my own life. What chutzpah to think of having and caring for a child on my own but what freedom to think of making the decision for myself!

The man I cared about at this time was Manuel Neri, a well-known Bay Area sculptor, someone I'd known for years. We kept separate residences because my Berkeley apartment was near the place where I was teaching. He lived nearer to Davis, the University of California campus where he taught, but we were together a good part of each week. His three younger children visited on weekends and were a great pleasure to me. I did not hide my desire to have a child of my own, but we did not make plans together. It was pretty clear to me that if I did become pregnant, I'd be on my own.

Once I learned I was pregnant for the second time, I faced the challenge I'd vowed I could take on—having this child on my own. I was more frightened and uneasy than I'd imagined I would be, terribly worried about how I would manage everyday life as a single mom, take good care of my child, and continue to be an artist. One night, I had a thrilling dream about an extraordinary sketchbook. In the dream, the book seemed to be Manuel's, and I was filled with a sense of great good fortune for being close to the maker of this incredible book. But when I awoke and thought about this dream, I realized that, since it was my dream, it was *I* who made the sketchbook. I vowed to buy my own sketchbook and work in it in collage.

Though I'd been making collage works for many years, the idea of making a sketchbook in collage took hold so strongly because I realized that when I became a mother, I would be unlikely to spend long hours in the darkroom. The collage sketchbook had one further appeal: California photography in the late 1960s and early 1970s was a very formal affair; attention to the smooth-surfaced fine print on manufactured paper was the perfectionistic goal, due to the influence of Edward Weston and Ansel Adams, both Californians who had perfected the fine art photo-print. I longed for the greater freedom with materials that painters like Bay Area artist William Wiley demonstrated when he rid himself of stretchers for his canvases and instead, accepting wrinkles, pinned the canvas to the wall through grommets he'd placed in the edges of the canvas. Collage on sketchbook pages would be my bid for this kind of freedom.

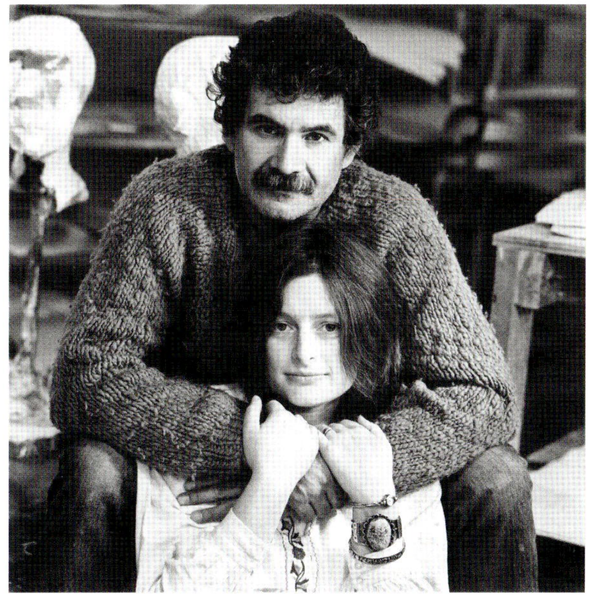

Above: Joanne with Manuel Neri, Benicia, by Mimi Jacobs, 1974

And so sometime in the days that followed my dream, I did buy such a sketchbook. I was about three months pregnant, and I made a collage that expressed everything I'd expected to feel—a bright yellow pear, standing for the pregnant body of a female, with outstretched legs and arms, fairly jumping for joy.

Illustrations from *Journal of a Miscarriage, 1973,* collage and pencil on sketchbook pages, all 11 inches × 14 inches; collection of Ms. Jeremy Stone and Mr. Paul Matz

Opposite: *Pregnant* from *Journal of a Miscarriage, 1973*

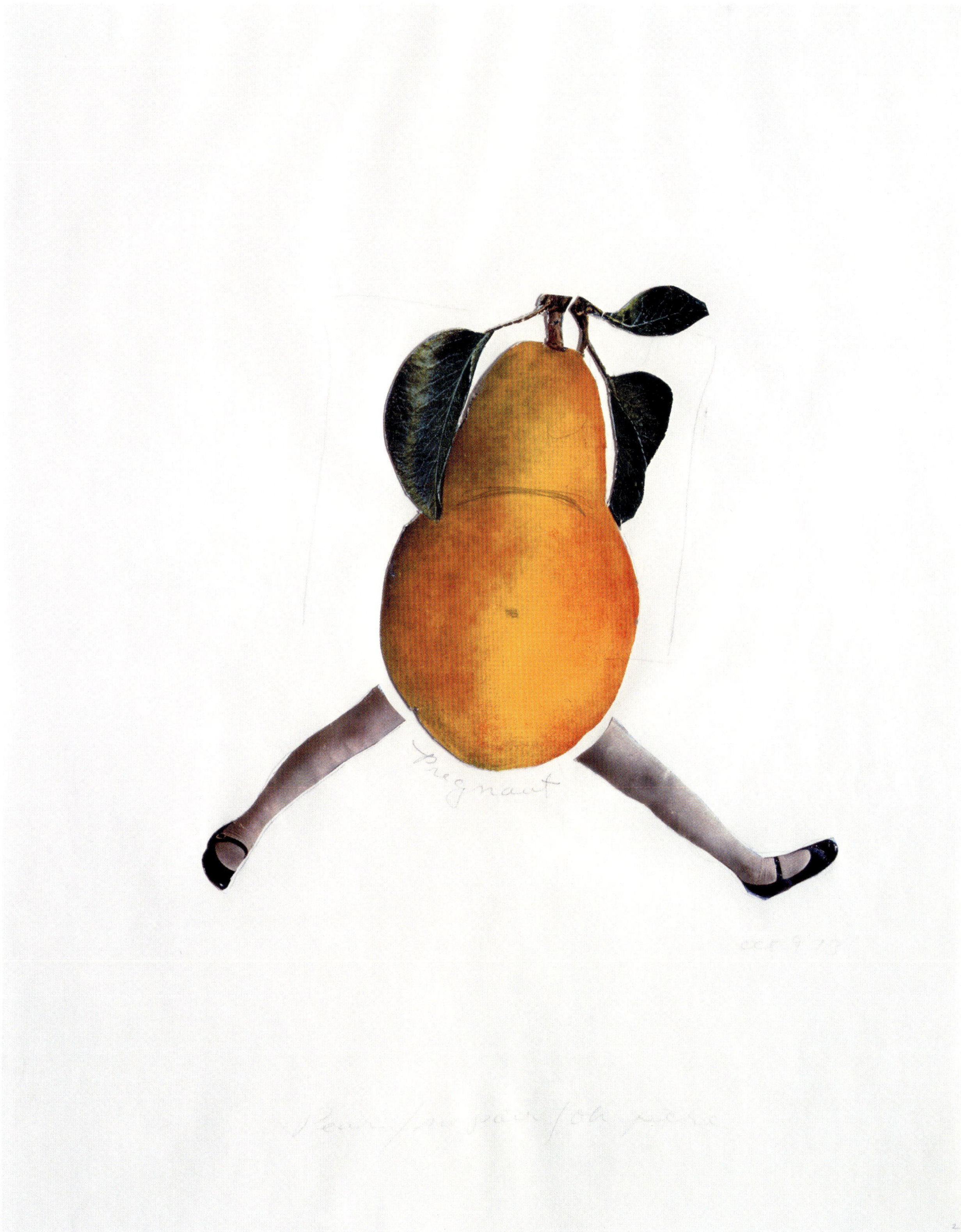
Pregnant

Within a day or so of this happy first entry in my sketchbook, I had a day of bleeding. I put blood on two pages of the book, nothing more. Just blood on the pages. Near evening of a day of terrible bleeding a friend took me to the hospital. I was having a miscarriage. Within a few days after I returned from the hospital, I found those bloodied pages and completed them, making the two journal collage pages *Rupture* and *Miscarriage/Ms. Carnage*.

Opposite: *Rupture* from *Journal of a Miscarriage, 1973*

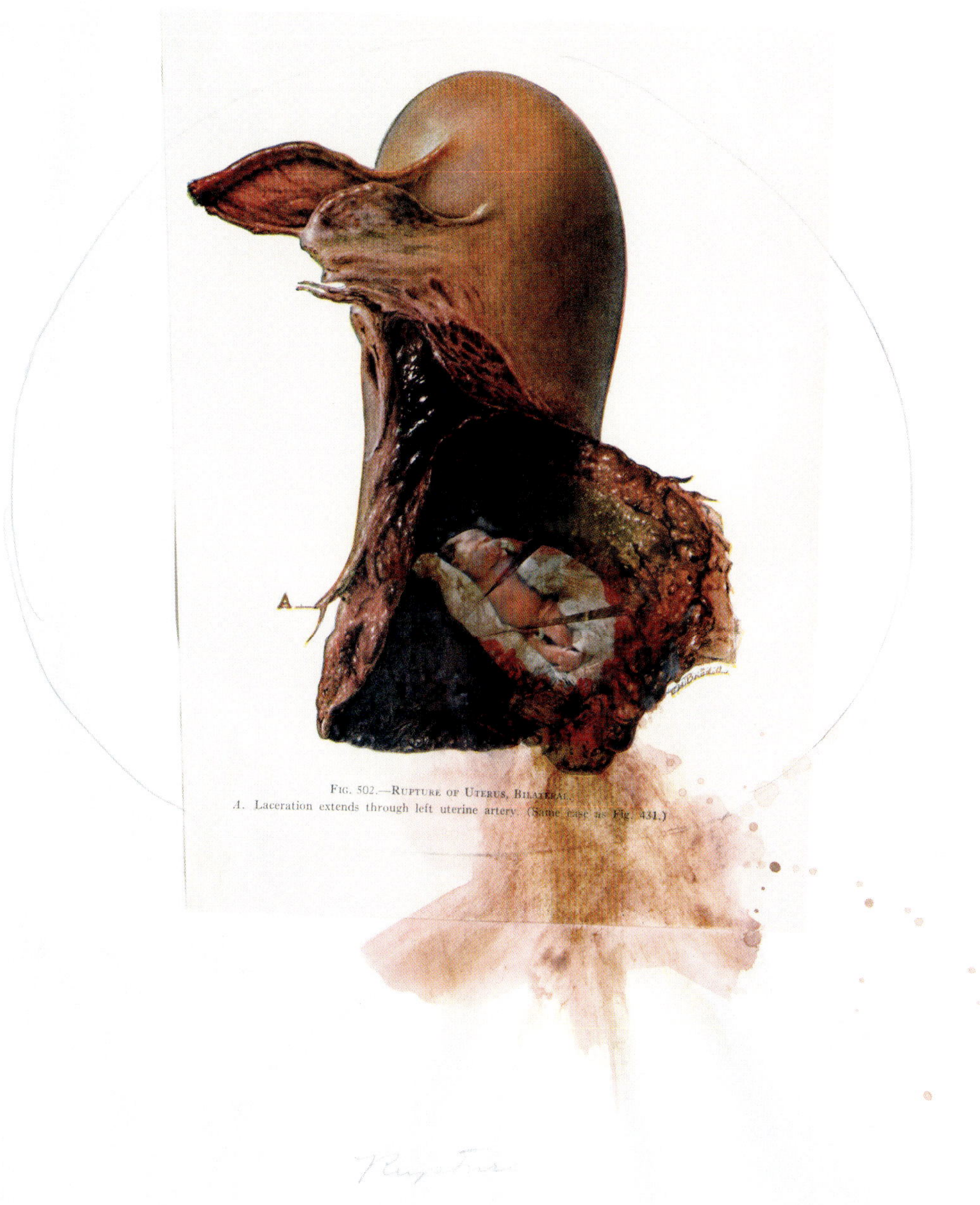
A
FIG. 502.—RUPTURE OF UTERUS, BILATERAL.
A. Laceration extends through left uterine artery. (Same case as Fig. 431.)

I wept and slept too much in the weeks that followed, struggling to move beyond loss and feelings of deep sadness that seemed to be unending. But I began to go out to stores that sold used books and old magazines, looking for material for the collages that were filling my sketchbook. One friend gave me the obstetrical textbook *William's Obstetrics* he'd had since medical school, and many of my collages depended on this contribution.

Opposite: *Miscarriage/Ms.Carnage* from *Journal of a Miscarriage, 1973*

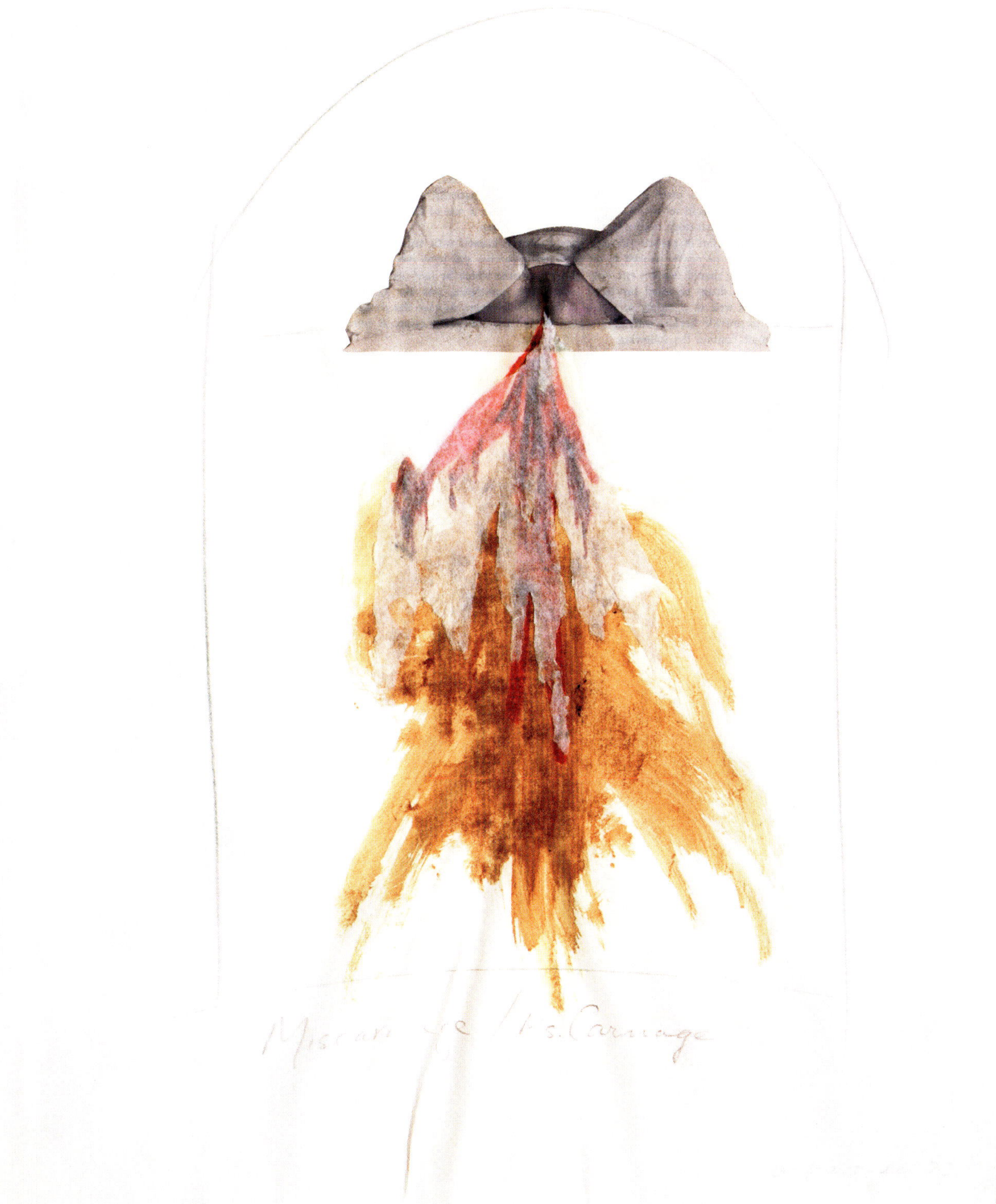

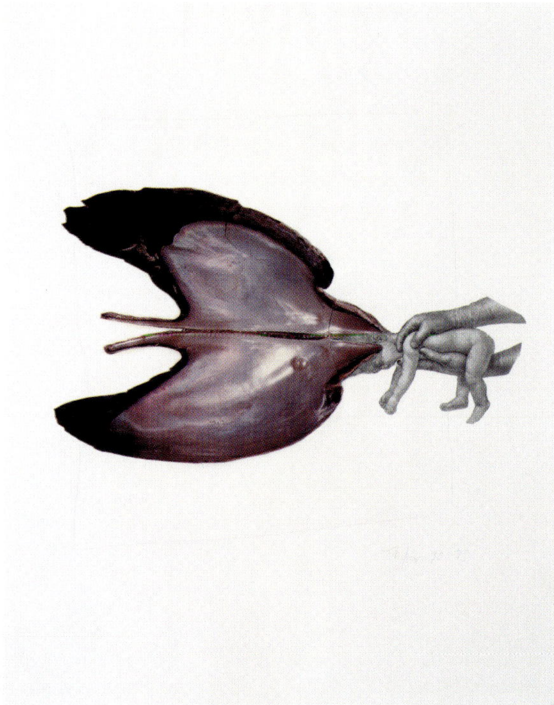

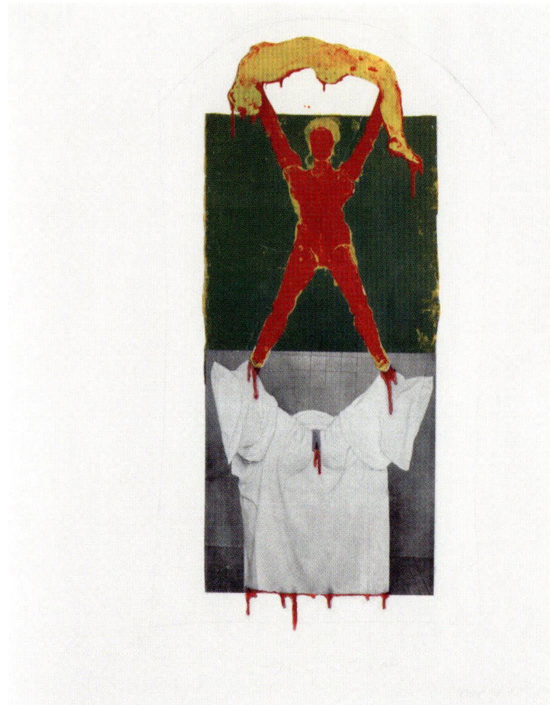

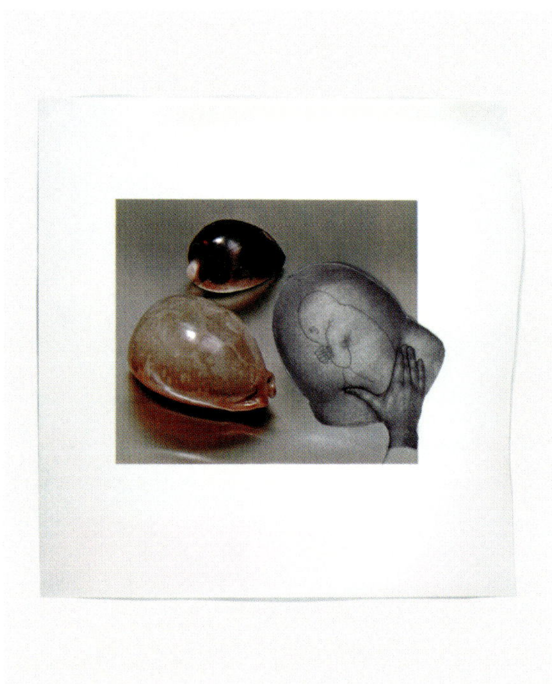

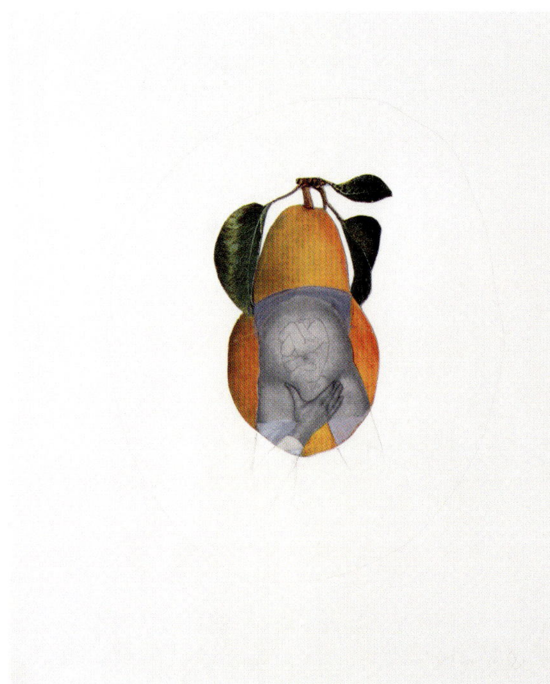

Above: From *Journal of a Miscarriage, 1973, clockwise, from upper left:* untitled (clam shell/birth), *Magic Act* (with painting by M. Neri), untitled (pear and embryo), untitled (cowry shells)

Opposite: *Now and Then* from *Journal of a Miscarriage, 1973*

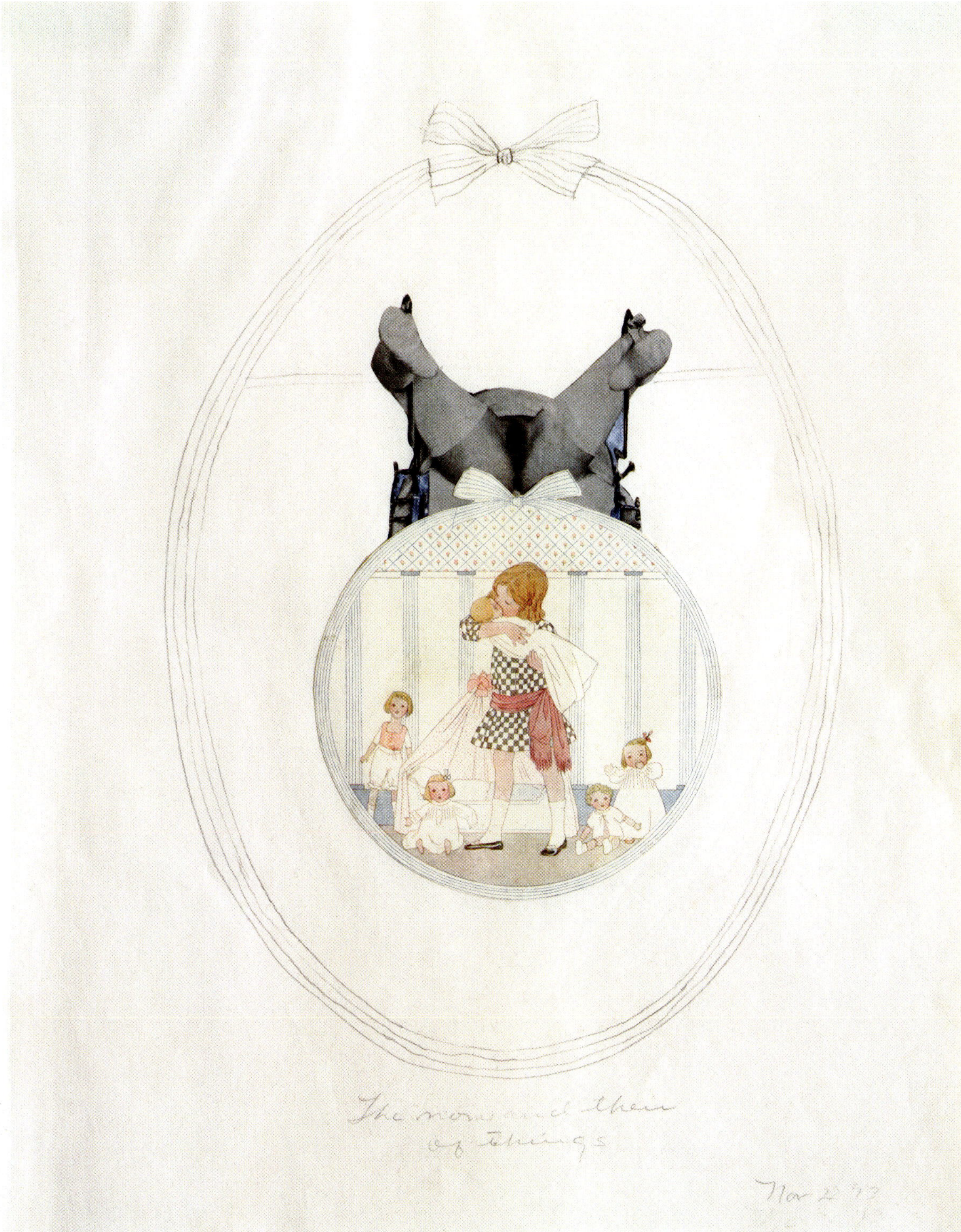

The actual journal has a slightly different chronological arrangement than the somewhat thematic groupings reflected here.

Some of the collages express my anger that stretched back a number of years, representing a harsh or distasteful sex act without a shared dream for a child. Images of violence and death appear intermittently throughout the journal, reflecting my dashed hopes and intermingled thoughts of death and loss.

Opposite: Untitled (woman/flower/snail) from *Journal of a Miscarriage, 1973*

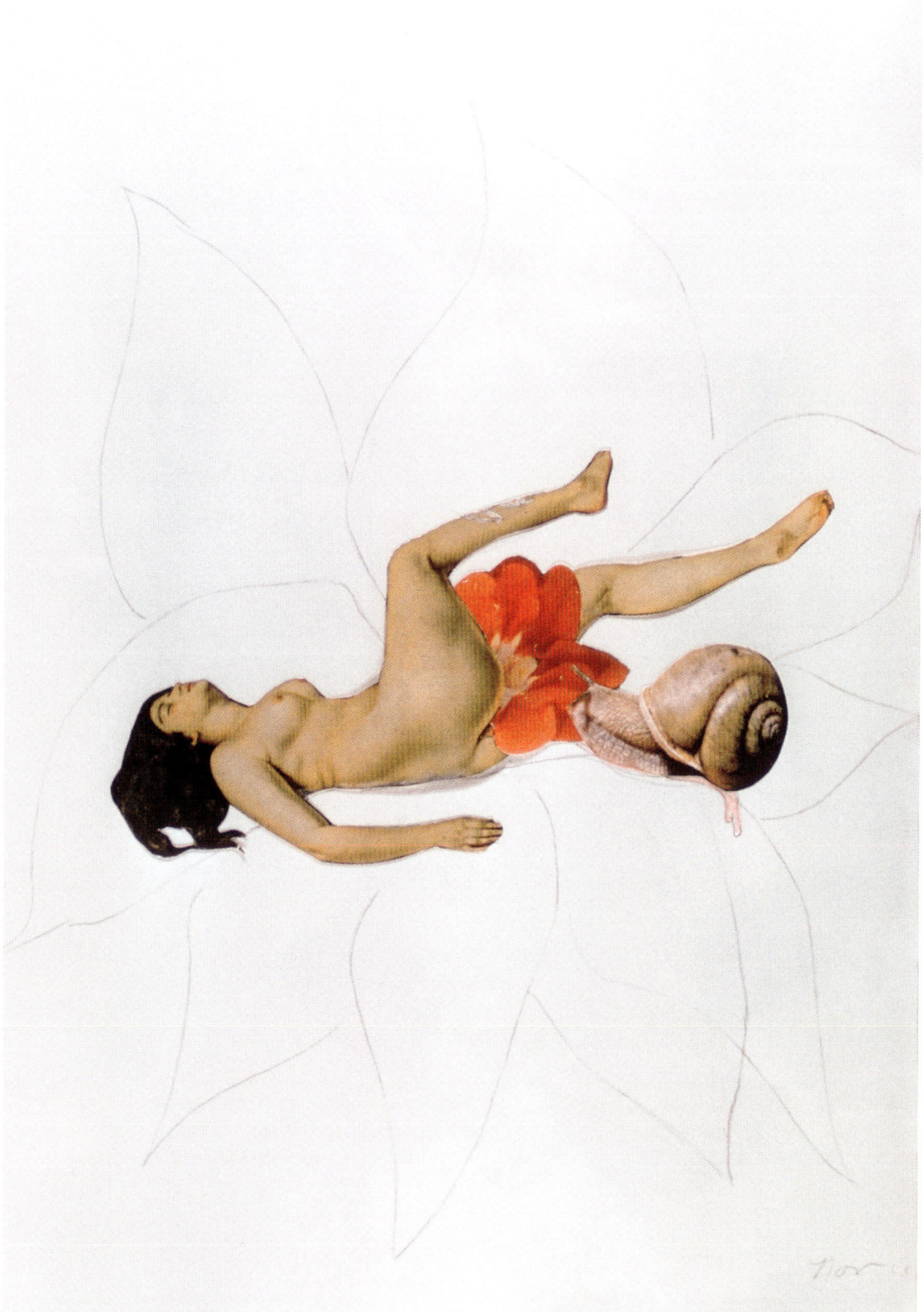

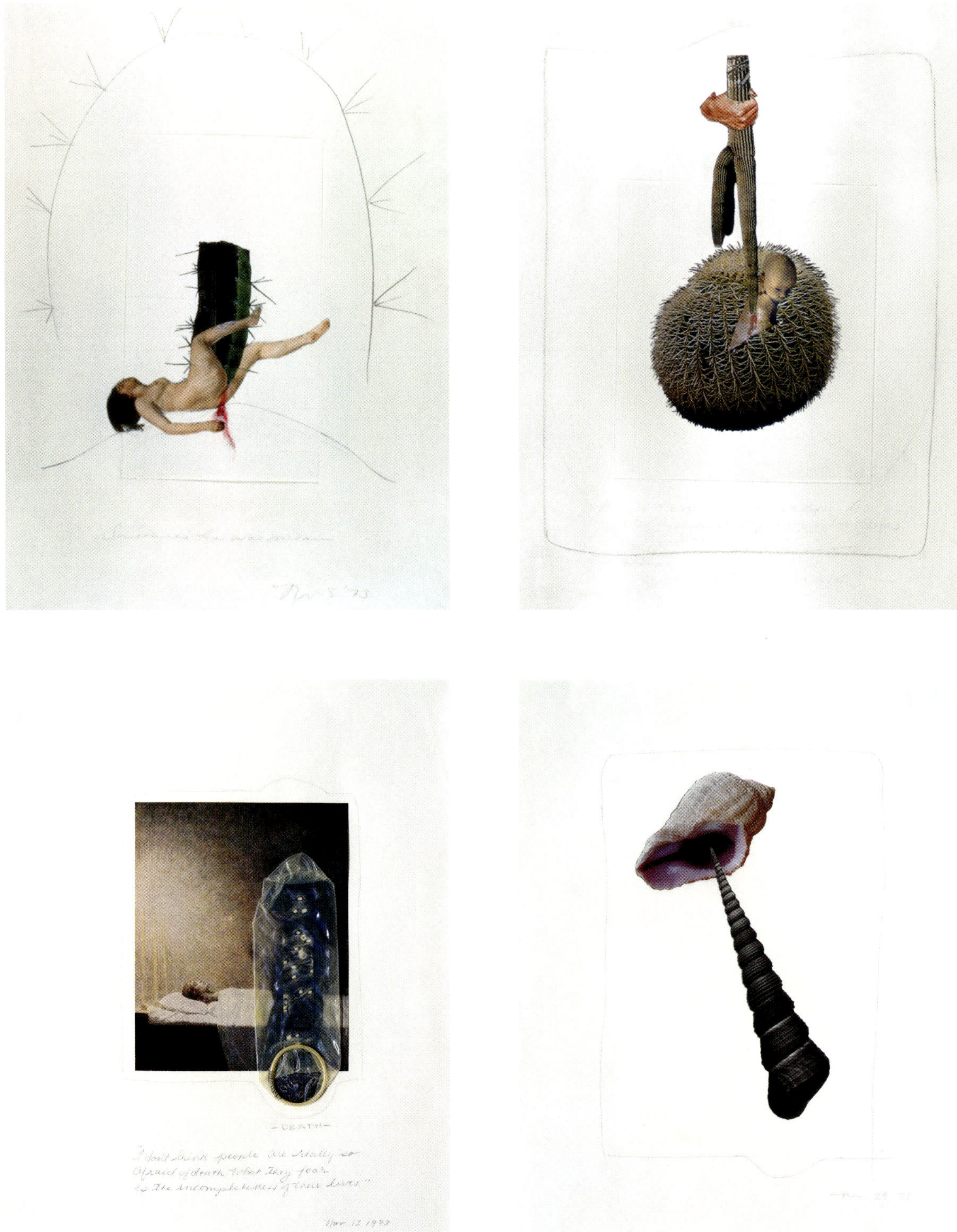

Above: From *Journal of a Miscarriage, 1973, clockwise, from upper left:* untitled (cactus rape), untitled (cactus stab), untitled (two shells), *Death*

Opposite: *Broken Heart Diagram,* from *Journal of a Miscarriage, 1973*

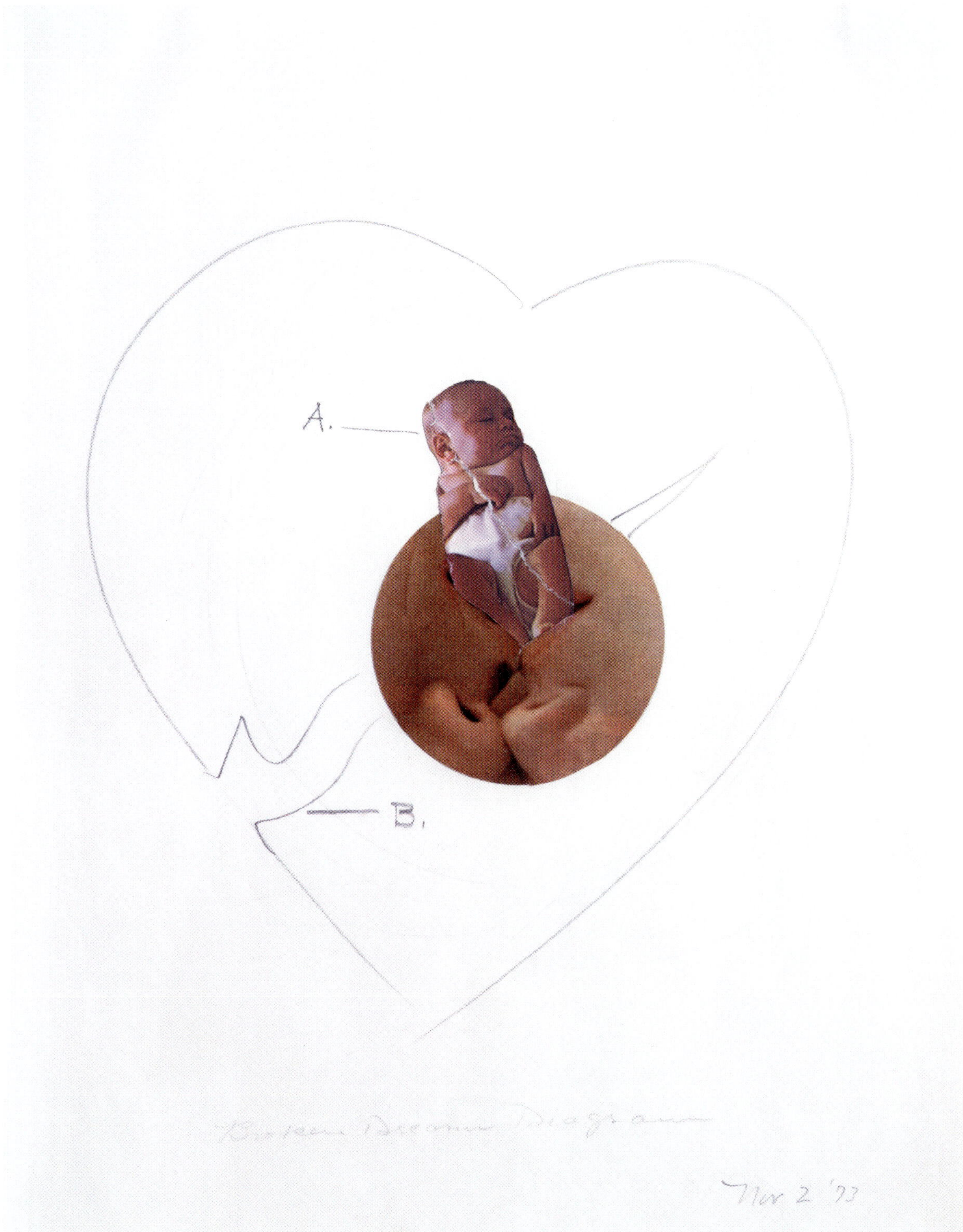
A.
B.
Broken Dream Diagram
Nov 2 '73

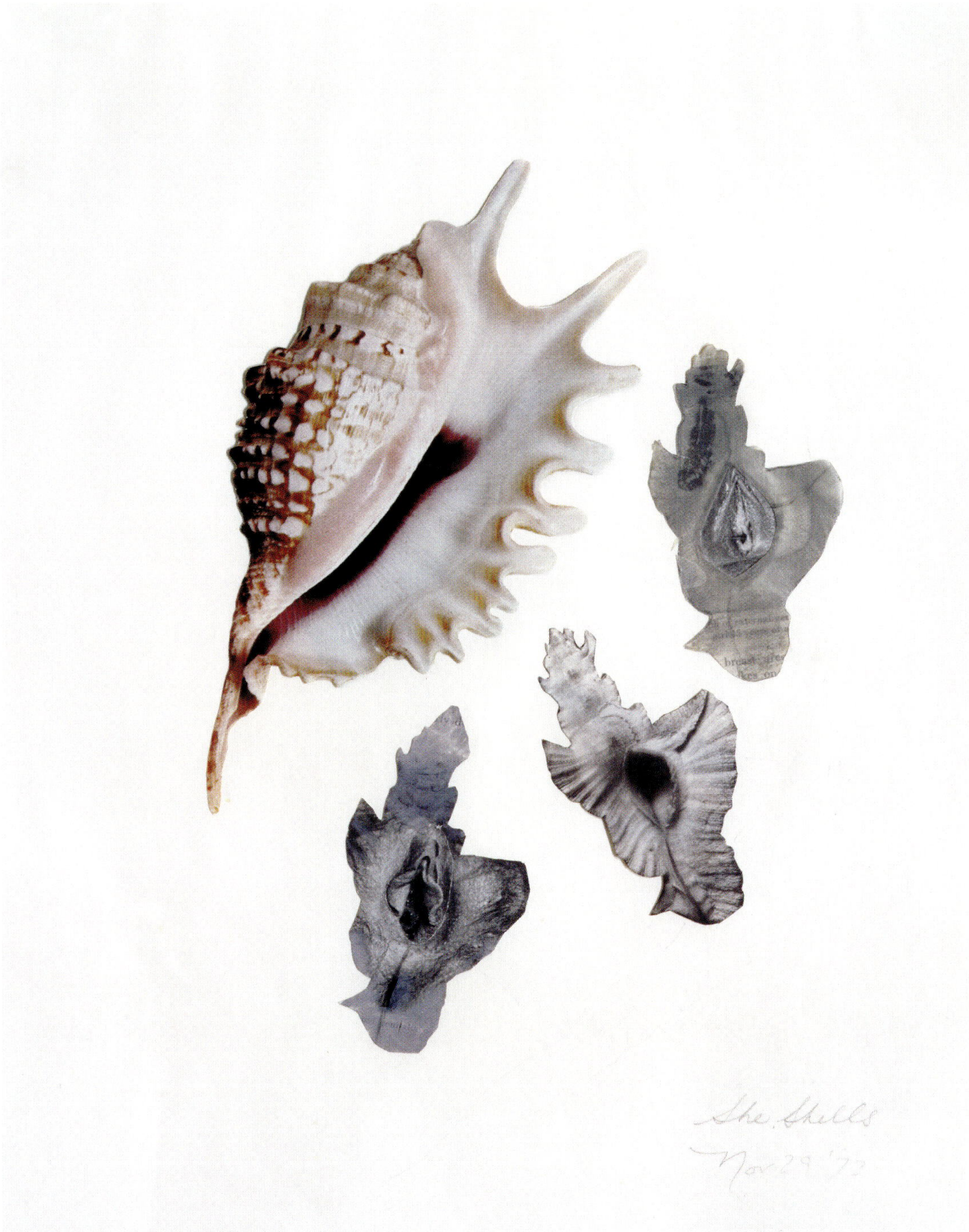

Above: *She Shells* from *Journal of a Miscarriage, 1973*

Opposite: Untitled (Joanne, frog, and sperm) from *Journal of a Miscarriage, 1973*

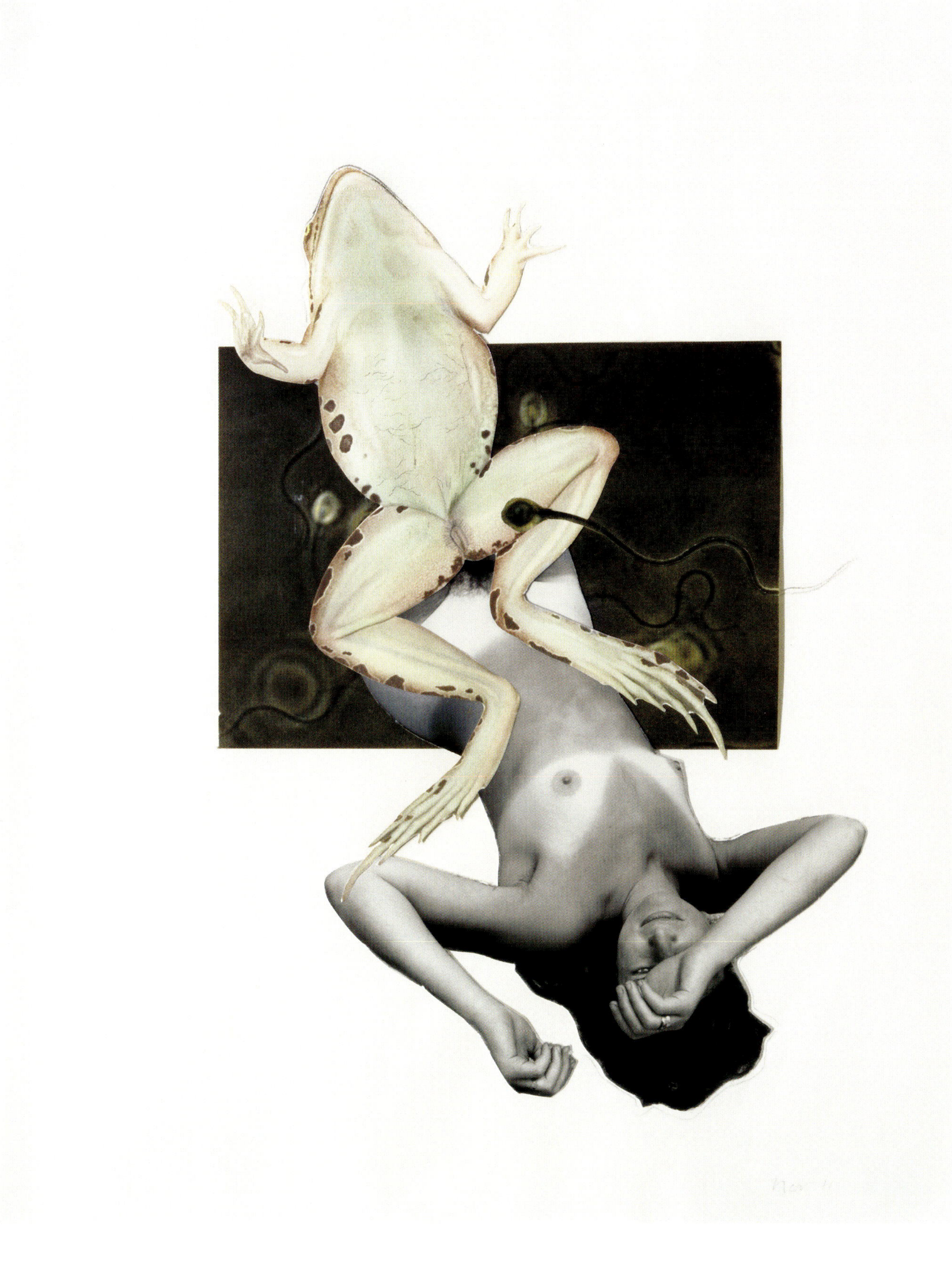

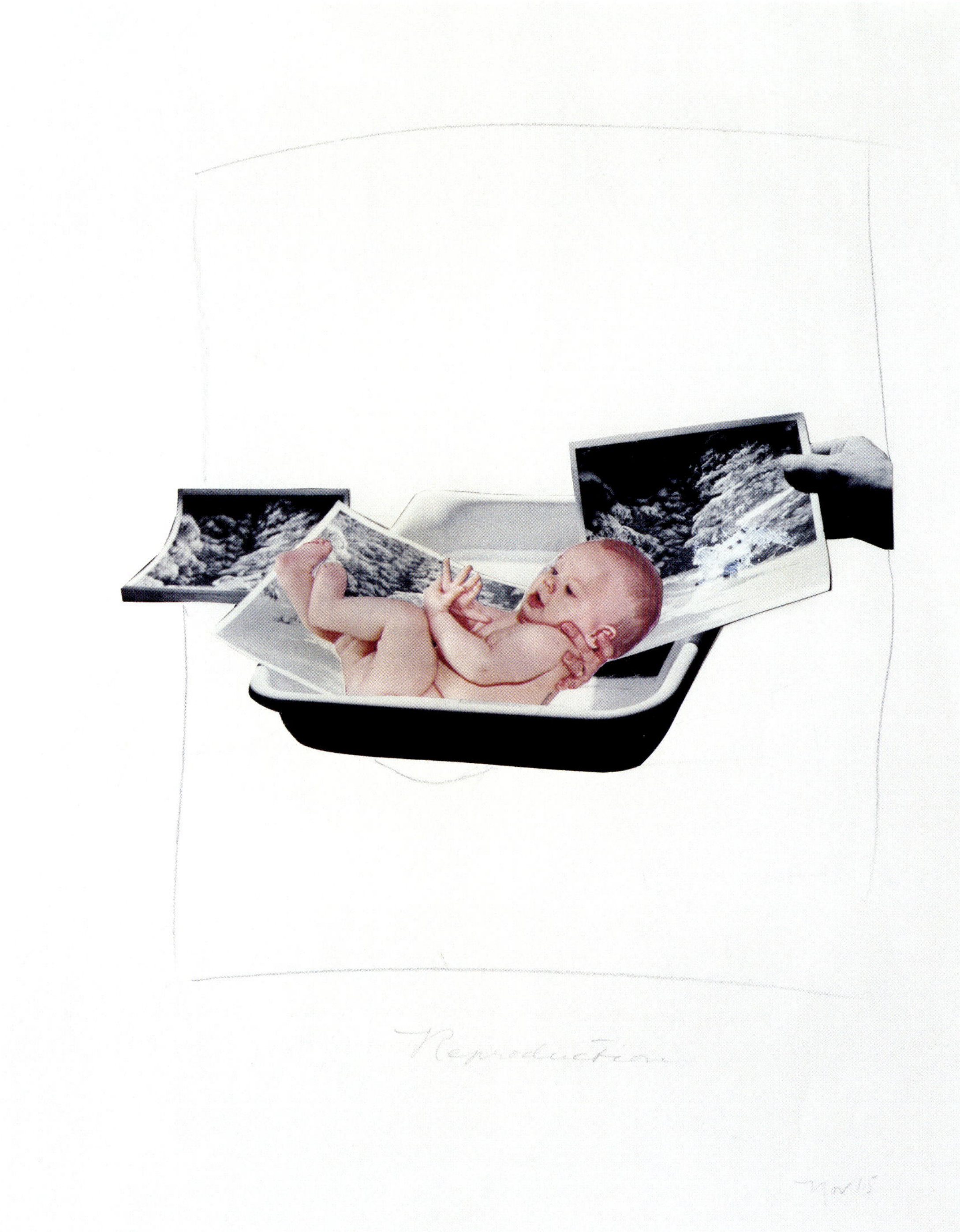

Above: *Reproduction* from *Journal of a Miscarriage, 1973*

Opposite: *Love Letter* from *Journal of a Miscarriage, 1973*

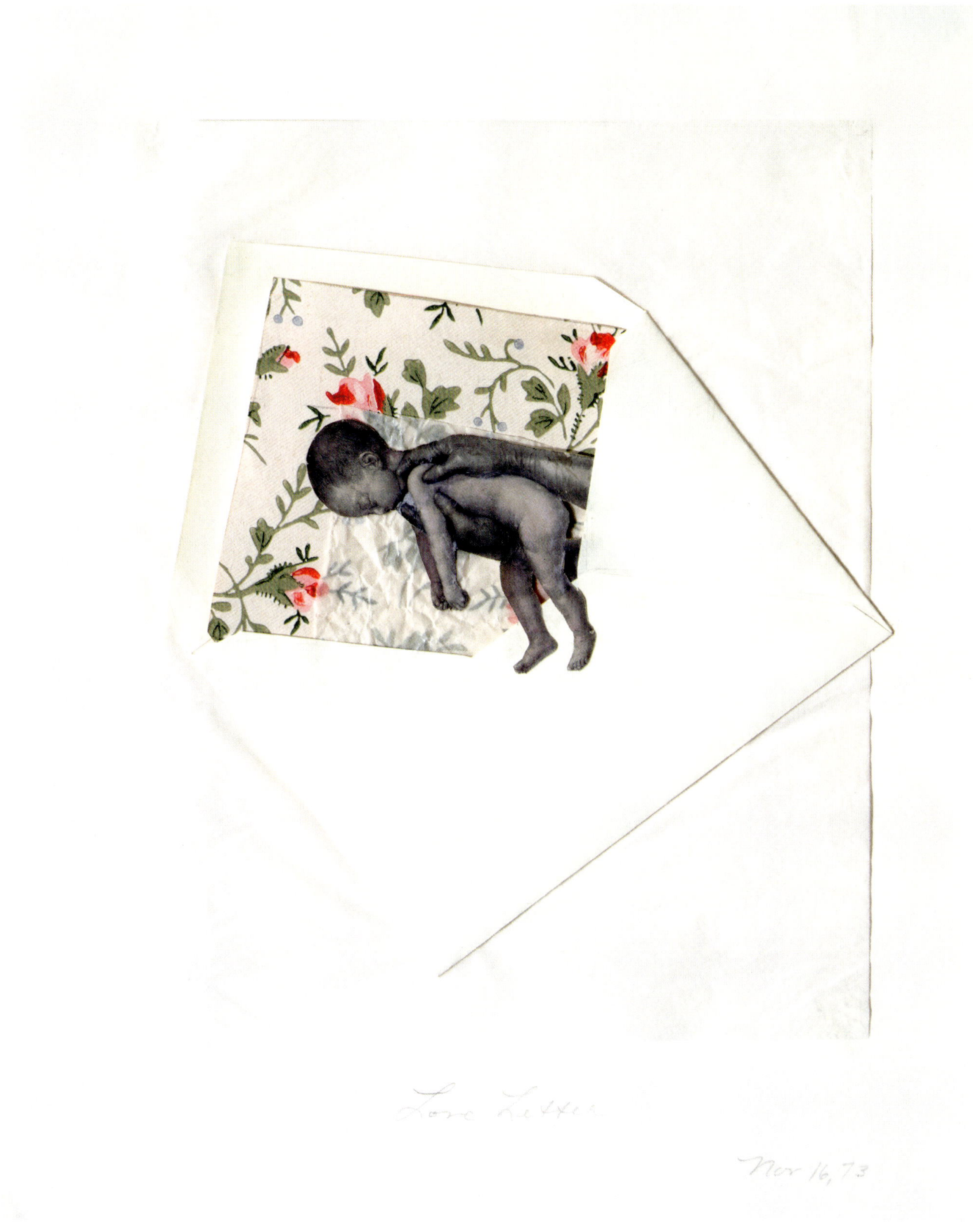
Love Letter
Nov 16, 73

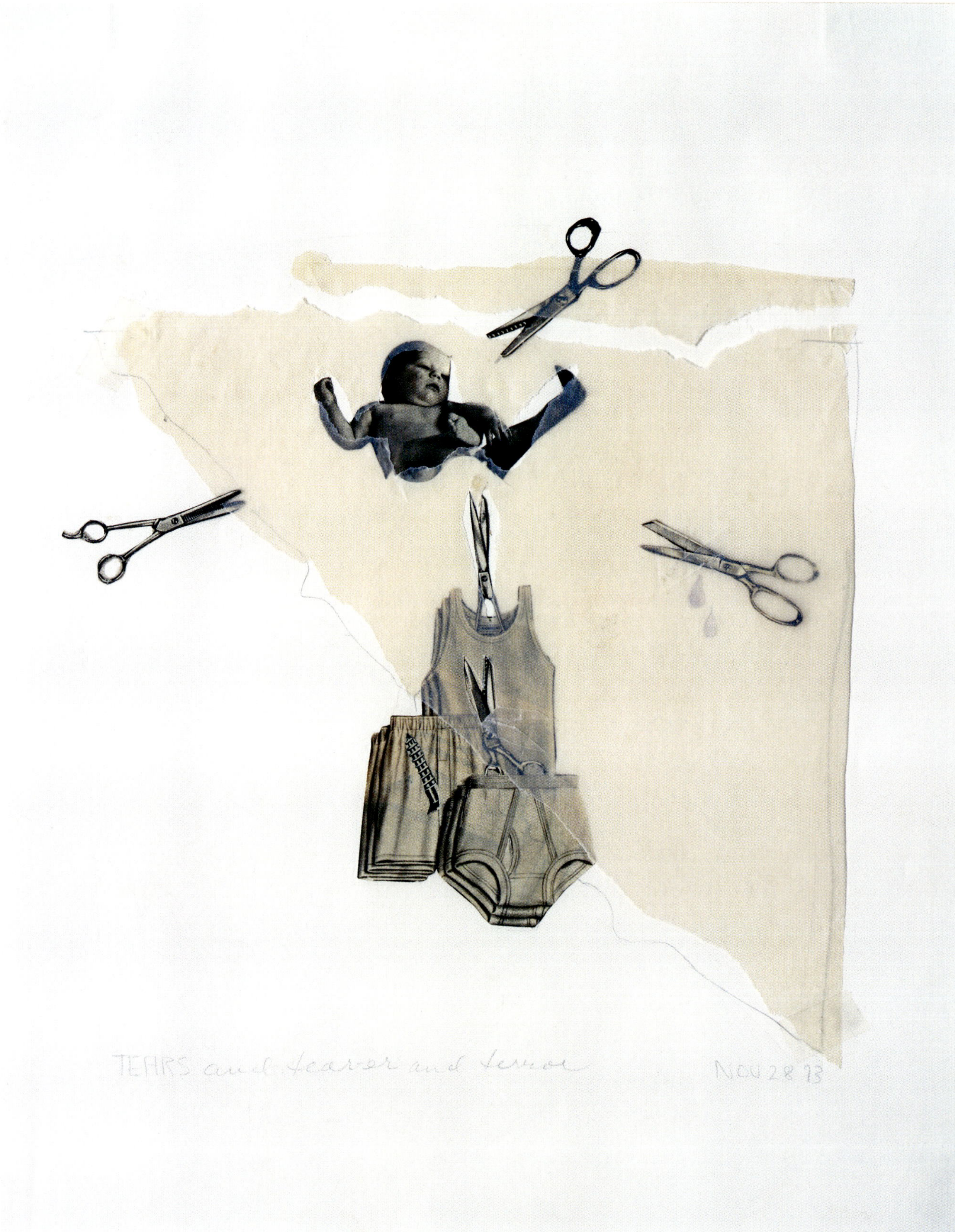
NOV 28 73

It might be difficult for a contemporary reader to appreciate how unusual it was at this time to make or find acceptance for art about an intensely personal subject like miscarriage. Artistic precedents that existed were largely unknown or rarely seen by artists of my generation. Not long after I finished the miscarriage journal, I discovered Frieda Kahlo's 1934 paintings about her own miscarriage. I felt a sense of connection to this work and gratitude to the newly active women's movement for its efforts to restore missing women artists to their rightful places in history.

With the expansion of the women's movement, artists began taking up subjects long considered off-limits for artistic representation and were pushing the limits with a range of new works. While I was finishing work on my miscarriage journal in 1973, the British conceptual artist Mary Kelly, perhaps feeling the same isolation as mother, feminist, and artist that I had felt, began her groundbreaking *Post Partum Document 1973–79,* which she published to acclaim in 1983. Surely a kind of feminist zeitgeist was at work on both sides of the Atlantic.

Judy Chicago's *Birth Project* (1983) was touted as the first work to deal with the subject of women's reproductive lives. While *Birth Project* was clearly not the first of such works, the claim underscores the isolation in which women artists were working at the time. Chicago's hard-won prominence as an artist no doubt served to create more opportunities for publications and exhibitions devoted to the subjects of childbirth and maternity, just as her 1971 project with Miriam Schapiro, *Womanhouse*, had focused attention on women's domestic lives and spaces. Feminist projects like *Womanhouse* were not only providing a climate that "permitted" West Coast women to make work they might not otherwise have made; they also were opening the door for West Coast exhibitions of such work.

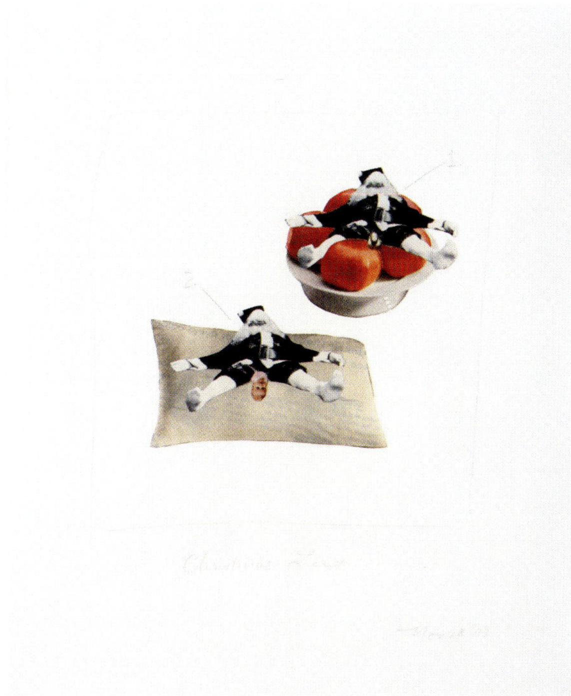

Opposite: *Tears/Tears* from *Journal of a Miscarriage, 1973*

Above: *Christmas List* from *Journal of a Miscarriage, 1973*

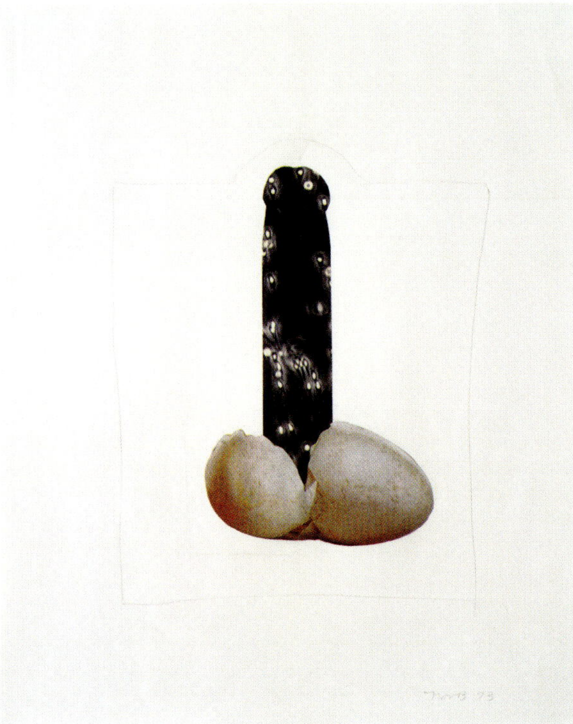

My miscarriage journal collages began to have an audience. In 1974, I had a show of one hundred works at the Diego Rivera Gallery of the San Francisco Art Institute. After the exhibit, the journal gained its formal name, *Journal of a Miscarriage, 1973*. The actual journal pages were separated, and each was set on the wall under glass. The curator handled the work in a gingerly fashion, mounting it in a somewhat set-aside space, separate from the main gallery, but I had no idea that, compared to what would happen in the next thirty years, this careful handling of the work would seem brave and forthright. Colleagues who saw *Journal of a Miscarriage, 1973* in California urged me to show the work in New York. In response to this encouragement, when I went east later that year to see my parents, I made appointments to show the work to several New York curators.

At the Museum of Modern Art, the chief curator of photography agreed to meet with me, but his assistant came in first. The assistant opened the work and began to page through. He saw only a few pages and was clearly appalled. He thrust the work back in its box with evident disgust, and we waited awkwardly for the chief curator's appearance. When the chief curator arrived, he paged through the work with great deliberateness, then condescendingly dismissed me with, "I think we all know about such things, don't we?"

The work of West Coast feminist artists had not yet penetrated the bastions of the East Coast art establishment.

Above: Untitled (egg and penis) from *Journal of a Miscarriage, 1973*

The history of *Journal of a Miscarriage, 1973* includes generosity and acceptance as well as outright rejection over many years. *Journal* was shown with great forthrightness in a 1980 retrospective of my work at the Laguna Gloria Art Museum in Austin, Texas. Jeremy Stone, a remarkable San Francisco gallery director, bought the entire *Journal* in the 1970s, framed every page of it, and showed these framed works in her gallery in 1985. No more than a few pages have been exhibited since, and the work was never published until the 1990s, when selections from its pages were reproduced in several books. Until now, *Journal* has not been reproduced in color or anything near its entirety. It has continued to be a difficult work to show. In 2005, for example, when a group of conference planners raised money for shipping the work to the University of Michigan, not one of the several secure and professional exhibition venues on campus agreed to exhibit the work.

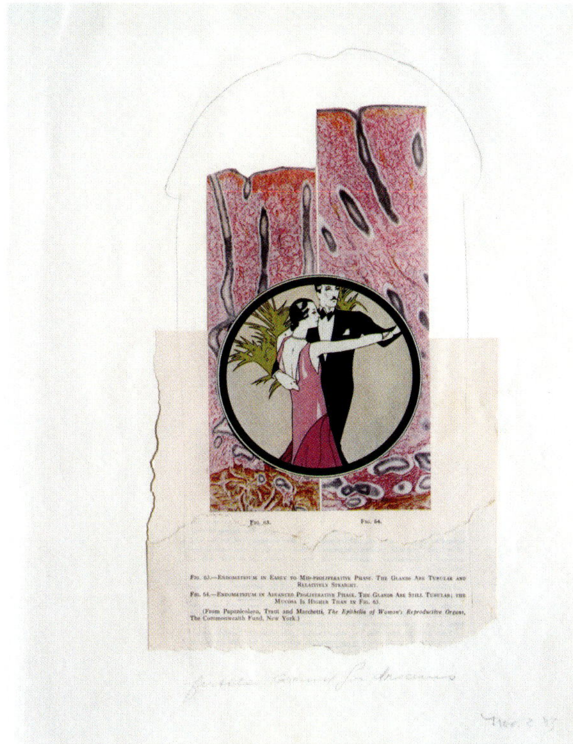

Above: Untitled (dancing couple) from *Journal of a Miscarriage, 1973*

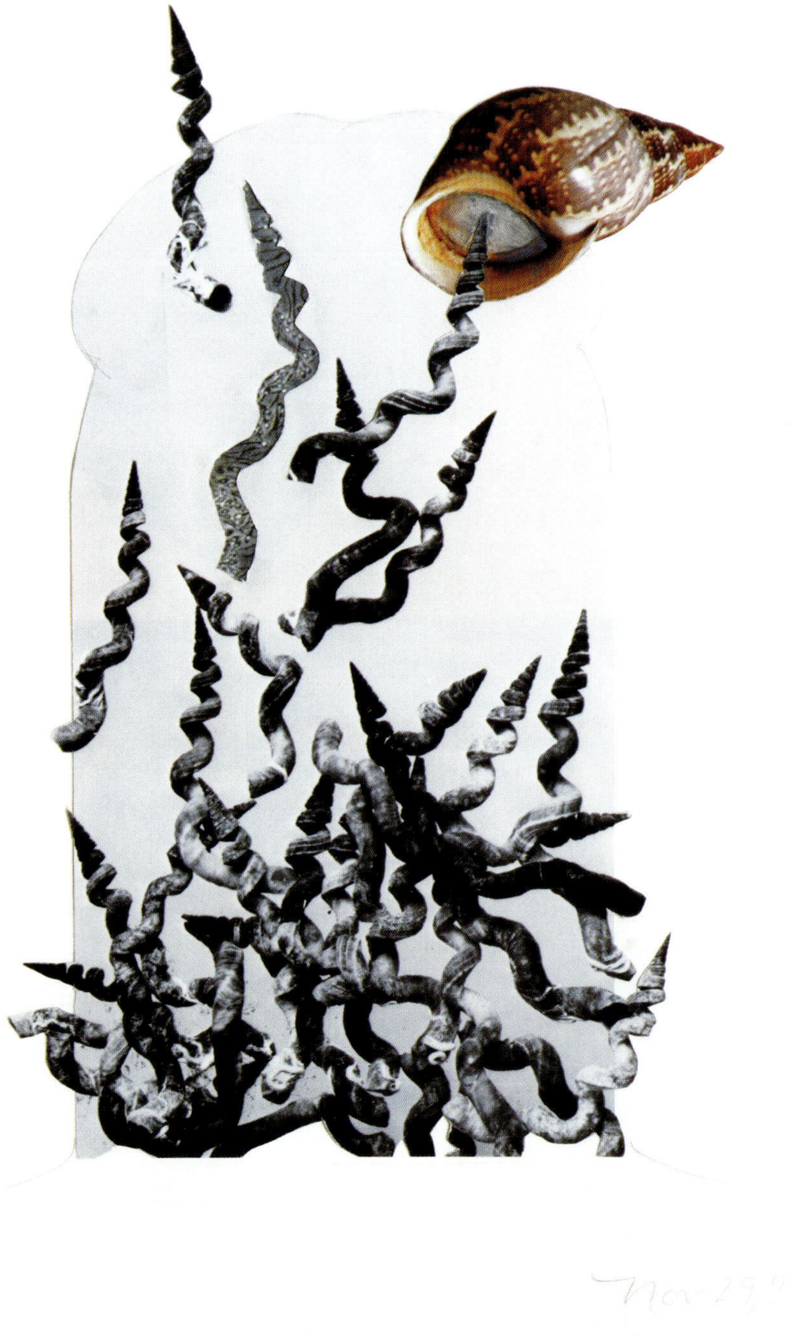

The museum, publishing, and gallery systems have served to restrict access to certain artists' work or subject matter. But artists' self-censorship is also a factor, especially for those artists (many of them women) who encounter resistance in the larger society. As intimate, sexually explicit, and "difficult" as some of my miscarriage images were, I wasn't troubled about exhibiting them, with the exception of two images.

Soon after I began the journal with the image of the happy jumping pear figure, I made two pages that expressed my ambivalence about the pregnancy. One combined my *Romanticism Is Ultimately Fatal* collage with a well-known, horrible picture of the dead, bloody, and abandoned victim of a botched abortion. The other image contained a note from my father, who gently tried to guide me and was inviting me to sound things out with him about my pregnancy. I cherished the letter, but I did not want its contents to be made public.
I represent here my own acts of self-censorship by crossing out the images.

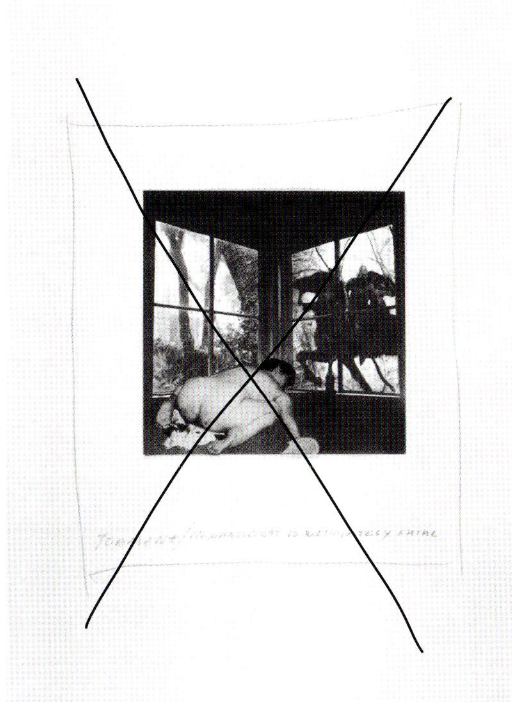

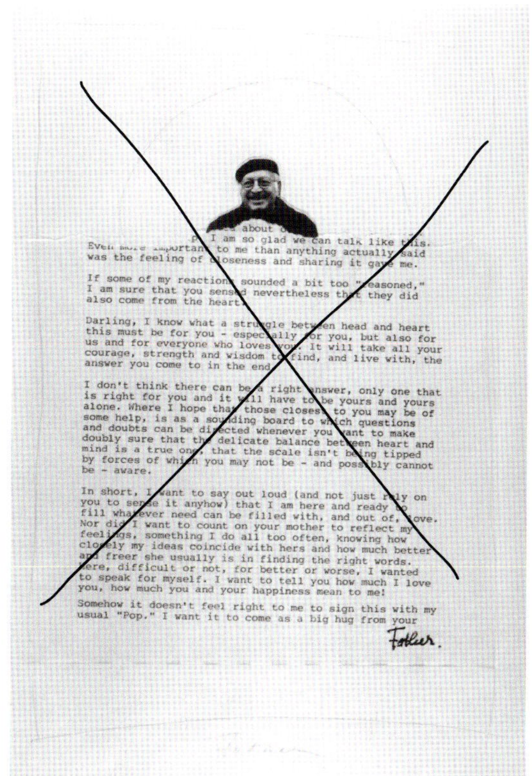

I am so glad we can talk like this. Even more important to me than anything actually said was the feeling of closeness and sharing it gave me.

If some of my reactions sounded a bit too "reasoned," I am sure that you sensed nevertheless that they did also come from the heart.

Darling, I know what a struggle between head and heart this must be for you - especially for you, but also for us and for everyone who loves you. It will take all your courage, strength and wisdom to find, and live with, the answer you come to in the end.

I don't think there can be a right answer, only one that is right for you and it will have to be yours and yours alone. Where I hope that those closest to you may be of some help, is as a sounding board to which questions and doubts can be directed whenever you want to make doubly sure that the delicate balance between heart and mind is a true one, that the scale isn't being tipped by forces of which you may not be - and possibly cannot be - aware.

In short, I want to say out loud (and not just rely on you to sense it anyhow) that I am here and ready to fill whatever need can be filled with, and out of, love. Nor did I want to count on your mother to reflect my feelings, something I do all too often, knowing how closely my ideas coincide with hers and how much better and freer she usually is in finding the right words. Here, difficult or not, for better or worse, I wanted to speak for myself. I want to tell you how much I love you, how much you and your happiness mean to me!

Somehow it doesn't feel right to me to sign this with my usual "Pop." I want it to come as a big hug from your

Father.

Opposite: Untitled (many spiral shells and one snail shell) from *Journal of a Miscarriage, 1973*

Top: Censored journal page (*Romanticism Is Ultimately Fatal* and 1964 police photograph of Gerri Santoro, left to die after botched abortion) from *Journal of a Miscarriage, 1973*

Bottom: Censored journal page (Letter from Dad) from *Journal of a Miscarriage, 1973*

Some of my strongest work seems to come from my capacity to meet anguish with artistic output. I've worried that I might be bound forever to court adversity in order to be a good artist. The often mythic life histories of artists had always seemed a confusing amalgam of boldness, poverty, misery, and triumph. I was miserable when I made the reprise of *Romanticism Is Ultimately Fatal* (one of the last pages in *Journal*), this time with a baby being trampled by the horse and riders. But as time passed and I embraced the idea of becoming pregnant again, I eventually realized that I could refuse the myth and misery of the artist and instead opt for happiness, believing that I could make a go of it for my child and me. I was taking chances with both my life and my art and picturing things about female life that I'd never seen pictured before.

Opposite: Untitled (horse tramples baby) from *Journal of a Miscarriage, 1973*

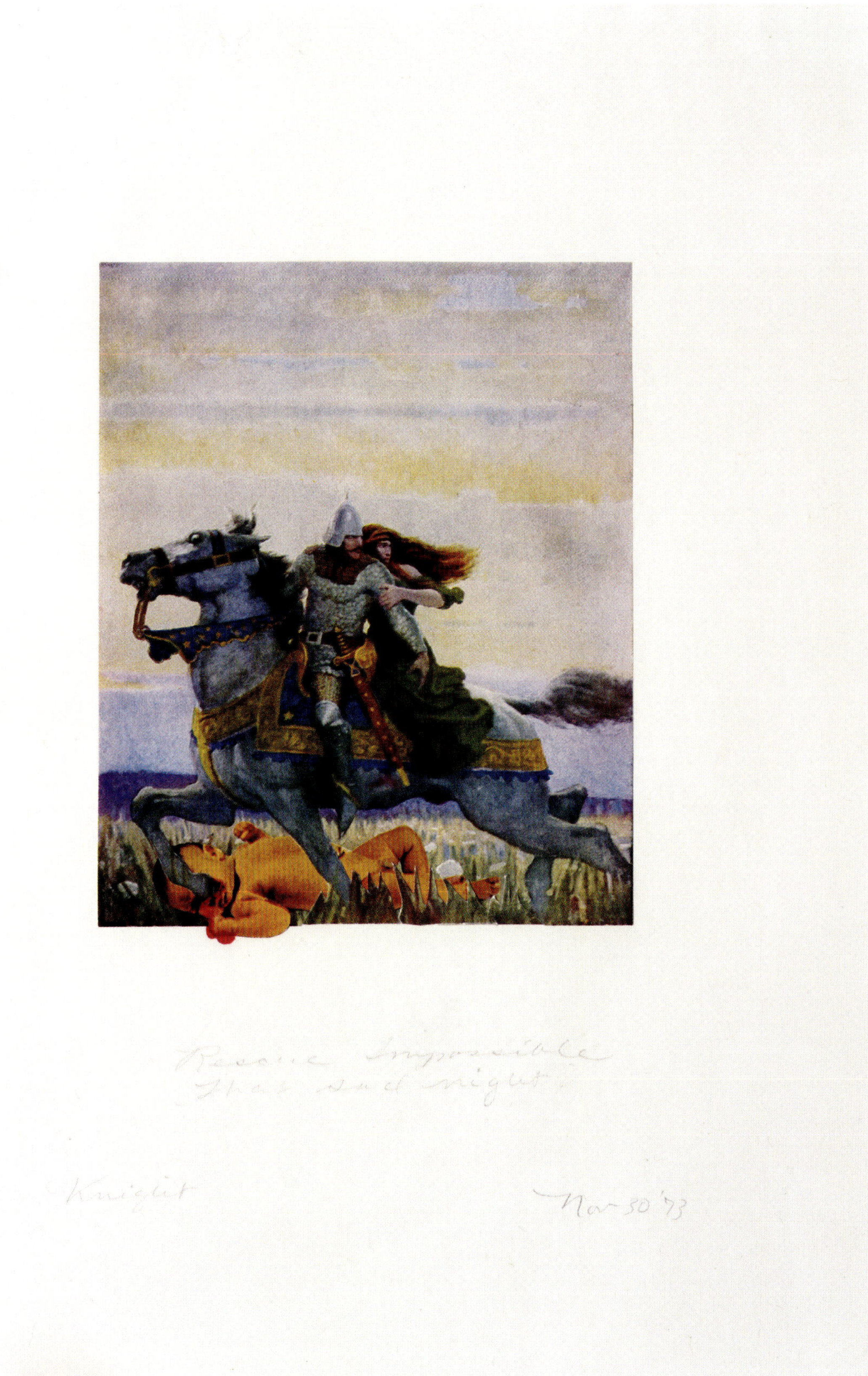
Rescue Impossible
Knight
Nov 30 '73

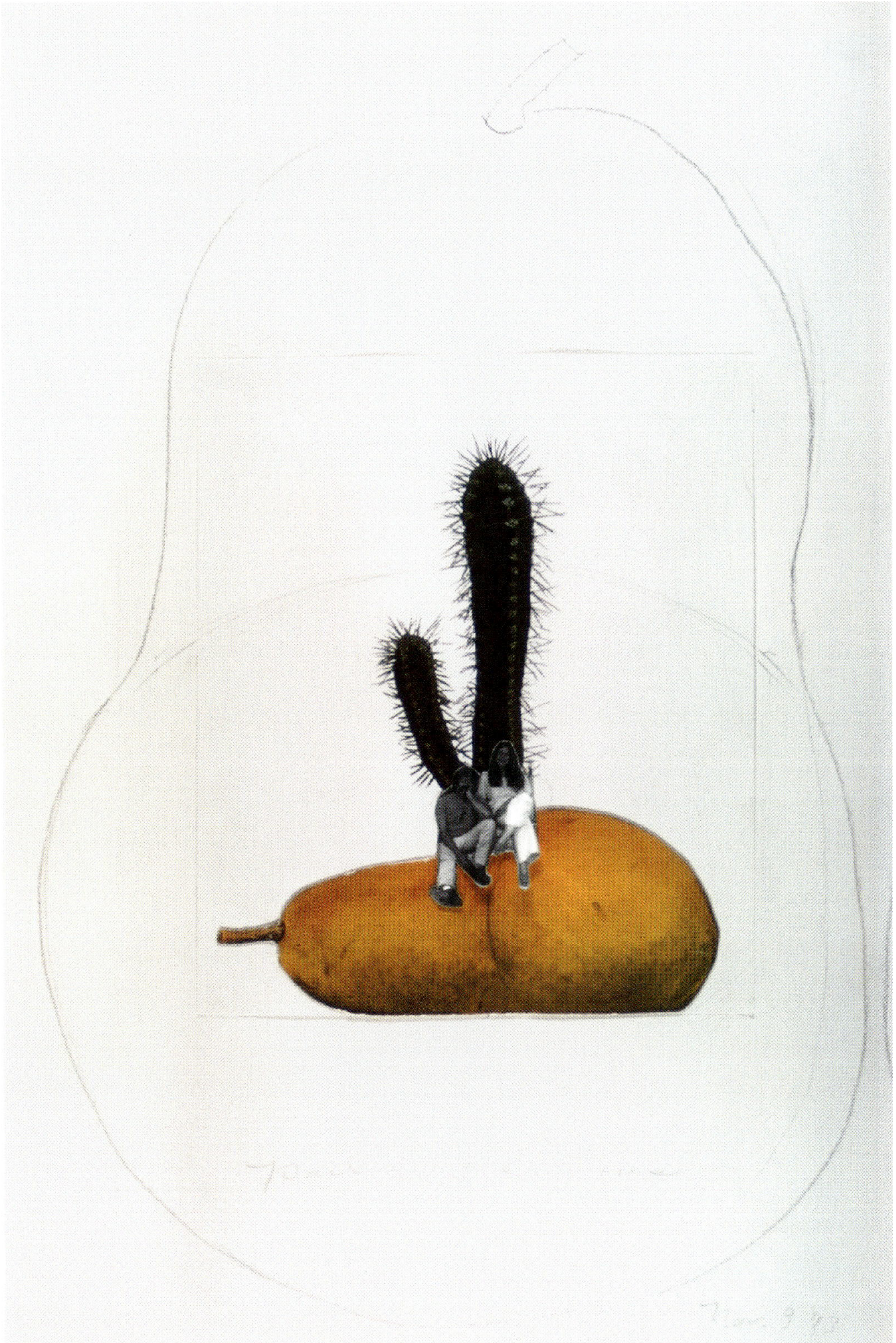

Above: Untitled (pear, couple [Manuel and Joanne], cactus) from *Journal of a Miscarriage, 1973*

In *Journal,* "tears" (the ripping of paper) and "tears" (the product of crying) appear in the collage *Tears/Tears,* which is among the many pages where I represent sadness, but after the initial bloody images, I also made images that play with words and pictures in a lighter vein: "reproduction," both photographic and maternal; "Christmas list," with Santa taking male and female roles. Images throughout the journal suggest sexual feelings and longings for the new prospect of a baby. After the miscarriage, Manuel and I maintained our residences in separate towns and teaching positions in different colleges but continued to see each other. Once in a while we would take off for a weekend and, for instance, drive down the coast to stay together in a hotel by the shore.

In these pictures more is hidden than is revealed. The multiple frames (two pictures) and the frame within a frame of the lower photo make one point of the picture the very act of framing—of inclusion and exclusion, things seen and unseen, made clear or obscured. In the mirror, the two prongs of the TV antennae reach toward the chandelier, serving as "equal" signs, visually pointing and equating: chandelier in mirror = TV on the dresser. Both represent potential sources of light, but neither illuminates a thing.

I remember lying there next to Manuel, whose feet poke up the sheets in the picture. While looking at the ceiling and waiting for him to awaken, I picked up the camera and recorded what I saw the morning after our daughter was conceived near the boardwalk and the amusement park in Santa Cruz at the Casa Blanca Hotel. Thus I became pregnant with Julia.

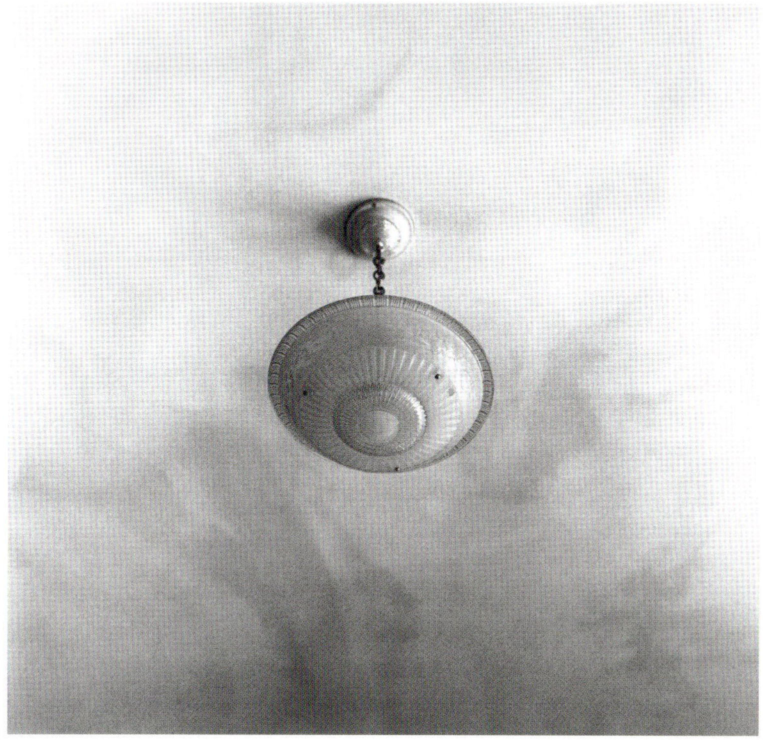

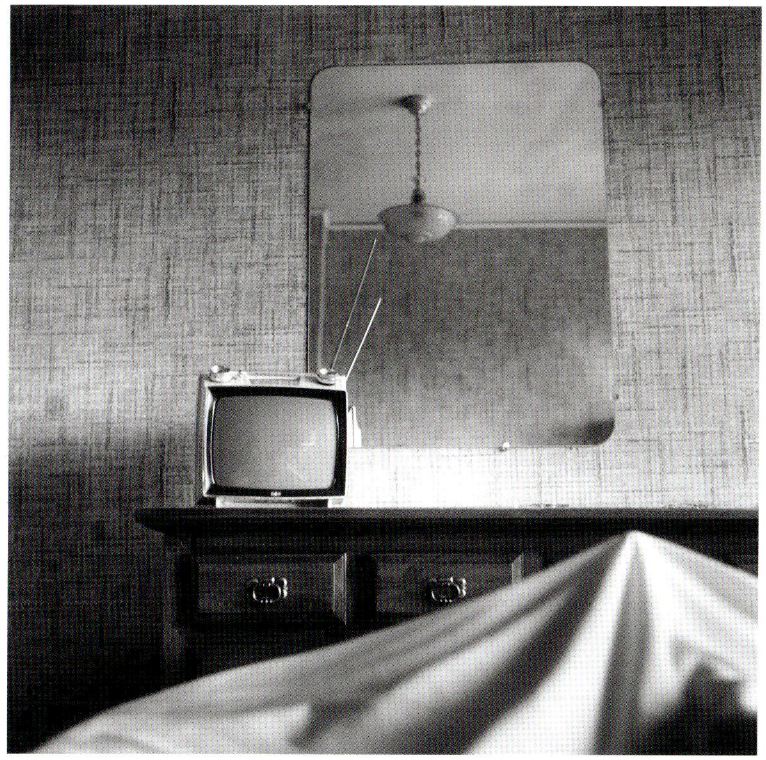

Above: Casa Blanca Hotel, Santa Cruz, silver prints, ca. 1974

Darkroom Alchemy

I've read many descriptions of being pregnant, including accounts of women who felt occupied, overtaken by another being, a loss of self. But I felt doubled, twinned, accompanied, wonderful. I had wanted this so much, and I loved the feeling of having my little company-keeper with me so completely while I was pregnant.

And yet, here I was, feeling that I was in midair having just jumped off a cliff. The ambivalence was gone, but I still had worries. How would I support us? How would I continue to be an artist? (Many friends were sure I wouldn't continue.) How would I (could I), in other words, continue to be "me"? For nearly five years I had worked from year to year in teaching programs with overlapping terms. I expected to give birth just as my current term was ending, and I did not yet have a promise of continued employment. I was under the weather a bit during the first few months of pregnancy, but as the months progressed, I felt well. The better I felt physically, the more expectant, resolved, optimistic, and contented I became.

Opposite: *Celebration,* cup and sperm (from post-*Journal* series), collage, 1973

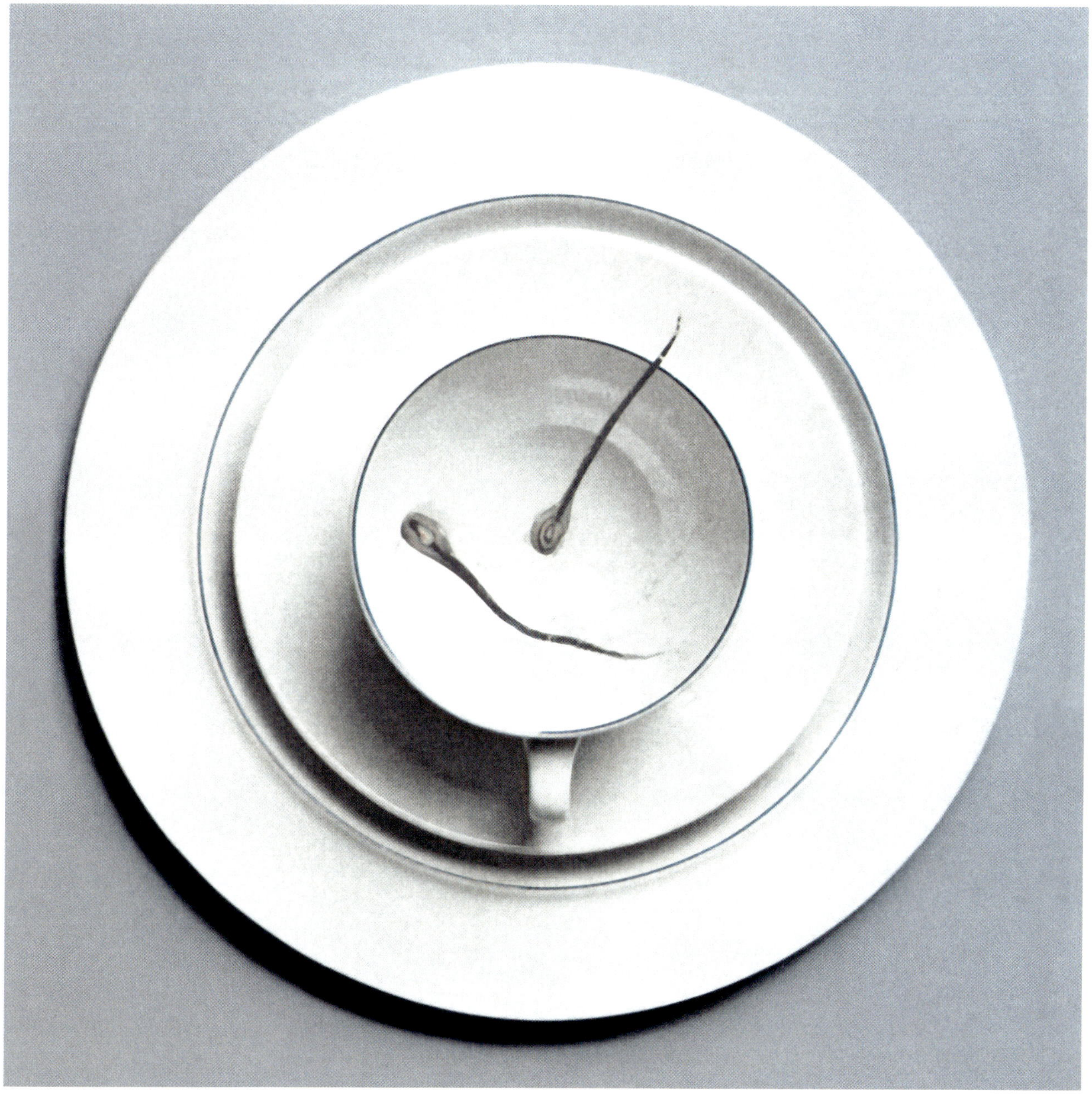

My parents worried about the stigma I might face as an unwed mother. In a local bookstore, I found a legal guide with contracts for unmarried persons who bought property together, lived in communes, or otherwise lived outside of the traditional married couple scenario. That I readily found such a book in Berkeley was a signal of the open atmosphere I felt around me. I was able to reassure my parents that Berkeley was a more tolerant place than they were imagining. I had a few acquaintances who expressed disapproval and one who used the term *bastard child* to refer to my situation. Though I didn't yet realize it, the older Julia got, the less unusual our lives would appear to new acquaintances. Most people wouldn't ask questions.

I had good friends who gave me two baby showers and provided their own children's outgrown items for the baby's room. The Art Department chair at Hayward State, where I had been teaching for the term, allowed me to use a substitute teacher for the last two weeks of my course. One night after I'd taught until 10:00 p.m. and just returned home, my water broke, completely on schedule. An hour later I got in a cab and took myself to the hospital. I had had nine months to make it clear to myself that I was doing this alone, so I did not dwell on how strange and admittedly a little sad it was to be alone just then. It was almost funny to think about the cab driver, who must have been wondering if I'd give birth in his cab. Just as I settled in at the hospital, labor began in earnest. After a few hours, my Lamaze coach arrived at the hospital, and I managed the natural birth I'd hoped for. During labor I thought, "How does anyone go through this pain more than once?" But when it was over and I held my tiny baby girl, I was so elated that I was sure I could fly to the moon. Julia Marjorie Leonard was born April 29, 1975.

My mother came a day after Julia was born and stayed for two weeks. Then my oldest friend, Harriet, came, and after that Elly with her daughter, Anna. And then—then I was on my own with my not-quite-four-week-old baby. It was during my mom's visit and Julia's second week on earth that I interviewed at Mills College for the part-time teaching job I would have for the next three years. I soon found additional teaching in two other college programs. Harrowing as it was to piece these work arrangements together, things in my life as a new mother were falling into place.

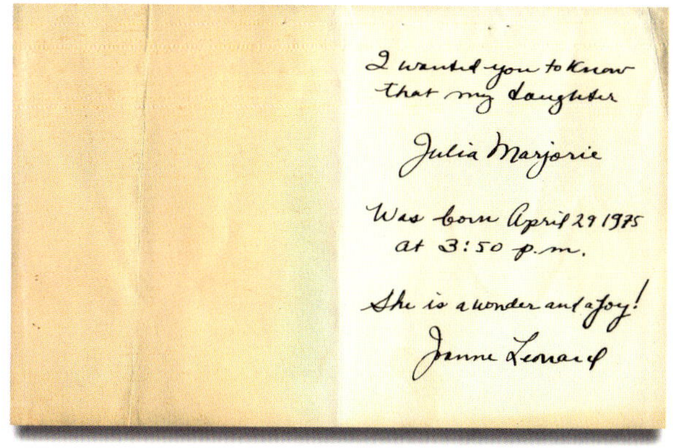

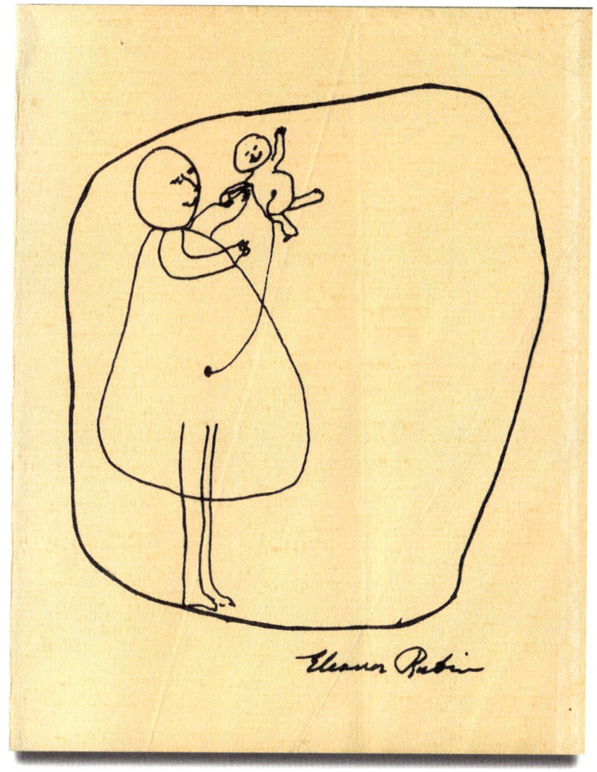

Above: Julia's birth announcement (with drawing by Elly)

Thursday May 21, '75

Dear Mom

Hurrah! Our little Julia weighs 7lbs l5 oz. 10 oz more in 6 days.

I got my work off to Seattle—now for the grant application. It is hard to get these things done but feels good to do them.

Harriet continues to be a big help. She took the laundry off to Susan's (her sister-in-law) today—she is definitely helping me a lot to eat regularly and well, and not too much.

I am So happy with my baby daughter, though I don't have time or words to tell you more about it properly.

If pop is home, give him a huge hug. We miss you both. Love, Joey

Julia weighed six pounds, eleven ounces, when she was born. My mom had gone back home when I wrote to her, with the pride of a breast-feeding mom, that Julia was thriving.

Opposite: *Julia, One Week Old,* silver print, 1975

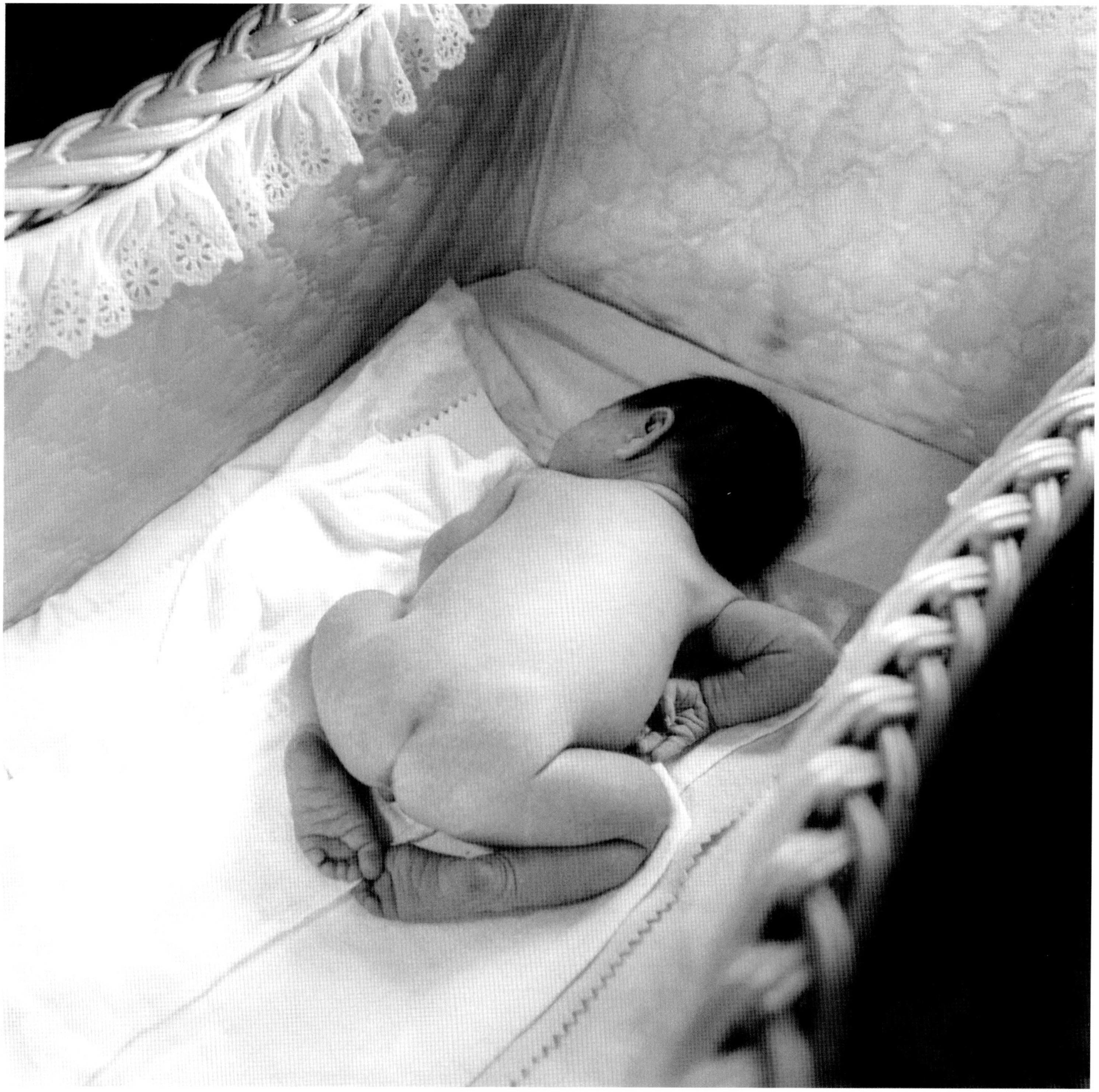

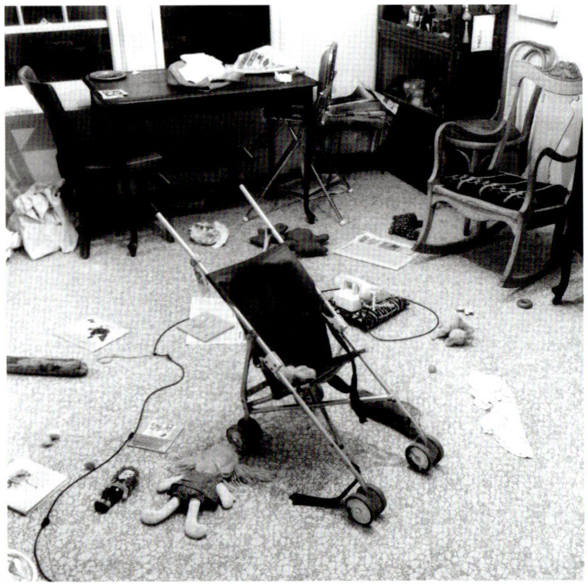

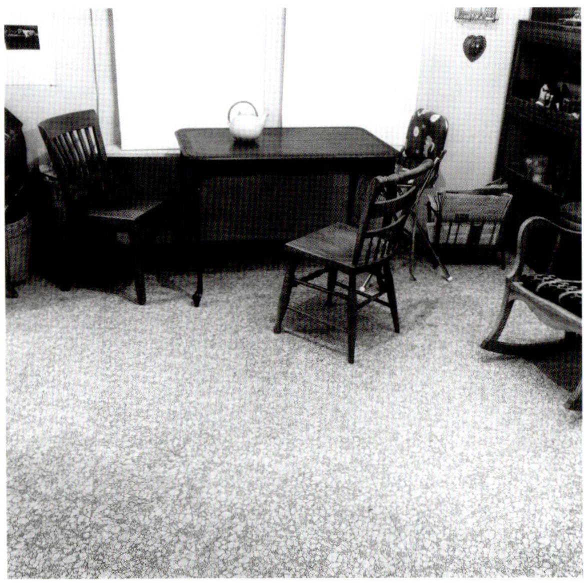

When Julia was born, we lived in an old shingled house in Berkeley that had been carved into apartments. Ours was in the back of the house. It was mostly quite ordinary, with surfaces of linoleum and Formica. But the bedroom (mine before Julia was born, hers afterward) was a closed-in former porch with the warm glow of rough-sawn redwood and a bank of wonderful windows along the outside wall.

One evening I sat down in our main room on my couch-bed and saw toys and clothes scattered everywhere. A total mess! Feelings of being alone and disconnected sometimes hit when I was tired. That night those feelings joined a long day's work and single parent life to leave me limp and despondent; I couldn't face the cleanup. Slumped on the couch, I turned on the TV and, wonderfully, found a biographical documentary on the setbacks, overcomings, and victories in the life of Eleanor Roosevelt. The portrait was a tonic, revealing the resilience of a woman who never won kudos for her role as homemaker but came into her own in a world arena. Suddenly, borrowing from her energy and inspiration, I got out a kitchen step stool to record the household chaos, then cleaned up and, savoring my small triumph on the home front, rephotographed.

Top: Living room/dining room/bedroom, messy view, silver print, 1976

Bottom: Living room/dining room/bedroom, tidy view, silver print, 1976

Opposite: Julia's bedroom, Josephine Street, Berkeley, silver print, 1975

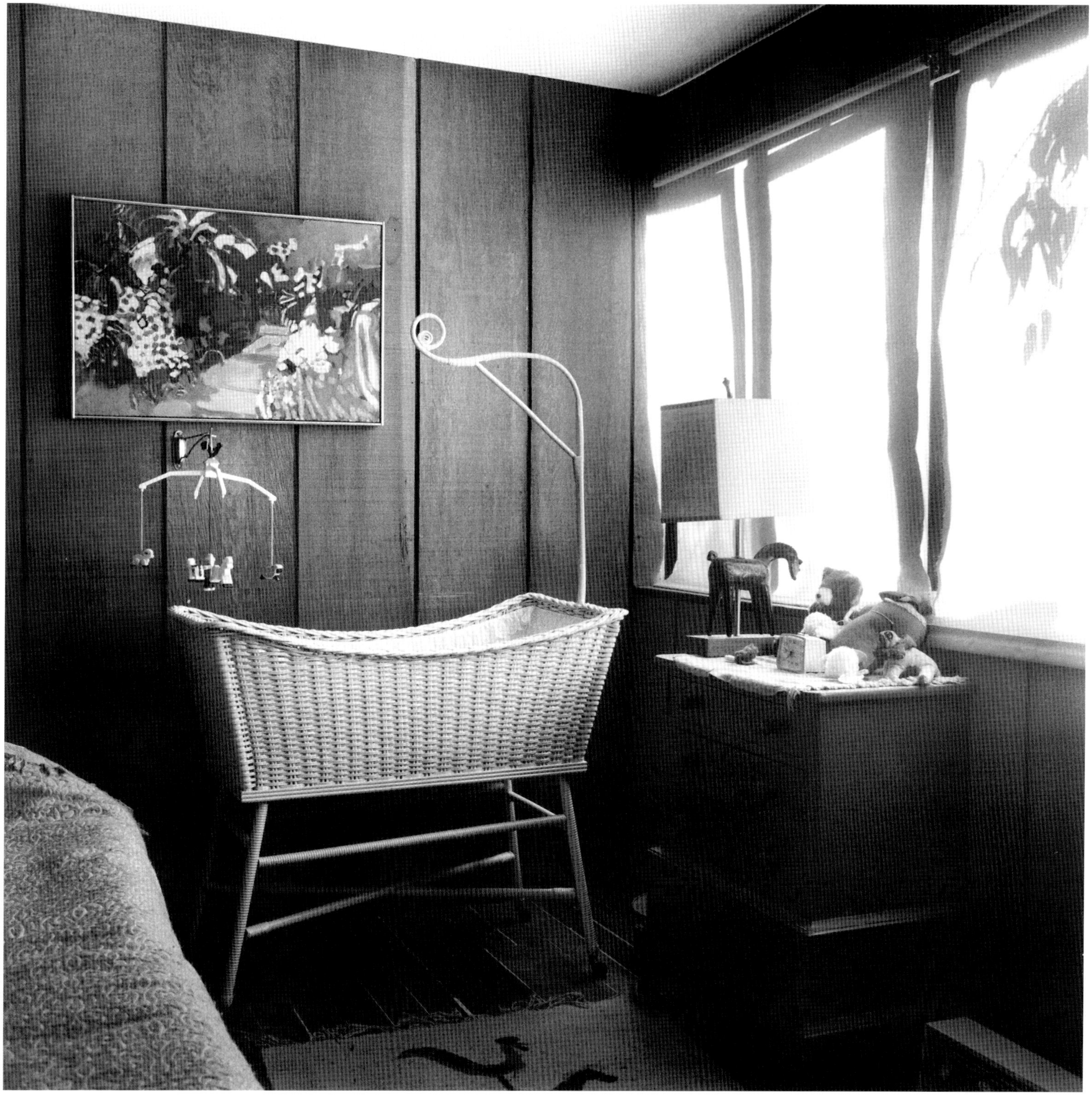

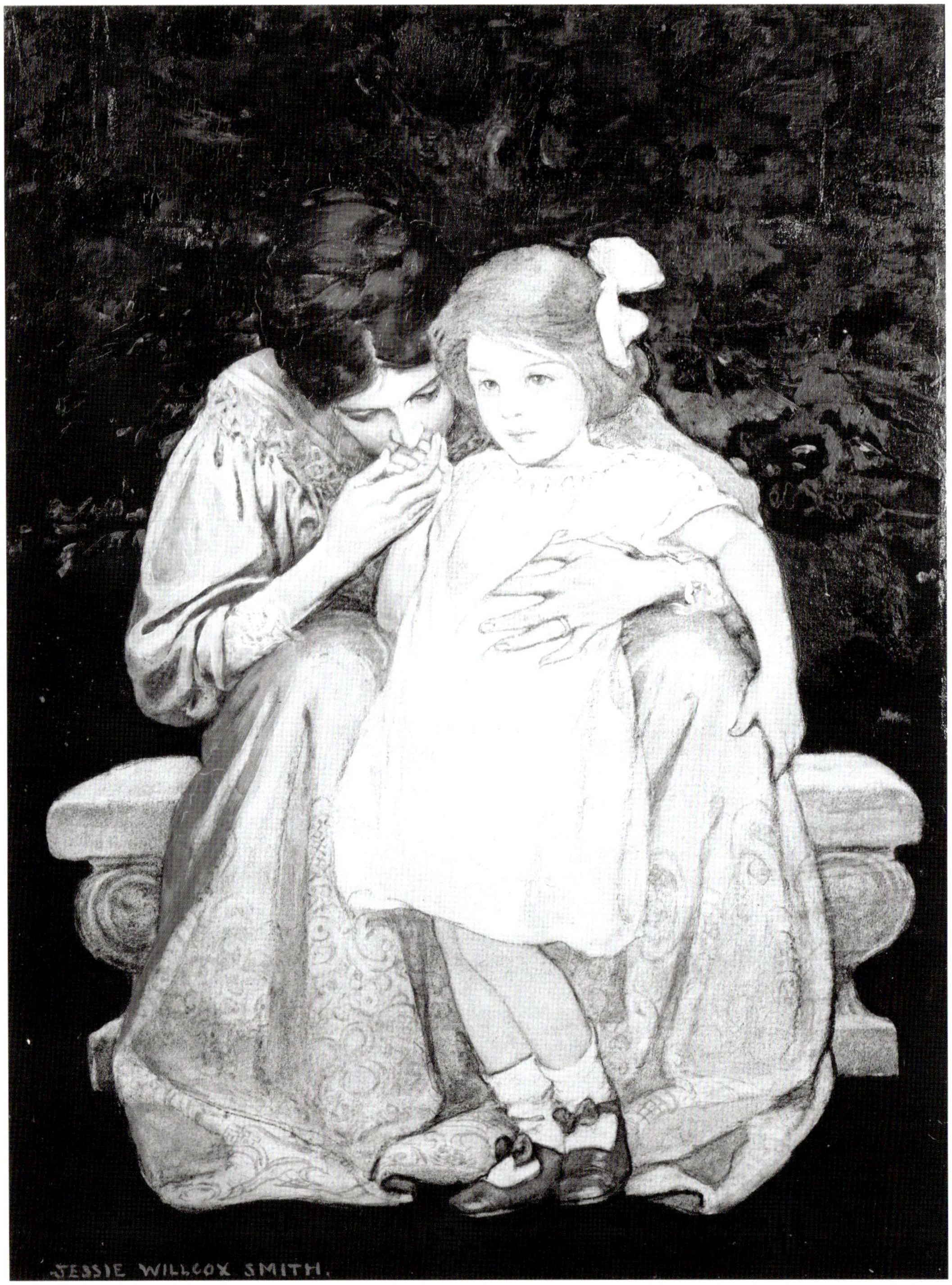

While we lived in that shingled house in Berkeley, a nine-year-old neighbor, Rachel Hannah, helped with Julia. It would have been easy to keep the roll of toilet paper, so prominent in this photograph of Julia and Rachel, from appearing. I could have framed the scene without it. I could have cropped it out later when making the print. I wanted that white paper roll *in* my picture to bring "reality" of place and moment, as well as intimacy, to the photograph of Julia wrapped in towels with Rachel. I have always been pleased that the loose section of white paper waves on the left side of the image, rhyming with Julia's waving arm on the right. Though my picture is a contemporary formulation, it also reflects my deep attachment to the work of Jessie Willcox Smith, the Victorian-era illustrator of children's books. One of the books my mother read aloud to us when Elly and I were small was *A Child's Garden of Verses*—her copy from her own childhood, with illustrations by Smith. Each illustration had delicate translucent paper covering it, which increased the anticipation every time we handled the pages—a sensation I try to evoke even today in some of my work.

Above: *Mother and Child* by Jessie Willcox Smith; collection of Jane and Ben Eisenstat

Opposite: Rachel Hannah (Fields) with Julia, silver print, 1975

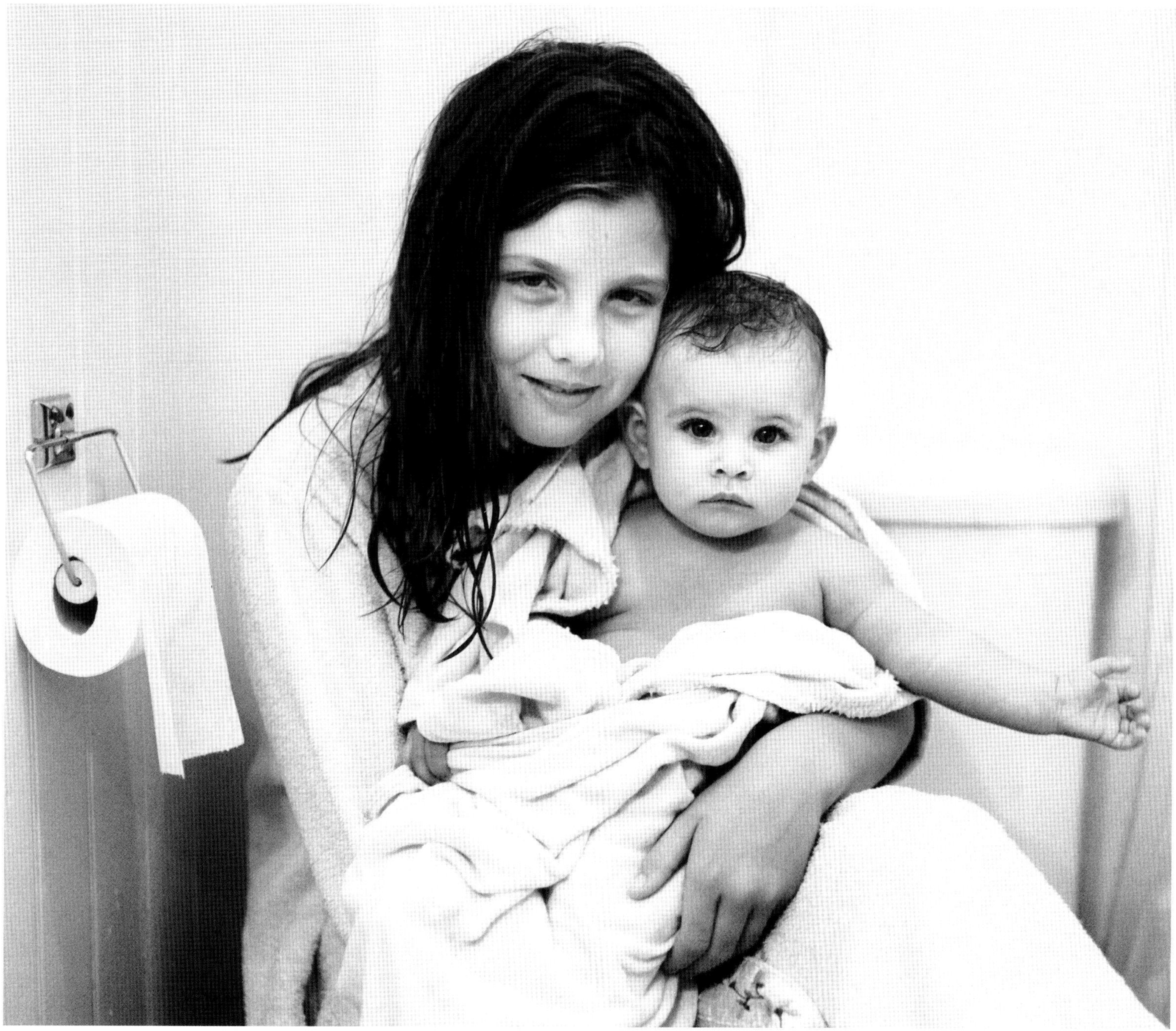

From a diary that I kept for a time during Julia's first year when I was commuting to the University of California, Davis (while teaching at Mills on alternate days):

. . . up at 5:20 AM, back at 7 PM. Leave the house at 7 AM. Drop Julia off at friend Sandra's, 5 min. away. . . . I stay with Julia 15 minutes then take off, meet car pool at 7:40 at rapid transit station. Park my car and . . . back to Berkeley at 6:15 p.m. back to Sandra. Home at 7 after nursing at Sandra's. . . . At first it was hell, now (after 5 weeks) it's working out o.k.

Opposite: Julia, first birthday, silver print, 1976; San Francisco Museum of Modern Art

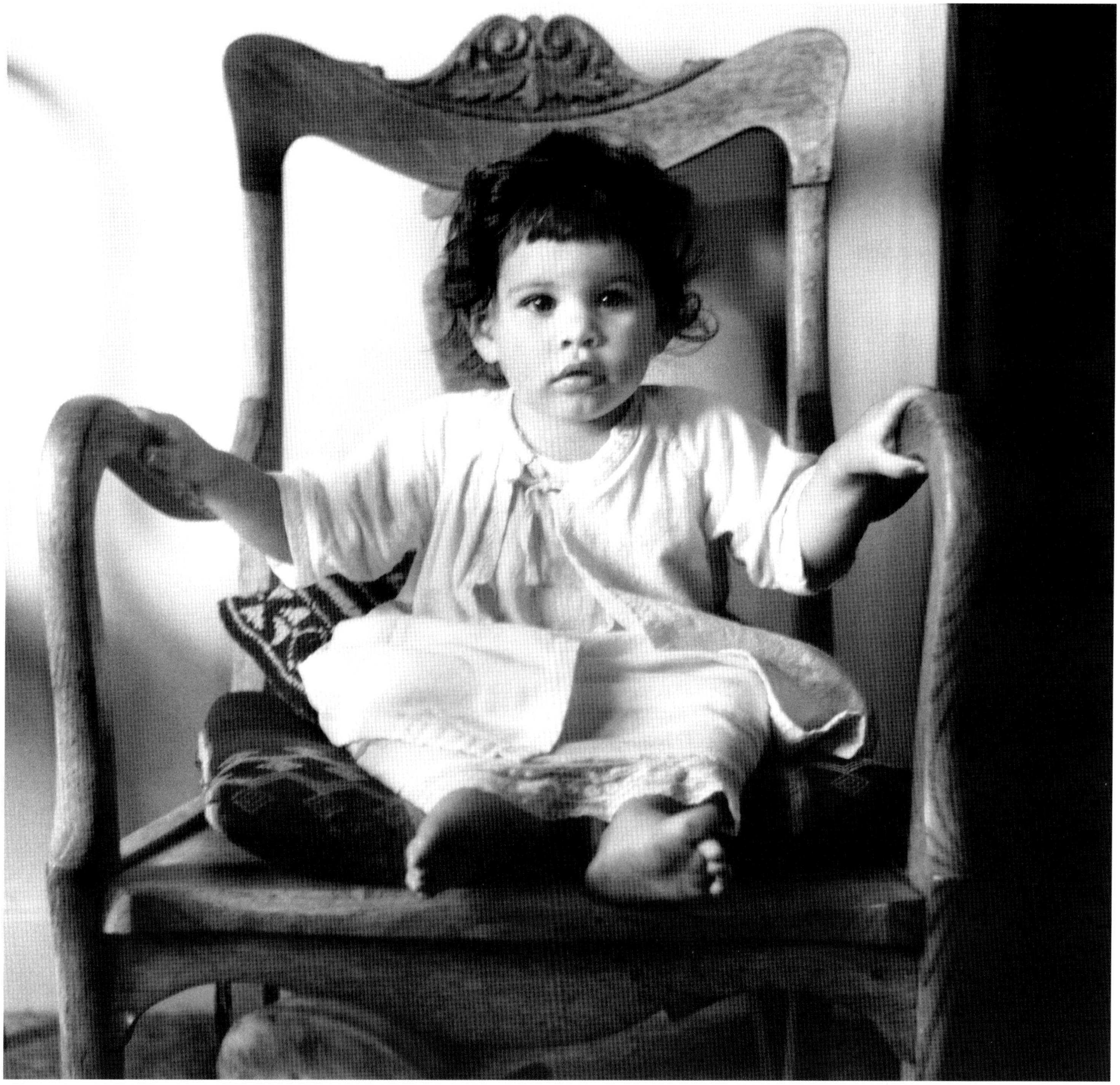

Mills College was now my only teaching job, and this gave me a more manageable schedule. But there were no benefits and no guarantee of long-term employment, two things that seemed newly essential. Very soon after Julia was born I applied and was asked to teach at the California Institute of the Arts in Los Angeles but found I couldn't say yes; I was too overwhelmed with being a new mother to pick up and move. Ironically, just after I said no, I was evicted from my apartment (the landlady wanted to move in there herself). I found a tiny house, and we stayed in Berkeley.

I continued teaching at Mills but, to increase my income, took a summer teaching job at Cornell University in upstate New York. After that summer away from Berkeley I had several more rounds of interviews, seeking a position that could lead to tenure and security for me and my two-year-old daughter. While I was applying in earnest, I lived in fear that I'd be hired, feeling that moving would be just too difficult. There were enough challenges just being a single mother alone in a long-familiar place and finding ways to keep going as an artist. But by 1978, I realized I had to find a long-term teaching position, even if it meant moving where I knew no one at all. I had two offers of employment to choose from and in 1978 was hired by the University of Michigan's School of Art and Design as a tenure-track faculty member who would teach photography and photo history.

Opposite: Julia on dark couch, silver print, 1976

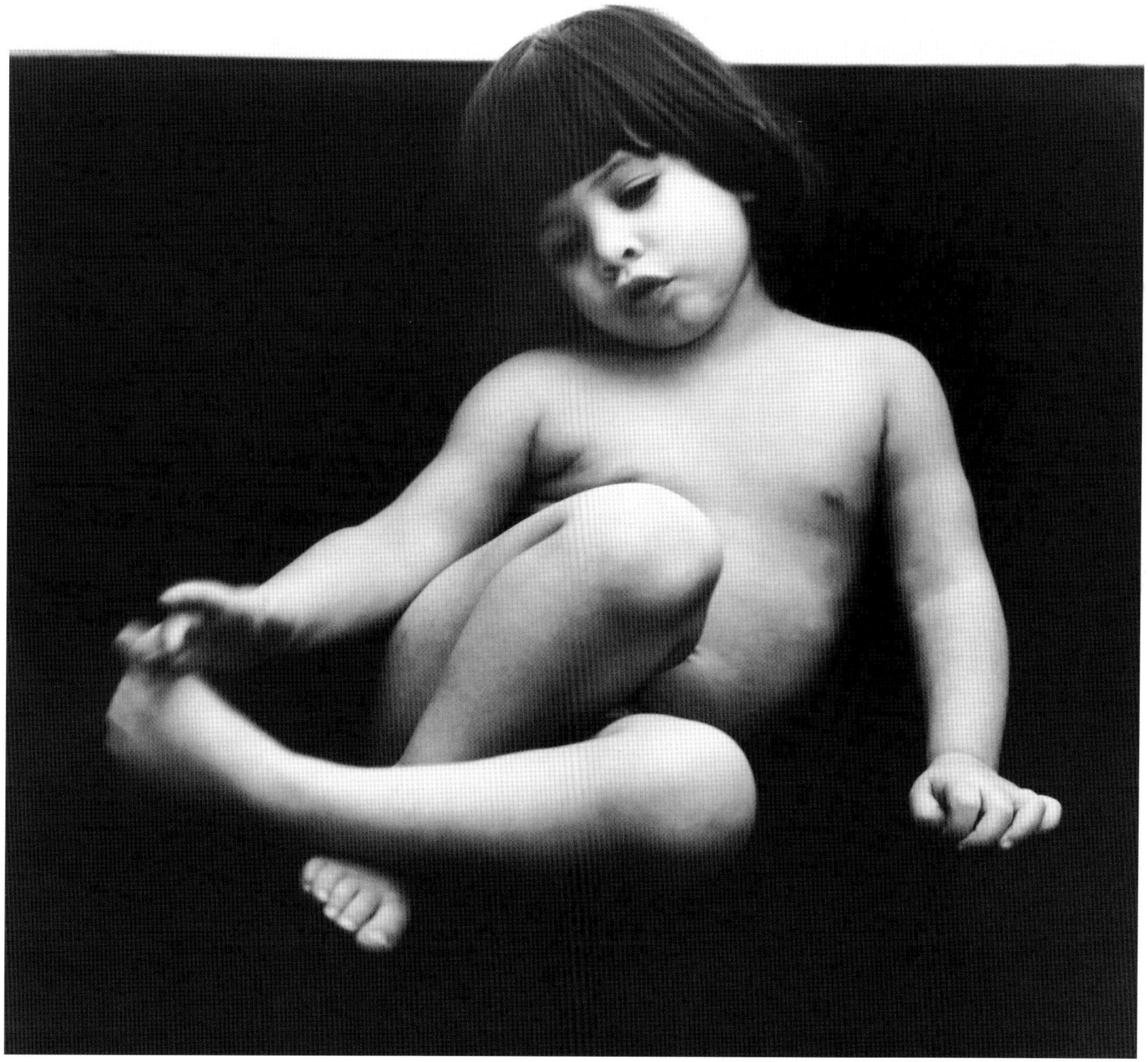

The summer I moved across the country with Julia and our dog, Puli, was one of the most harrowing of my life. As I packed, I begged for Julia's forgiveness for a summer with so few moments of fun and promised repeatedly that as soon as we got to Ann Arbor we'd get a swing set for our new backyard. And we did. I bought it even before the furniture caught up with us by truck. But first it had to be assembled, so there was the laying out of stove bolts and lock washers and wing nuts and a myriad of small items of which hitherto I'd never heard. Hours and hours later (even into the next day!), with many missteps and much frustration, I finished. And then, there it was! We both loved that it was there, a promise kept. It was more difficult to begin building my darkroom, weeks into my first term. But without it, I wasn't the photographer I had been "at home" in California. Getting it built was crucial.

House hunting in California had included keeping an eye out for a back porch or breakfast nook that could serve as a darkroom. In Michigan, almost every house I saw had a basement—and ranch-style one-story houses like mine had basements under the full length of the house, big basements. I found a carpenter, a widower with a small child. I didn't have a design—we just talked about what I needed, and he set to work. When the darkroom was complete, I had an eight-foot sink, temperature-control gauges, and two faucets. After making do with tiny makeshift darkrooms over the years, I thought that this one was great, but its features may now sound quaint in the computer age, when more and more "darkroom work" (including some of mine) is done at a desk.

Opposite: Julia, half asleep, silver print, 1977

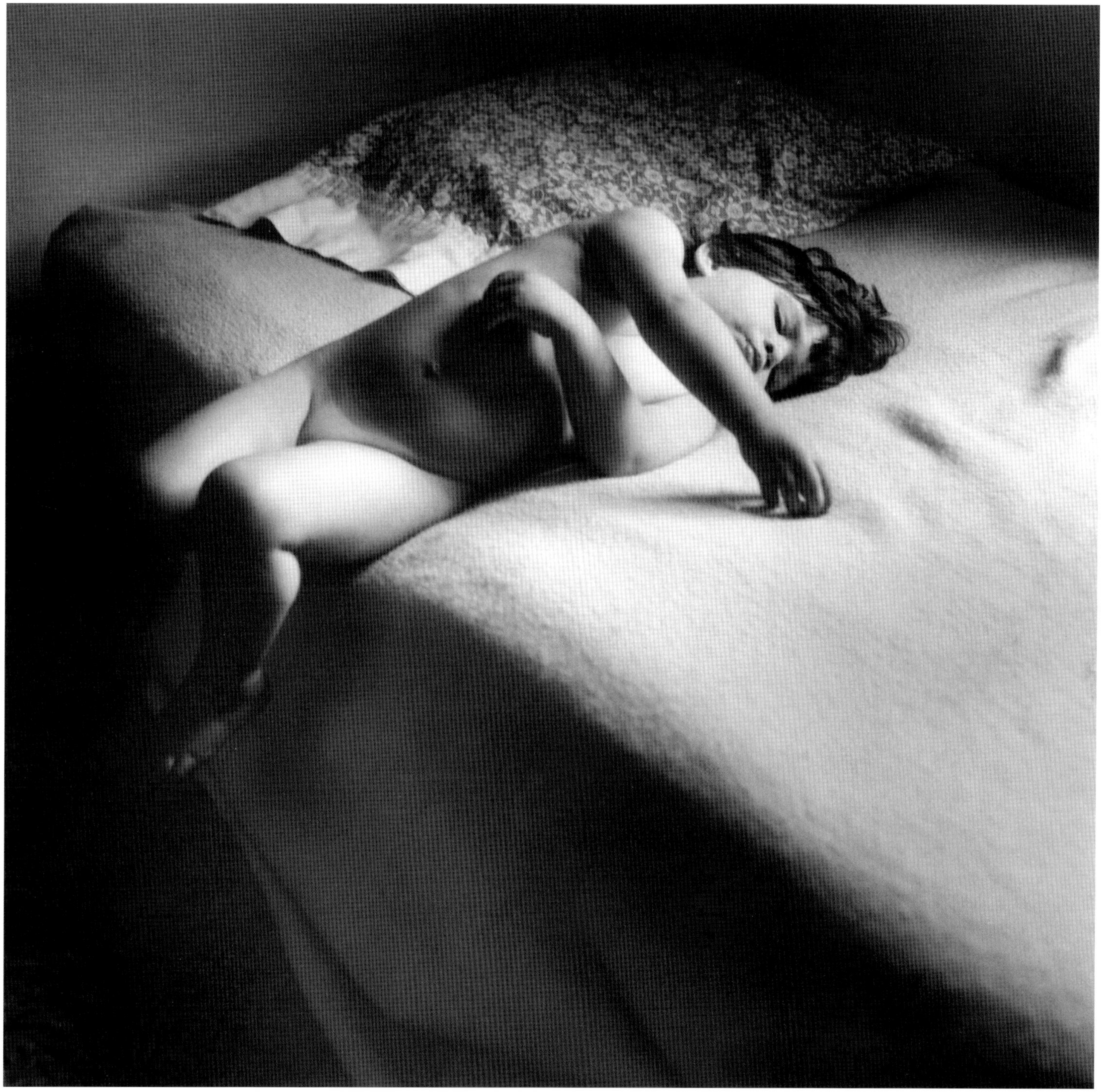

I not only had to get my darkroom built, but I also had to learn the history of photography quickly enough to teach it. In addition, I had to make the hundreds of slides I'd need to teach the course. I'd blithely said, "Of course I can teach photo history" when getting hired seemed to depend upon it. I knew it would be difficult, but I had no idea *how* difficult. Studio classes—where I gave hands-on lessons in photography to eighteen or twenty students—were held on North Campus, several miles from the University of Michigan's Central Campus. My slide-lecture photo history class had fifty students the first term and nearly double that the second. But the slides I needed for the class existed only at the slide library on Central Campus at the Department of the History of Art. And that library's slide-borrowing regulations conflicted with both my teaching needs and my parenting responsibilities.

Beginning immediately and continuing over the next two years, I had to make the slides myself. And the difficulties of teaching the course included not only the slide making but also more reading in the history of photography. I was also preparing for a ten-year retrospective solo exhibition of my work at the Laguna Gloria Art Museum in Austin, Texas. After two years of teaching the history of photography, I was desperate to stop. This demanding course consumed the time and energy I needed for exhibition preparation and new creative work. It robbed me of assignments to teach studio courses that I could face with more confidence and left me deeply unhappy. I told the dean, "I simply can't keep teaching the history of photography any longer. If that means I have to look for another position, so be it." I really thought that it might be the end of my job. But my gamble paid off. He agreed I'd given it my best shot and let me teach only studio courses since that is what I preferred. I began enjoying the university much more—visiting Central Campus more often; making friends among faculty in other departments, including Women's Studies; finding my stride as a teacher; and taking up my camera anew. Though there would be some rocky times ahead, this was a turning point for me, as I had the great good fortune to find a community of wonderful friends and colleagues at that time.

Opposite: Julia with bird water whistle, silver print, ca. 1978

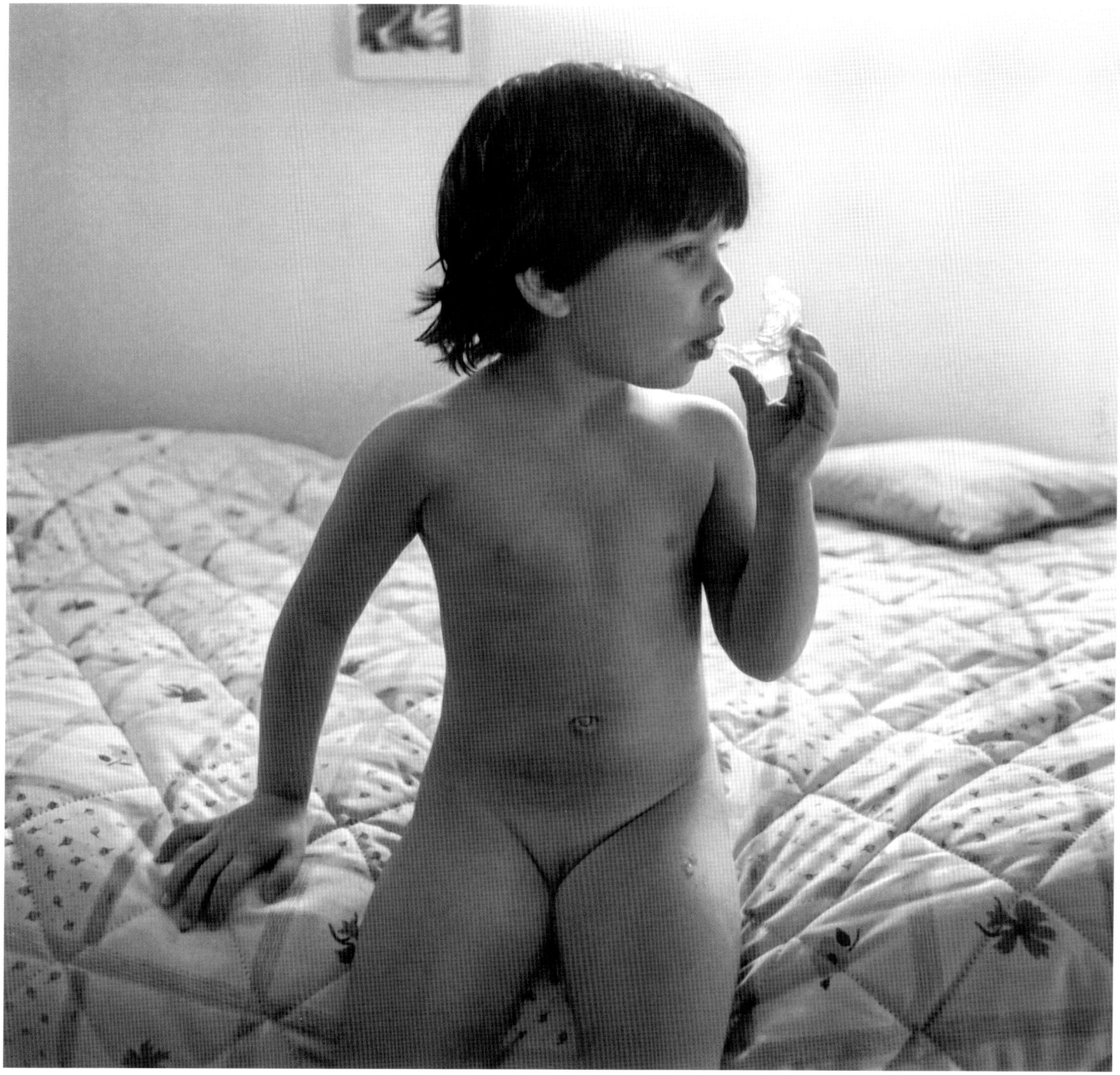

A mother who makes *hundreds* of pictures of her child (as I have) may simply be performing and exaggerating activities of maternal absorption and devotion. There is a popular notion that women's creativity is "natural," that procreative and creative forces in women are part and parcel of the same womanly instinct. Then what could have been more "natural and motherly" than the picture-taking mother that I had become? But a mother's act of paying close and frequent attention to her child through photography can be read in many ways, including as devoted and attentive or as horridly intrusive, too objective, and thus cold, exploitive, or even pornographic.

(The texts on this page and the next are adapted from my essay "Photography, Feminism and the Good Enough Mother," in *The Familial Gaze*, edited by Marianne Hirsch.)

Opposite: Julia series

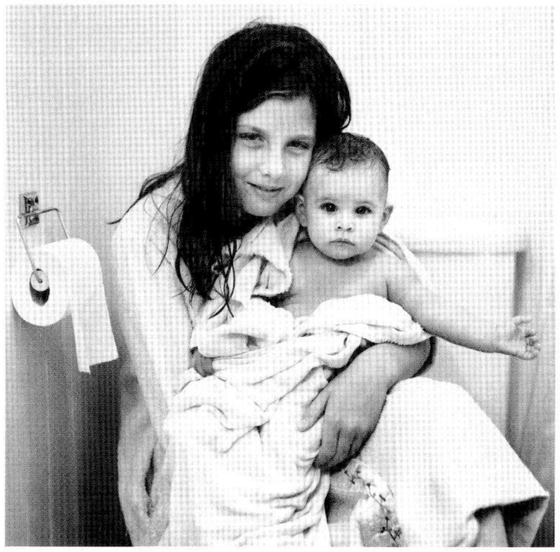
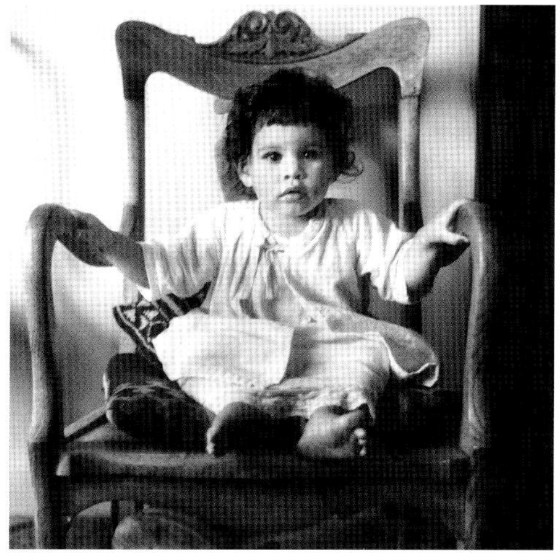
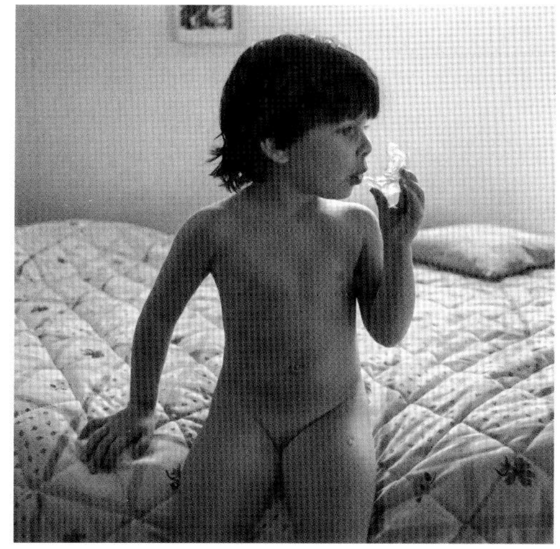
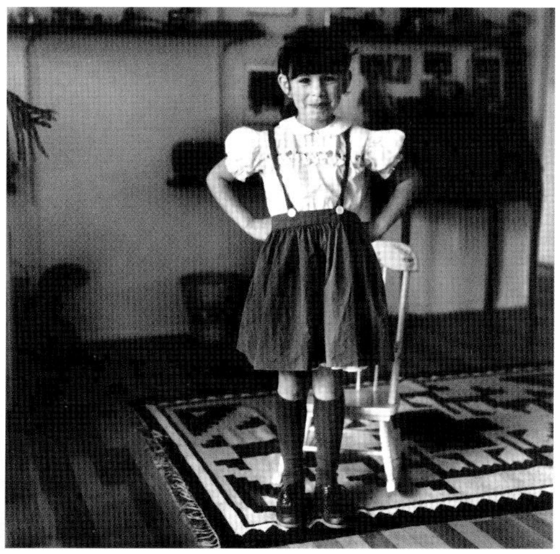
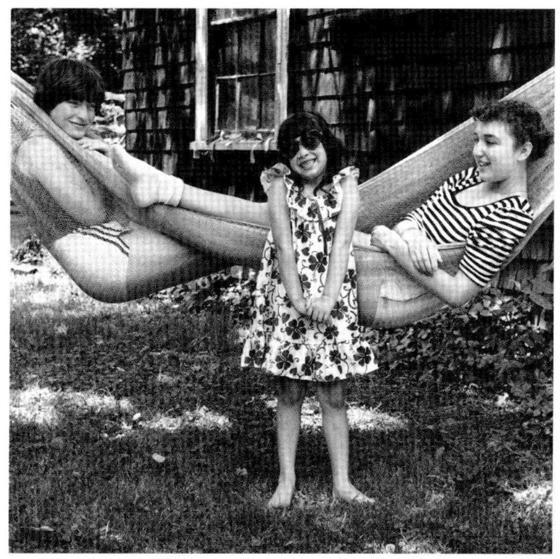
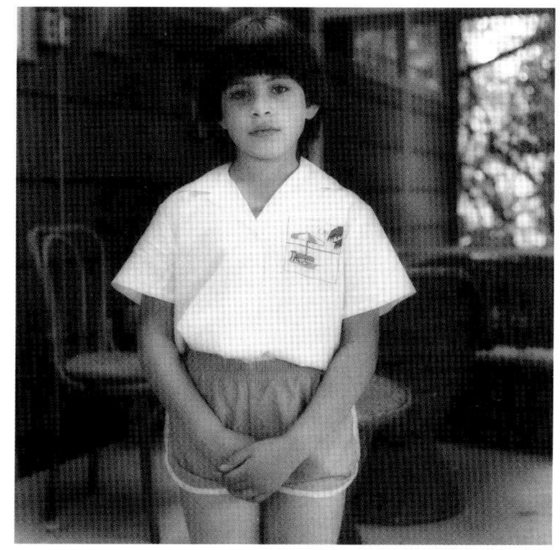
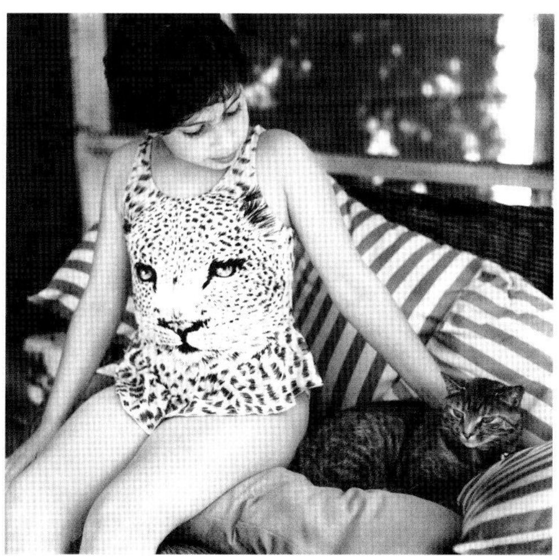
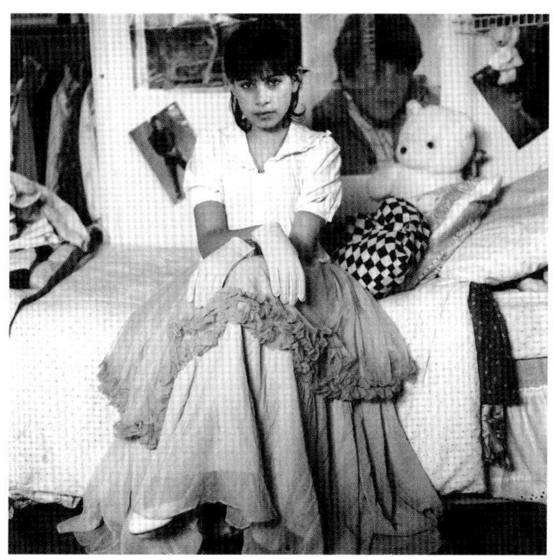
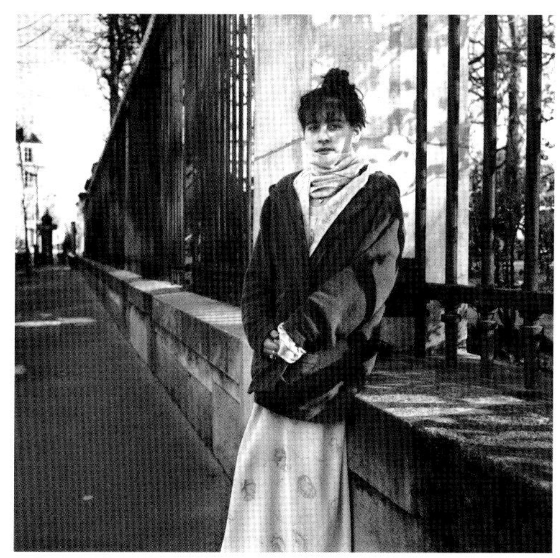

When Julia was an infant, she slept through much of my picture-making attentions. But over the years she definitely became complicit in the making of her own image, thus prompting me to think about this enduring partnership between artist and model, between Julia and me, her mother/photographer. Years later, Julia wrote her own words about my photograph of herself as a newborn. As important as it is to me to know what she thinks now about my photograph of her, or what she remembers about moments and places in our lives, I can't take Julia's words as the answer to my questions about the photograph, its impact, and its meaning. For one thing, try as we might, she and I could never rid ourselves of the mother-daughter power dynamics of our situation. For example, when she was little, she may have sought to please me by posing for a photograph and, when she was older, to manipulate me by withholding a picture-taking moment I'd wanted. In these and similar situations, each of our responses was too intricately linked to the other dynamics of our lives to sort them all out into one coherent story and explanation. Her comments reflect on a few of the "realities" and contradictions about family life embedded in this image by me, as the maker of it, by Julia (its subject), and by viewers (who have become the audience for the work).

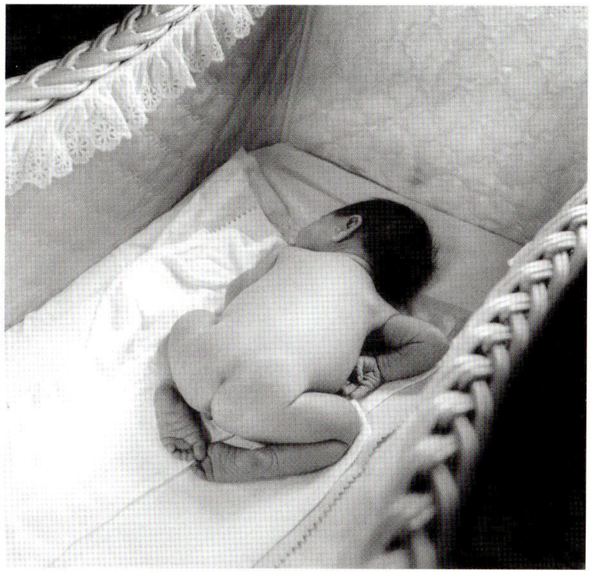

This photo has always felt so loving and warm as though you see this baby through eyes of someone who loves and knows this baby like a "view" as opposed to just a snapshot or a family photo. When I was younger this photo and other photos from [our] small green house made me wish I could remember more about the time we lived in San Francisco [Bay Area]. Now I remember the answers you gave me to all my questions [when] I asked you about things like my yellow room with the long white shades, the [gold] fish . . . that I killed, Puli [the dog] rolling me over, the snails [I collected from our fence posts], eating too many strawberries on my birthday, playing under the yellow blanket in your bed in the living room. The list goes on. I feel that this and all other photos of me before I could remember help me remember being a baby.

(Julia Marjorie Leonard)

Julia concludes that my photographs provide memories of things that happened when she was too young to remember. Her report of her own memories is for me exquisitely visual and tactile at the same time—of things she saw and touched. She saw yellow light in her room—a dark back room turned sunny with paint. She squished her fish but didn't mean to kill it. My bed was in the living room, just as she remembers it, and I remember the fun of hiding under the covers together.

Remembered, too, are the limitations the details in Julia's writing about her memories make clear—that our little two-person single-parent family had so far lived in an apartment and a tiny house, each with only one bedroom (hers, so I could shut the door for/on her at night and have the rest of the house to myself). It wasn't until we had moved to Ann Arbor that I had a bedroom of my own.

Opposite: Julia with hands on hips, silver print, ca. 1982

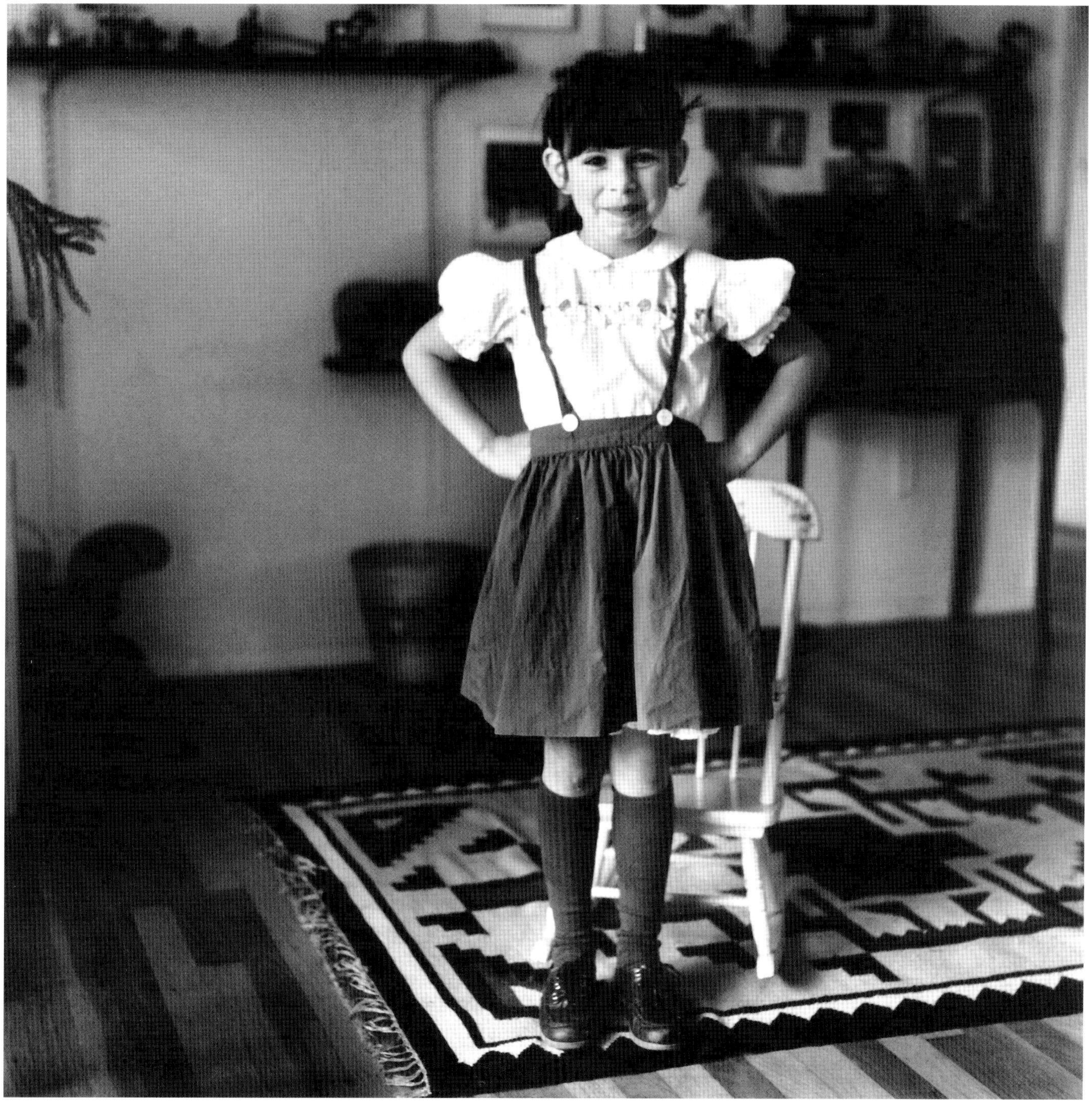

Each detail Julia remembers has a story, a history, and an economic foundation that makes the moments depicted seem less idyllic, more complex. Does the absence of these narrative details make a photographic distillation of a moment into a lie, half-truth, or fiction? Sometimes the use of collage has helped me address such complexities, but photographs are in a sense always collages, layered as they are with levels of "realities"—the photographer's, the subject's, the viewer's.

Opposite: Julia with camp shirt, silver print, ca. 1987

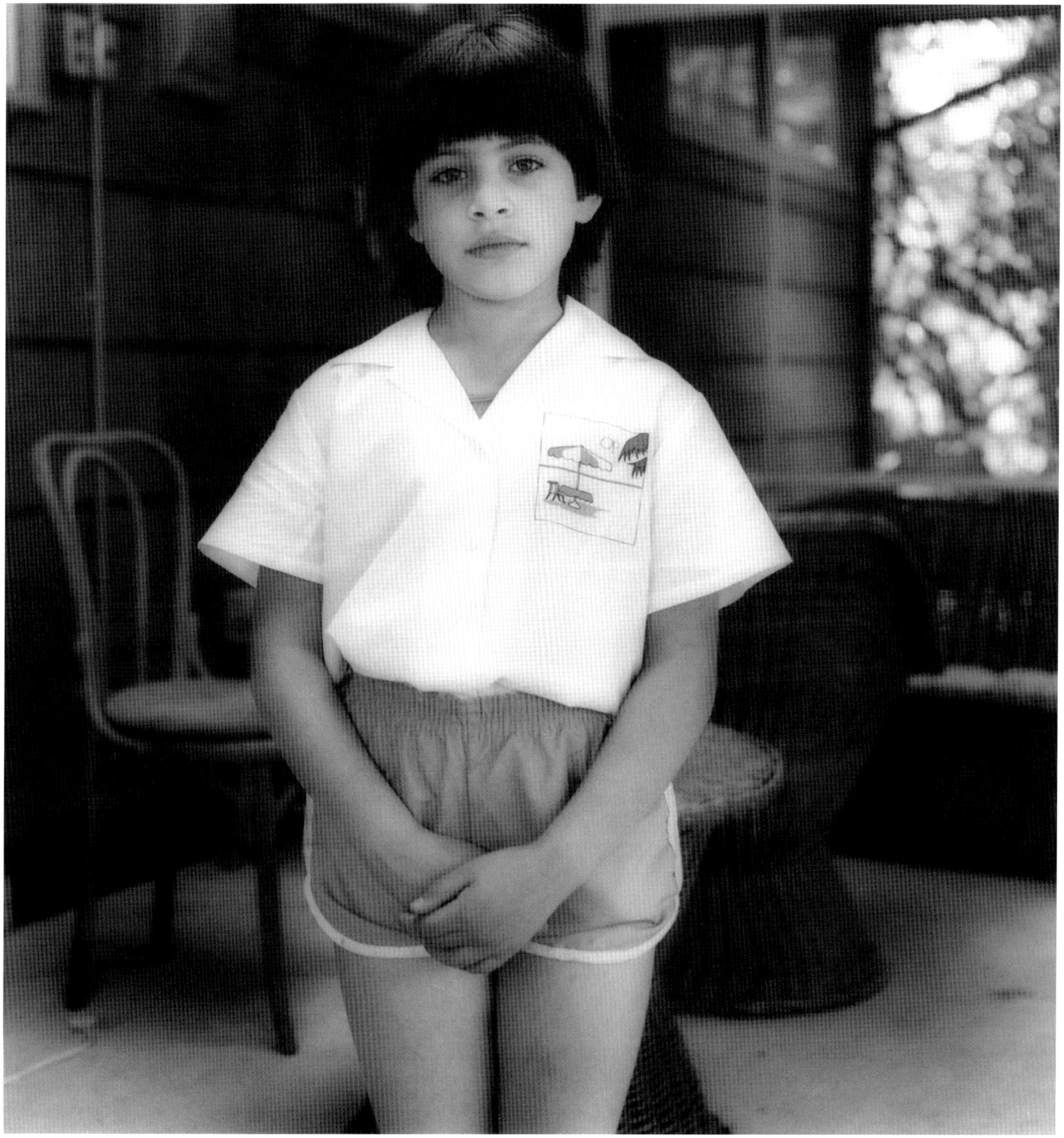

If collages can in effect layer photographs with meanings, this made-in-the-darkroom collage may be a good example. While the academic year had me in its grips, I'd hardly had time for a good look at my little girl. When the end of the term brought relative peace, I looked at her anew and saw change; she could do so many new things that only a year ago I could not have imagined. Though I don't think the phrase literally came to mind, it was as though she'd "sprouted wings," and that idea is something of what my new work that spring reflected.

I made *Winged Ones* in 1983, when the cicadas in Michigan emerged after seventeen years of underground hibernation. I found a cicada wing on the street, then found a cicada on a nature walk I'd signed up for to learn more about these ubiquitous insects. While the effect is that of collage, the actual technique is called "cliché verre" because I've made a negative (*cliché* in French) from the cicada wing by attaching it to the glass (*verre*) along with my camera-made negative. Then I made a photo print from the conglomerate "handmade" negative.

Opposite: *Winged Ones* (Julia with cicada wings), silver print and cliché verre, 20 inches × 24 inches, limited edition, 1985; Detroit Institute of Arts and private collections

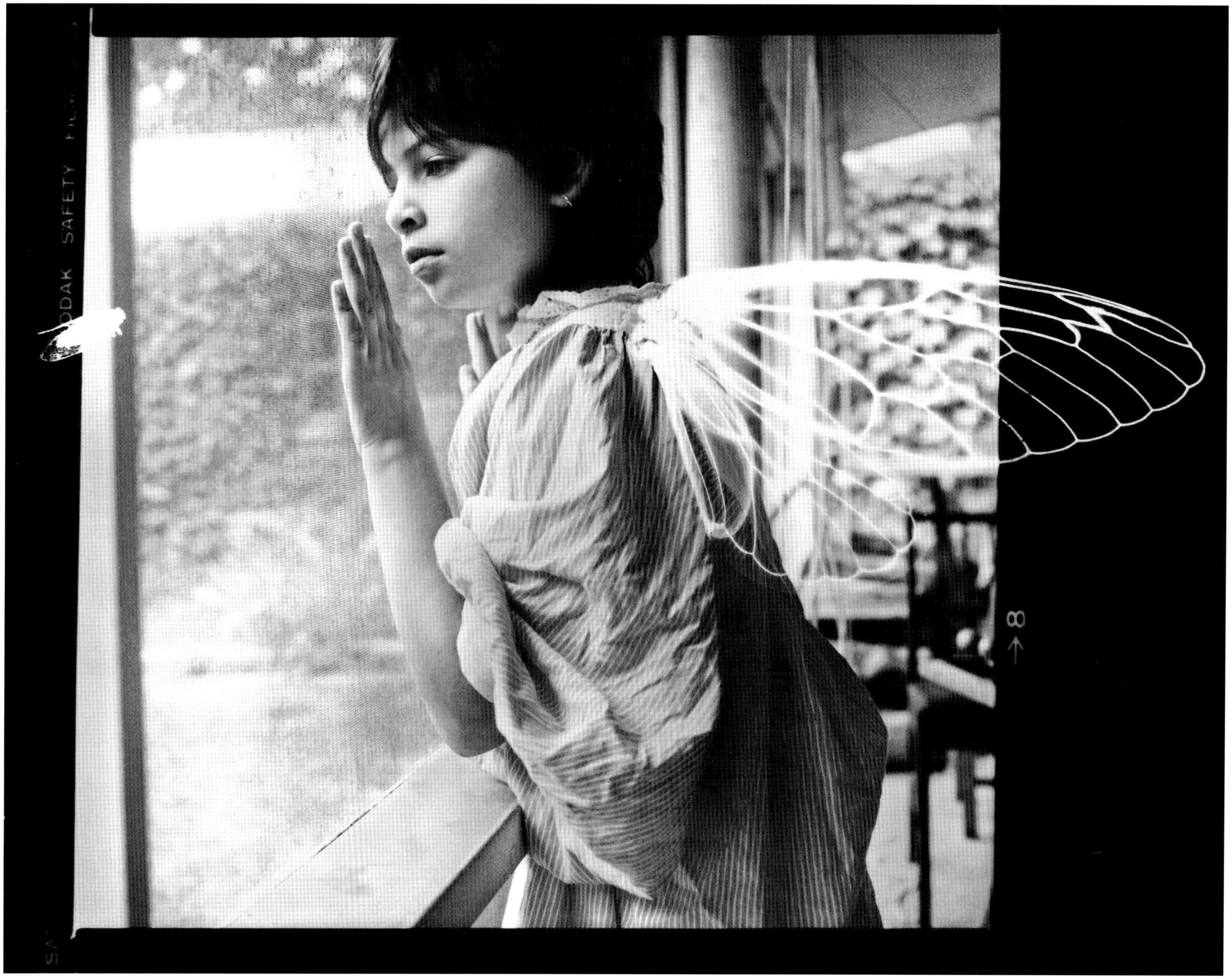
ODAK SAFETY

Julia and the Window of Vulnerability is one of my best-known works. It was a career milestone when it was reproduced in full color in *Gardner's Art through the Ages* (1991).

The story of this work's creation offers an alternative story to the big "ah ha" moments with lightbulbs going off over the creators' heads that are the common stuff of artists' biographies.

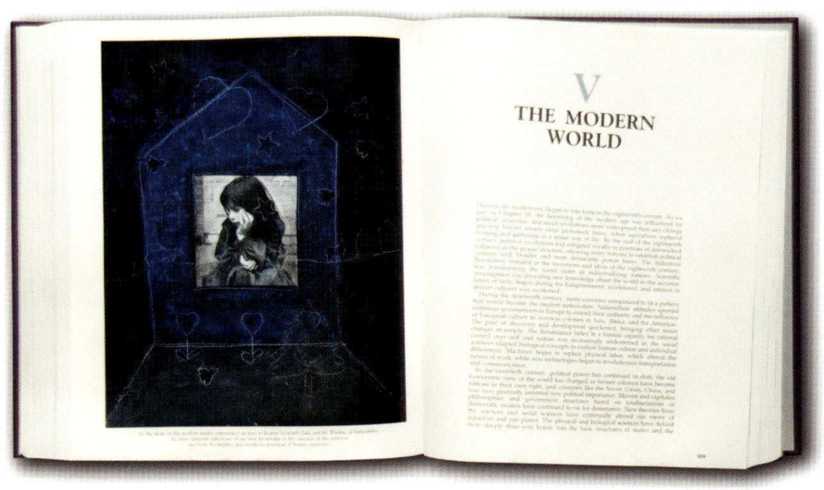

Opposite: *Julia and the Window of Vulnerability* (I), silver print with chalk pastel, 1983; collection of René di Rosa

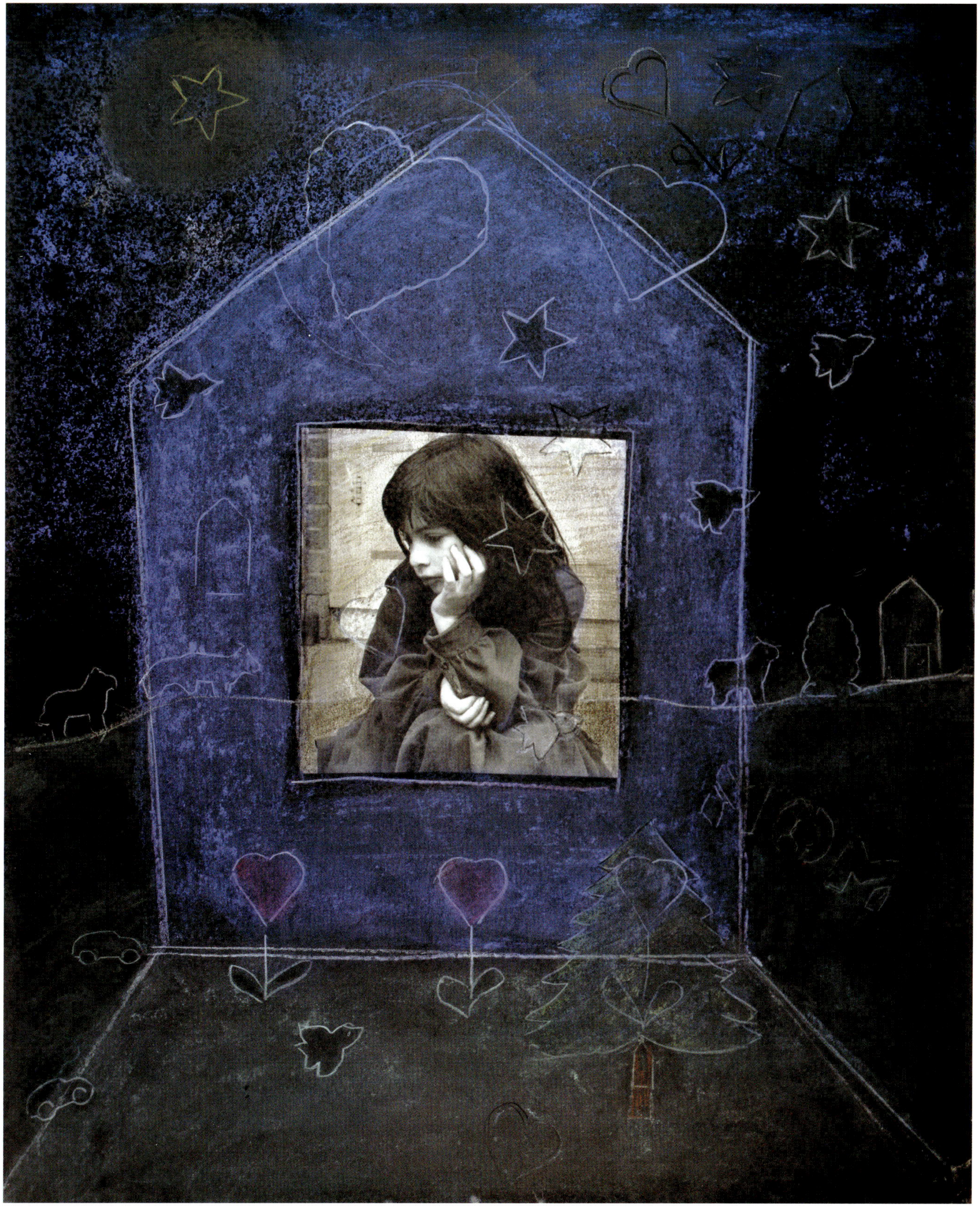

How's your work going?" people would ask, and I sometimes wanted to shout, "What do you mean, how is it going? When do you suppose I get a chance to do it?" But I didn't say anything except "fine." The summers, after the school term had ended, held more opportunities for art making, but I felt tense about competing needs and desires: I wanted to spend time with Julia, but also to concentrate on my artwork, and to teach a summer course for added income. It took me awhile to discover how to balance everything, but sometimes we had fun. We went swimming together during Ann Arbor's often hot and humid summer season. We found a giant luna moth and made a little house for it to live in until we could get it to Julia's science camp counselor. We loved lighting Fourth of July sparklers and watching from one of the highest spots in Ann Arbor while fireflies brightened the near distance and fireworks lit the higher reaches of the summer sky.

That summer I made *Julia and the Window of Vulnerability;* what I called my "studio" was a small, crowded bedroom that housed eight four-drawer filing cabinets full of negatives, prints, and papers. A small table and chair that I'd bought at a local resale shop took up every inch of the remaining space. I remember sitting and working out the details of the *Julia and the Window of Vulnerability* pieces at that table. There were four variations when I finished. I worked with great intensity and remember how important it was to me to suggest something of my heightened anxieties about the world and Julia's safety, particularly in the political climate of that time when the United States and the Soviet Union competed for supremacy by heating up the nuclear arms race. On the other hand, the very real heat of summer brought Julia and me closer to each other as we found moments to sit together at a lakeside, in a park, or on our own screened porch.

In 1983 President Reagan was building up huge stockpiles of antiballistic missiles. Enough missiles were already on hand, I had read, to destroy the world many times over. The president justified the missile buildup's huge expense by saying it would help the United States close a "window of vulnerability," a phrase I found poetic and suggestive for my imagery.

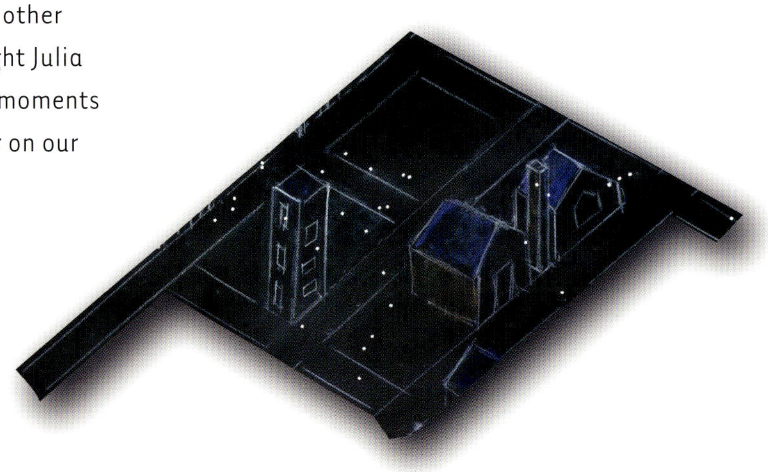

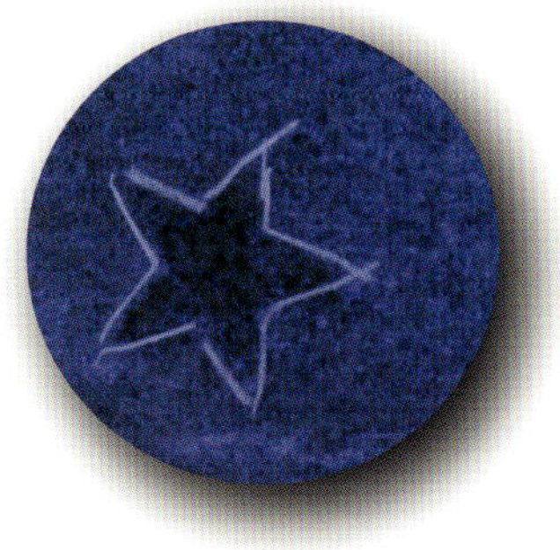

There is a meaning of the word *vulnerability* that I didn't consciously consider at the time, the kind *inside* a home. Even as a child, I'd been the more volatile one. Elly was more controlled; I'd strike out. Altogether I am a bit more of a renegade than Elly, more ready to stand and fight.

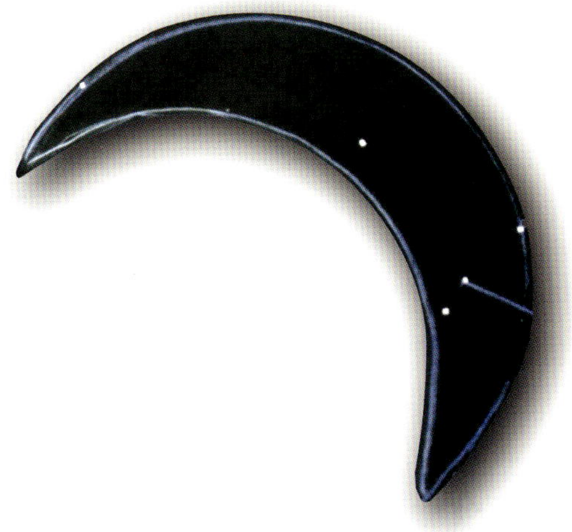

With Julia, though, the issue of hitting revealed something else. I learned that hitting out was newly a gesture of weakness, a bid for control. I was moved to strike out if I got into a corner, ran out of any sense of authority, was too completely without resources in handling a child who was herself often a rebel, with me as her main target. I found my temper very frightening but sought professional help in time and managed to keep things from going out of control.

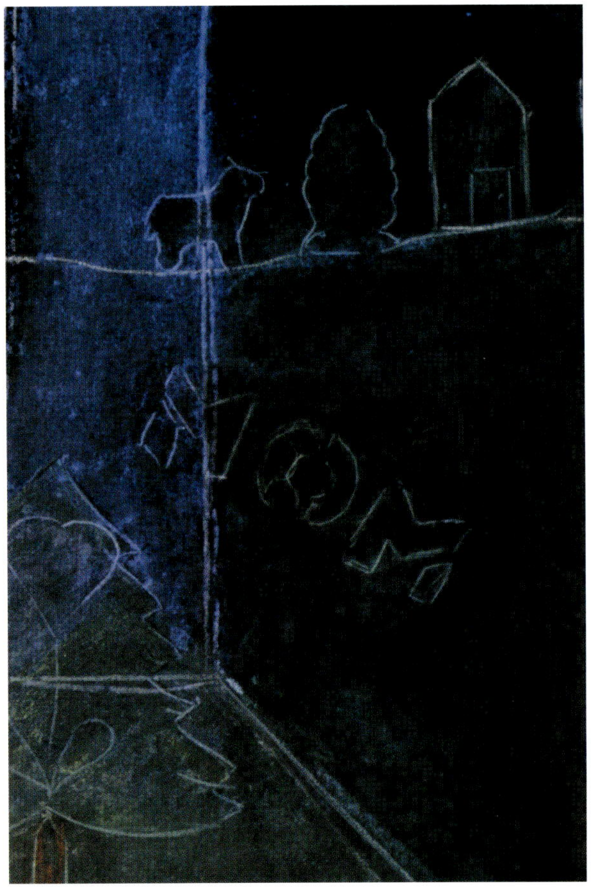

With white pencil I traced the outlines of small cars, trees, and hearts onto the surface of the photo, guided by a book of stencils and tiny wooden blocks that were Julia's. The stencil book had the word *mom* in it, and I stenciled that, too, onto the surface of my print. When the work was published in *Gardner's*, I was tickled that the word *mom* had made it into fine art history; I felt I'd created a kind of Trojan horse that carried the word *mom* from my world at home to the halls of history, on behalf of mother-artists everywhere.

To make *Julia and the Window of Vulnerability*, I used a color negative and printed it on black-and-white photo paper. The color negative was from a snapshot of Julia wearing a new dress my sister Barbara had made for her, with room to grow. That Julia looks a bit swallowed up in the garment and a little downcast (for reasons we can no longer remember) made the photograph work for my purposes. In the darkroom I created the dark surround as well as the stars. After the processed photo paper dried, I drew on it with chalk pastels. Pastels don't combine easily with photo paper, but I *had* to use them because I love the vivid blues they allow. I tend to think of all of my "altered" photographs as collages, as the motivations are similar, layering additional images and ideas onto photographs through drawing. Though today I could use digital methods to achieve similar effects, doing so would not provide the pleasure I recall of sitting at my little table transforming my photos by drawing directly on them.

Opposite: *Julia and the Window of Vulnerability* (II), silver print with chalk pastel, 1983; collection of Wanda and Joe Corn

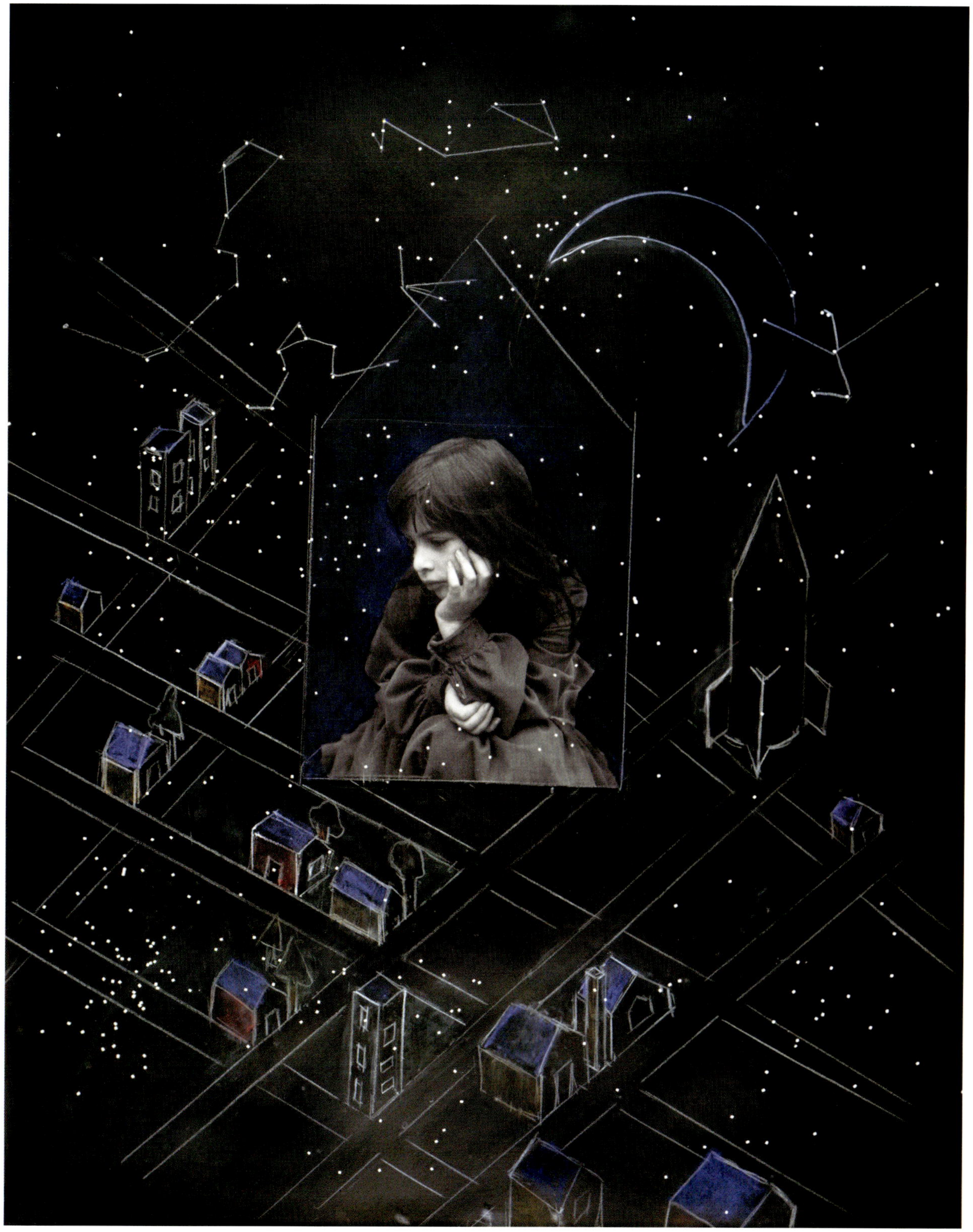

In the photograph here, Julia, perhaps eleven or twelve, seemingly born with a sense of costume and fashion, has layered herself with skirts, petticoats, and a veiled, wry look. The picture gives me a pang other mothers might share, for I recognize in Julia's hooded glance that she has begun to pull away. Soon enough, she would be entering her teen years.

With teen years and high school, when Julia's focus became her friends, my chances to photograph her were few and far between. She loved Polaroid cameras and began to document her own life quite wonderfully. Occasionally, vacations and travel brought us together; though sometimes the going was bumpy, I did get a few pictures along the way.

Opposite: Julia, preteen with frilly skirt and gloves, silver print, ca. 1987

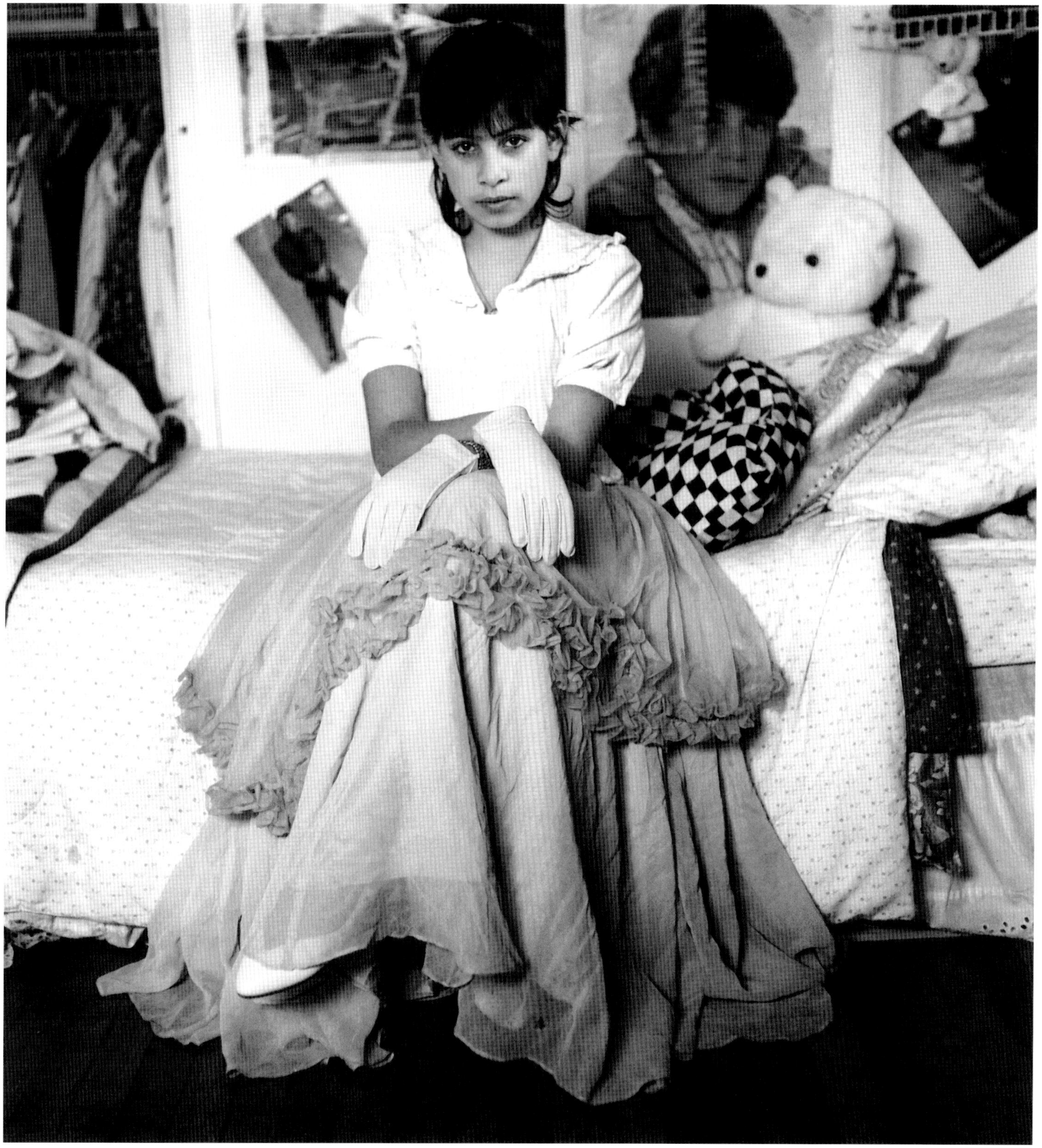

We were at war with each other almost from the moment we arrived in Paris for a brief vacation during a school holiday. Julia was about eighteen. Following the sleepless overnight flight from Michigan, we arrived at our tiny hotel and both collapsed. I had hoped we could sleep for a few hours and then look for dinner somewhere, but Julia did not want to wake up until it was far too late to find anything decent open. Her stubborn reaction set the stage for what would be five days of conflict and negotiation. She rarely wanted to eat at any standard mealtime and never where and when I wanted to. I'd find some wonderful restaurant recommended by friends, and she'd glower and not eat while I ordered and tried to enjoy my meal. Later, when all we could find was lousy food, she was content to eat. It wasn't cheap, and it was plenty annoying. On the other hand, Julia loved the museums, providing enthusiastic and observant company.

It annoyed Julia so much when I spent time trying to read maps that we mostly just headed for the Metro and accepted the simple maps and directions the token sellers would sketch for us. Thus it took me until our last morning to realize that, heading in a different direction from our subway stop, we would find the Luxembourg Gardens virtually right behind the hotel. We spent a lovely hour or so there, and when we stepped back outside the gardens, I took a picture of Julia posing by a fence of iron bars. Sometimes amazing things happen for the camera! The kiosk at the end of the street echoes the arrangement of Julia's hair. We should claim we planned it.

When we arrived home, I heard Julia tell friends, "We had a great time."

Julia moved to San Francisco, went to art school, and now lives and works in that city, so opportunities for taking her picture have become increasingly scarce.

Opposite: Julia at the Luxembourg Gardens, Paris, silver print, ca. 1997

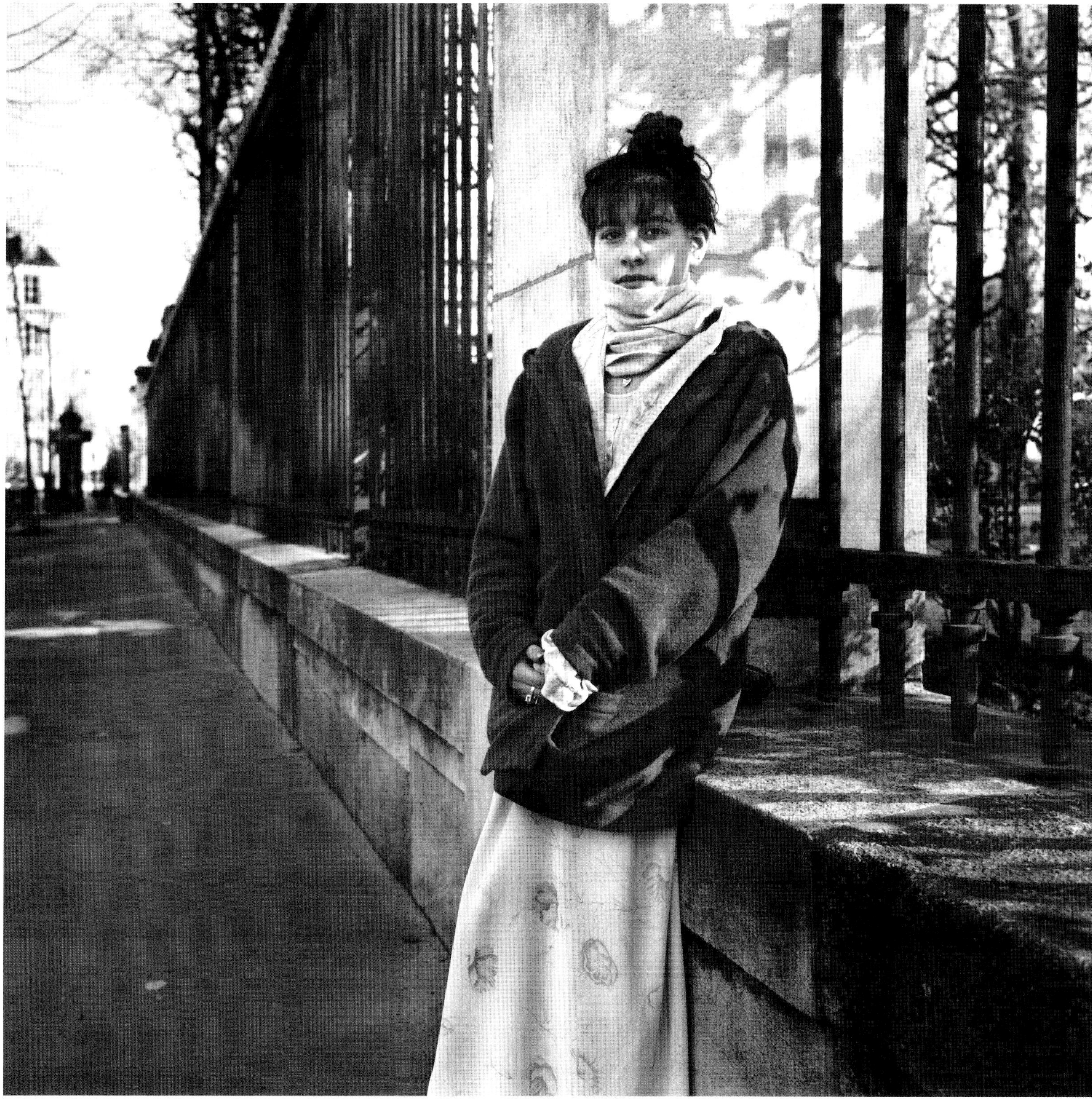

Recently, Julia, now in her thirties, sent me a photograph she made at her father's house. It is a "photo collage" she made by capturing multiple reflections on glass surfaces. Julia, wearing blue (my favorite color), is casting reflections of that blue into my framed picture of her. She created this layered and nuanced self-portrait with me in mind, knowing I'd love it and would enjoy seeing that her father had hung the picture.

Opposite: Self-portrait reflected in Joanne's *Winged Ones*, by Julia Marjorie Leonard, 2004

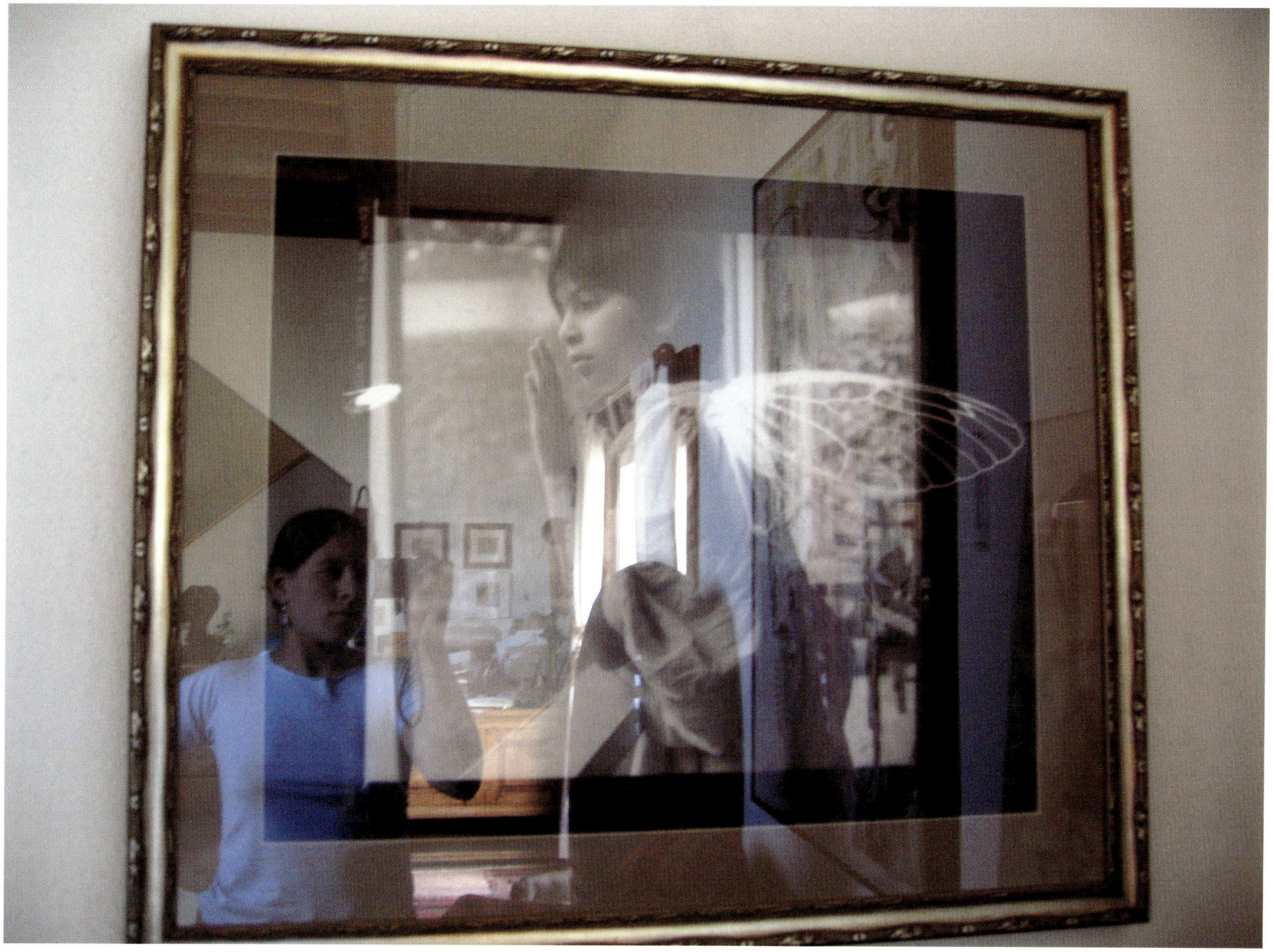

Home Industry

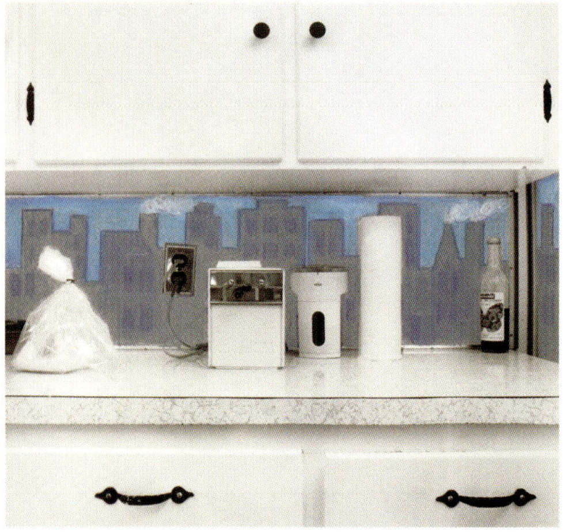

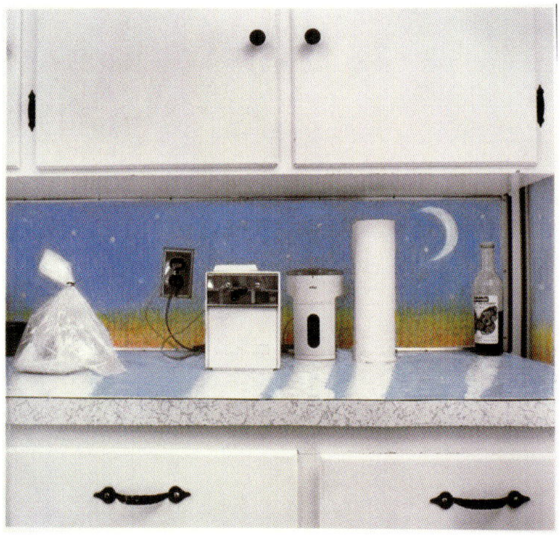

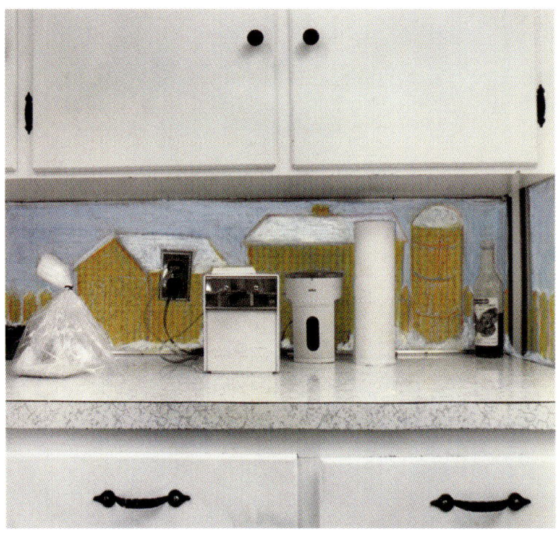

Shortly after I arrived at the University of Michigan, I was invited to a social event that allowed me to meet some of my colleagues and their spouses. I especially enjoyed talking to a painter and his wife, a psychiatric social worker. I was determined to get to know them and immediately invited them and their children to dinner. As a single parent/artist/professor, I was always behind: on housecleaning and grocery shopping, course preparation, exhibition planning, grant writing, studio time. All too often, I failed to reserve time for Julia, time we needed for relaxing and playing together. Only the fact that life in a new town was lonely would have induced me to engage in hostesslike activities for an entire precious weekend day. By that evening, though, I felt prepared and eagerly awaited my company. I was dumbfounded when I answered the door and saw one wife, two children, no colleague. "Oh," my colleague's wife quickly explained, "he needed some time in the studio and wanted me to take off with the kids and leave him to work. So here we are." Of course I wanted to know them both and would have been happy if she as well as he had become my friend, but instead (with his wife's cooperation) my colleague had erased our professional equality and made my invitation serve his needs. I was hurt, and I was furious.

When critics reviewed this work, they sometimes suggested the images had something to do with a woman trapped in a kitchen, longing for release. I began the series thinking I was responding to the many joking questions people asked about my response, as a transplant from California, to Michigan weather. But, ultimately, if the set of images succeeds, it's because it suggests, I think, something more complex about the tensions and pulls of the world inside and the world outside "home"—which included my university responsibilities.

Above: Countertop Landscapes and Skylines series, silver print with water-soluble wax pastel, all 13 3/8 inches × 14 inches, 1979

Top: *Countertop Industry;* collection of Abby Stewart and David Winter

Middle: *Countertop Moonscape;* collection of Amon Burton, Jr., and Linda Burton

Bottom: *Countertop Barns;* collection of Suzanne Hanson

Opposite: *Countertop Snowing,* water-soluble wax pastel and gouache, 6 ½ inches × 6 ¾ inches, 1980

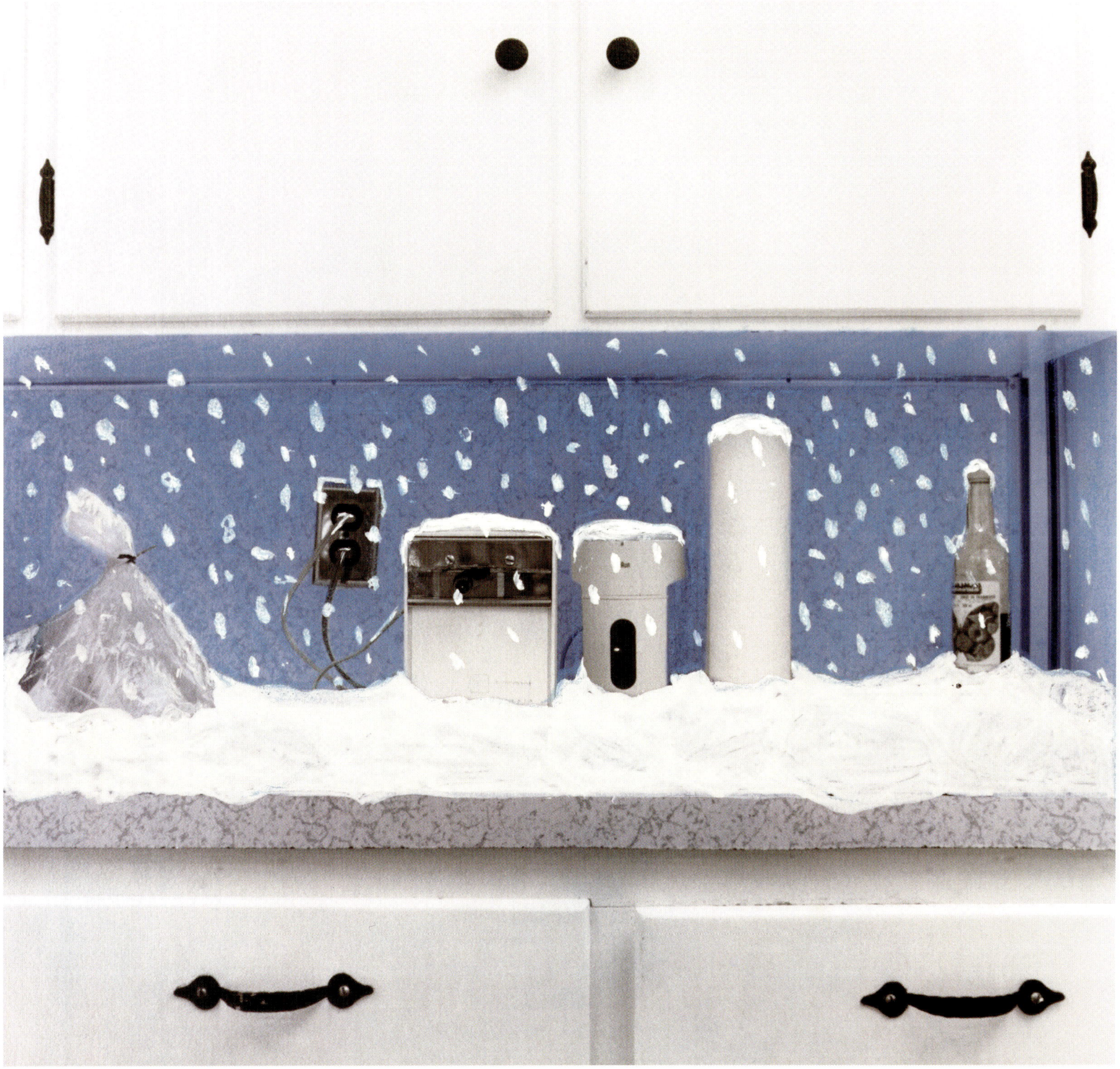

There was a time while Julia was small that life was especially difficult. I was teaching an additional course for the Women's Studies Program—a course on women artists that I'd fought to have added to the curriculum and then suddenly got drafted to teach. I could not pick up Julia from her after-school sitter until after 10:00 p.m., when a four-hour Art School studio course ended. I was working on an exhibition. And on top of it all, a fibroid tumor was now causing so much bleeding that I sometimes did not make it through the day without going home at least once to change clothes.

During this stressful time I came home one night and almost plowed into two garbage cans that someone had placed in the middle of my driveway. I had to get out of the car and move them. After I had parked my car and arrived at my front door, I found this note: "Please take in your trash cans promptly after the trash pickup. Is it really so hard? Your new neighbor, Bob, across the street."

While I put Julia to bed, I was fuming and exhausted; I wanted the refuge of bed and sleep. But how dare he? I was so angry that I could not sleep, so I wrote him a note. In the morning I left a note on his door that said something like: *Yes, it is hard, but you probably have no experience that would allow you to understand. You probably do not raise a child alone and put in overtime at work. If having my trash cans disappear promptly from the curb is so important to you, why don't you take them in for me? I'd water your plants or feed your pet sometime when you are on vacation. You are new to our neighborhood and haven't yet figured out how to be a good neighbor. Time to start out on a different foot?*

My neighbor came over the next day to apologize.

Opposite: *Keeping My Hand In,* white pencil and collage on silhouette paper, 10 inches × 15 inches, 1997/98

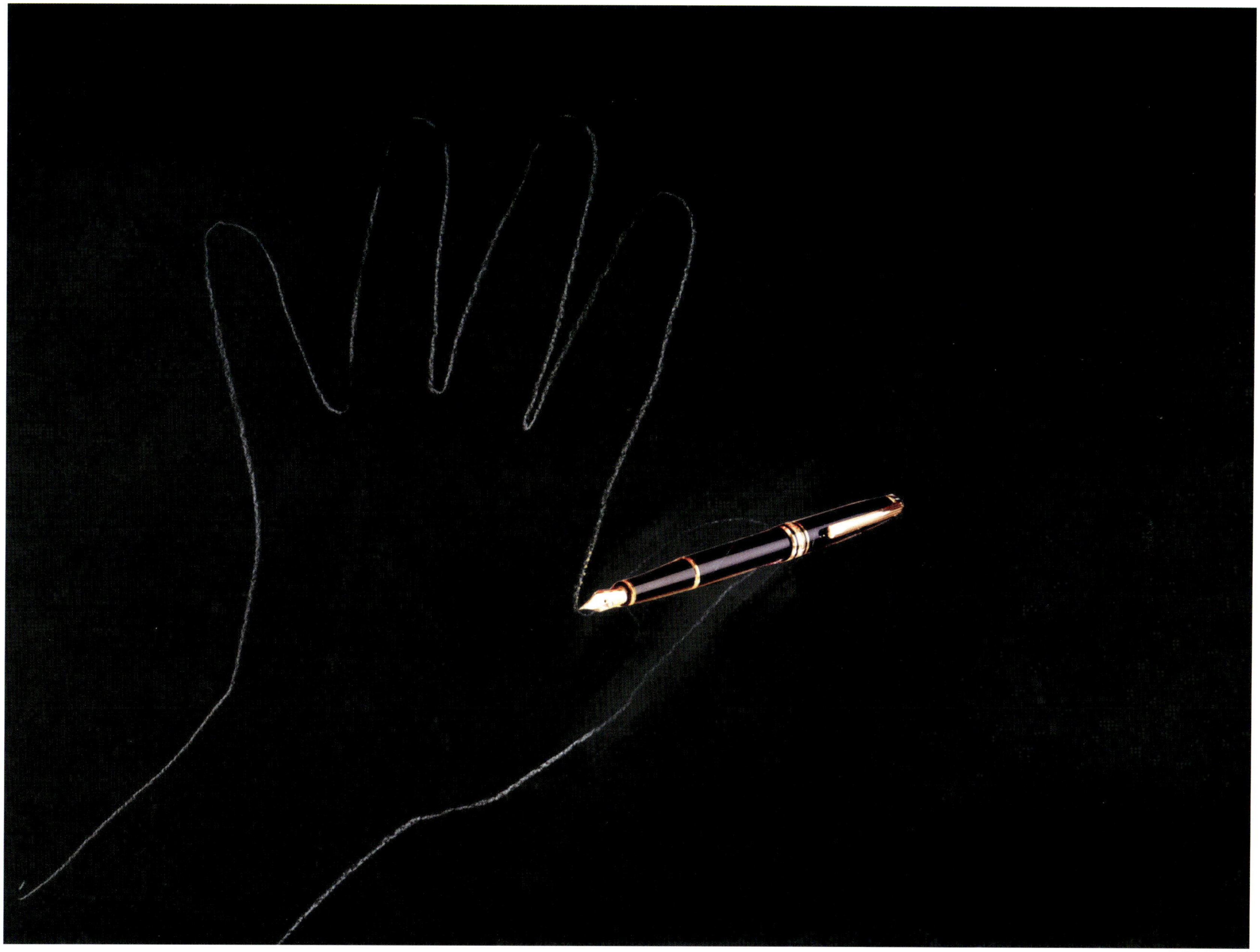

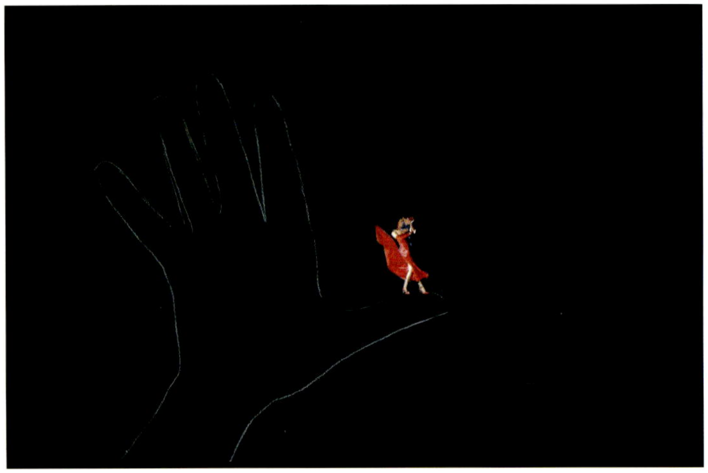

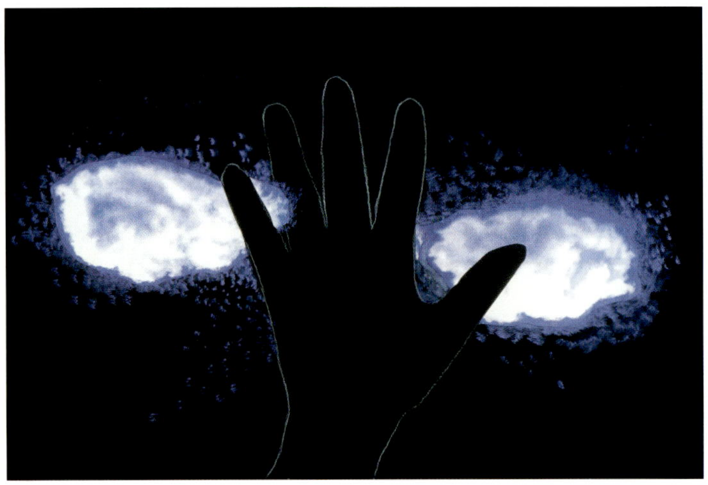

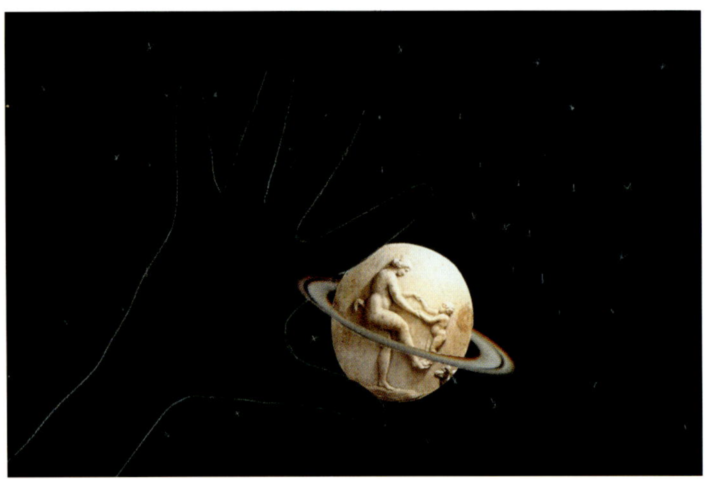

This set of images combining outlines of my hand with collage started out as a challenge to myself to use a minimal and repeatable image or idea throughout a set of works. The repeated hand might seem to be only a playful device, lacking heart. Yet it was also part autobiographic impulse, "keeping my hand in," leaving a trace of myself. The phrase "keeping one's hand in" also refers to the act of "keeping going." Teaching, parenting, and meeting the very demands of daily life seemed to swamp me, and so a straightforward visual problem allowed me nearly to trick myself into believing I could make art when I felt too busy.

Above: From the Keeping My Hand In series, drawing and collage on silhouette paper, 10 inches × 15 inches, 1997/98

Top: *Hand and Dancers*

Middle: *Hand in Clouds*

Bottom: *Hand and Mother/Child Medallion with Saturn's Rings*

As I tried to open my bedroom window the other day, a portion of the wooden frame, old and rotted, fell to the ground. That's life. I know. I know. But the rounds of calls, the visits from repair people, and other related tasks send me into such a frenzy that I am almost literally kicking and screaming. I'm thinking that my life is a complete disaster; my thoughts skip straight to the end of summer—I panic that classes will start any minute and I'll never, never get this work I want to do done and . . . x@#$%^&*!! Not healthy, sensible, productive. The opposite. Sometimes I find myself unbearable, and my mood sinks.

In the Winter Window series, I wanted the "reality" to be the coldness of winter, the "invented" world to be the home interior. I seem to use cups in my work as a way to represent aloneness. To make this set of images, I printed the winter scenes from my own garden, making the exposure small in the middle of a large sheet of paper, as I had done for *Window of Vulnerability*. Then I covered the winter scene and reexposed the paper (very briefly) to create a light gray tone (or longer for the darker tones). Collage provided bowls, cups, and vases.

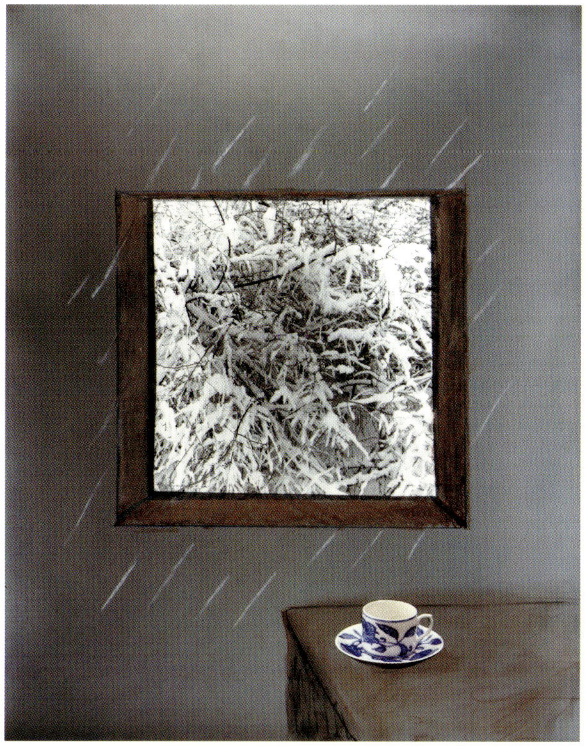

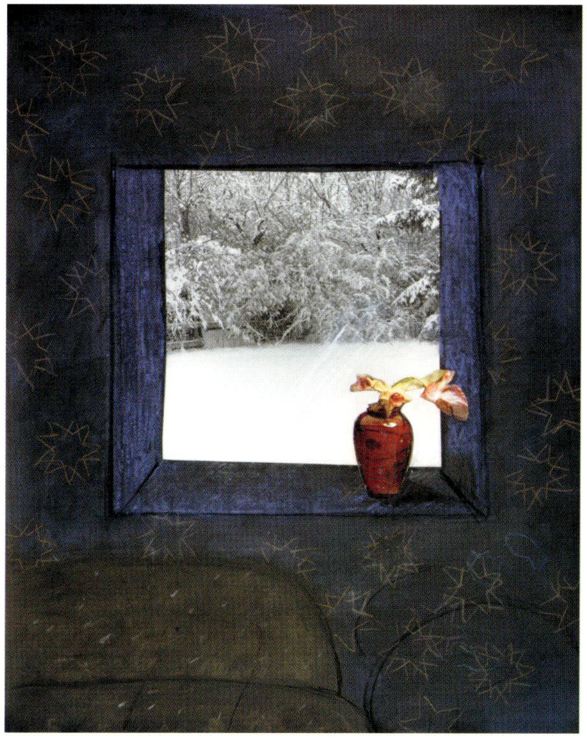

Above: From the Winter Window series, silver print with chalk pastel and collage, 11 inches × 14 inches, 1983; collection of Dorothy Stewart

Top: Winter Window (with white and blue ceramic cup)

Bottom: Winter Window (with red vase)

Mirror Images

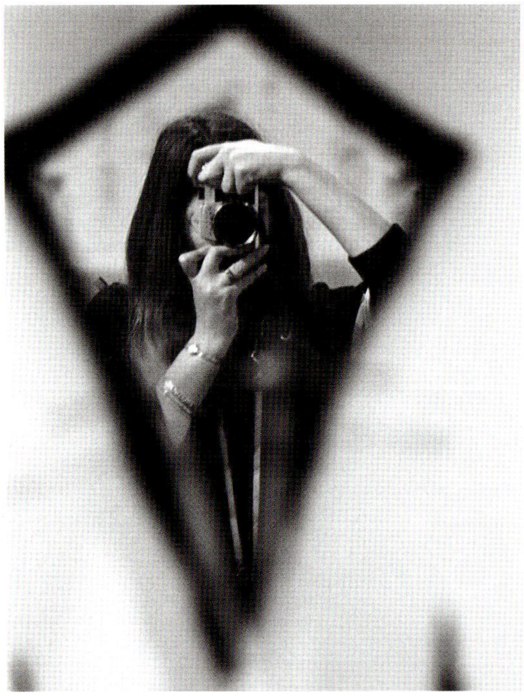

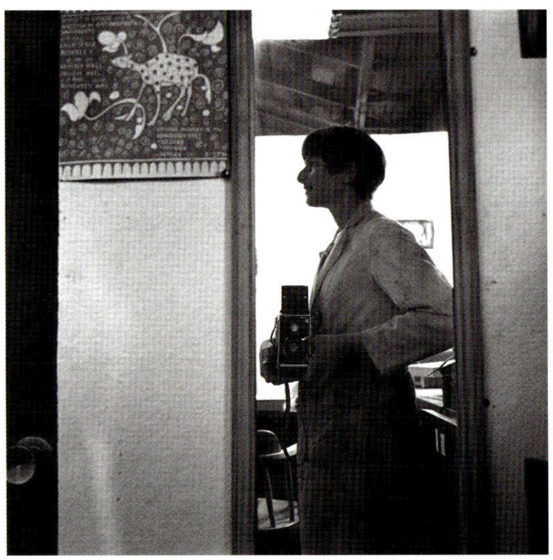

In both my artwork and my teaching, autobiography, self-portraits, and mirrors are recurring themes. About midway through my more than twenty-five years of teaching at the university, I taught a course called Photography, Ethnography, and Autobiography with a colleague. Our students, women and men, came from several programs and departments. We both put in huge amounts of time preparing for this one-time-only course offering. There was a vast amount of reading to be done of material that was largely new to me. As a result of the course, my colleague, a social scientist, received recognition from her college for her innovative, cross-disciplinary teaching. I received the lowest evaluation and merit salary increase of my teaching history. When I asked my dean about it, I was told, "Your project, rather than contributing to the school, appeared to be one largely responding to self-interest." "Self-interest?" I queried. "Well, yes, they [the Art School's executive committee members, who award merit and recommend salary increases]—said it was a women's class." It was hard to tolerate this treatment, especially during a time when Julia was still young and we were still very much struggling to make ends meet.

I suspect that mirrors may fascinate all photographers. Historically, the photograph itself was once called a mirror with a memory. Though I'd say that in general I have not been much of a self-portraitist, I do have a folder of pictures I made by snapping pictures of myself in the mirror while, from time to time, I used up the last few frames in a roll of film. In the diamond-shaped mirror that a colleague remarked resembles the vulva, I'm holding a camera to my eye. But that's not the style of camera I most prefer. A twin-lens camera is what I like best because it allows one to look down into a specially made glass surface (the "ground glass") to see and frame the picture. With such a camera, held *below* my face, I can make conversation and have direct eye contact with my photo subjects.

Top: Joanne in mirror (self-portrait with 35-mm camera, at San Francisco Art Institute), silver print, ca. 1974

Bottom: Joanne in mirror (self-portrait with 2 ¼-inch format camera), silver print, ca. 1971

I recognize now, in pictures I took years ago, a reversal of the usual practice in making "nudes." Usually the nude is a female, and even if we don't see the artist (painter or photographer), we sense we are looking through what the film theorist Laura Mulvey would call the "male gaze," a gaze that projects its fantasies onto the female figure.

Though the term *male gaze* was not in my vocabulary, I was at the time exploring my relation to male artists and the nude. In this collage, one of a set of collages that I worked on around 1973, I'd created a fun and funny reversal of things I'd absorbed in art school. I remember the strange atmosphere in drawing classes of men and women who were looking at the same nude model; I had no language for the odd difference between the men's looking and the women's. Today I am more enlightened about gender issues in photography, and I explore them in my teaching.

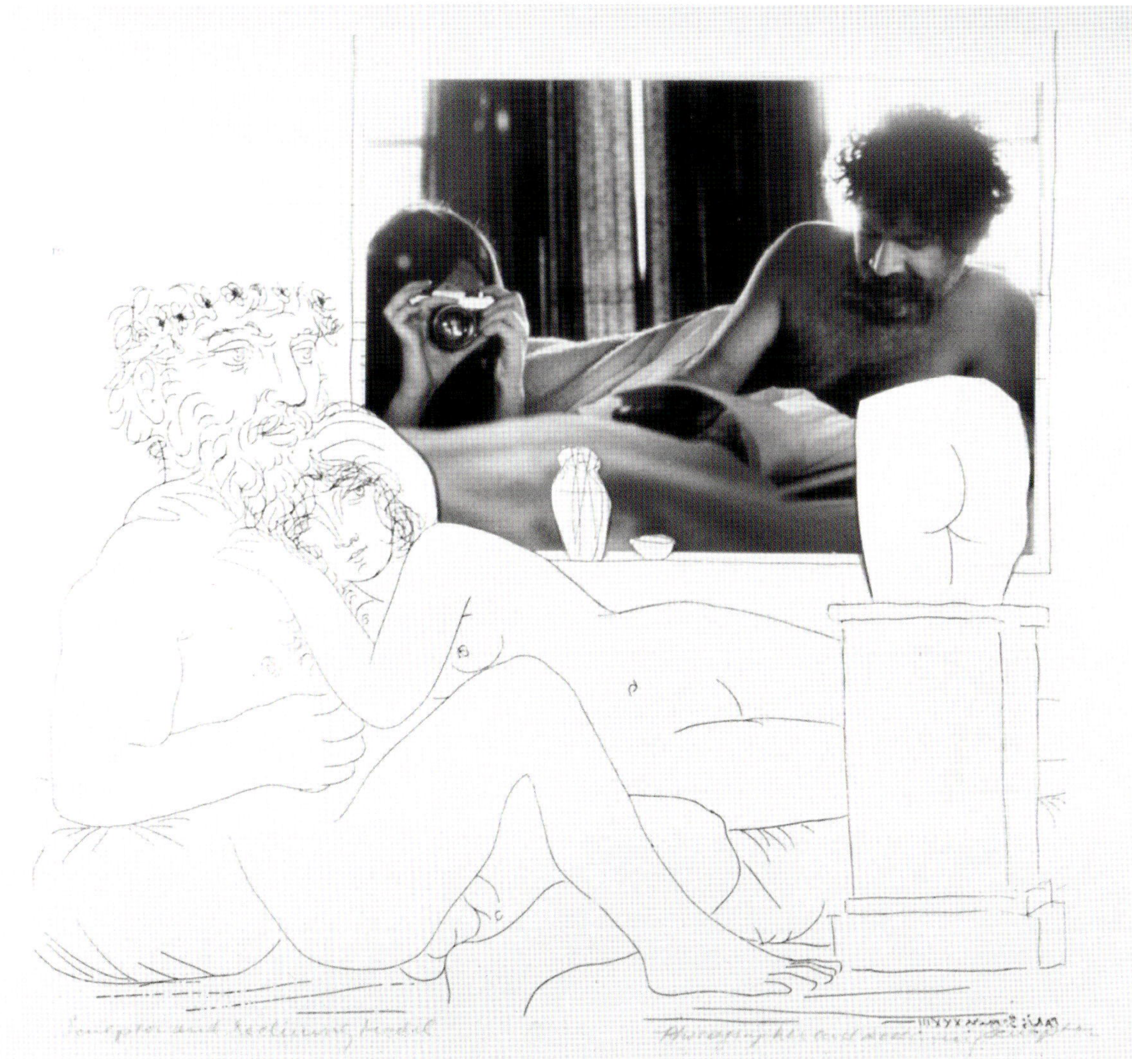

Above: Picasso collage (with Manuel and Joanne), collage and silver print, approximately 7 inches × 7 inches, 1973

Time Frames

Moments of Being combines my interest in autobiography with my growing fascination with understanding memory and how to represent remembering in visual terms. This ninety-two-inch-long scroll marked the first time I used the scroll form and reflects the continuing (since the Dreams and Nightmares series) exploration of transparency and translucency. It is one of the first works where I used the translucent paper known as glassine.

I made *Moments of Being* in the mid-1980s after I'd read the book *Moments of Being: Unpublished Autobiographical Writings* in 1985, a collection of posthumously published autobiographical writings by Virginia Woolf. In one essay in the collection, Woolf likens memory to a net suspended in water from corks, where the corks (like the few moments that one remembers over the years) are all that rise to the surface. Woolf's vivid textual imagery of memory in her writings interested me hugely; I used a set of alphabet rubber stamps to stamp passages from Woolf onto the glassine.

Opposite: Detail from *Moments of Being*, collage on off-white paper with stamped lettering and additional collage on glassine overlay; detail is approximately 14 inches × 28 inches; entire work is approximately 26 inches × 74 inches, 1990

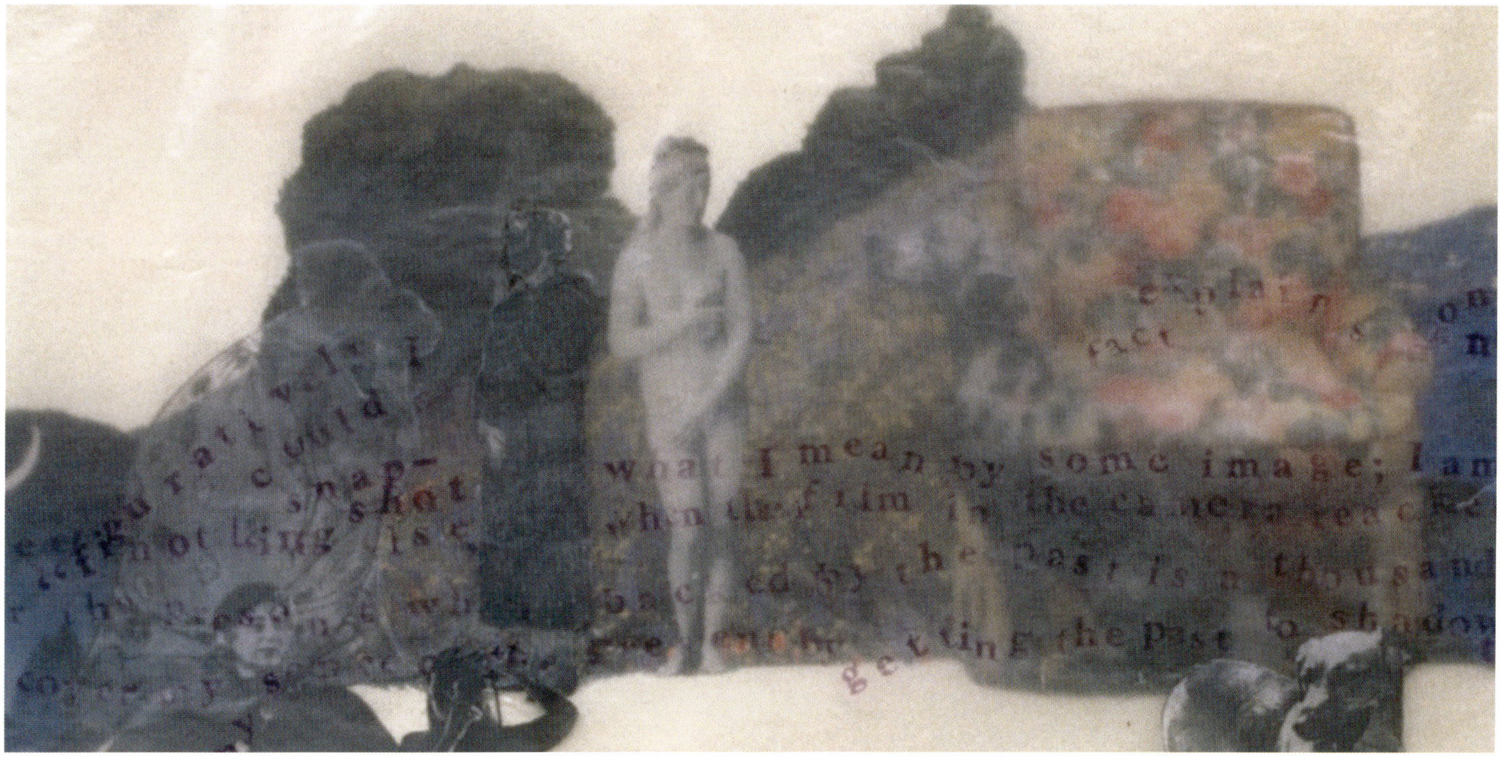
what I mean by some image;
getting the past

For *Moments of Being* I found that I could print my photographs on especially thin, or "document weight," photographic paper. I discovered that, by waxing the thin photographic prints or photocopied pages, I could make these items translucent. I bought a deep fryer, melted paraffin wax in it, and then dipped the small photographic bits I'd cut out of larger photographs into the wax. I glued those to the surface of the underlying drawing paper. Thus transparency is apparent in some places on this underlayer as well as when the piece has its glassine layer superimposed. One of the ideas I had about the overlay was that it veils the underlying imagery and creates a kind of distance suggesting memories obscured by time, as in Woolf's wonderful word picture of remembering: "lying in a grape and seeing through a film of semi-transparent yellow," a quote I found in "A Sketch of the Past" in *Moments of Being*.

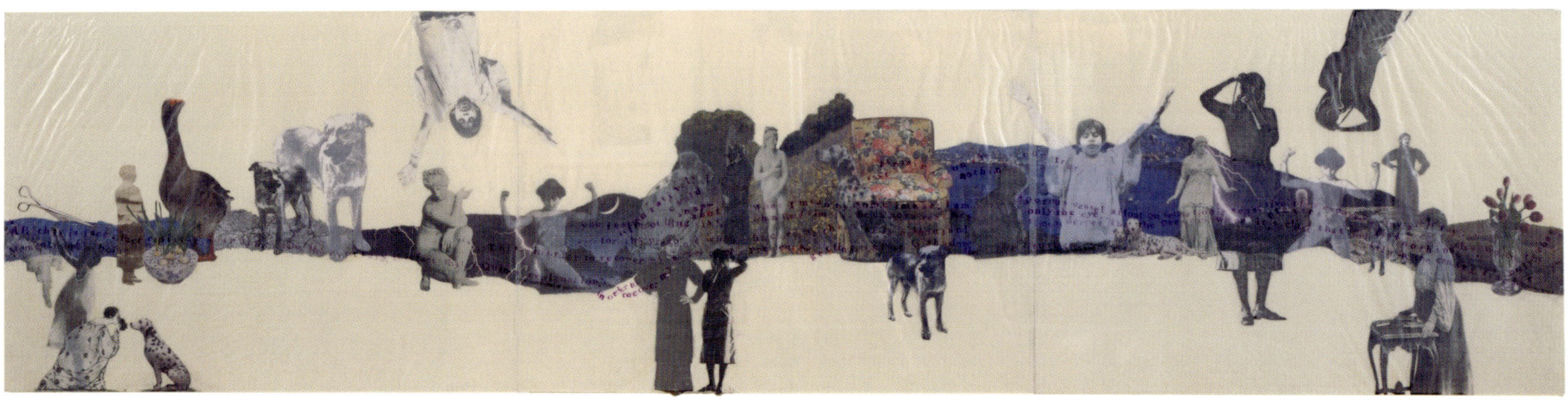

Above: *Moments of Being* (with glassine layer in place, as intended for exhibition)

Opposite: *Moments of Being* (with glassine layer lifted to provide clearer view of collage elements)

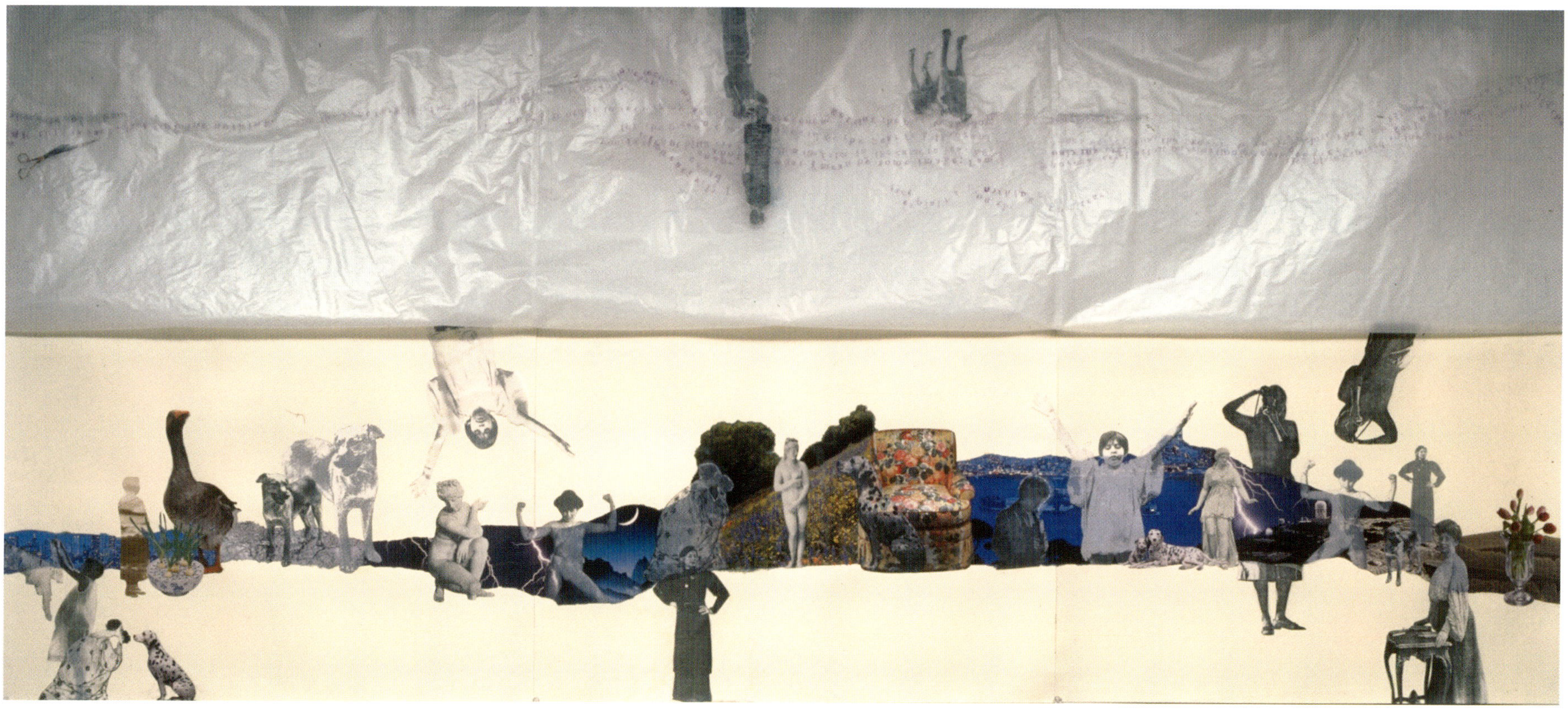

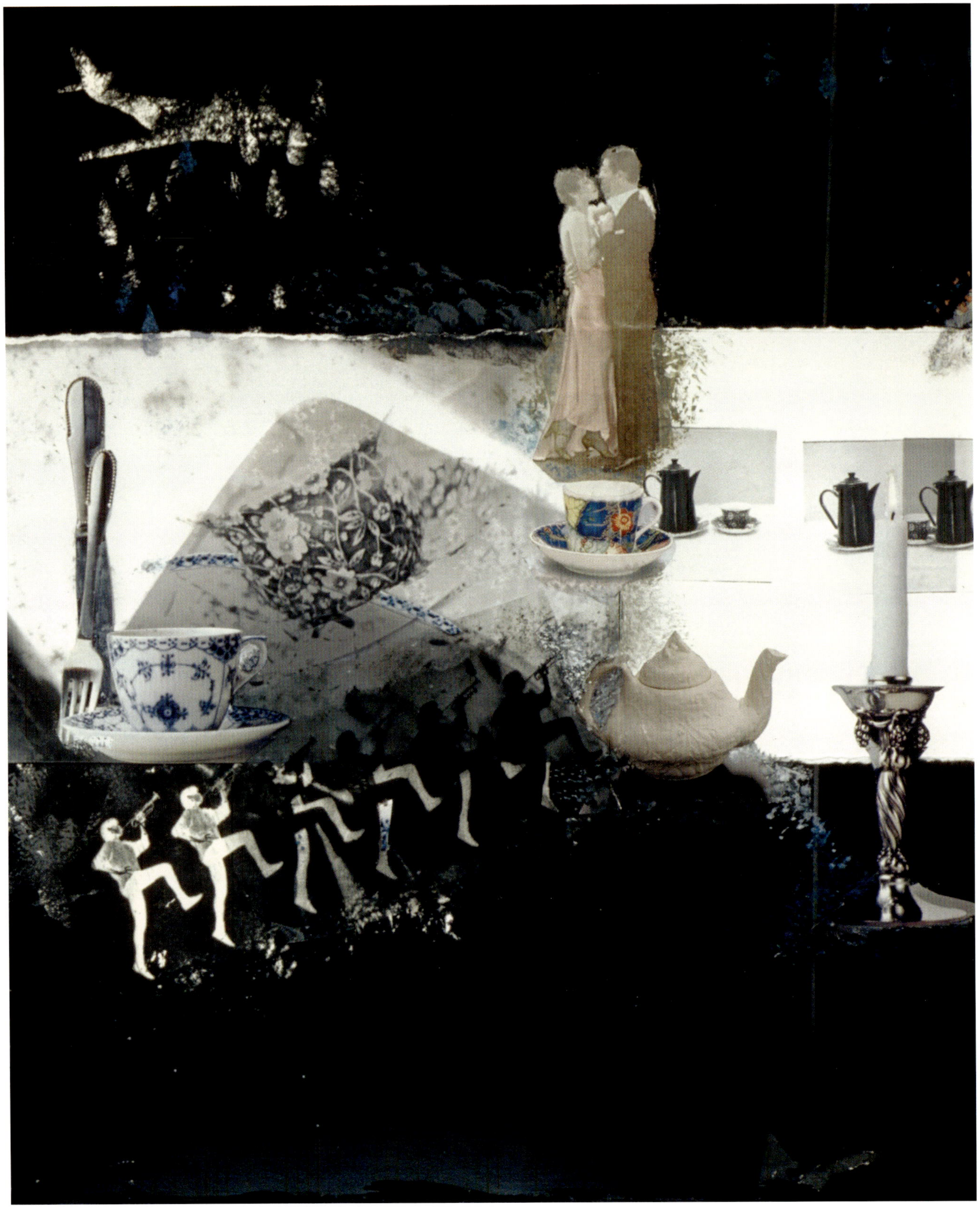

I made *Roots and Wings* when my parents were elderly. My dad had liver cancer, and my mom's memory was failing. In this piece, I sought to suggest a continuum from my parents to my daughter—a passage of time. I've used a cup and coffee pot or teapot to refer to myself alone, here as in other works. Additional imagery in this work suggests the things my parents and their children have survived: war, the threat of nuclear annihilation, the march of time. There are references to art, courtship, and romance (restaurant tables, ballroom dancers) and a framed photograph of my parents (one of the last of them together—my dad died shortly afterward, in 1988). Stars, comets, rockets, and lightning make their appearance, and, from sheet music to the parading marching band, there are references to music (my father's field). Julia is here, too, aligned with the wings of the title, ready to take flight while "rooted" in ways that connect her to my parents.

This piece is over five feet long. The teapot and cups, airplane, Julia and wings, marching band, nuclear explosion, stars, raindrops/tears are printed onto the surface of black-and-white photo paper using photocopies on clear acetate and darkroom methods of contact printing from the acetate "negatives." The roots are actual roots (as opposed to a picture of roots) laid on the photo paper to make their own shadow-image—thus, a "photogram." Some items were clipped from books and magazines, then collaged onto the surface of the photo paper. With gouache paint I added color and provided transitions between collaged-on images and the underlying surfaces.

Opposite: Detail from center section of *Roots and Wings,* detail approximately 20 inches × 30 inches

Overleaf: *Roots and Wings,* silver print of photographs and photograms with collage and gouache, approximately 24 inches × 60 inches, 1988; collection of Barbara Raymond

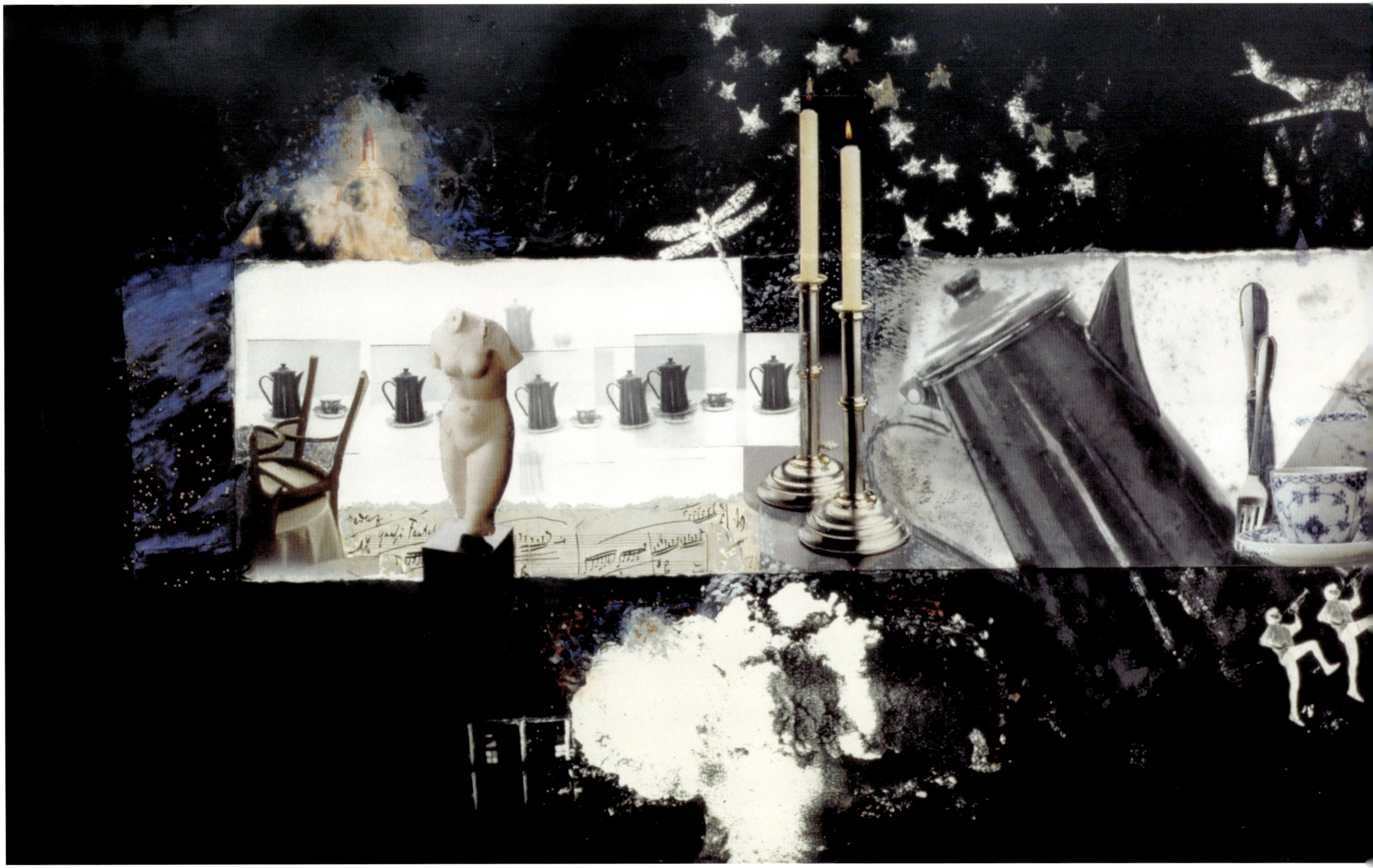

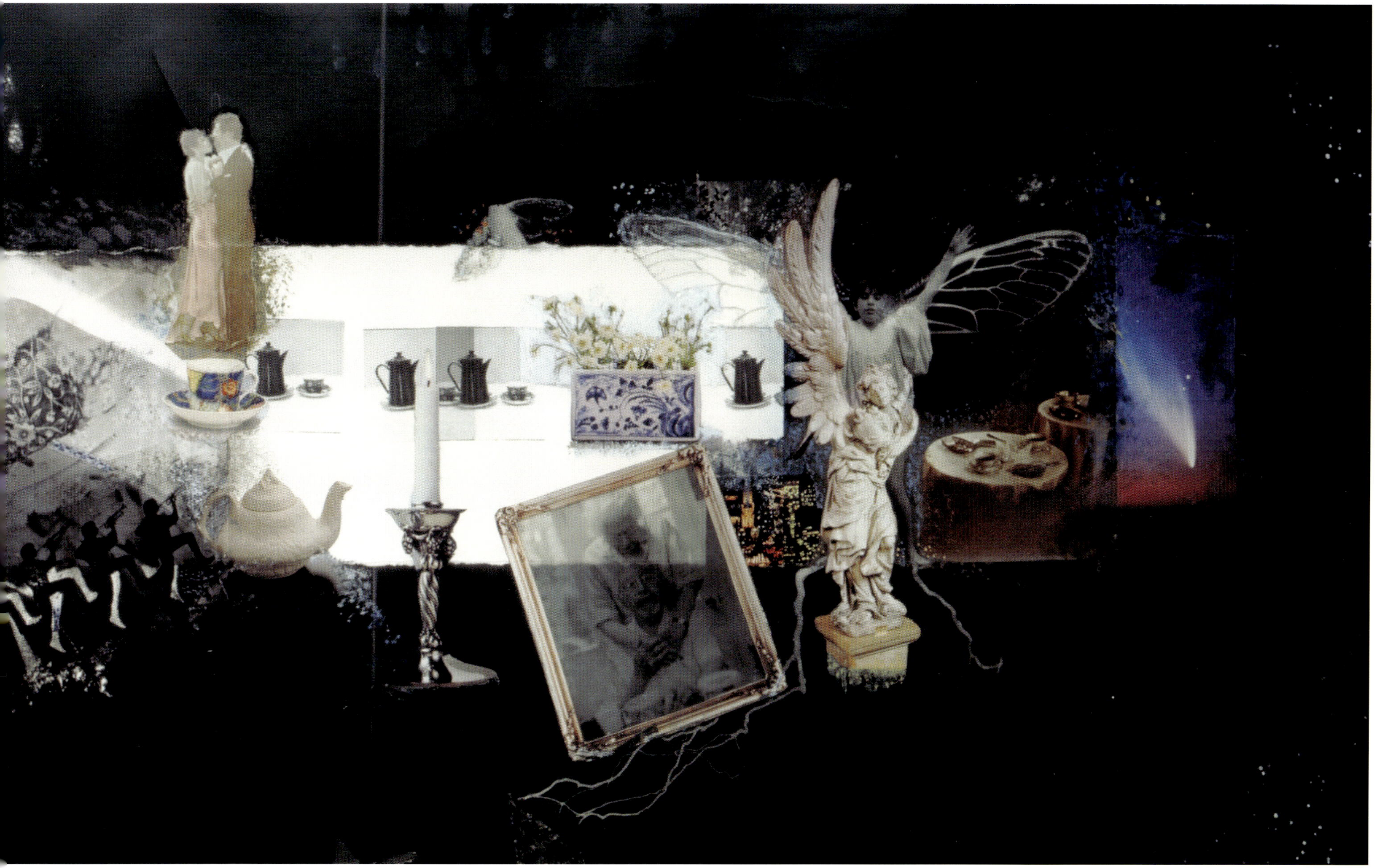

As the years have gone by I have worked increasingly to find a visual vocabulary that describes female worlds, female lives. I have created a number of photo collage series highlighting family resemblances and twinning among the women of my family, who appear so similar at times as to be indistinguishable; they merge or stand in for one another. The issue of likeness is central to my family history of twins, but I've tried to deal with the problem that Timothy Dow Adams refers to: "too exact a likeness would in fact result in a difficulty with identification." I try to show that family resemblance does not erase differences in outlook, generations, life events, and economic circumstances. I am concerned with creating images of my own family that do not objectify, stereotype, and constrain the women pictured but rather give voice, space, energy, and history to my female subjects, women of four generations in my own family.

When I create photo collage, I fragment the original photographic "truths" by rearranging sequences, layering images in time and space, and (in later work such as my Not Losing Her Memory series) placing words on and around the photographs. Using my female subjects' words and my own, I write text in, and the lines of writing resemble roads making connections between territories, between generations, but refusing conquest: I do not make over my subjects' voices into one voice or my own voice. I create an atlas for further study, a geography of identity with uncertain boundaries. The work engages multiple viewpoints, disrupts ideas about "the facts" in photographs and in the autobiographical forms that chart life stories.

Opposite: *Geography of Identity,* swimming figures cut from silver print portraits on reproduction of map, approximately 18 inches × 18 inches, ca. 1994

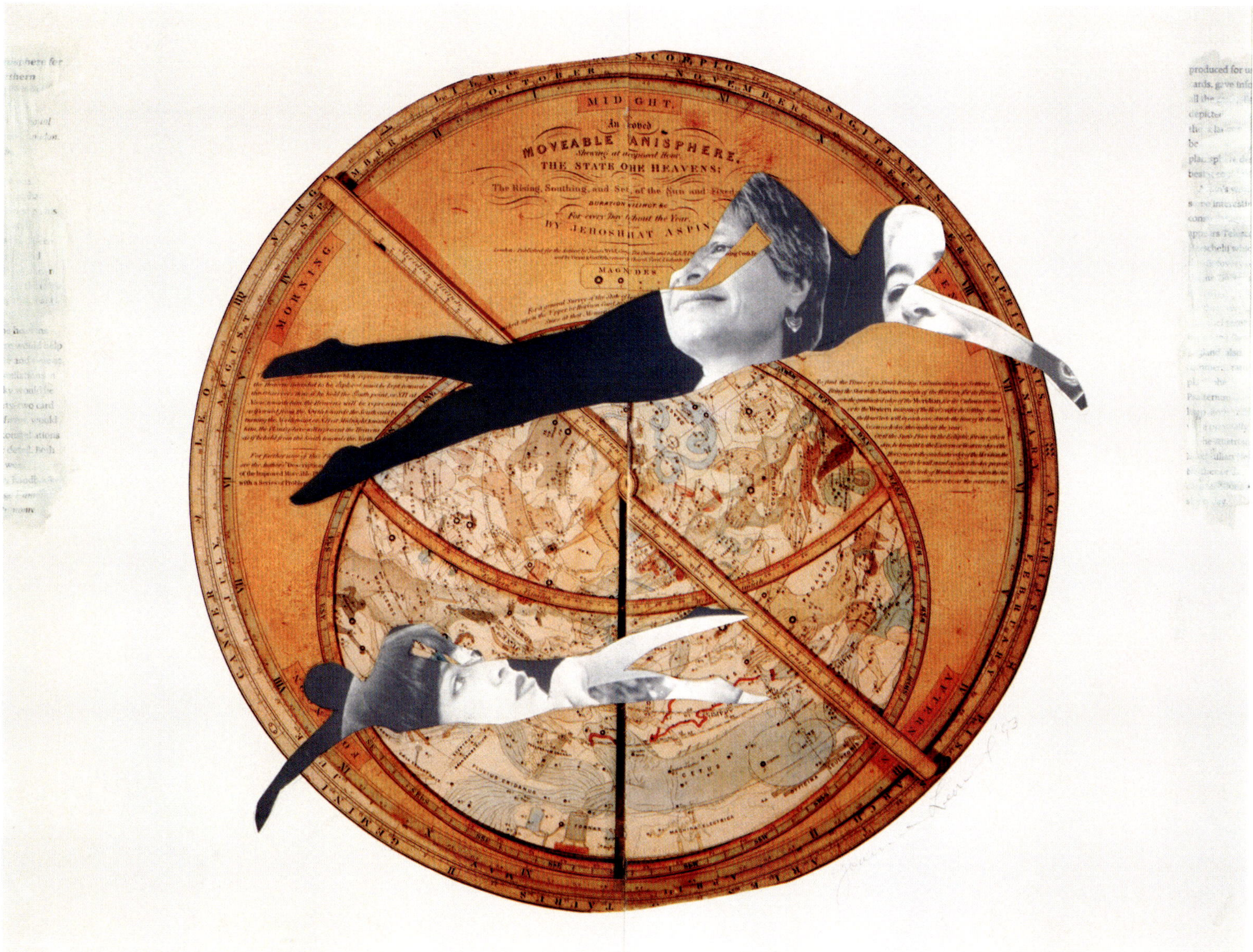

A Picture and a Thousand Words

Exploring issues like female identity and biography and visually representing memories became urgent quests as my mother declined from Alzheimer's disease. I struggled to represent her lapses while attempting to suggest, in pieces combining text and images, stories she could no longer remember. Absence and loss are all but unrepresentable through traditional photography since photography inherently depends on presence—a presence recorded by the camera. The collage series that evolved is the one I called Not Losing Her Memory: Stories in Photographs, Words, and Collage. *Four Generations, One Absent* is one of the earliest collages from that series and one of my first works to include a great deal of handwritten and stamped text. I doubt that I would have become nearly so involved with text in my images—and even text *as* image—had I not, about this time, discovered Charlotte Salomon's (1917–43) paintings from the early 1940s.

In a series of small studies for *Four Generations, One Absent* before arriving at a final larger (16 × 20) version with the three photo portrait heads, I made a set of smaller (8½ × 11) studies in which I tried out various texts and stand-ins for the four generations of the title: dogs, furniture, and outlines filled with flowers or newsprint stood in for the three portrait heads. In the final version and all the studies, I represented my mother by an empty space because her mental decline as well as inability to travel meant she was absent (figuratively and literally) when I traveled to Los Angeles to photograph Elly and Julia at what had once been my grandmother's house.

The series Not Losing Her Memory: Stories in Photographs, Words, and Collages is comprised of nearly sixty works in two groups made in 1991–92. The two groups are (1) a set of 16-inch × 20-inch silver print photo-works often featuring writing and collage, and individually titled; and (2) a set of small studies called *Frieze,* 8 ½ inches × 11 inches, mostly without individual titles, most on black (silhouette) paper but also on various papers such as glassine, typewriter paper, and wallpaper samples. Many of the *Frieze* works were studies for one piece, *Four Generations, One Absent.* The works from *Frieze* were exhibited in a continuous line (no spaces between works) underneath the 16-inch × 20-inch works.

Opposite: *Four Generations, One Absent,* silver print from laser-copy transparencies with writing, stamped lettering, and collage, 16 inches × 20 inches, 1991–92

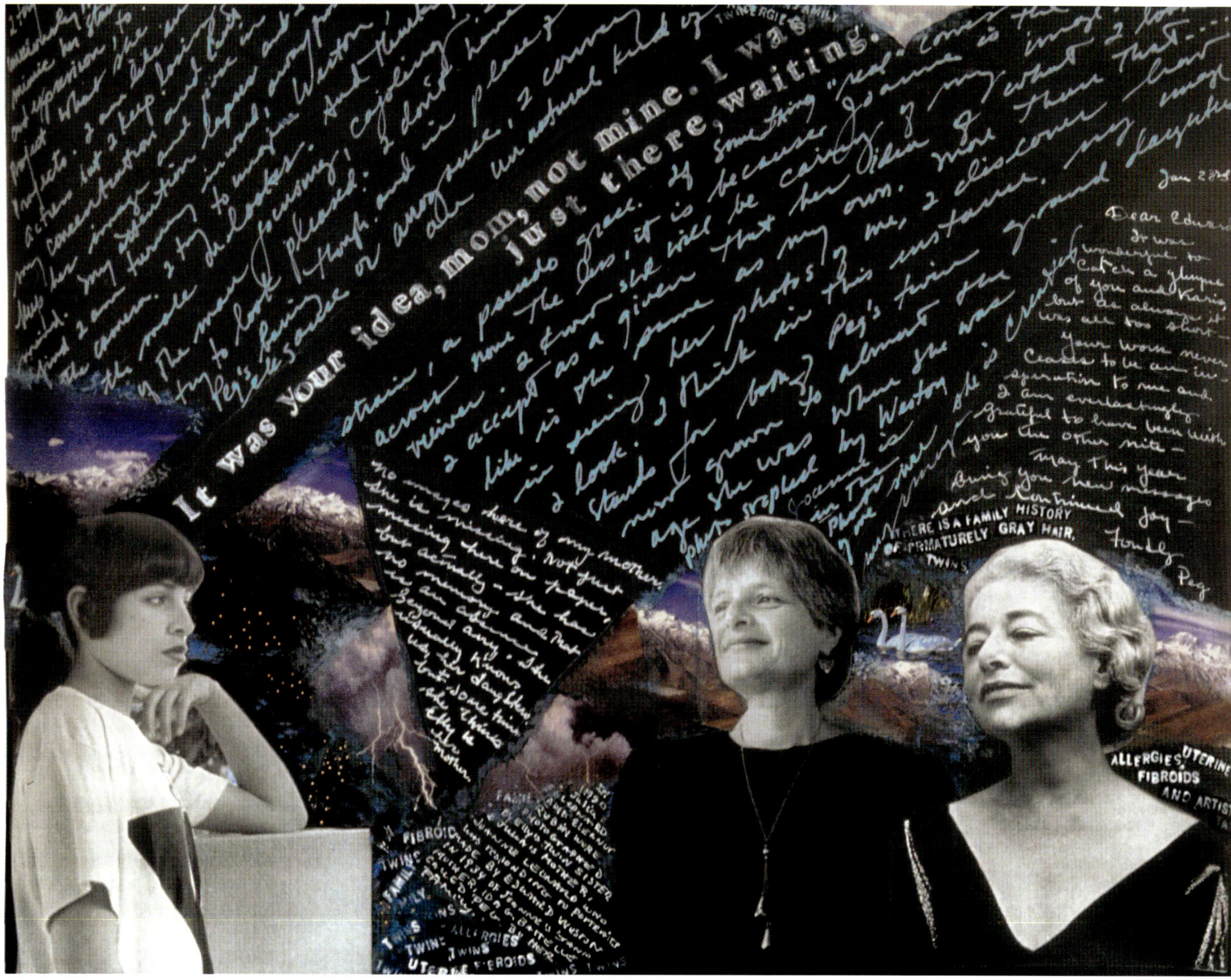
It was your idea, mom, not mine. I was just there, waiting.
ALLERGIES, UTERINE FIBROIDS

At the same time that I began the Not Losing Her Memory series, in 1990, my sisters and I wrote a three-part essay called "Caring and Grieving: A Mother's Story in Three Voices" about caring for my mom. I adapted my part of the essay and place that writing here and in the following pages as background to my series Not Losing Her Memory. Under the text of my story runs the set of studies for *Four Generations, One Absent*, collectively called *Frieze*, which were exhibited as a broad horizontal band running under the larger works in the exhibitions of Not Losing Her Memory.

In some of the studies for the Not Losing Her Memory series, using white ink on transparent paper helped give the text an illusive, evanescent quality reminiscent of the qualities of memory. When the words are clear in a place within the work, they surface from the background much like a retrieved memory comes into view in the mind's eye. Transparency serves also to evoke the act of seeing through—through the invisibility that age imposes on the lives of women.

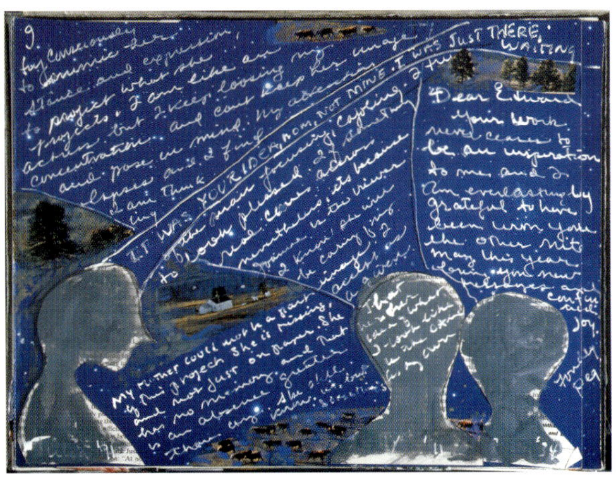

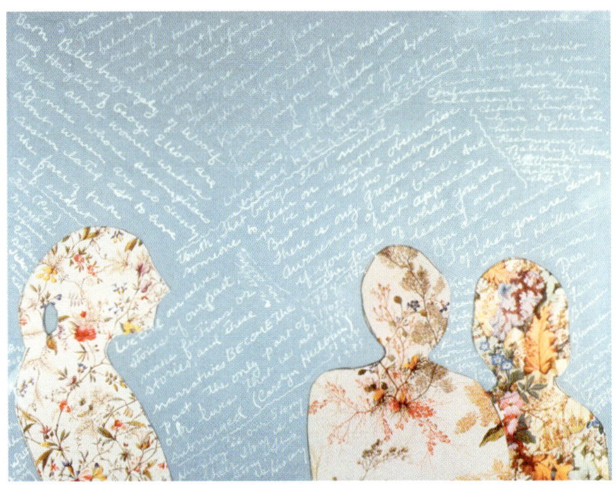

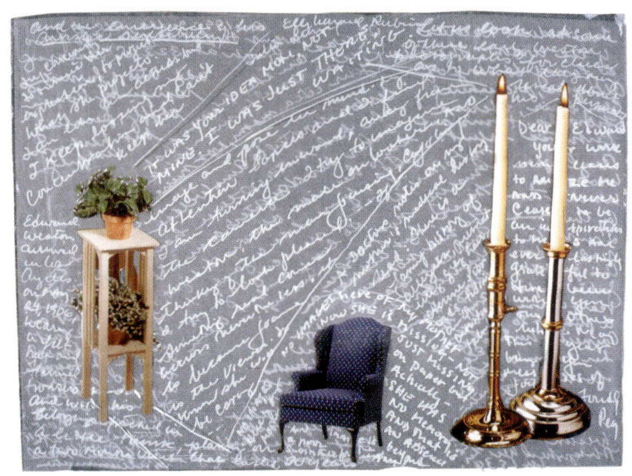

Above: From *Frieze,* studies for *Four Generations, One Absent,* each 8 ½ inches × 11 inches

Left: study on blue ground

Middle: study with flowered heads

Right: study with plant stand, chair, candlesticks

Opposite: From *Frieze,* study for *Four Generations, One Absent,* with flowered heads, glassine with white ink

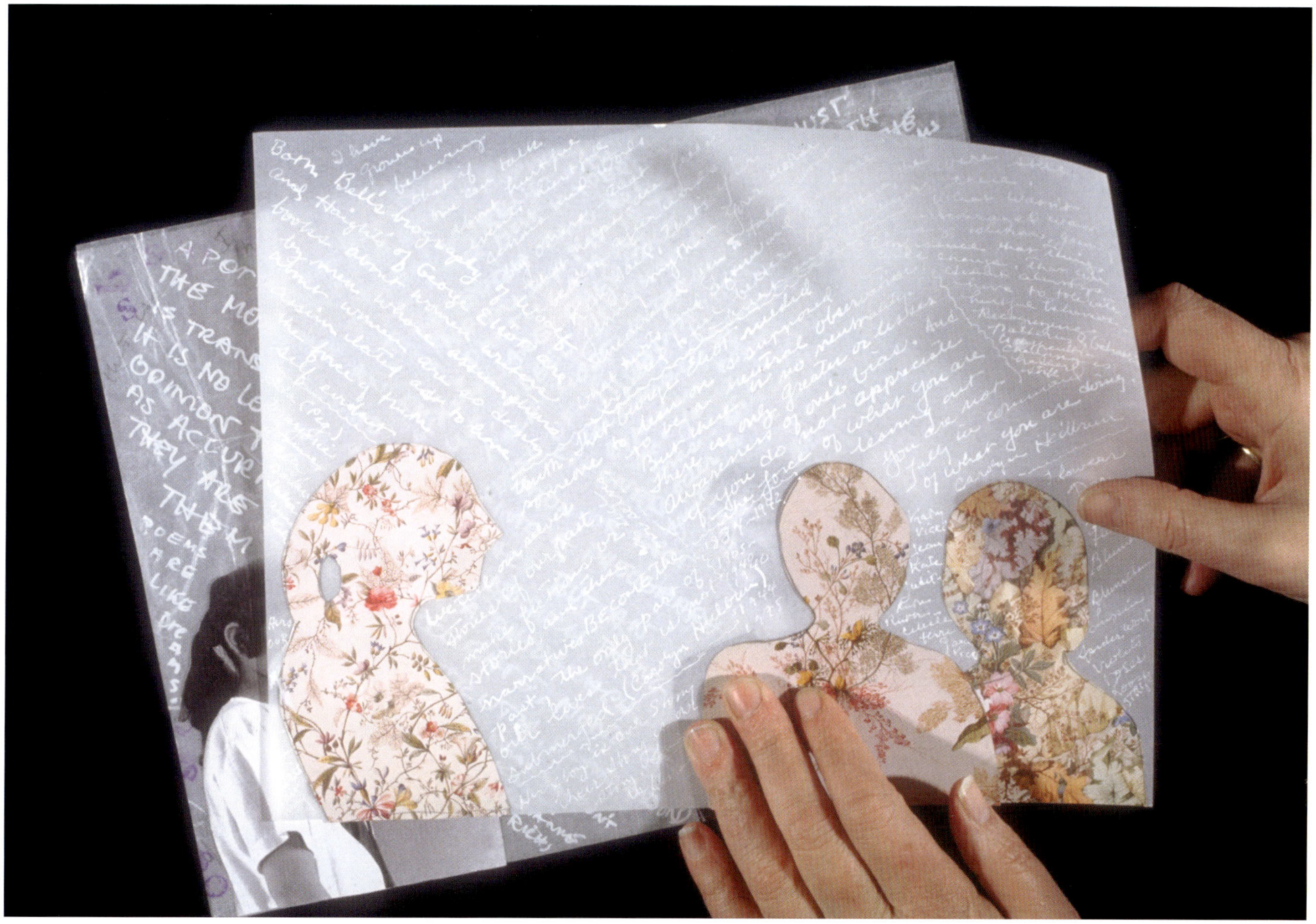

I have never been certain what brings me to use versions of a starry sky repeatedly, but here it is the dominant imagery of a particularly important small study from *Frieze*. In this study there are stars, the predictable three heads with an empty space, and the text from the doctor's list of our female family traits: "There is a family history of allergies, twinning, prematurely gray hair, uterine fibroids . . . and artistic talent." The words *twinning*, *allergies*, and *fibroids* float among the stars, suggesting constellations around the heads of the three women. Some of these phrases from the medical report are also tucked into areas of *Four Generations, One Absent*.

Opposite: From *Frieze,* study for *Four Generations, One Absent,* heads with stars and words, silhouette paper and white ink

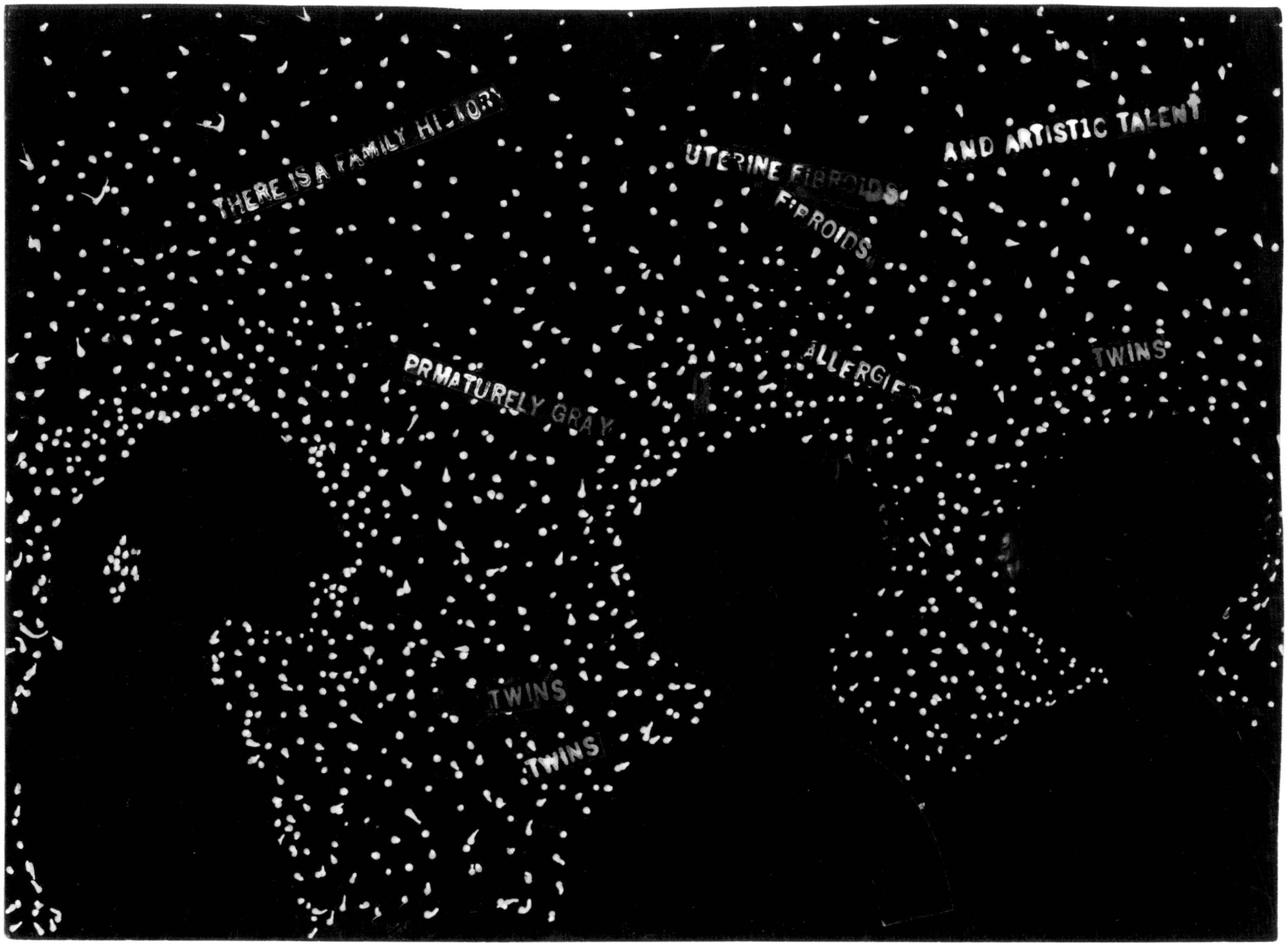
THERE IS A FAMILY HISTORY
UTERINE FIBROIDS
FIBROIDS
AND ARTISTIC TALENT
PRMATURELY GRAY
ALLERGIES
TWINS
TWINS
TWINS

Elly, Barbara, and I are accustomed to being successful, but at the time of my mother's decline, we could not succeed, though we continued to dream of rescuing our mother from the terrors and destruction of her dementia.

Over the process of caring for my mother hovered the dark shadow of our earlier failures to reach and comfort our father. He was truly mortified at what was becoming of Mom, who, as he knew, had always feared dementia in old age. He denied her decline in order to protect her from confronting her disease. But his denial of her situation cut him off and had a terrible cost: he was angry beyond all imagining. He died hating the world for the same failure his daughters had to accept: the failure to stop the dreadful process of my mother's loss of herself. During the weeks leading to his death, he seemed to forget his love for us and declared only his disappointments. My sisters and I were angry too at the loss of our mother, and sometimes we directed our anger toward each other, even though we mostly knew how lucky we were to have each other to depend on through this difficult time.

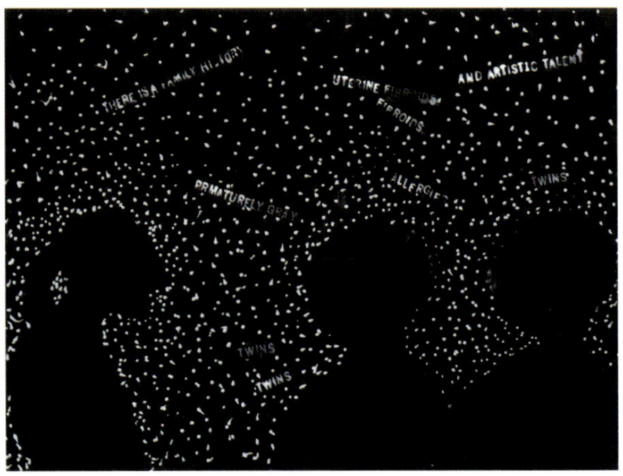

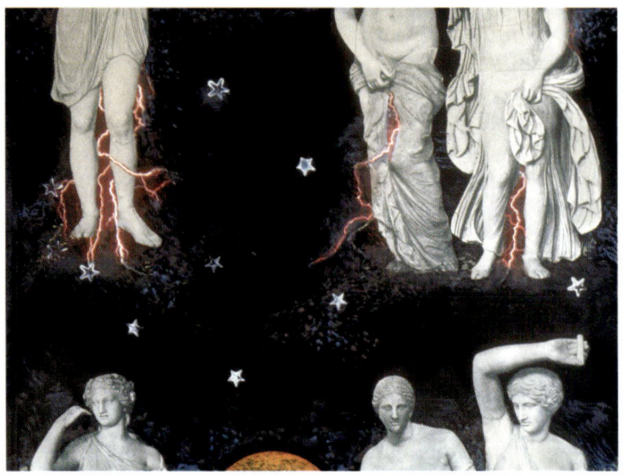

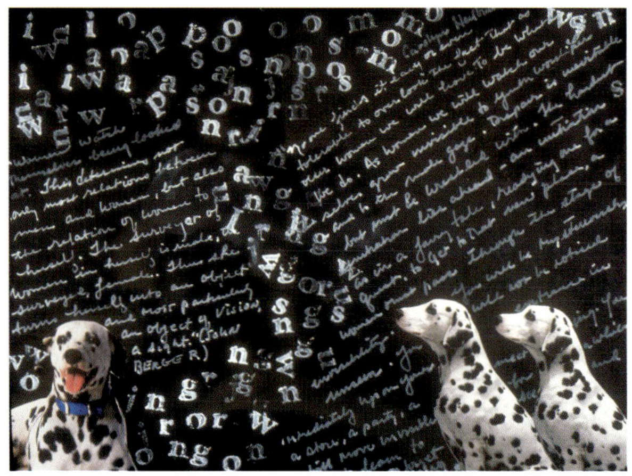

Above: From *Frieze,* studies for *Four Generations, One Absent,* each 8 ½ inches × 11 inches

Left: heads with stars and words

Middle: figures and heads with lightning and stars

Right: dalmatians, alphabet letters, words in white ink

We did not share equally in the care of my mom. She was in a nursing home in the Boston area near Elly and David. Elly visited her every day while continuing her work in her studio and at her job.

Barb lived in New Hampshire, which meant she could frequently drive to Boston. Her expertise as a family therapist as well as her geographic proximity were a great help to Elly and my mom.

I lived far from Boston and could do little to help Elly with the enormous number of day-to-day tasks associated with my mom's care. During this time, I curtailed my lifelong habit of sharing with Elly the ups and downs of daily life, fearing my reports might seem trivial. Our twin relationship had meant that we had always been tuned in to each other, and there were days when I felt one of the greatest losses from my mother's situation was losing Elly.

On my many visits to Boston I often felt miserable. I wanted so much to be part of mom's care and fantasized about moving to Boston to care for her, forgetting in those moments that I also had a daughter at home and a job I needed. And yet there were times when, having flown to Boston to visit mom in the nursing home, I could barely wait to leave, to whisk Elly away, to go home with her, and to leave the wrenching sadness of my mother's environment.

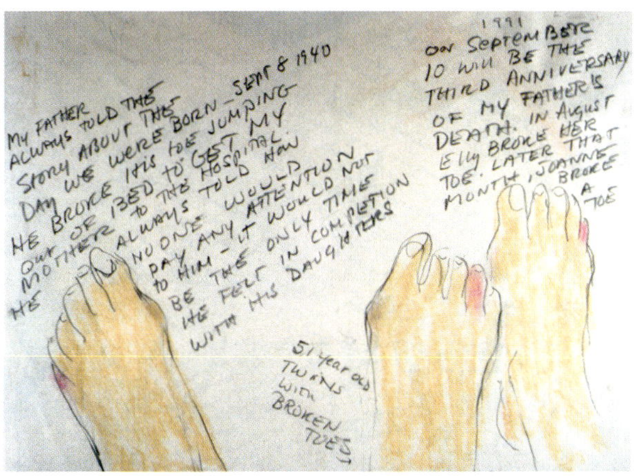

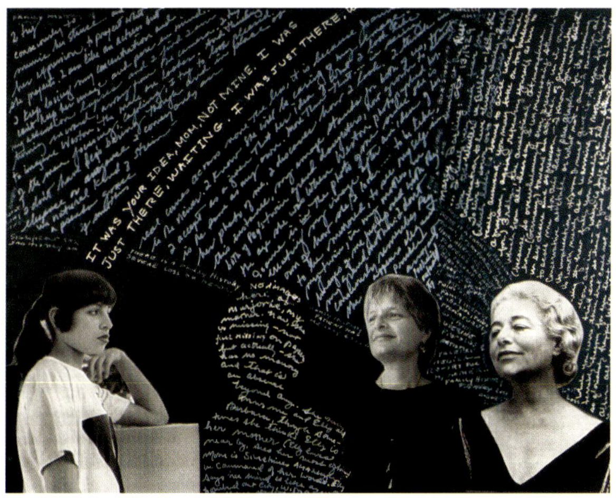

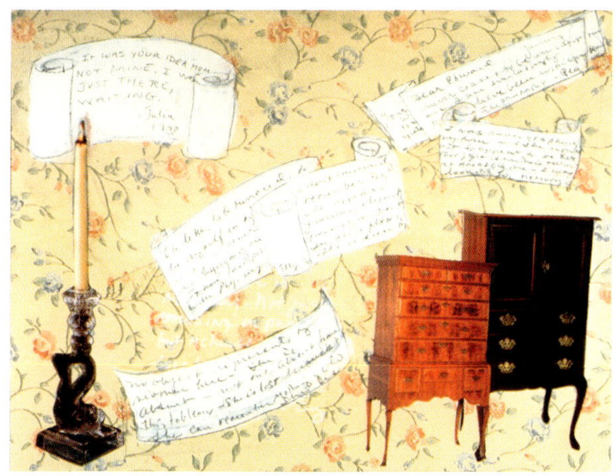

Above: From *Frieze,* studies for *Four Generations, One Absent,* each 8 ½ inches × 11 inches

Left: three feet with broken toes

Middle: four portrait heads and one head with text

Right: candlestick and two bureaus

Imagine for a moment that you are coming along with me on a visit to see my mother. We decide to put lunch off a little while in order to join Mom for lunch at the nursing home. When we arrive on her floor, at first we cannot find her. "I saw Marjorie down on the other wing," some helpful aide may say, recognizing us as we search. As we head in the direction indicated, I may turn my head as if in recognition and then shrink back, horrified to realize I have turned momentarily toward the wrong white-haired figure moving slowly and without purpose in her wheeled chair, so similar in appearance do residents here seem to become. Now we spot Mom and go to her. "Hi Mom, it's Joey. I know Elly told you I would come today." "Ooooh," she might moan, and seem for a time unable to emerge from her sad sounds and lost meanderings. But with a little conversation, a little straightening of her garments, and a few strokes of her hair, little by little, in a few minutes, she clearly is taking comfort, looking like herself, and on a good visit, taking real pleasure in recognizing us, knowing that Elly and I are there for a visit, and talking with us, rising from her chair with surprising strength, taking a stroll.

As we depart, we witness my mom's almost instant withdrawal, her return to a lost state. Our visit replicates those that Elly makes daily, with their near miracle of transformation and sustained connection. Even though it was painful to see the toll that these visits took on Elly, I wished that she could be there even more often, so that my mother need never become, as Elly described her, "that tiny planet lost in orbit."

Conversation: My Mother and Her Mother has my mother talking to her mother, but their ages are reversed; in this composite image, my mother is older than her own mother and tells two memories of her mother. For the text I used two contradictory stories Mom had written at different moments, long ago. Visually, by allowing the two texts to interrupt and cancel each other, I'm suggesting how memories frequently refuse to coalesce into one coherent narrative.

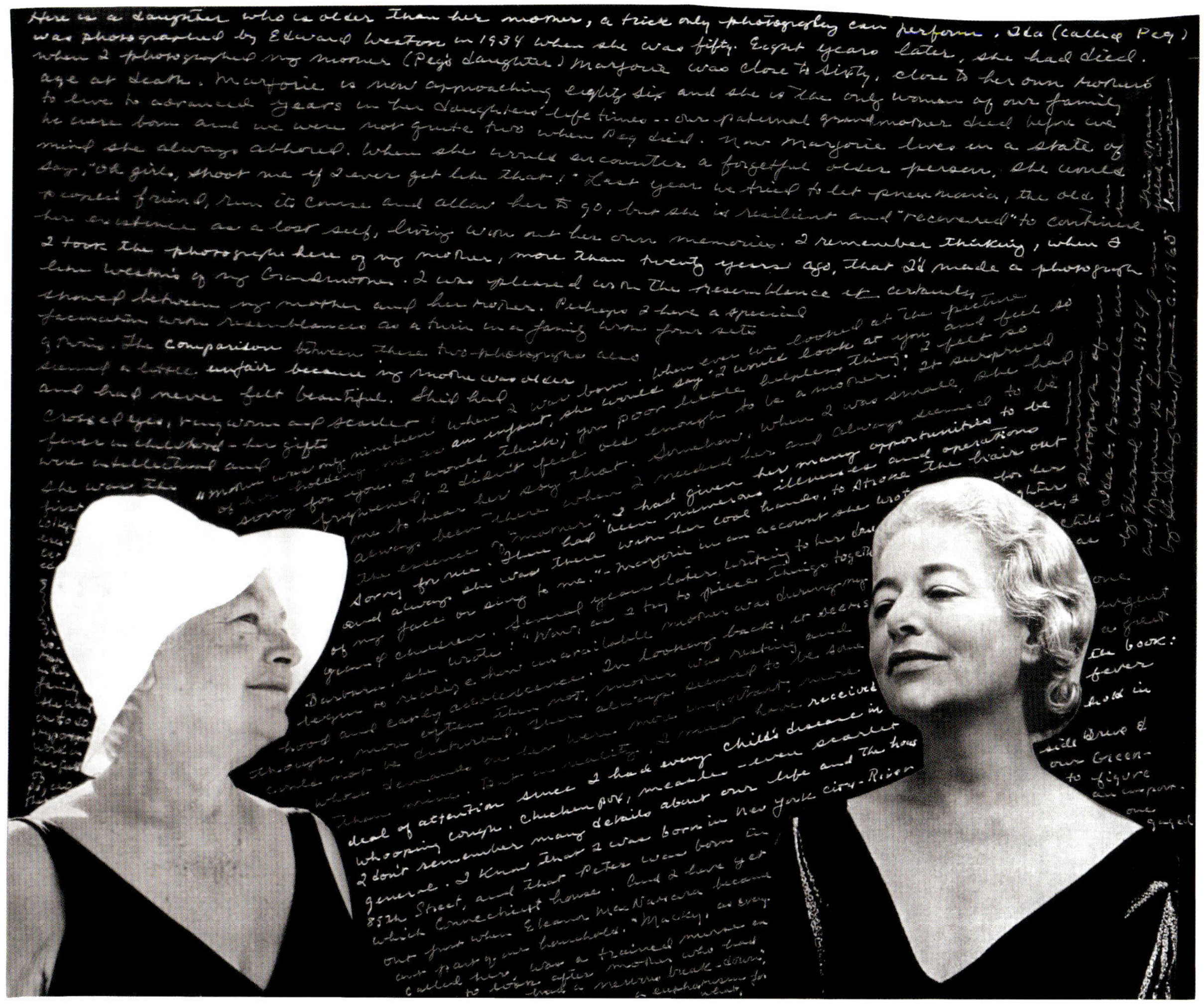

Above: *Conversation: My Mother and Her Mother,* silver print from laser-copy transparencies, 16 inches × 20 inches

During my parents' later years and respective illnesses, I struggled with my role as photographic recorder. At the time of my father's illness and death from cancer I wrote: "Though photography is my usual expressive form, my camera has always sought the beauty and light in a moment. I have taken no picture in weeks. Before me are scenes unbearable on first sight—nothing feels as if it could be contained by the camera's frame. The house is filled with an atmosphere of darkness; I am the last person to want to turn on the floodlights, or click the shutter now." My response was similar during the time of my mom's illness, and I took hardly any photographs in the later stages of her decline.

The making public of something that was never meant to be placed into the public realm is a form of "outing," a struggle for control over personal histories. When confronted with a confused elderly person, my mother had often said, "Shoot me if I ever get like that." While I believe she would have applauded the politics behind my desire to give the nearly unthinkable subject of dementia a form and forum for public dialogue, she would have been personally mortified by being exposed as a demented person.

Clearly there are tensions between what I might "expose" as a photographer and my mother's feelings, feelings that, as a good daughter, I would honor. I also face this dilemma from another direction: when I write or make art about life with my daughter, I risk exposing things she might prefer not to have made public.

Elly found a scrap of paper and sent it to me. Inscribed on it was my mother's incomprehensible written message. What did she want to tell us?

I rented a little house for the summer on the shore in Massachusetts. I was going there to work, to be alone, but also to be near Elly and my mom. But a hurricane came and flooded the house. I went back and photographed the hurricane damage, which was like the damage to our mother's mind. A brutal wind had stolen everything that had been her, and whatever remained was now adrift, lost.

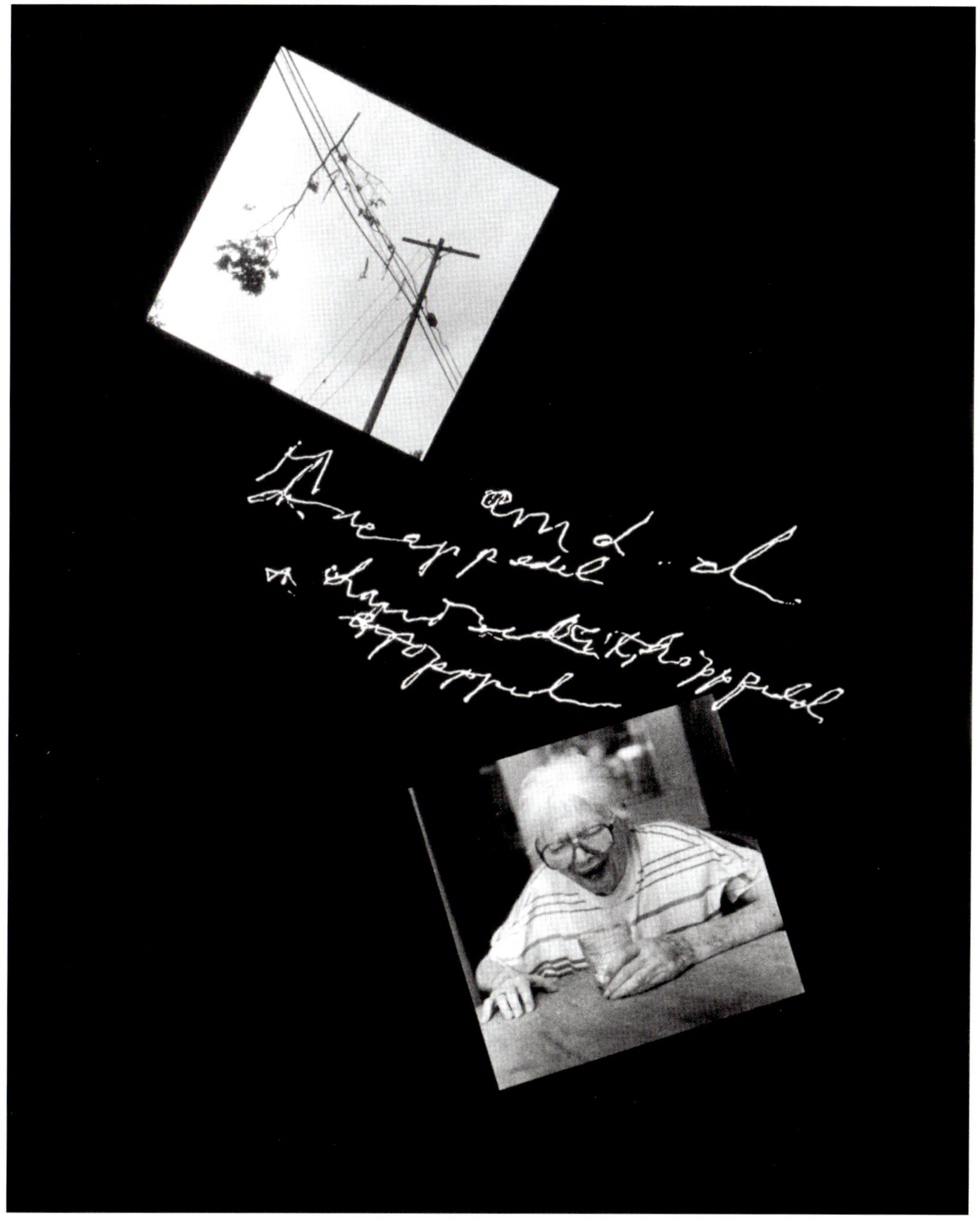

Above: *Devastation,* silver print from laser-copy transparencies, 20 inches × 16 inches

In *The Personal Is the Political and Vice Versa* there are scattered words that carry phrases such as "we don't believe her," "forget it," and "she waited too long to talk about it." Elly, Barbara, and I still felt the familiar presence of our mother's body and gestures but, because of her memory losses, could never again hear her stories directly from her. She had indeed waited too long to tell any untold stories. I was listening to the radio broadcast of the Anita Hill–Clarence Thomas congressional hearings as I worked during the summer of 1991. For an entire day I listened to the allegations that Hill's memories of sexual harassment were faulty and that her testimony was not credible. These phrases blended with thoughts of my mother's anguish at forgetting and her loss of the ability to speak. Phrases like "forget it," "they exaggerate," "she waited too long to talk about it," and "her memory is defective" clearly belong in both realms, the personal and the political.

Also in the news that summer was an incident at the University of Michigan highlighting contentions that the Holocaust had never happened. Political dementia. Text in this piece tells of my grandmother's isolation as a Jew living in the gentile city of Greenwich, Connecticut. This text and other family stories make trails through the territory of personal and world history, as ribbonlike bands of text trace lines across the surface and between the photo images that compose *The Personal Is the Political and Vice Versa*.

Opposite: Detail from *The Personal Is the Political and Vice Versa,* silver print from laser-copy transparencies, with white ink and gouache; detail approximately 7 inches × 10 inches; entire piece is 16 inches × 20 inches

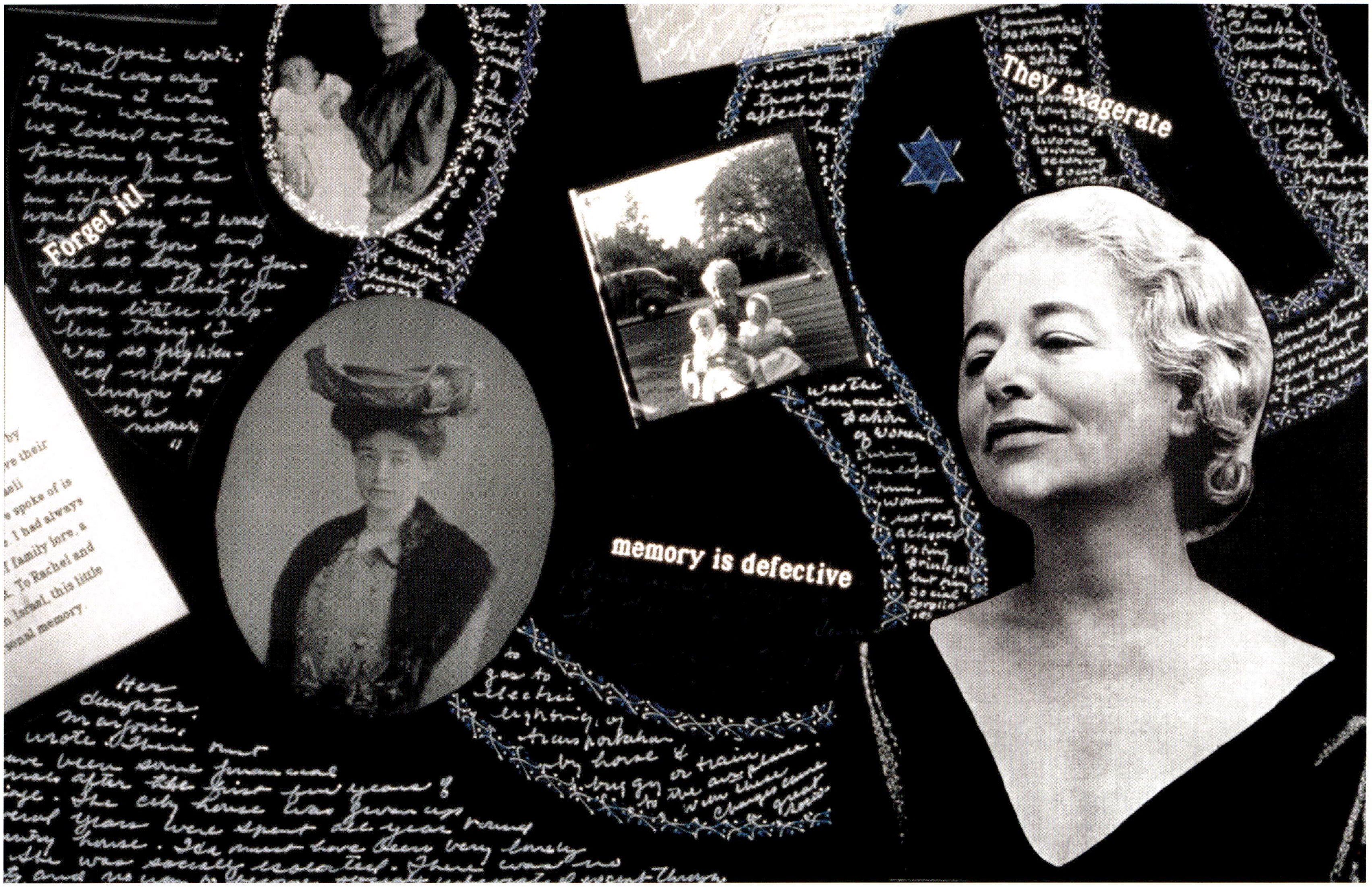
Forget it!
They exagerate
memory is defective

The title *Book of Names* comes from the open book in the work's lower right corner (and perhaps echoes the name "Book of Life" that is part of the story and ceremony of the Jewish high holiday Yom Kippur). The open book in my collage is inscribed with names of women in, or important to, our family. In some medieval works of art women hold open books and narrative is suggested by lines of horizontal frames. I found again the stratified storytelling and the ladder connecting the layers in an ancient Babylonian relief. I took inspiration from these visual storytelling devices and incorporated them into my piece *Book of Names.*

As I continued the series Not Losing Her Memory I sometimes used standing figures instead of the portrait heads that characterized *Four Generations, One Absent* and *Devastation*. In *Book of Names*, I used the standing figures, photo collage, pictures of ladders, and text to create visually the steps between past and present, grandmothers and grandchildren, wealth and lesser circumstances. Text here is in the small scroll Elly holds. It relates the story of my taking the photographs: "In 1990 Joanne traveled with Elly and Julia to Los Angeles." In Los Angeles, I photographed Elly and Julia and they photographed me. We were reinterpreting a set of 1934 photographs by the renowned California photographer Edward Weston, my grandmother's friend whom she had commissioned to make a set of portraits of her in her own milieu. While we photographed, we tried to be ourselves while thinking of Weston's subject, Peg, and how she had chosen to represent herself and her home. That home was the location of our photographs, but when I took up my camera there, it was a borrowed setting—this suggests just one of the problems in expecting these photographs to tell their own story. None of us now posing for my camera "belonged" in such a setting of million-dollar houses, nor did any of us still live in Southern California.

Opposite: *Book of Names,* silver print and collage, handwriting, and stamped stars, 16 inches × 20 inches

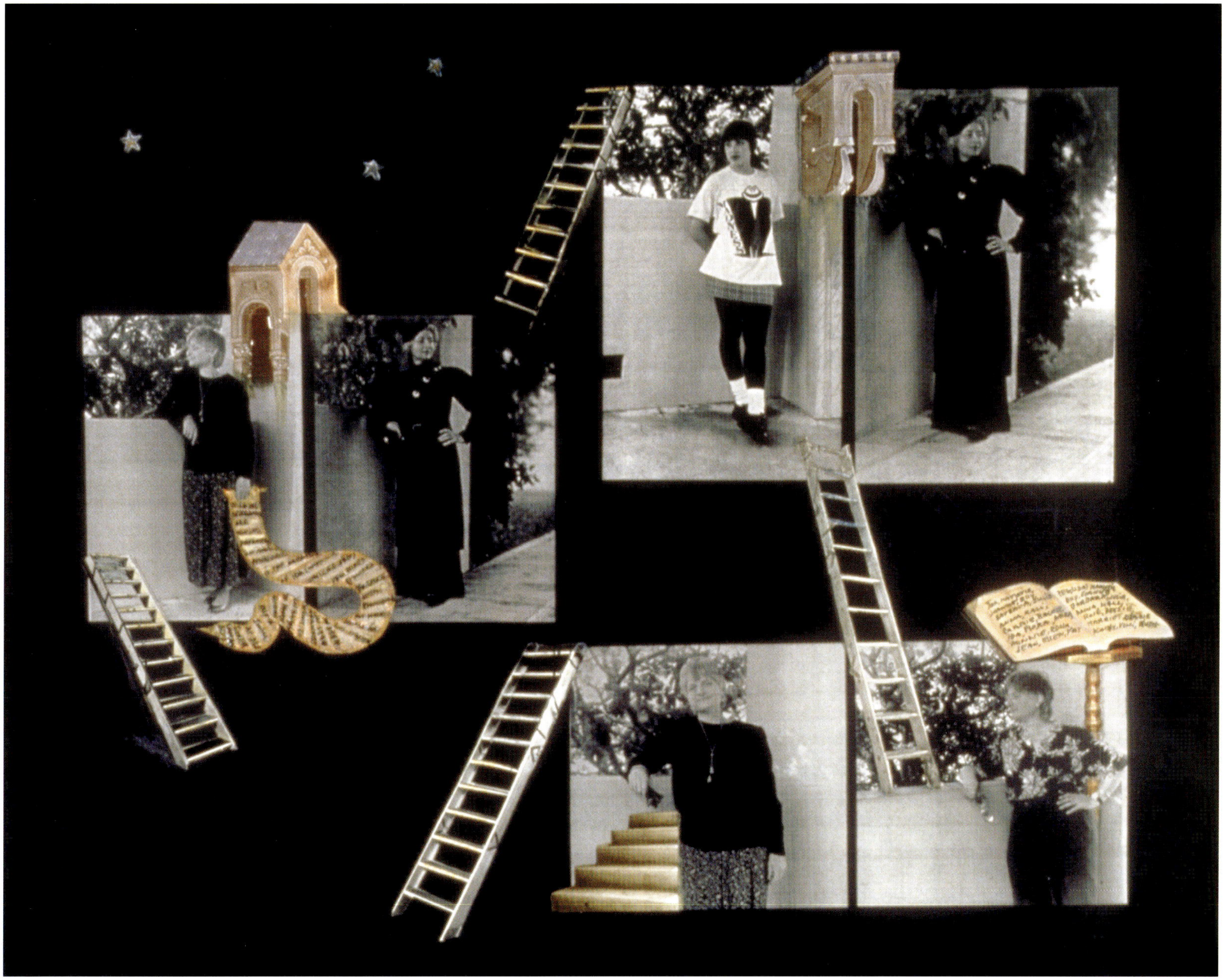

In *Daycare Documents,* another work from the Not Losing Her Memory series, I included stories about daycare arrangements as a way of comparing my grandmother's and my mother's family and economic situation to my own. I was particularly emphasizing the downward economic turn my own status as single-parent head of household signaled in our female family history.

The collage contains bits of pages with accounts my grandmother, mother, and I had written. My own page has notes from my early days with Julia, when I was commuting between home and jobs. My mother's and grandmother's pages, from baby books they each kept, reveal their relatively light duties because of the household help and baby nurses they were able to hire during their early years as mothers.

Opposite: *Daycare Documents,* silver print from laser-copy transparencies with collage and white ink, 16 inches × 20 inches

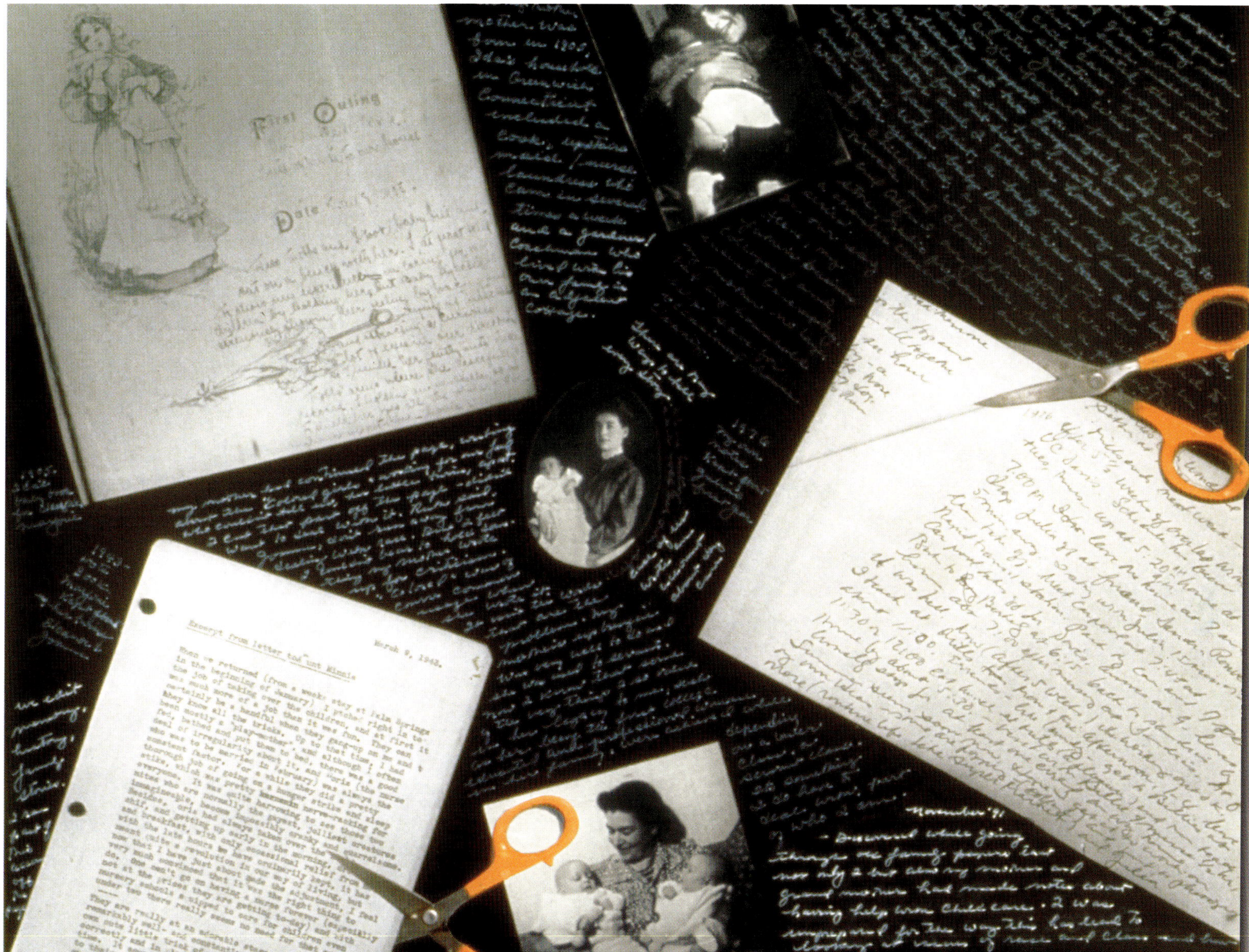

First Outing
March 9, 1942.

At most we're allowed a few months

of simply listening to the simple line

of a woman's voice singing a child

against her heart. Everything else is too soon,

too sudden, the wrenching-apart, that woman's heartbeat

heard ever after from a distance,

the loss of that ground-note echoing

whenever we are happy, or in despair.

from "Transcendental Etude" by Adrienne Rich

Opposite: Detail from *Map of That Ground-note,* silver print from laser-copy transparencies with collage, white ink, translucent plastic stars and leaves; detail approximately 8 inches × 10 inches

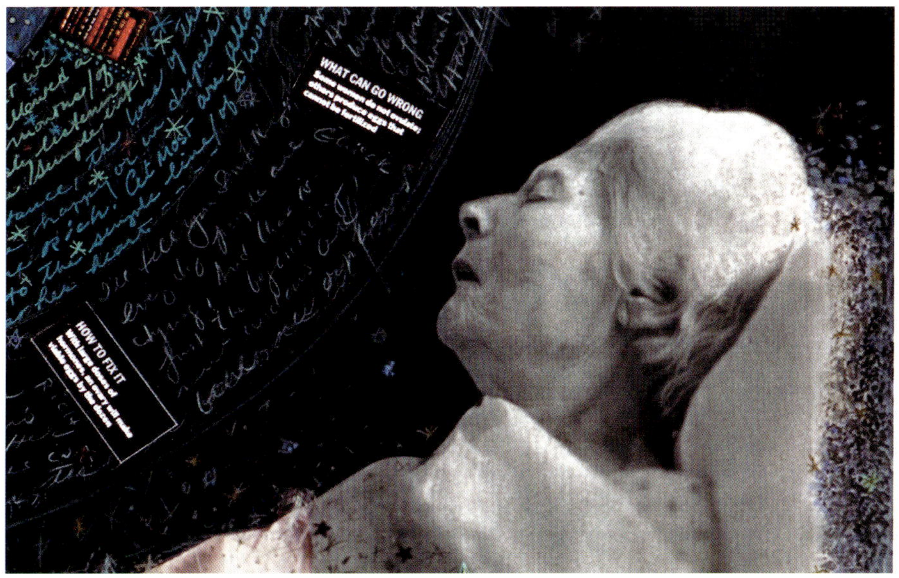
WHAT CAN GO WRONG
Some women do not ovulate; others produce eggs that cannot be fertilized
HOW TO FIX IT

In *Map of That Ground-note* I wanted to return to the profile portrait photographs of my daughter, sister, and grandmother I'd been using in the Not Losing Her Memory series, but this time, instead of using text to evoke my mother—or rather my mother's absence in the empty space where she should have been—I would bring her into view. I used one image from when she was very close to death. Since I'd been so reluctant to photograph her then, I had only a few photographs from the end of her life from which to choose. I had another photograph that I'd taken years before that greatly resembled Weston's profile portrait of my grandmother, showing my mother as a vital older woman in a sun hat. I added this to the lineup of heads. I called the piece *Map of That Ground-note* in homage to Adrienne Rich's line "loss of that ground-note" in "Transcendental Etude," a poem she wrote about the death of her mother.

A circle is the "eye" or "I" of this piece, and it rolls in from the left as part of an unwinding spiral that trails a section, already unwound, a trail of words. In the uppermost left corner is a reproduction of the fifteenth-century Italian artist Giovanni di Paolo's *The Creation of the World and the Expulsion from Paradise*. My piece repeats di Paolo's circle, if not precisely its themes. A line from a Louise Glück poem fills some of the lines of the path: "I'll tell you something: Everyday / people are dying. And that is just the beginning." Texts representing women's stories, women's lives, and women's reproductive health ("what can go wrong?" and "how to fix it") make up the circle.

Opposite: Detail from *Map of That Ground-note,* detail approximately 8 inches × 10 inches

Overleaf: *Map of That Ground-note,* silver print from laser-copy transparencies with collage, white ink, translucent plastic stars and leaves, 19 inches × 42 ½ inches, ca. 1994; collection of Diane M. Kirkpatrick

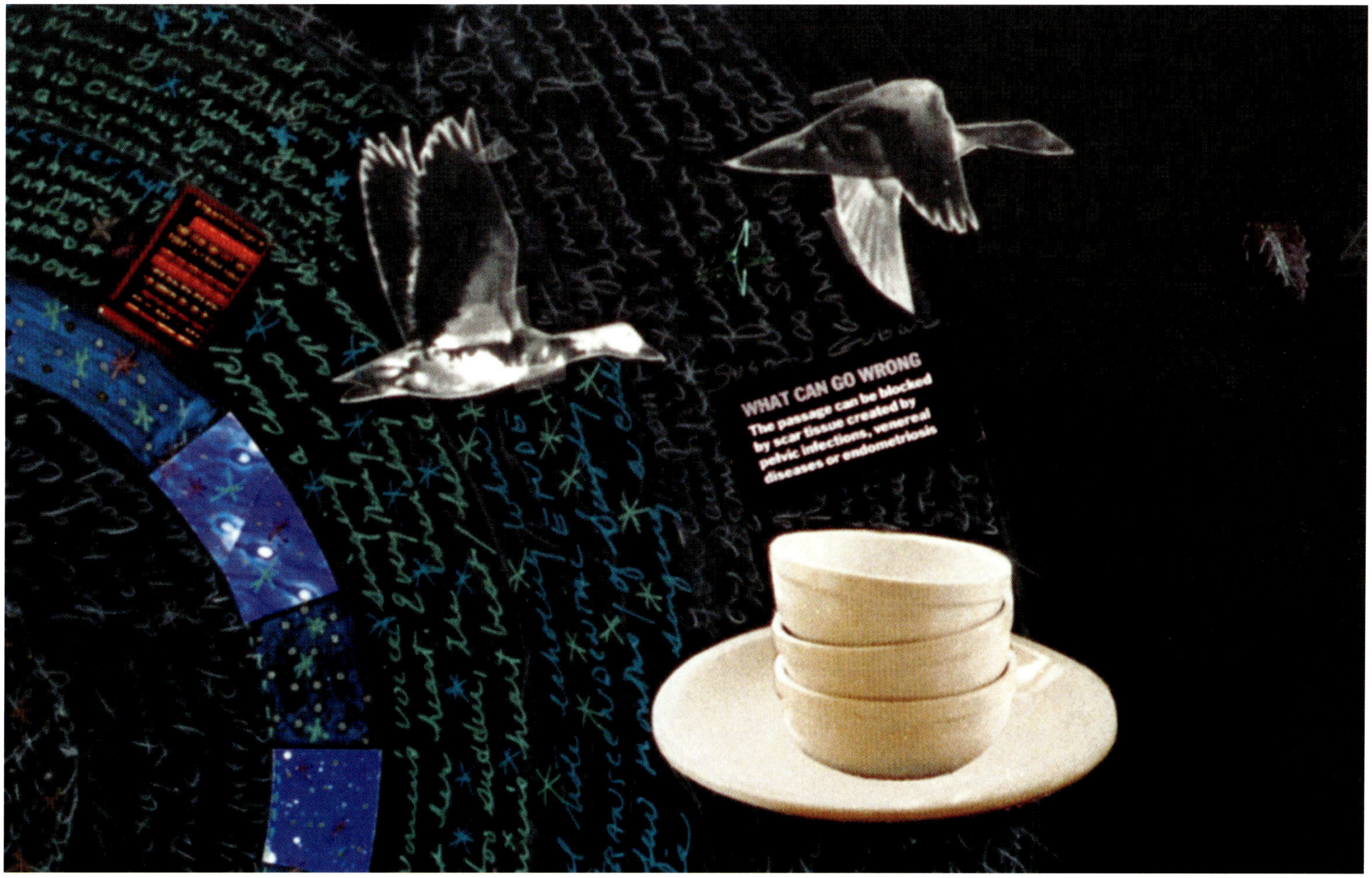
WHAT CAN GO WRONG
The passage can be blocked
by scar tissue created by
pelvic infections, venereal
diseases or endometriosis

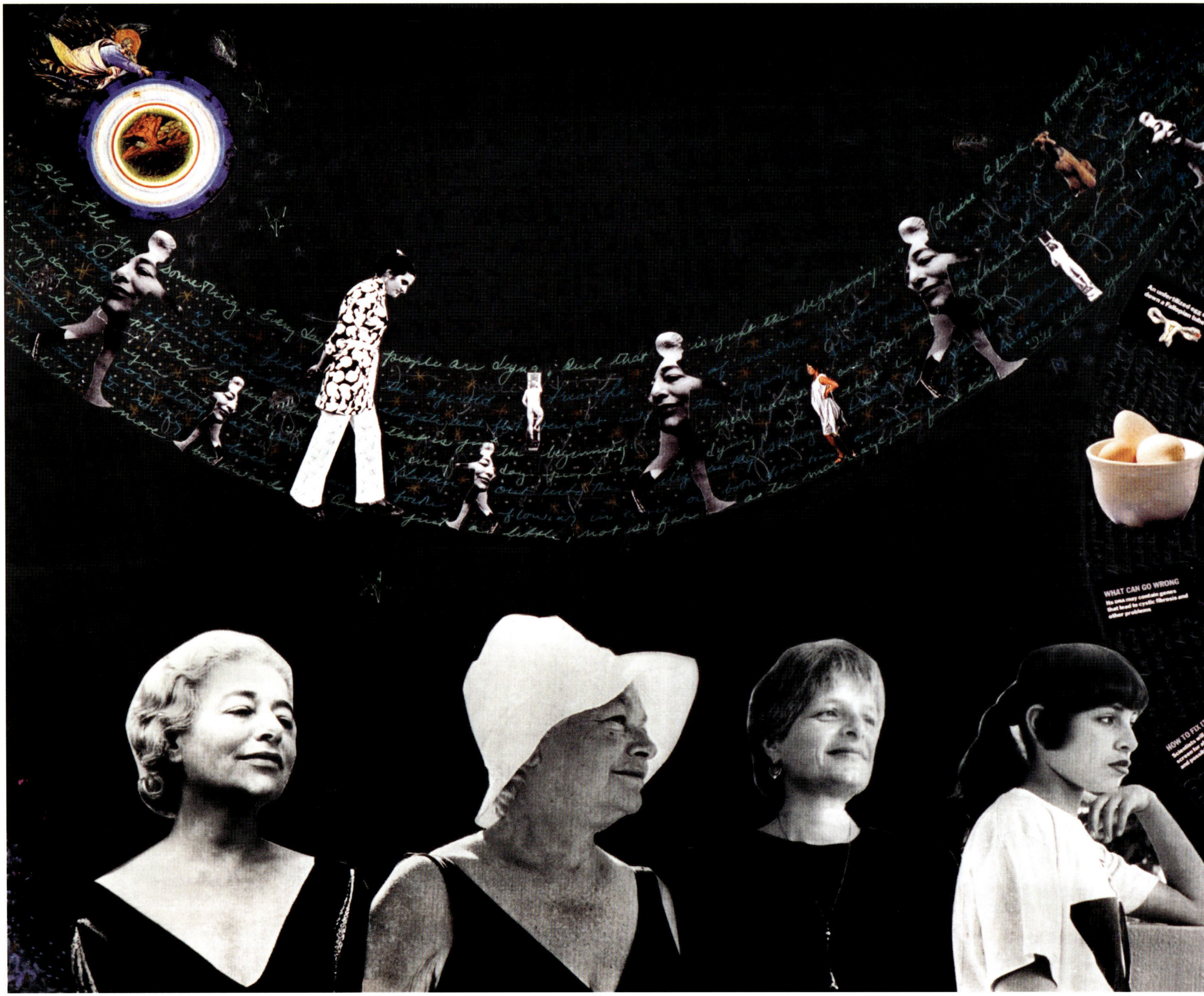
WHAT CAN GO WRONG
HOW TO FIX IT

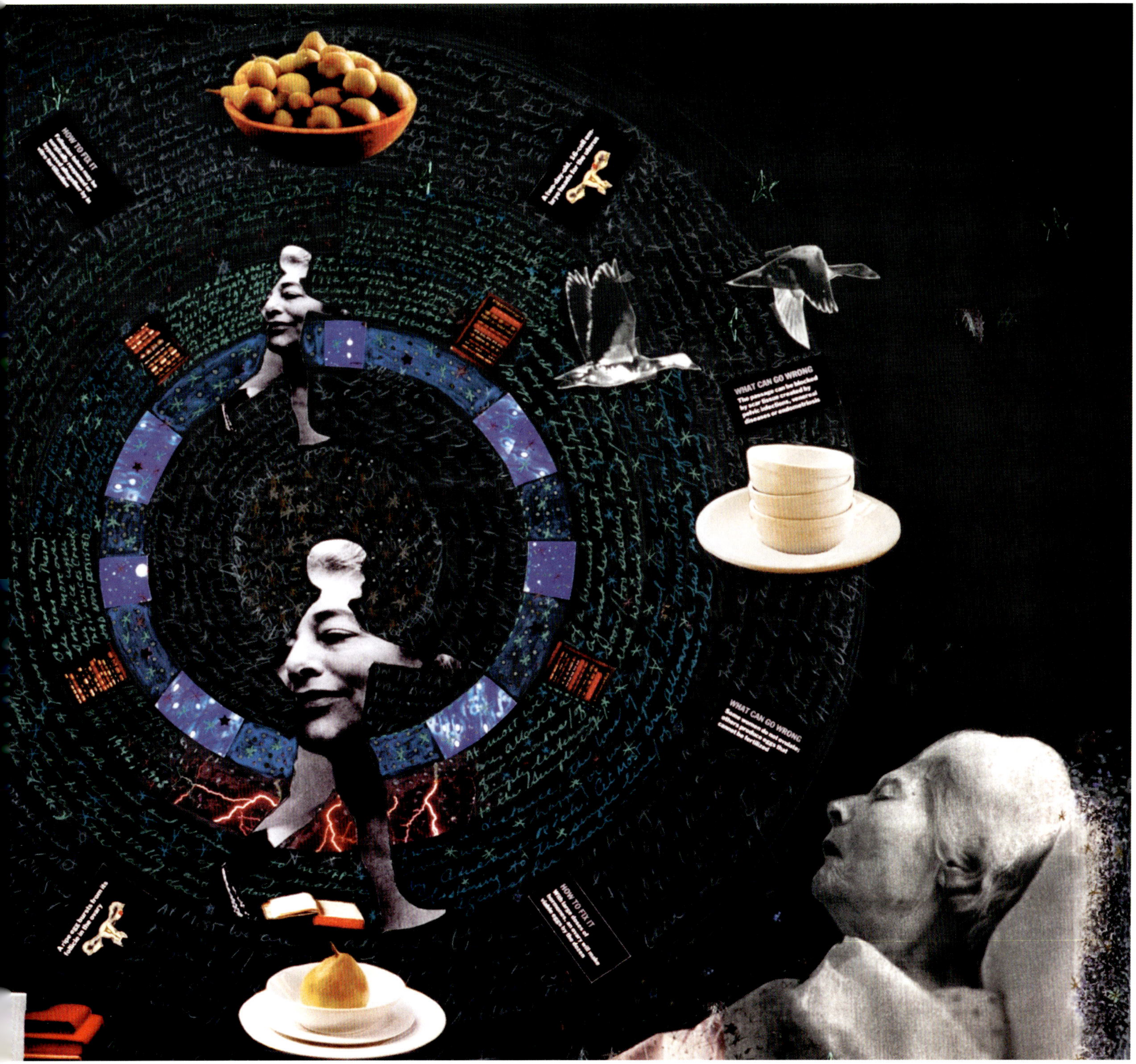
HOW TO FIX IT
WHAT CAN GO WRONG
WHAT CAN GO WRONG
HOW TO FIX IT

Family Pictures

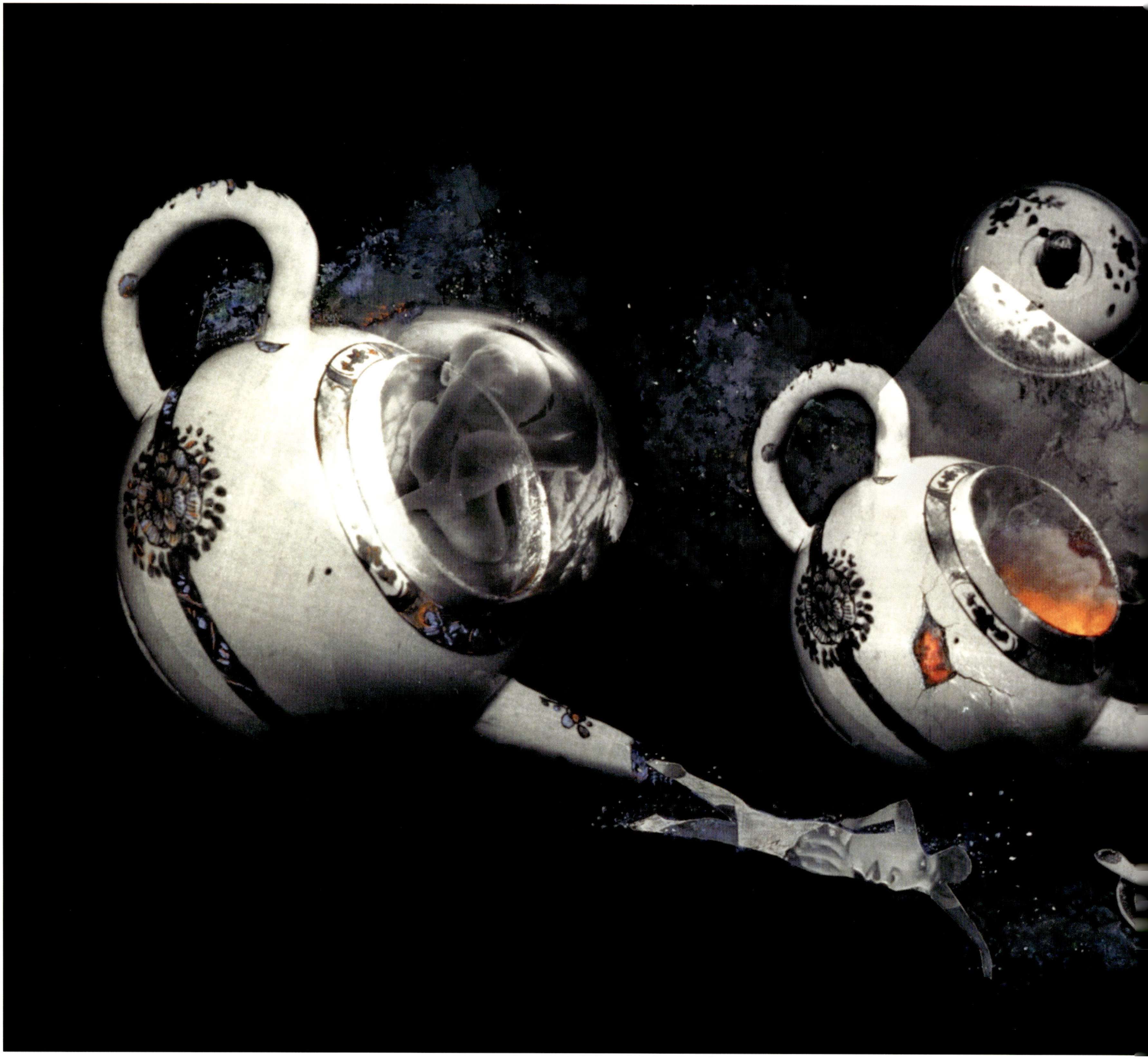

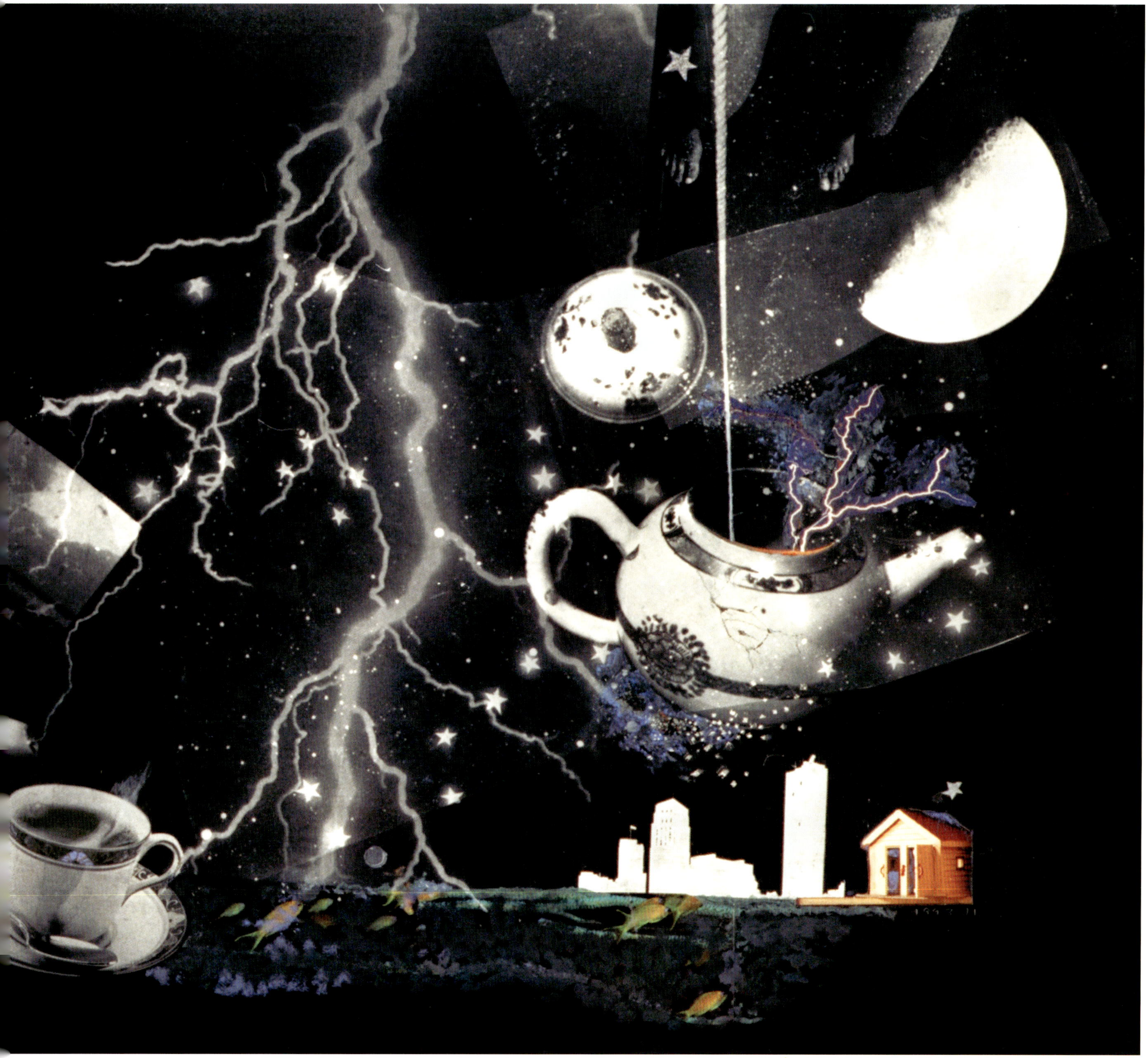

When I began *Letting Her Go with Difficulty,* I had just finished the Not Losing Her Memory series. As I wrote in my essay "Photography, Feminism and the Good Enough Mother," I was startled when Elly told me she saw *Letting Her Go with Difficulty* as another work dealing with my mother's death. I had to agree that the loss of my mother was a theme in this new work, though I had not consciously intended it to be. When I began the mural-format collage (four feet long), what I had in mind was to suggest my daughter's stormy emergence into her own life, away from family. Pain, rupture, departure, fracturing are all present. I wanted to depict hearts breaking, physical damage, and pain but found I could not wreak havoc upon my images of Julia, myself, or even generic female forms.

For a time every image that came to mind was either unbearable in its violence or as obvious as the phrase "broken-hearted." The teapot continued to be a theme of mine. I'd used it, along with teacups, to suggest companionship (two cups) and solitude or loneliness (the teapot or one cup on its own). I painted directly on the scroll-like print, making the pot look broken and then mended (further to the right) through the use of paint.

When I began to picture the teapot breaking and mending in this tableau, the issues of who was leaving whom seemed unclear. My own struggles for self and identity within the roles of mother and artist were part of the imagery of damage and repair. I had conflicts about the use of the photograph of an unborn fetus, so often used as an antiabortion image by the right-to-life movement. I risked that association, hoping to claim the image to my own purpose here. I wanted to show new life emerging into the battle for connection and autonomy. I wanted the anger to have force, to suggest its explosive nature. I used fiery images that came from photographs of volcanoes that I clipped from magazines and collaged onto the surface of my photo paper. The surface qualities that result from direct applications of paint and collage to photo paper give this work a completely different look than that of a digitally produced Photoshop work, yet these differences are far more apparent when one sees the original than when one views a reproduction.

I had stepped out of the frame in *Julia, One Week Old* to take a view, a perspective, from a distance. Separation had been the issue from the beginning, and I was continuing to explore separations in *Letting Her Go with Difficulty*.

Previous Spread: *Letting Her Go with Difficulty,* silver print from laser-copy transparencies, with collage and paint, approximately 20 inches × 48 inches, ca. 1993

Opposite: Detail from *Letting Her Go with Difficulty,* left side of scroll

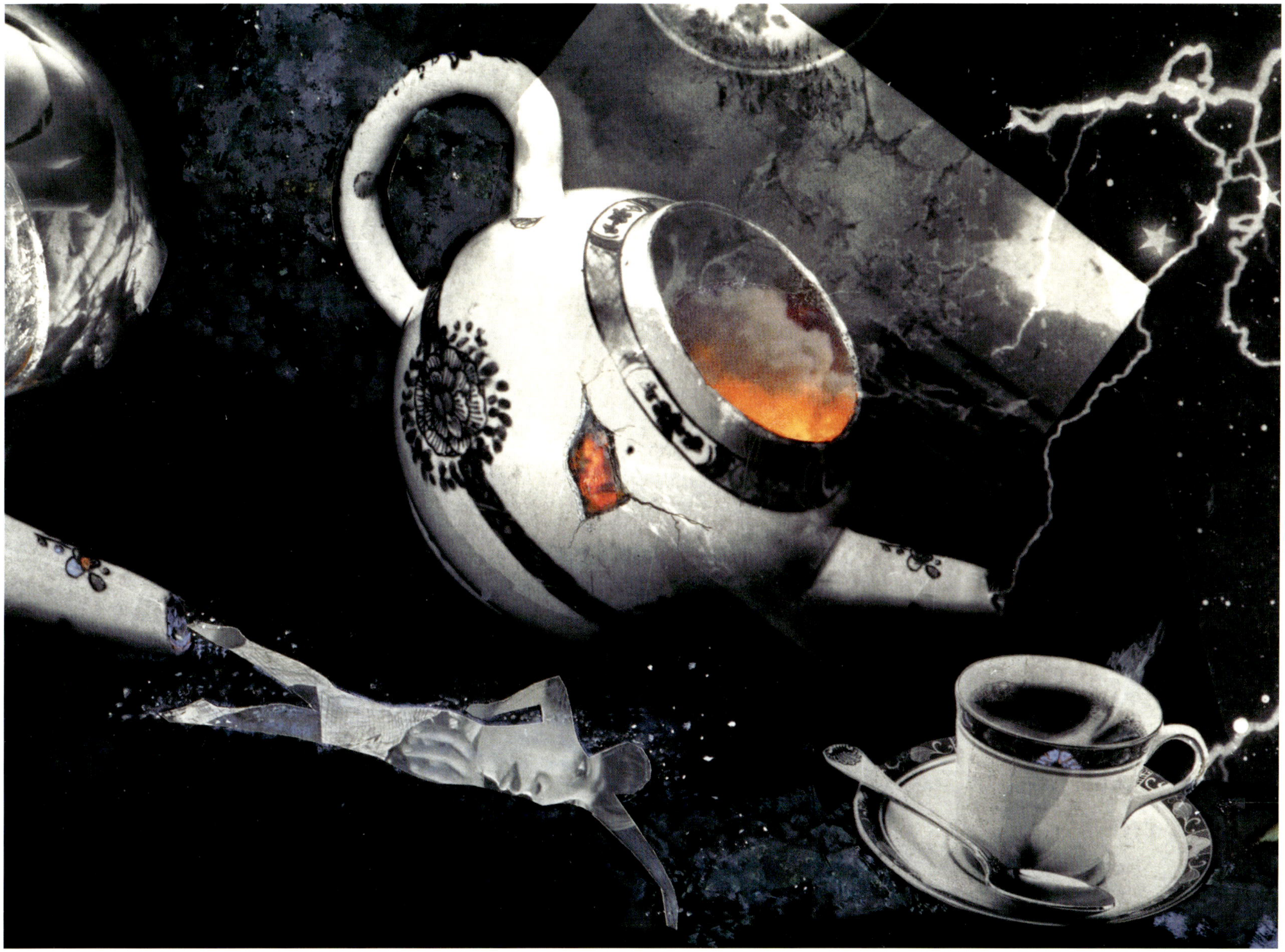

Opposite: *Running in the Family,* double-sided scroll on glassine paper, approximately 10 inches × 9 feet, 1998

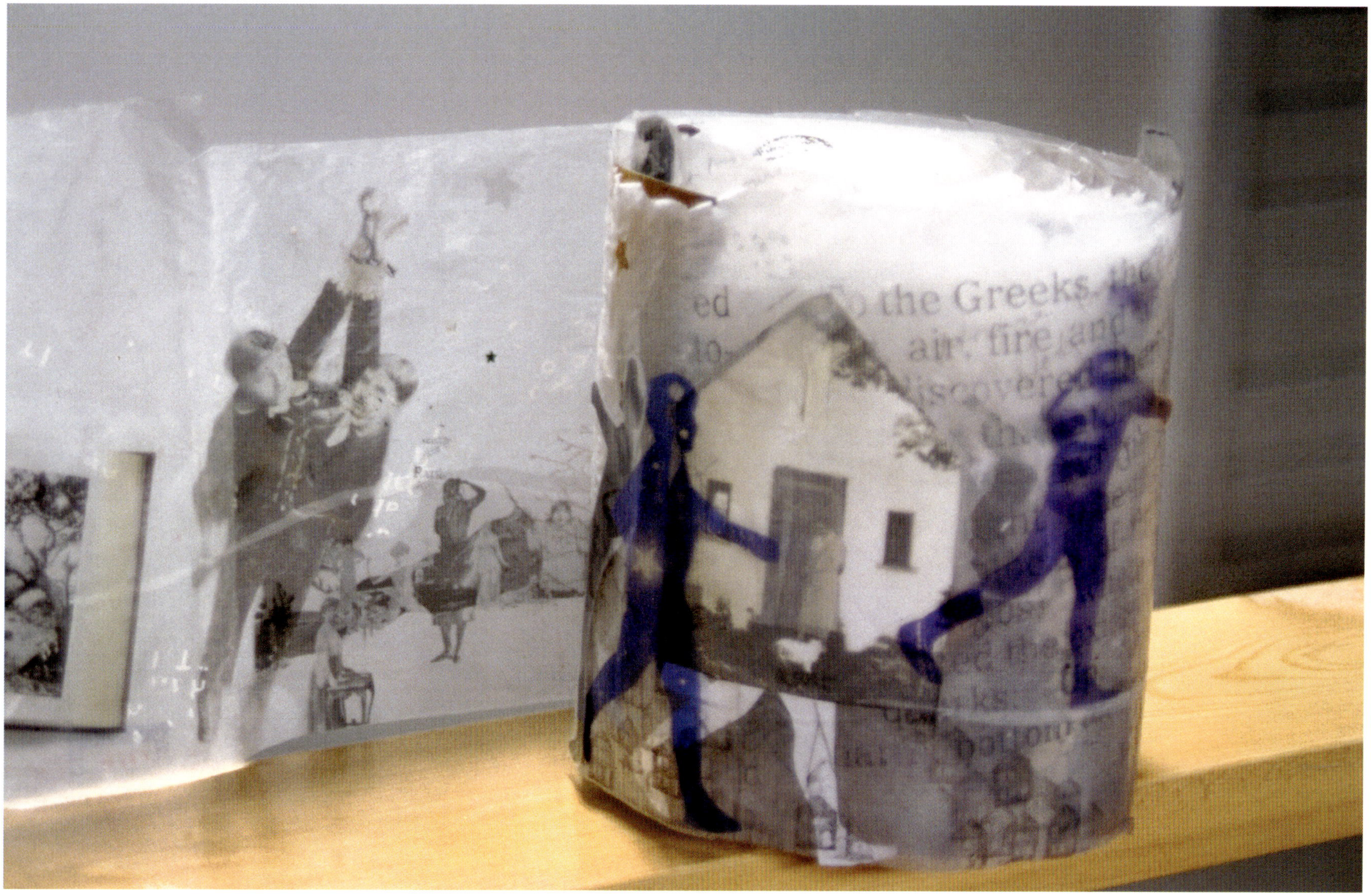
the Greeks
air, fire and

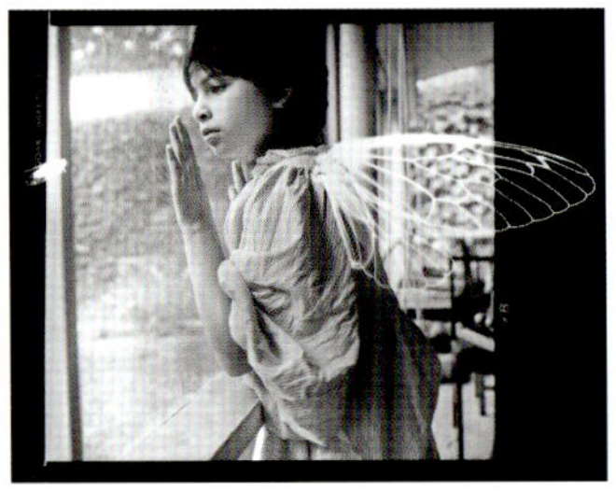

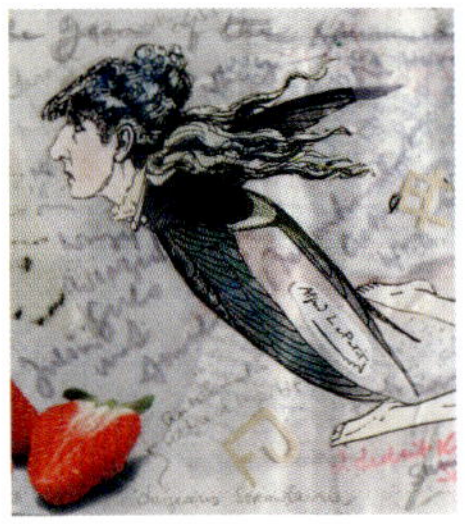

Giving myself challenges such as making pieces larger or longer, working on two-sided pieces, and extending work on my family after completing the Not Losing Her Memory series: these are the themes and points of departure for the piece *Running in the Family*. This work has visually interpenetrating texts and images on two sides of a nine-foot-long translucent scroll. When exhibited, it has usually remained partly rolled, exposing only a portion of its length and providing a clue to an important dimension of its intended meaning: that time is "caught up" in the scroll; some passages are only partially revealed, only partially available.

Over the years I've created a lexicon of imagery that I bring along from piece to piece. This work uses twins, houses, windows, my mother, multiple generations of women in the family and their histories, coffee cups, family documents, and references to anti-Semitism, among a number of themes that travel with me from older works and get taken up again in works that come later.

In the rolled segment of the scroll one sees a small house in the shape of the sort small children draw (as in the small house shape surrounding Julia, for instance, in *Julia and the Window of Vulnerability*). There are also conjoined twins: the ultimate twins, the ultimate—and horrifying—closeness.

There are figures that walk and run through the piece. Close inspection reveals that they walk or run depending on the angle at which they are placed on the page, but each is in fact identical; all are cut from a photograph of my grandmother's face and thus carry her portrait with (and in) them.

Two winged females in profile appear in segments of *Running in the Family*. One is from *Winged Ones*, where I added cicada wings to a picture of Julia. The other is a winged portrait sketch of the actress Sarah Bernhardt. The winged woman in profile intrigued me. When I discovered this was an anti-Semitic caricature of Bernhardt, I used the image without addressing the issue of anti-Semitism. But in *Reel Family*, which I made soon after *Running in the Family,* anti-Semitism is one of the central themes.

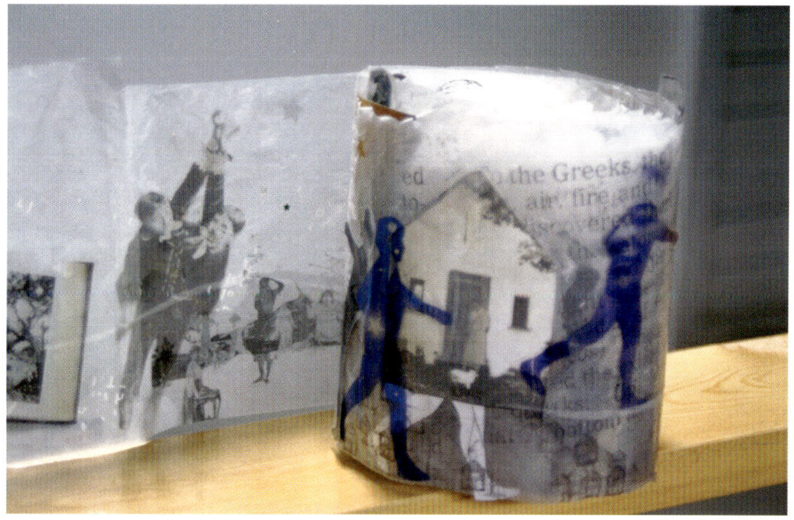
the Greeks

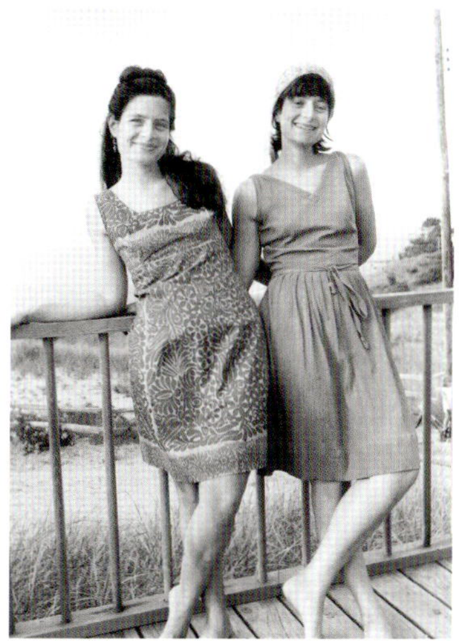

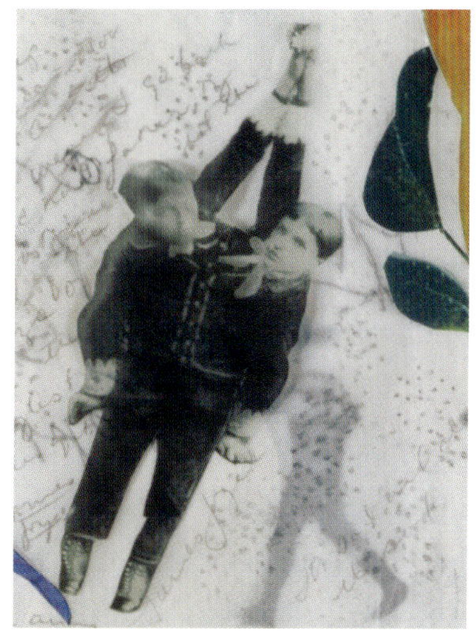

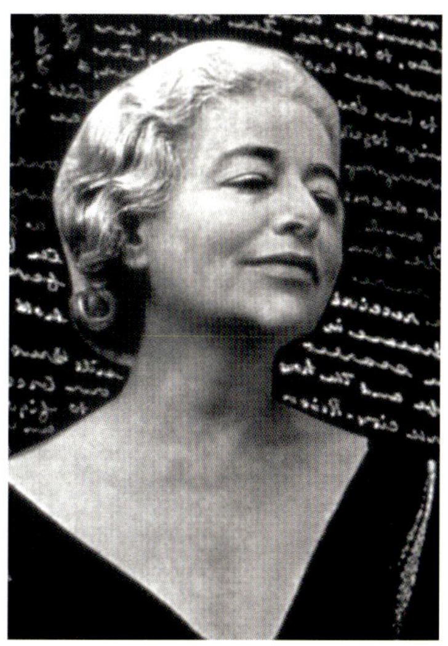

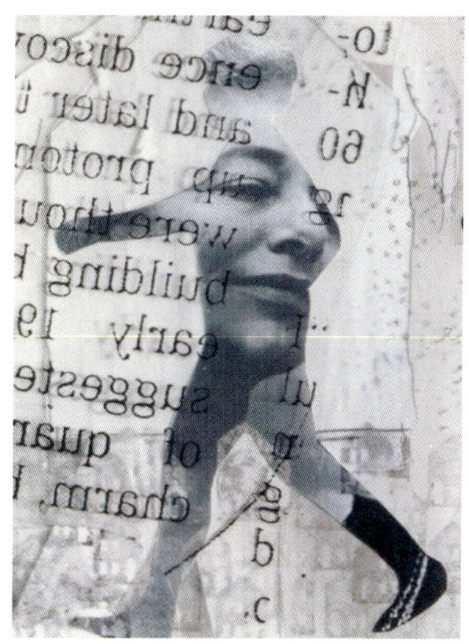

The questions of influence and parallelism in artistic practice are fraught subjects; for an artist to admit influence can undermine a claim to "originality." Being both a feminist and a twin prepared me to stop defining artistic achievement in terms of the lonely, singular journeys that are so much a part of the usual artists' memoirs and biographies. For me, feeling connected to other artists through artistic themes and ideas is energizing, comforting, and gratifying.

Nancy Spero made works that resemble scrolls. In one exhibition I saw, Spero's "scroll" ran all the way around the room, stenciled directly onto the walls. Her work engages subjects such as the torture of women; draws on facts, figures, and images from the news or human rights publications; and is executed on solid walls. It stands in contrast to my work, which draws from family stories and photographs and is executed on filmy translucent paper. Yet influences such as Spero's and the influences of many other artists have operated almost like conversation—enriching my work and me. I don't want such valuable input, particularly from other women artists, to go without mention.

Opposite and Overleaf: Views of four lengths of *Running in the Family,* double-sided scroll, 7 ¼ × 9 feet; each detail approximately 2 ½ feet wide

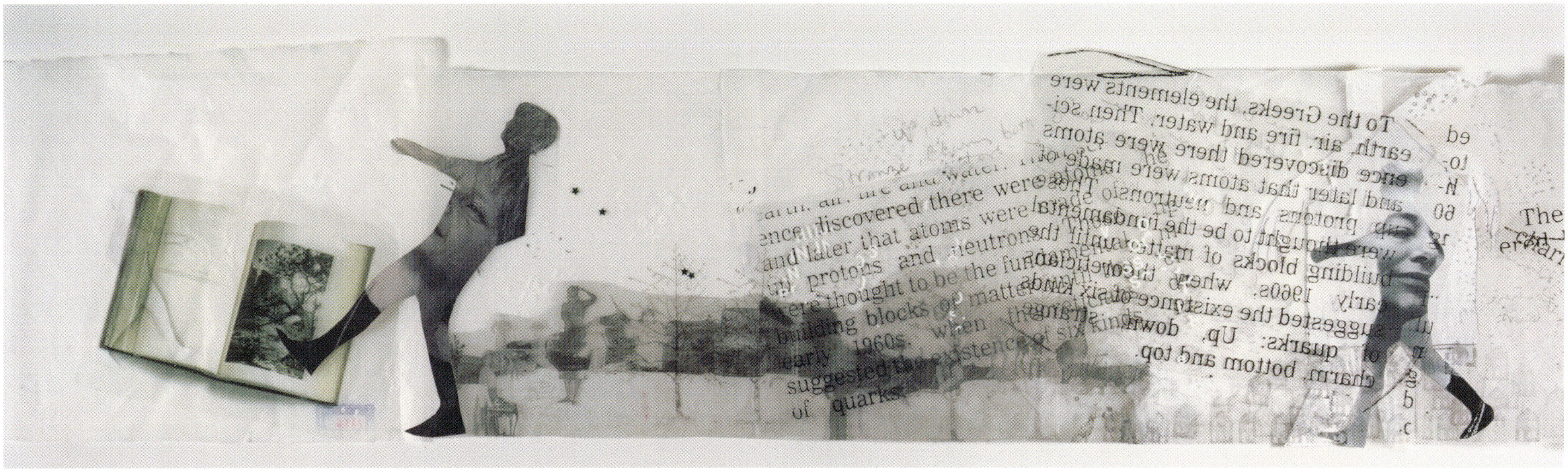
To the Greeks, the elements were
earth, air, fire and water. Then sci-
ence discovered there were atoms
and later that atoms were made of
building blocks of matter
early 1960s, when
suggested the existence of six kinds
of quarks: Up, down
charm, bottom and top.

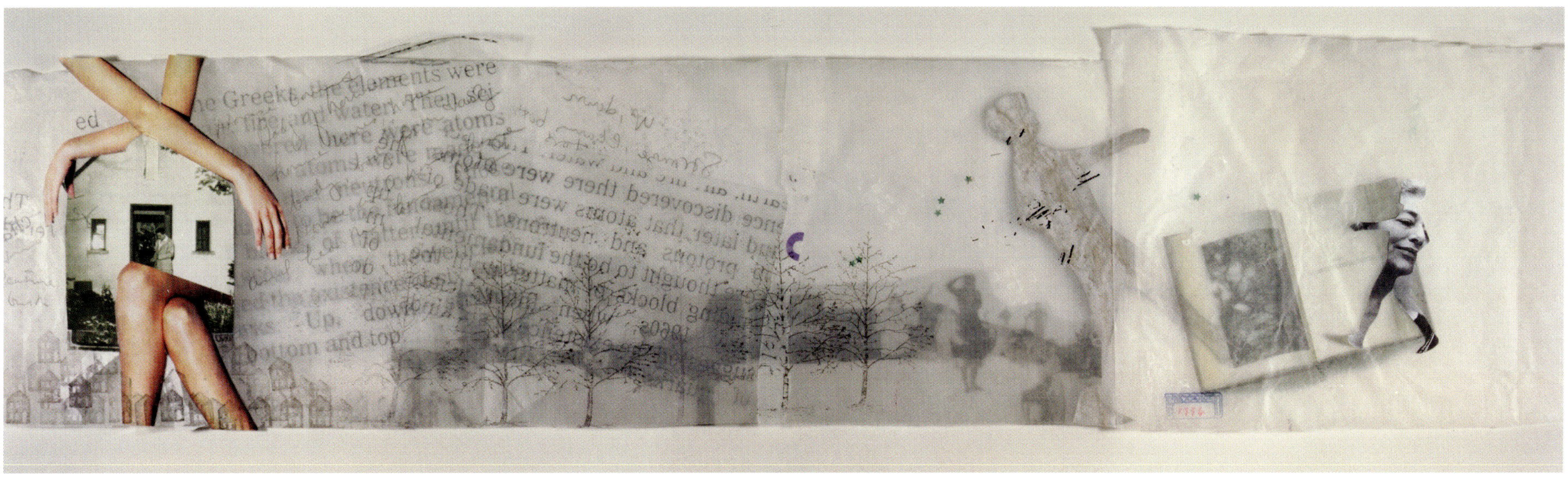

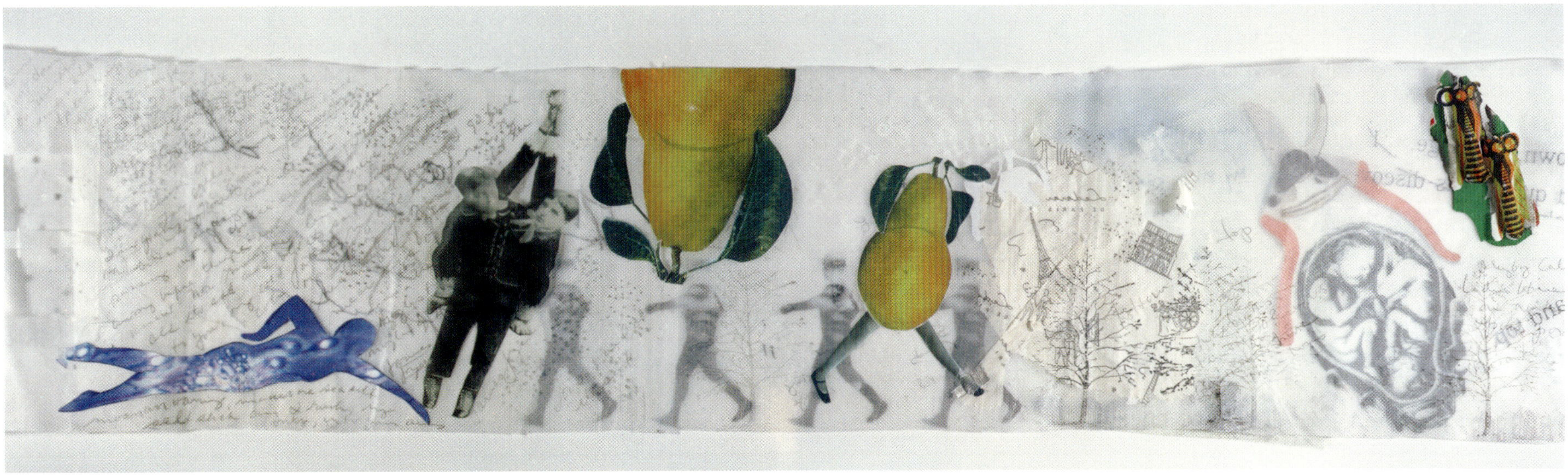

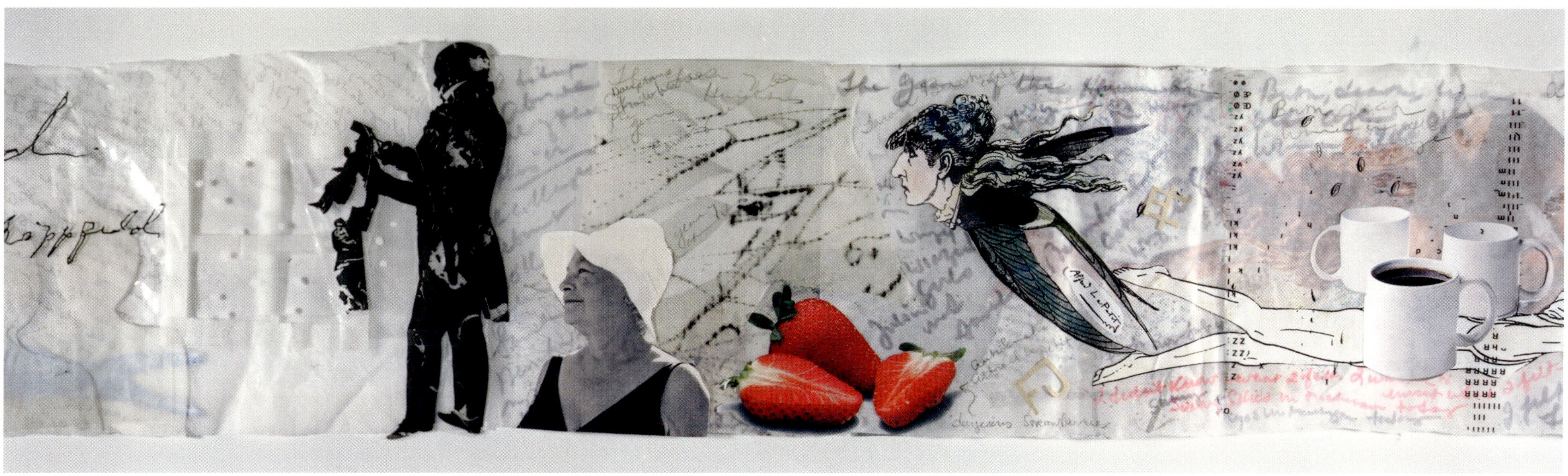

My father was uncomfortable talking about family trees or ancestors, subjects that are painful for many Nazi-era European Jews. But my mother's brother, born in the United States, loved family history. Uncle Peter was the keeper of the family portrait paintings from my mother's side of the family, including the two hanging on the wall of my uncle's house depicting Henrietta and Lazarus Rosenfeld, my great-grandparents. Henrietta and Lazarus came to America from Bavaria in the 1850s to escape anti-Semitism and repressive laws at home. When Peter's wife, Aunt Pat, sold the house, she donated the Rosenfeld portraits to Temple Beth Emeth, the synagogue in New York City that my great-grandparents had attended. More than thirty years after I took the photograph of the portraits and living room, my aunt was cleaning out a closet in that very room and found a satin-lined wallet filled with newspaper clippings. The gift to me of that wallet and its trove of clippings launched the scroll work *Reel Family*.

Opposite: Living room with piano and portrait, home of G. Peter and Patricia Lee Rosenfeld, Los Angeles, silver print, 1968

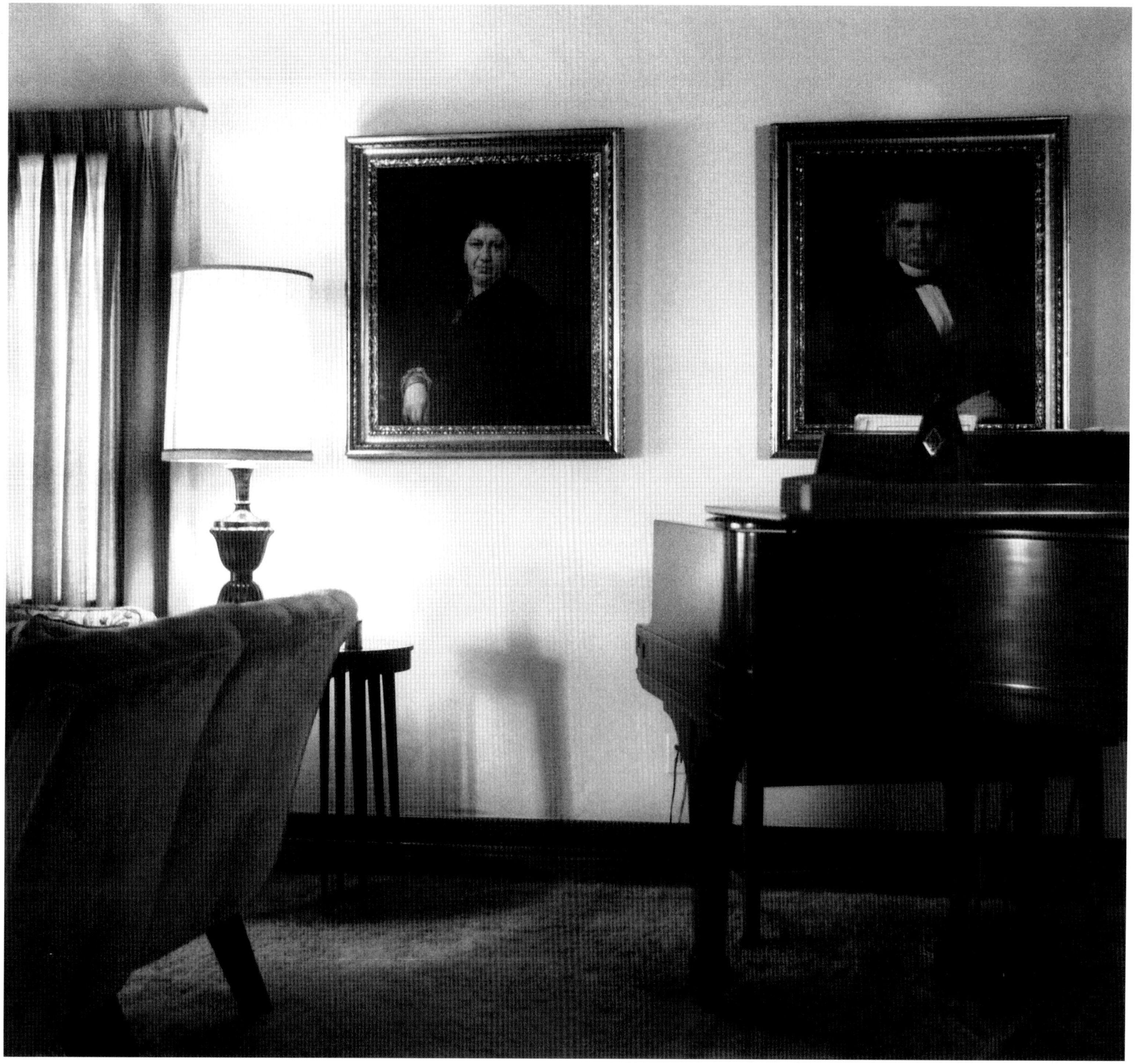

My first twenty-first-century work, *Reel Family,* is a twenty-two-foot scroll on translucent paper that, in a covert reference to my childhood in Hollywood, resembles an unrolled stretch of motion picture film. It also resembles a medieval scroll (I've "illuminated" details using gold and silver paint), and for a while, when I worked on it, rolling it from both ends to access middle sections, it resembled a Torah.

The clippings in the wallet my aunt gave me were from 1877. They were virulently anti-Semitic letters to the editors of New York newspapers. They concerned an incident between the financier Joseph Seligman and the hotelier Conrad Hilton that a historical account about that period called the "Seligman-Hilton Affair." Seligman had been turned away from the Saratoga Union Hotel because of a policy prohibiting Jews. A prominent figure in his day, Seligman went public with the story, expecting outrage on his behalf. Instead, many letter writers responded by praising Hilton and offering negative stereotypes of Jews as legitimate reasons why Seligman and other "Hebrews" should be kept out of good hotels. Puzzled over why my family had saved those clippings all these years, I turned up the fact that Seligman and his wife were the two friends who figured most prominently in a family album my great-grandmother kept. In my scroll work I wove the story of my great-grandparents' exodus from Bavaria and references to the anti-Semitism their friend encountered, using pictures from Henrietta's album, pictures and documents concerning immigration, details of the 1877 letters, family photographs, as well as other items.

Remaining art in this section from *Reel Family,* various detail views of scroll on glassine with collage from scanned objects (such as book pages and photographs), 29 ½ inches × 22 feet, 2000; Institute for Research on Women and Gender, University of Michigan

Opposite: Detail from scroll, *Reel Family,* wallet with newspaper clippings

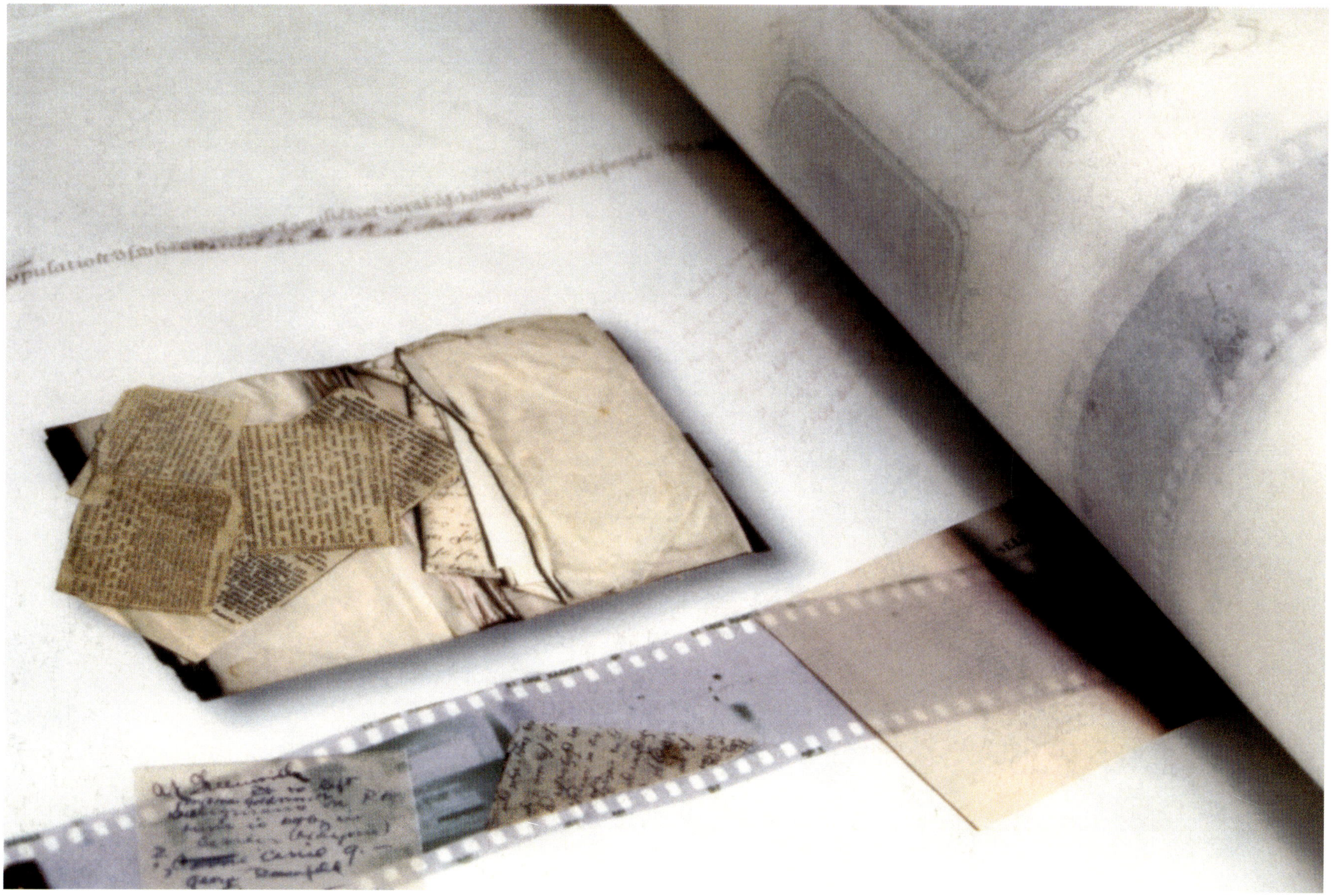

Three lines run through the twenty-two-foot length of *Reel Family*.

In the top line, text taken from newspaper headlines on the days I worked on the piece joins the story of an 1850s wave of immigration that brought my great-grandparents to the United States. Sail ships and steamships, the ocean liners of the day, travel on this wave of text.

In the middle line are reproductions of photographs, letters, book pages, immigration documents, and newspaper clippings, reproduced at near actual size.

In the bottom line, segments of a slightly oversized reproduction of a piece of film run the length of the scroll, where bits of items from the other two lines, greatly reduced in scale, are repeated.

Opposite: Detail from *Reel Family,* three lines of text and images

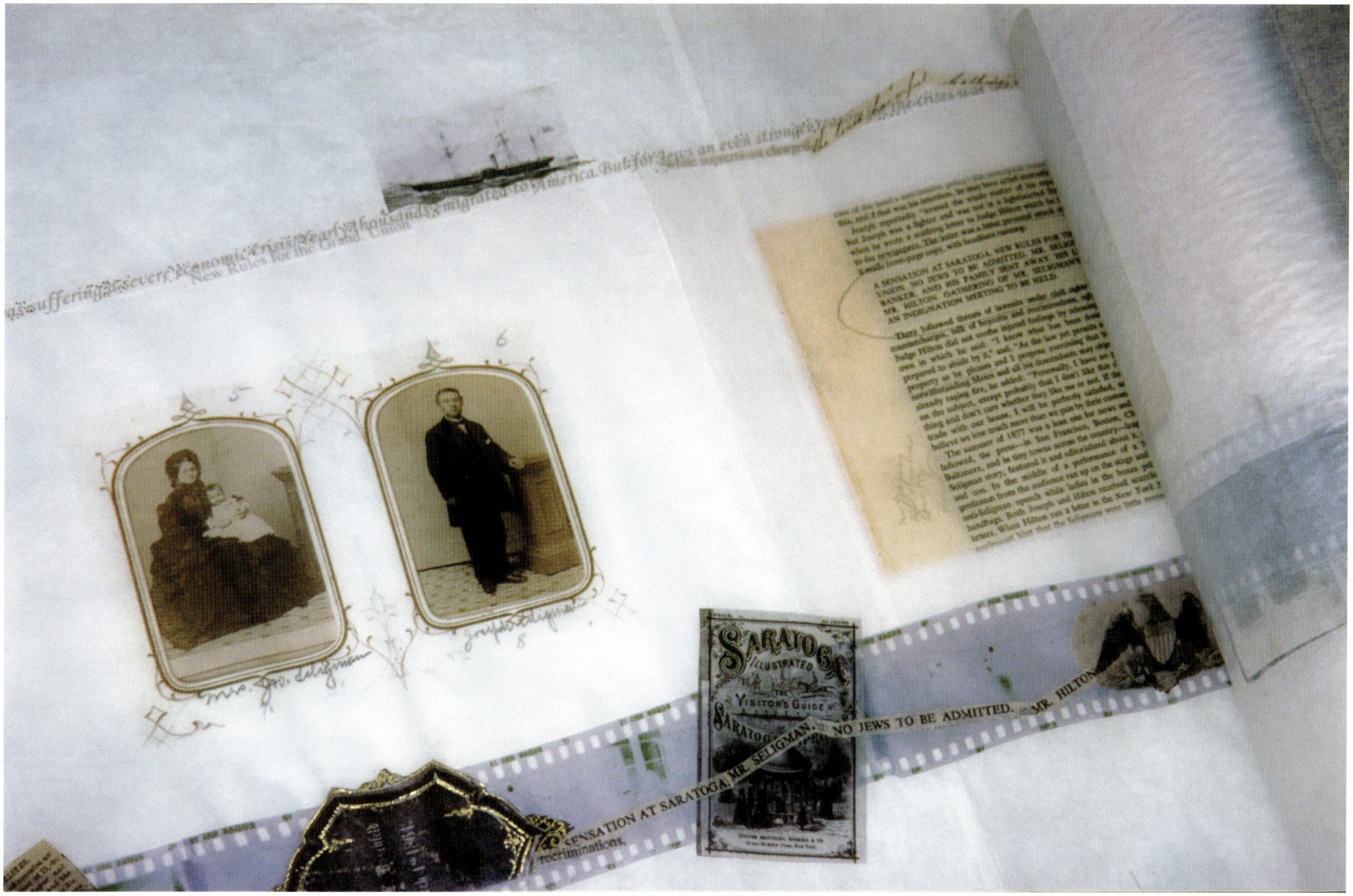
New Rules for the Grand Union
A SENSATION AT SARATOGA. NEW RULES FOR THE GRAND UNION. NO JEWS TO BE ADMITTED.
AN INDIGNATION MEETING TO BE HELD
SARATOGA ILLUSTRATED
THE VISITOR'S GUIDE
SENSATION AT SARATOGA MR. SELIGMAN NO JEWS TO BE ADMITTED. MR. HILTON
recriminations

Digital scanning, printing, and image control played a role in *Reel Family*. I scanned many items that appear in the middle and lower registers, and Photoshop made it easy to resize the pictures to make them fit where I wanted to place them. Through digital means I also created shadows to give the illusion that some items sit on the surface. I attached all of the hundreds of bits of my twenty-two-foot collage to glassine, and I was able to give translucency to the photographs and documents that appear throughout the scroll by printing them digitally onto vellum.

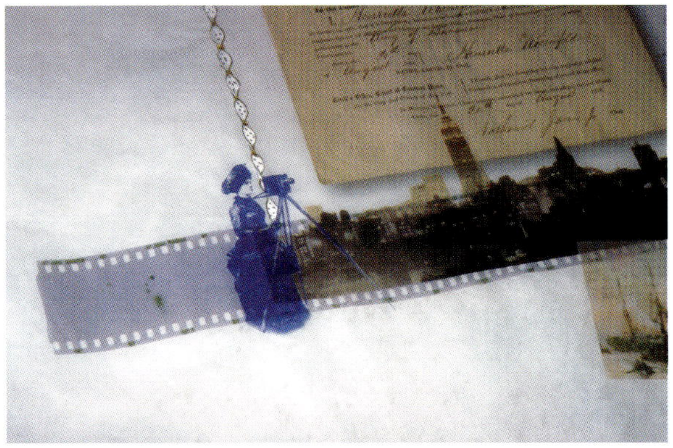

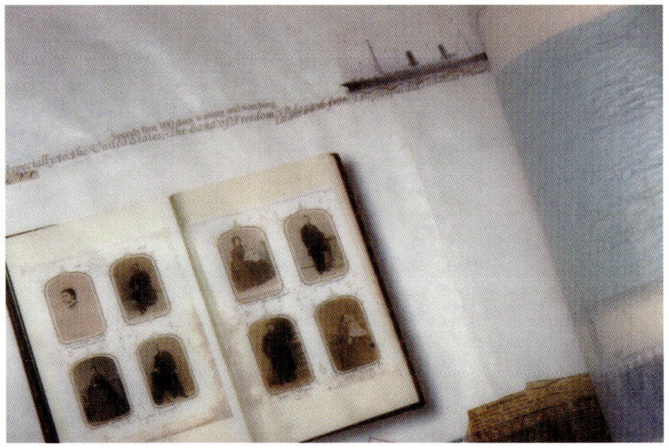

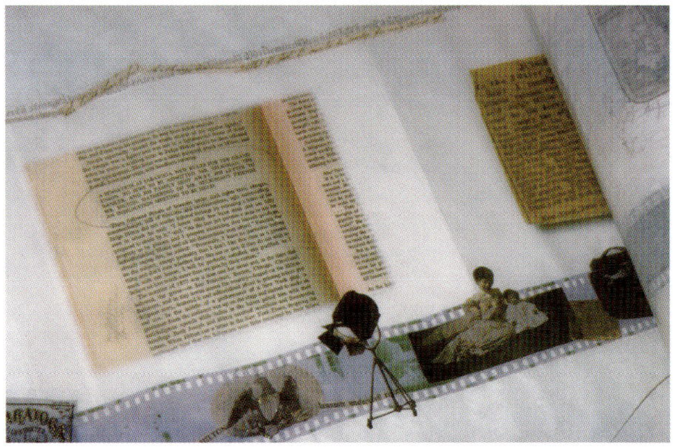

Above: Detail from *Reel Family, left end of scroll:* woman, cityscape, and immigration document; family album, ship; book page, spotlight

While Julia was growing up, my studio continued to be a crowded little room, but after my parents died and my sisters and I sold their home, I was able to add a real studio to my house. This loftlike half-story addition made it possible for me to work on larger pieces and also provided a view from the upstairs studio down into the living room. And it's that view that allowed me to make the only photograph of my twenty-two-foot scroll that shows some of its length.

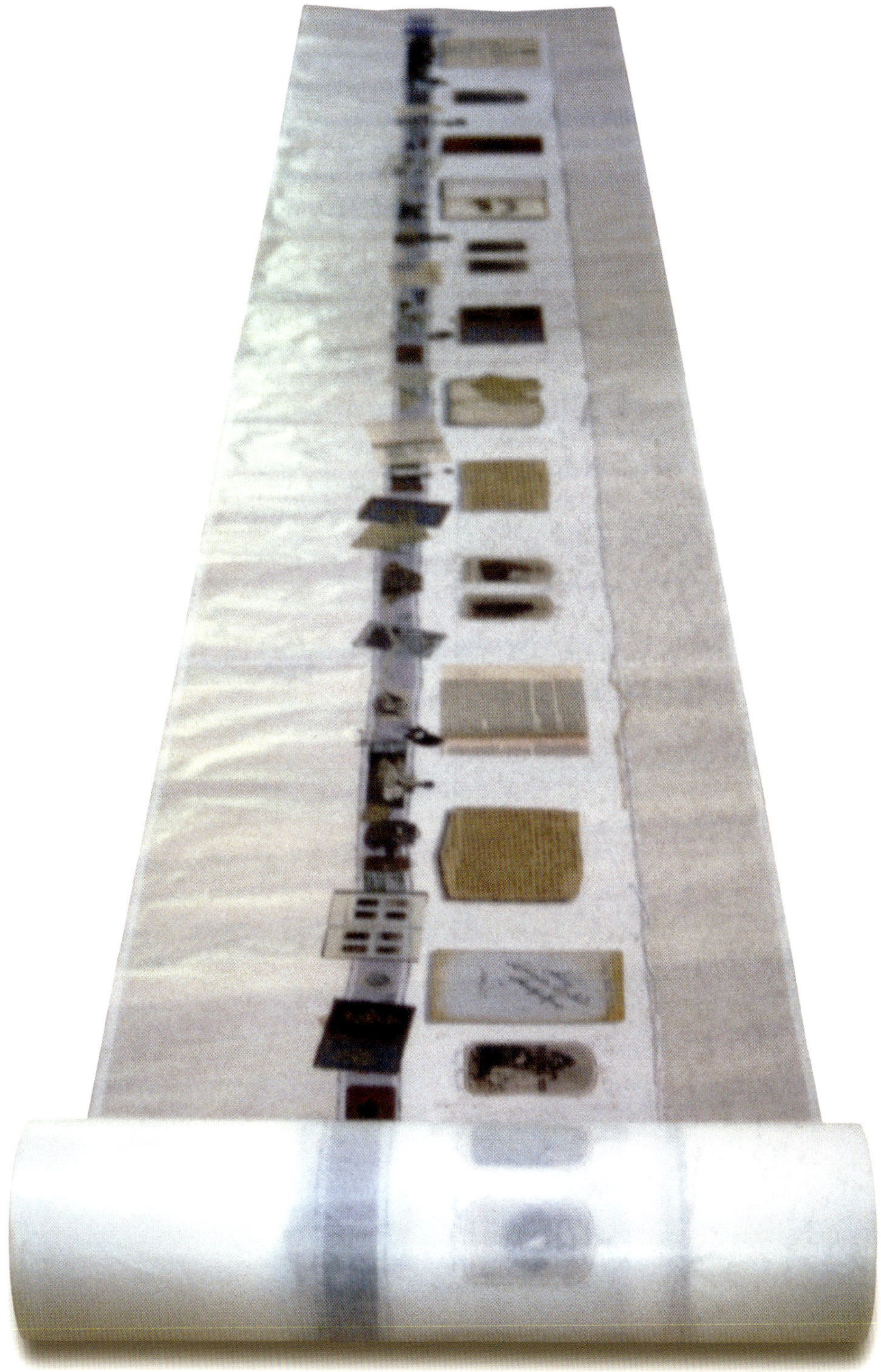

Above: Scroll, *Reel Family,* seen from above

Photo Finish

An event like the attack on the World Trade Center in 2001 is riveting. So many of the images from that September morning have been repeatedly shown that after awhile the news pictures repeat endlessly in one's mind. Yet, as an artist, what can I do with these images? How can I respond? (I can't; it's overwhelming.) How can I not? (It's such an important part of recent experience.) When the horror and immediacy of the tragedy recede from direct view, I'm left with some of the word-images. One of these is "twin towers."

Conjoined twins have also made the news recently. Some spectacular cases of babies joined at the head have been major stories in the past few years. From Iran, two handsome and articulate conjoined twenty-nine-year-old sisters were each so determined to be released from their appalling, endless, and completely merged selves that they risked death for surgical separation. And they both died in surgery. In the case of conjoined babies, I often miss the follow-up stories and don't know how each twin fared after separation.

Over and again in rebroadcasts, the twin towers separated and collapsed. I had hoped to make a collage work about the twin towers but found myself making one in which the towers play a small role in an overall theme of repetition, twinning, and separation caught in the glare of spotlights. From the news: twins who were driving in separate cars collide. From the war: twin brothers were serving in Iraq, and one is reported to have died. And in the realm of every day: hands are twins, joining and separating as they clap (applauding the war?). The old-fashioned film camera has twin reels that feed film through the camera. My twin sister in a large floppy white hat bends over her girl and boy twins, little Anna and Joe. Conjoined twins stand towerlike, together. I divide a drawing of a twin constellation from a Persian star chart into two heads, two bodies, two sets of legs and feet. The whole of *Twins: Conjoined and Separated* is a circle of repeating ideas and forms on translucent paper with gold-leafed borders. The piece takes details from the public sphere and blends them with my recurrent personal themes of twins, women, separation, and family.

Opposite: *Twins: Conjoined and Separated,* glassine with gold paint, watercolor, scanned photographs, constellation map of Gemini, newspaper clippings; 17-inch diameter circle on 22-inch × 20-inch square glassine sheet, ca. 2003

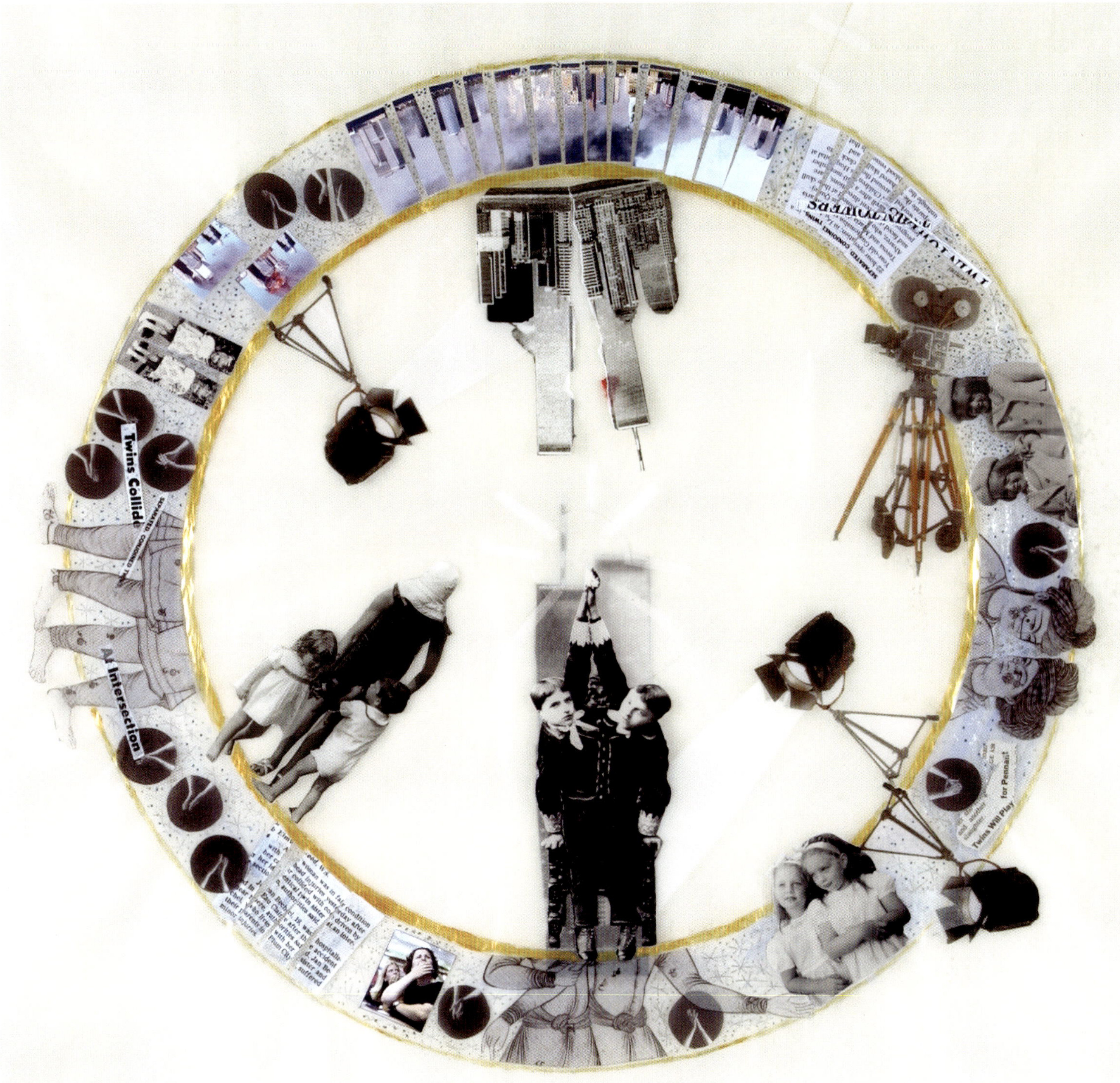
Twins Collide
At Intersection
Twins Will Play
for Pennant

Autobiography is not the story of a life; it is the recreation or the discovery of one. In writing of experience, we discover what it was, and in the writing create the pattern we seem to have lived. It is a revelation . . . to the reader and the writer. . . . Simply put, autobiography is a reckoning.
— *C. Heilbrun,* The Life of Gloria Steinem

Where does a mother's story end and a daughter's begin? That might be, after all, the central question of this book, the point of the autobiographical approach I've taken in putting this book together—to discover the lives in my own images, to remember the stories of my mother, to give the stories to my daughter, and to anyone else for whom these ideas and themes resonate.

Opposite: *In My Mother's Garden* from *Frieze,* Not Losing her Memory series, collage and white ink on silhouette paper, 8 ½ inches × 12 inches, 1991/1992

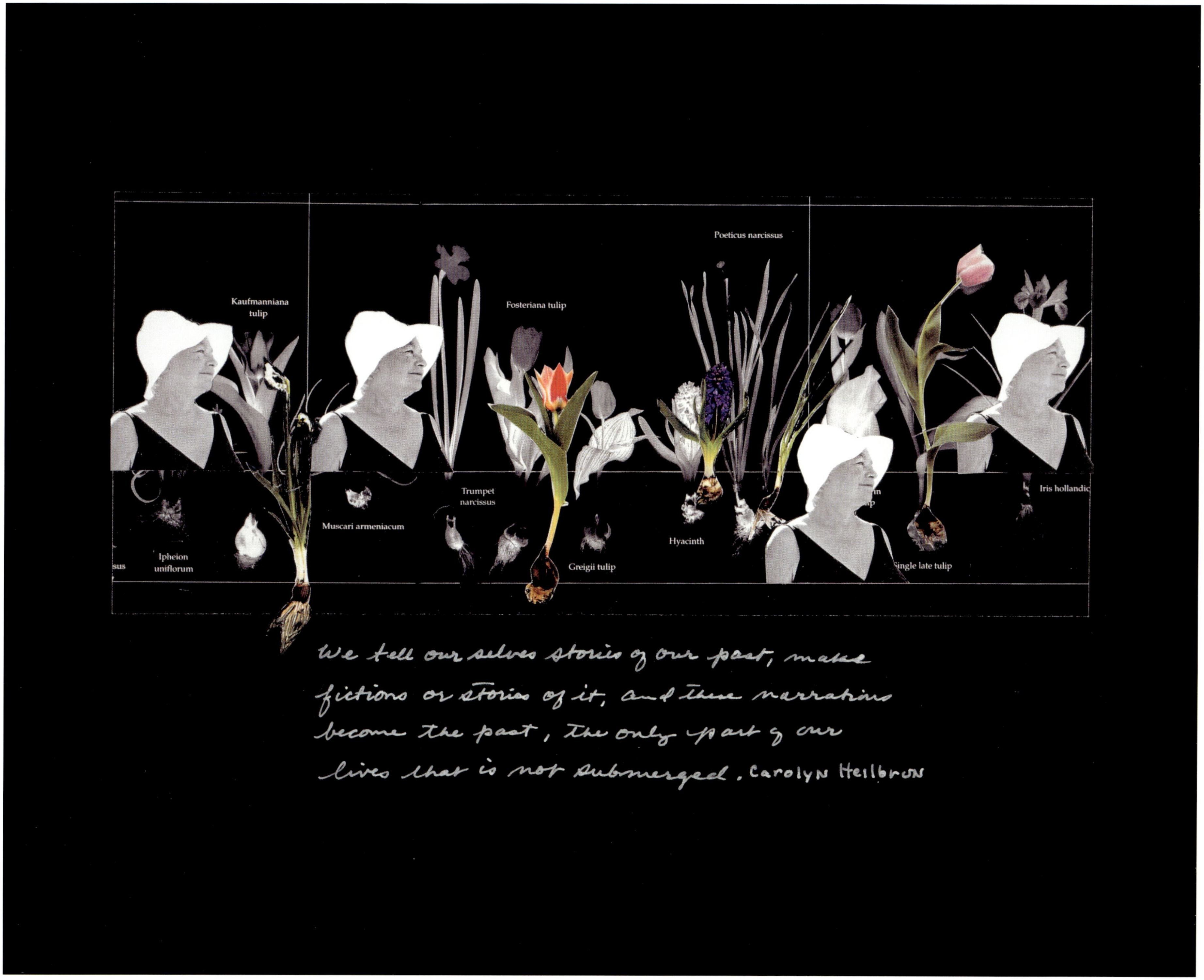
Kaufmanniana tulip
Fosteriana tulip
Poeticus narcissus
Trumpet narcissus
Muscari armeniacum
Ipheion uniflorum
Hyacinth
Greigii tulip
Single late tulip
Iris hollandic
We tell our selves stories of our past, make
fictions or stories of it, and these narrations
become the past, the only part of our
lives that is not submerged. Carolyn Heilbrun

Works Consulted

Adams, Timothy Dow, ed. *Autobiography, Photography, Narrative.* Special issue of *Modern Fiction Studies* 40, no. 3 (fall 1994).

Alexander, Christopher, Sara Ishikawa, and Murray Silverstein, with Max Jacobson. *A Pattern Language.* New York and Oxford: Oxford University Press, 1979.

Birmingham, Stephen. *Our Crowd: The Great Jewish Families of New York.* New York: Harper and Row, 1967. See esp. chap. 18.

Connell, Evan S., ed. *Woman by Three: Photographs by Joanne Leonard, Michael E. Bry and Barbara Cannon Myers.* Menlo Park, CA: Pacific Coast Publications, 1969.

Cook, Blanche Wiesen. *Eleanor Roosevelt.* Vol. 1, *1884–1933.* New York: Viking, 1992.

Eastman, Nicholson J. *William's Obstetrics.* 10th ed. New York: Appleton, Century, Crofts, 1950.

Glück, Louise. "A Fantasy." In *Ararat,* 16–17. New York: Ecco Press, 1990.

Goldstein, Laurence, ed. *The Female Body: Figures, Styles, Speculations.* Ann Arbor: University of Michigan Press, 1991.

Heilbrun, Carolyn. *The Education of a Woman: The Life of Gloria Steinem.* New York: Dial Press, 1995.

Heilbut, Anthony. *Exiled in Paradise: German Refugee Artists and Intellectuals in America from the 1930s to the Present.* Berkeley: University of California Press, 1983.

Hirsch, Marianne, ed. *The Familial Gaze.* Hanover, NH: University Press of New England, 1999.

Janson, H. W. *History of Art.* Rev. Anthony Janson. New York: Harry N. Abrams, 1986.

Leonard, Joanne. "Caring and Grieving: Part II." *Michigan Feminist Studies: Gender and Health,* no. 11 (1996–97): 99–110.

——. "Couple and Baby (Sonia Palmer and Fletcher Beasley)." Photograph. In "Prize Winning Pictures," by Richard Schnickel. *Life,* December 25, 1970, 80.

——. "Miscarriage/Ms. Carnage and Other Stories: A Visual Essay." In *Discourses of Sexuality: From Aristotle to AIDS,* ed. Domna Stanton, 297–311. Ann Arbor: University of Michigan Press, 1992.

——. "Not Losing Her Memory, Stories in Photographs, Words and Collage." In *Autobiography, Photography, Narrative,* ed. Timothy Dow Adams. *Modern Fiction Studies* 40, no. 3 (fall 1994): 657–85.

——. "Photography, Feminism and the Good Enough Mother." In *The Familial Gaze,* ed. Marianne Hirsch, 293–310. Hanover, NH: University Press of New England, 1999.

——. "Portfolio, 'Romanticism Is Ultimately Fatal' and 'Lost Dreams.'" Reproductions of photo collages. *Ms. Magazine,* June 1974, 92–93.

Mohr, Richard D. *Gay Ideas: Outing and Other Controversies.* Boston: Beacon Press, 1992.

Nochlin, Linda. "How Feminism in the Arts Can Implement Cultural Change." *Women and the Arts, Arts in Society* (spring–summer 1974): 86.

Rich, Adrienne. "Transcendental Etude." In *The Fact of a Doorframe: Poems Selected and New 1950–1984,* 264–69. New York: Norton, 1978.

Smith, Jessie Willcox. *Mother and Child.* Oil and pastel. In *Dream Blocks*, by S. Michael Schnessel, cover and 13. New York: Thomas Y. Crowell, 1908.

Sontag, Susan. *On Photography.* New York: Farrar, Straus, and Giroux, 1977.

Woolf, Virginia. *Moments of Being: Unpublished Autobiographical Writings.* Ed. Jeanne Shulkind. 2d ed. New York: Harcourt Brace, 1985.

Exhibitions

Artist's Chronology

Selected One-Person and Two-Person Exhibitions

2000 Correspondence(s), with Eleanor Rubin. Institute for the Humanities, University of Michigan, Ann Arbor, MI.

1995 Not Losing Her Memory. Schlesinger Library of Women's History, Radcliffe College, Cambridge, MA.

Not Losing Her Memory: Stories in Photographs, Words and Collage. University of Michigan Museum of Art, Ann Arbor, MI.

1988 Photographs and Photo Collages. Jeremy Stone Gallery, San Francisco, CA.

1987 Greenwood/Henke/Leonard Recent. Detroit Institute of Arts, Detroit, MI.

Twin Sisters: A Visual Connection, with Eleanor Rubin. Sarah Doyle Gallery, Brown University, Providence, RI.

1985 Ten Years. Jeremy Stone Gallery, San Francisco, CA.

1981 Photo/Trans/Forms, with Judith Golden. San Francisco Museum of Modern Art, San Francisco, CA.

1980 Inside and Beyond, ten-year retrospective. Laguna Gloria Art Museum, Austin, TX, and University of Michigan Art Museum, Ann Arbor, MI.

1975 Photographs and Collages. Bristol Polytechnic Art Gallery, Bristol, England.

1974 100 Photographs and Collages. Diego Riviera Gallery, San Francisco Art Institute, San Francisco, CA.

1972 Sapporo Olympics. Bank of America World Headquarters, San Francisco, CA.

1971 Leonard, Irene Poon, and Chris Enos. San Francisco Museum of Art, San Francisco, CA.

1969 Recent Photographs: Joanne Leonard. Seligman Gallery, Seattle, WA.

1968 Our Town. M. H. de Young Memorial Museum, San Francisco, CA, and Dartmouth College, Hopkins Center, Hanover, NH.

Group Exhibitions

2006 Disturbing the Peace, with Deborah Bright, Donna Ferrato, Holly Hughes, Carol Jacobsen, Susan Meiselas, Martha Rosler, Connie Samaras, Clarissa Sligh, and Pat Ward Williams. Bibro Gallery, New York, NY.

2004 About Face (Portraits). Denise Bibro Gallery, New York, NY.

2003 Duet. Ceres Gallery, New York, NY.

The Art of Aging. Hebrew Union College–Jewish Institute of Religion Museum, New York, NY.

2002 Camera Della Donna. Sheppard Fine Arts Gallery, University of Nevada, Reno, NV, and Heuser Art Gallery, Bradley University, Peoria, IL.

2001 Capturing Light, Masterpieces of California Photography, 1850–2000. Photographs in the Collection of the Oakland Museum of California, Oakland, CA.

Camera Della Donna. Elaine Jacobs Gallery, Wayne State University, Detroit, MI.

2000 Camera Della Donna. Tyler Rome Gallery, Rome, Italy.

1998 From the Sniper's Nest: Art That Has Lived with Lucy Lippard: The Collection of Lucy Lippard. Santa Fe Museum of Art, Santa Fe, NM.

1997 Eye of the Beholder: Photographs from the Avon Collection. International Center of Photography, New York, NY.

1996 The Familial Gaze: Dick Blau, Christian Boltanski, Darrel Ellis, Joanne Leonard, Sally Mann, Lorie Novak, Larry Sultan, Art Spiegelman, and Sarah Wells. Hood Museum, Dartmouth College, Hanover, NH.

From the Sniper's Nest: Art That Has Lived with Lucy Lippard. Originating at the Center for Curatorial Studies Museum, Bard College, Croton on Hudson, MA, and traveling.

1995 Imagined Children, Desired Images. Davis Art Museum, Wellesley College, Wellesley, MA.

Enigmas and Abstractions: Photographs from the Permanent Collection. Detroit Institute of Arts, Detroit, MI.

1992 Reframing Women's Health. New Works Gallery, University of Illinois at Chicago, Chicago, IL.

1990 Familial Territory. Hampshire College, Amherst, MA.

Photographers Collect Photography. Center Galleries, Center for Creative Studies, Detroit, MI.

1989 Post Photo. Hearst Art Gallery, St. Mary's College, Morago, CA.

Urbanology: Social Engagement. Focus Gallery, Detroit, MI, catalog.

1988 Through the Looking Glass. Bernice Steinbaum Gallery, New York, NY, and traveling.

Children of Our Times, a Photographic Essay: 1900–1988. Stephen Wirtz Gallery, San Francisco, CA.

Rites of Spring. University of Michigan Art Museum, Ann Arbor, MI.

1987 Andy Grundberg, *New York Times* Critic, Selects. Detroit Focus Gallery, Detroit, MI.

Gallery Artists. Jeremy Stone Gallery, San Francisco, CA.

1986 Baby Pictures. Santa Barbara Museum of Art, Santa Barbara, CA.

1985 Extending the Perimeters of 20th Century Photography. San Francisco Museum of Modern Art, San Francisco, CA.

Facets of the Collection, Light: From Illumination to Pure Radiance. San Francisco Museum of Modern Art, San Francisco, CA.

1984 International Competition and Exhibition of Women Photographers. Eighth Street Gallery, Los Angeles, CA.

Untitled. San Francisco Camera Work Gallery, San Francisco, CA.

Lensless Photography. IBM Gallery of Art and Science, New York, NY.

The Nude in Modern Photography. Society of Western Museums, traveling to seven museums and galleries throughout Canada and the United States.

1983 Lensless Photography. Franklin Institute, Philadelphia, PA.

Reframing Women's Health. New Works Gallery, University of Illinois at Chicago, Chicago, IL.

1982 Resource/Reservoir; Collage and Assemblage. San Francisco Museum of Modern Art, San Francisco, CA.

Contemporary Photography as Phantasy. Santa Barbara Museum of Art, Santa Barbara, CA.

New American Nudes. Contemporary Photography Gallery, Massachusetts Institute of Technology, catalog and book.

Recent Works. Grey Art Gallery, New York University, New York, NY.

Photography, with John Pfal and Olivia Parker. College of the Mainland Gallery, Texas City, TX.

1981 Facets of the Collection: The Nude in Modern Photography. San Francisco Museum of Modern Art, San Francisco, CA, catalog and traveling show.

Women/Image/Nature. Tyler School of Art, Temple University, Philadelphia, PA, catalog, and traveling to Anderson Gallery, Rochester Institute of Technology, Rochester, NY.

1979 Thirty Works by Fifteen Artists. Judah L. Magnes Museum, Berkeley, CA.

Five Year Anniversary Exhibition. 112 Green Street Gallery, New York, NY, catalog.

Insights. Marcuse Pfeifer Gallery, New York, NY.

1978 The Nude Male. Halsted Gallery, Birmingham, MI.

The Nude Male. Marcuse Pfeifer Gallery, New York, NY.

Out of the House. Whitney Museum of American Art, Downtown Branch, New York, NY.

Reflections: The Child in America. John F. Kennedy Center for the Performing Arts, Washington, DC.

Women See Men. Massachusetts Institute of Technology, Cambridge, MA.

Photocriticism. Art Gallery, University of Massachusetts, Amherst, MA, catalog.

1977 Book Works. Rare Book Room, Library, Mills College, Oakland, CA.

The Male: A Woman's View. San Francisco Camera Work, San Francisco, CA.

First Exhibit of Permanent Collection of Photography. Stanford University Art Museum, Palo Alto, CA.

American Photography: Past into Present. Seattle Art Museum, Monsen Collection, Seattle, WA.

Photo Synthesis. Herbert F. Johnson Museum, Cornell University, Ithaca, NY.

Untitled. 112 Green Street Gallery, New York, NY.

1976 The Eyes Have It. Fine Arts Museum of San Francisco, Downtown Center, San Francisco, CA.

1975–76 Women of Photography—An Historical Survey. San Francisco Museum of Art, San Francisco, CA, and traveling to Museum of the University of New Mexico, Santa Fe, NM; Wellesley College Museum, Wellesley, MA; Sidney Janis Gallery, New York, NY; and Rice University Art Museum, Houston, TX.

1975 Ten Teachers of Creative Photography. Friends of Photography Gallery, Carmel, CA.

1974 Directions, '74. Focus Gallery, San Francisco, CA.

1973 Women's Image. Boston University, Boston, MA, and traveling to Threads, Floating Foundation of Photography, New York, NY; and Women U.S.A., Laguna Beach Museum of Art, Laguna Beach, CA.

1972 Summer Light. Light Gallery, New York, NY.

Critic's Choice. Focus Gallery, San Francisco, CA.

1971–72 Photo Media. Museum of Contemporary Crafts, New York, NY.

1971 John D. Phelan Awards Exhibit. Oakland Museum, Oakland, CA.

1970–74	American Photographers. American Arts Documentation Centre, University of Exeter, Exeter, England, and traveling.
1969–70	Vision and Expression: Contemporary Photographers. George Eastman House, Rochester, NY.
1969	The City of Man. Bergman Gallery, University of Chicago, Chicago, IL.
	California Photographers. Pasadena Art Museum, Pasadena, CA.

Selected List of Public Collections

1970–2006	Detroit Institute of the Arts, Detroit, MI
	San Francisco Museum of Modern Art, San Francisco, CA
	Crocker Art Museum, Sacramento, CA
	Stanford University Art Museum, Palo Alto, CA
	University of Massachusetts Art Museum, Amherst, MA
	International Museum of Photography, George Eastman House, Rochester, NY
	American Arts Documentation Centre, University of Exeter, Exeter, England
	Oakland Museum, Oakland, CA
	U.S. State Department, Art in Embassies Collection

Publications

Writing and Images by Joanne Leonard

2002	"Marlene and Me" (essay with thirty-four images, many in color). In *Changing Focus: Family Photography & American Jewish Identity,* ed. Laura Levitt. *The Scholar & Feminist Online,* www.barnard.edu/sfonline. New York: Center for Research on Women at Barnard College.
1999	"Photography, Feminism and the Good Enough Mother" (essay with color plate *Letting Her Go with Difficulty* and six other images). In *The Familial Gaze,* ed. Marianne Hirsch, 293–310. Hanover, NH: University Press of New England.
1997	"Caring and Grieving: Part II" (essay with reproduction of *Romanticism Is Ultimately Fatal*). *Michigan Feminist Studies: Gender and Health,* no. 11 (1996–97): 99–110.
1995	"Not Losing Her Memory, Stories in Photographs, Words and Collage" (essay with nineteen images). In *Autobiography, Photography, Narrative,* ed. Timothy Dow Adams. Special issue of *Modern Fiction Studies* 40, no. 3 (fall 1994): 657–85.
1994	"Not Losing Her Memory: Images of Family in Photography, Words and Collage" (essay with five images from Not Losing Her Memory photo collage series). In *Changing Perceptions of Aging and the Aged,* ed. Dena Shenk and W. Andrew Achenbaum, 3–9. New York: Springer.
1992	"Miscarriage/Ms. Carnage and Other Stories: A Visual Essay" (essay with seven photo collages). In *Discourses of Sexuality: From Aristotle to AIDS,* ed. Domna Stanton, 297–311. Ann Arbor: University of Michigan Press.
1987	With Eleanor Rubin, eds. *Sisters, A Complex Destiny,* published by the editors with funds granted by the Massachusetts Foundation for Arts and Humanities.

1976 "October Dreams" (photo collage). In *From the Center: Feminist Essays on Women's Art,* by Lucy R. Lippard, 32. New York: E. P. Dutton.

1974 "Portfolio, 'Romanticism Is Ultimately Fatal' and 'Lost Dreams'" (color reproductions of photo collages). *Ms. Magazine,* June 1974, 92–93.

1973 "Portfolio: Photographs by Joanne Leonard" (eight photos). *Creative Camera,* no. 103 (January 1973): 6–9.

Selected Critical Writing by Others

2004 *Romanticism Is Ultimately Fatal* (color reproduction of photo collage with discussion). In *History of Art: The Western Tradition,* by H. W. Janson, 6th ed., rev. A. F. Janson, 940. Englewood Cliffs, NJ: Prentice Hall.

2003 *Reel Family* (detail of photo collage). In *Jewish in America,* ed. S. Blair and J. Freedman. Special issue of *Michigan Quarterly Review* 42, no. 1 (winter 2003): frontispiece.

2001 *Children Hugging* (photo, biography and photo of artist, discussion). In *Capturing Light: Masterpieces of California Photography, 1850–2000,* ed. Drew Heath Johnson, 236, 338, 200. Oakland, CA: Oakland Museum.

2000 *Four Generations, One Absent* (photo collage). In *Light Writing & Life Writing: Photography in Autobiography,* by Timothy Dow Adams, 241. Chapel Hill and London: University of North Carolina Press.

Sonia, 1966 (photo), two images from *Journal of a Miscarriage, 1973* (discussion). In *Pregnant Pictures: The Work of Women in the Age of Mechanical Reproduction,* ed. Sandra Matthews and Laura Wexler, 47–48, 78–79. New York and London: Routledge.

1998 *Julia, One Week Old* and *Family Album* (photos with discussion). In *Pictures of Innocence: The History and Crisis of Ideal Childhood,* ed. Anne Higonnet, 140–41, 209. London: Thames and Hudson.

1994 *Granddad and Twins* and *Father and Daughter* (photos). In *Dads,* by Bruce Velik, 2, 31. New York: Harmony Books.

1992 *Joanne Leonard: Not Losing Her Memory—Stories in Photographs, Words and Collage,* with catalog essay by Lucy Lippard (eleven photo collages on cover and 6–9). Ann Arbor: University of Michigan Museum of Art.

Julia, One Week Old (photo). In *Baby, Baby, Sweet Baby,* by Bruce Velick, 24. San Francisco: Pomegranate Art Books.

Of Things Masculine (photo collage with discussion). In *Gay Ideas: Outing and Other Controversies,* by Richard D. Mohr, 191–92. Boston: Beacon Press.

1991 *Julia and the Window of Vulnerability* (photo collage, color plate, and discussion). In *Gardner's Art through the Ages,* 9th ed., ed. D. Kirkpatrick, H. de la Croix, and R. Tansey, xv, 358, 1056. San Diego: Harcourt Brace Jovanovich.

Three images from *Journal of a Miscarriage, 1973.* In "The Body in the Woman, the Story in the Woman: A Book Review and Personal Essay," by Ruth Behar, in *The Female Body: Figures, Styles, Speculations,* ed. Laurence Goldstein, 268, 277, 306. Ann Arbor: University of Michigan Press.

1988 *Julia with Eclipse* (photo collage). In *Through the Looking Glass,* by John Perreault and Bernice Steinbaum, 33. New York: Bernice Steinbaum Gallery.

1986 *Romanticism Is Ultimately Fatal* (photo collage with discussion). In *History of Art,* by H. W. Janson, 3d ed., rev. A. F. Janson, 781–83. New York: Harry N. Abrams.

1984 *Sad Dreams on Cold Mornings* (photo collage with discussion). In *Photography in California 1945–80,* by Louise Katzman, 54, 57, 91, 93. San Francisco: San Francisco Museum of Modern Art, and Manchester, VT: Hudson Hills Press.

1981 *Julia, One Week Old* (photo). In *New American Nudes,* by Arno Minkkinen. Dobbs Ferry, NY: Morgan & Morgan.

1980 *Of Things Masculine* (photo collage). In *The Male Nude in Photography,* by Lawrence Barnes, 64. Waitsfield, VT: Vermont Crossroads Press.

1979 *Inside and Beyond, Photographs by Joanne Leonard,* with a catalog essay by Lucy Lippard (color cover and seven other images). Austin, TX: Laguna Gloria Art Museum.

Sonia, 1966 and *Rachel and Julia in Rocker* (photos). In *The Family of Women,* ed. Jerry Mason, 107, 124. New York: Ridge Press, Grosset and Dunlop.

Noel, Falicitas, and *Child with Mask* (photos). In *La famille des enfants: un panorama photographique mondial de l'enfance,* ed. Jerry Mason, 51, 52, 89. Paris: Ridge Press, Flammarion et Cie.

Variations on a Sleeping Theme and *Self-portrait with Frog and Sperm* (photo collages with discussion). In *In/Sights: Self-Portraits by Women,* comp. Joyce Tenneson Cohen, vii, 16, 17, 124. Boston: David R. Godine.

1977 *Bruce in Mirror* and *Ben at Two* (photos). In *Women See Men,* ed. Yvonne Klamus, Rikki Ripp, and Cheryl Wiesenfeld, 46–47. New York: McGraw Hill.

1976 *Two Views in the Morning: Umbrella Stand* (photos). In *American Photography, Past into Present: Prints from the Monsen Collection of American Photography,* ed. Anita Mozley, 116. Seattle: Seattle Art Museum.

Falicitas (photo). In *Women See Women,* ed. Yvonne Kalmus et al., 65. New York: Thomas Crowell.

Take the Key and Lock Her Up (photo collage with discussion). In *Photo/Synthesis,* ed. Jason Wong, 13. Ithaca, NY: Herbert F. Johnson Museum of Art, Cornell University.

1975 *Romanticism Is Ultimately Fatal* (photo collage with discussion). In *Women of Photography: An Historical Survey,* ed. Margery Mann and Ann Noggle. San Francisco: San Francisco Museum.

1972 *Sad Dreams on Cold Mornings* and *Lost Dreams* (color reproductions of photo collages with discussion). In "Darkroom Transformations," in *Life Library of Photography: Frontiers of Photography,* ed. Richard L. Williams, 88–89. New York: Time Life Books.

1970 *Sonia, 1966* (photo). In *Life Library of Photography: The Great Themes,* ed. Richard L. Williams, 14. New York: Time Life Books.

Couple and Baby (photo). In "Prize Winning Pictures," by Richard Schnickel. *Life,* December 25, 1970, 80.

1969 *Masked Boy* (photo). In *Vision and Expression: An International Survey of Contemporary Photography,* by Nathan Lyons, 18. New York: Horizon Press.

Thirty-one photographs. In *Woman by Three: Photographs by Joanne Leonard, Michael E. Bry and Barbara Cannon Myers,* ed. Evan S. Connell, 1–31. Menlo Park, CA: Pacific Coast Publishers.

Acknowledgments

My indebtedness is beyond calculation. This book would simply not exist without the help, support, affection, and inspiration of those listed here.

First and foremost, my thanks and gratitude to my parents, Marjorie (1905–92) and Alfred (1909–88), whose presence I feel daily in everything I do; and to the rest of my family, who have offered their help and suffered my neglect as I concentrated on the book: my daughter, Julia; my sisters Elly and Barbara; and Carol Jacobsen, who has been like family throughout, probably hearing more of the complaints during hard times and cheers during happier ones than any other person except Elly.

To my most significant and treasured teacher, the photographer/anthropologist John Collier Jr.; and to gallery and museum people who have shown and championed my work, particularly Theresa Heyman (Curator of Photography at The Oakland Museum of California Art, who brought my archive of West Oakland work to the museum's permanent collection) and Jeremy Stone (Jeremy Stone Gallery). Also to those friends and neighbors who allowed my photographs of them to be used in this book.

To Celeste Novak, architect of my wonderful home studio, where I spent countless hours working on my book, as well as to the School of Art and Design for generously assigning me the studio where I sorted photographs and worked on the book's design.

To my friends, family, and colleagues at the University of Michigan who read this manuscript (in some cases, many times) and who offered invaluable suggestions, particularly Margaret Lourie, who provided invaluable professional editing and collegial support. Other cherished and crucial readers were Abby Stewart, Sidonie Smith, Kali Handelman, Kristin Hass, Diane Kirkpatrick, Carol Jacobsen, Helen Nestor, David Rubin, Elly Rubin, Joanne Reuss, Ruth Reynolds, Andrea Sankar, Cathy Smillie, Sarah Trinkaus, Harriet Whelan, and Reneé Rose Shield.

To the feminist artists and scholars from whom, as editors, authors, correspondents, and friends, I've derived support for my work: Sidra Ezrahi, Anne Higonnet, Marianne Hirsch, Lucy Lippard, Griselda Pollock, and Mimi Schapiro.

To the senior executive editor at the University of Michigan Press, LeAnn Fields, without whose interest, friendship, editing skills, and patience this book would never have happened. And to everyone else at the University of Michigan Press whose work has been essential to this book's success.

To Bryan Rogers, dean of the School of Art and Design, without whose general and generous support I could not have succeeded, and to other School of Art and Design administrators, faculty, and staff, whose support I have felt so keenly. To student assistants from the Undergraduate Research Opportunity Program (UROP) Xuelun (Brandon) Li and Seungyeon (Sunny) Chung, who helped with the image selection process, as well as UROP students from earlier years who helped me put my years of photographs into reasonable order.

To the campus units that provided funding for my work on the book and toward meeting the costs of publication: the Institute for Research on Women and Gender; the School of Art and Design; Rackham School of Graduate Studies; Office of the Vice President for Research; Office of the Senior Counselor to the President for Arts, Diversity, and Undergraduate Affairs; the Frankel Center for Judaic Studies; and the Office of the Provost. And to the private parties who gave money to help produce the book: Judith Adell; Dare Association Inc. of Cambridge, Massachusetts, and its president, Michael Lamport Commons; and Sarah Trinkaus.

To the American Academy in Rome, where I spent nearly six weeks as a visiting artist and scholar and began to write the text. And to the colleagues there who offered useful criticism as well as encouragement.

To John Palmer for his extraordinary skill in creating and correcting the scans from which the book's fine reproductions were made. To David and Peter Smith and Vicci Veenstra for photography of my artwork and to Foto One and Precision Photo, which provided photo services. And to my invaluable studio assistant and incomparable friend, Karen Zaher, an artist in her own right.

Finally, to all those, no less dear or important, whom I have not managed to acknowledge in print, I express my heartfelt gratitude.

Page 11
Picture taking and posing, *clockwise from left:*

Eleanor Whelan (O'Neill), Julia Leonard, Hillary Whelan (Reyl), and Harriet Whelan, Villers-en-Ouche, France; silver print, 1979

Leroy family, with Eleanor (Whelan), Julia (Leonard), and Hillary (Whelan), Villers-en-Ouche, France; silver print, 1979

Hillary Whelan photographing Eleanor Whelan, Los Angeles, silver print, ca. 1973

Tony Veit and others photographing Susan Veit and others, Ann Arbor, silver print, mid-1980s

Pages 35 and 36
Four old friends with babies and reunion of lifelong friends: Sonia (Mathias) Beasley, Judy Fuss Adell, Harriet (Blumstein) Whelan, and Jeannie Kamins

Page 51
Pairs, *clockwise from left:* wedding preparations, West Oakland, 1970; couple watching television, West Berkeley, 1976; girl and man with guitar, West Oakland, mid-1960s; couple on couch, Barbara and Leo Reed, West Oakland, mid-1960s

Page 67
Sleeping series, *top row, from left:* dog at Manuel's, *Another Morning* (sleeping house guest), Elly

middle row: Julia, my dad, Bruce (Merida, Mexico)

bottom row: Julia; dogs at Manuel's; Palmer, Sonia, and Monica

Page 73
Dreams and Nightmares series, *left to right, top to bottom: Merida Morning; Lost Dreams; Death for a Wife; Erotic Dreams; Last Dreams of September, Cold Weather Coming; Sad Dreams on Cold Mornings;* San Francisco Museum of Modern Art

Page 143
Julia, *top row, from left:* Julia with Rachel, first birthday, with water whistle

middle row: hands on hips, with two girls in hammock (her cousin Anna and friend), in camp shirt

bottom row: in cat bathing suit, preteen with frilly skirt and gloves, in Paris

Page 152
Photograph by Patrick Young

Page 222
Details, *from left to right: Julia with Wings;* Sarah Bernhardt caricature, detail from *Running in the Family*

Page 223
Details from various works, various sizes, *left to right, top to bottom: Running in the Family;* Joanne and Elly; conjoined twins (probably the Tocci brothers), detail from *Running in the Family*; Joanne's grandmother (photo by Edward Weston, 1934), detail (reversed) from *Conversation: My Mother and Her Mother;* walking figure made from portrait of grandmother

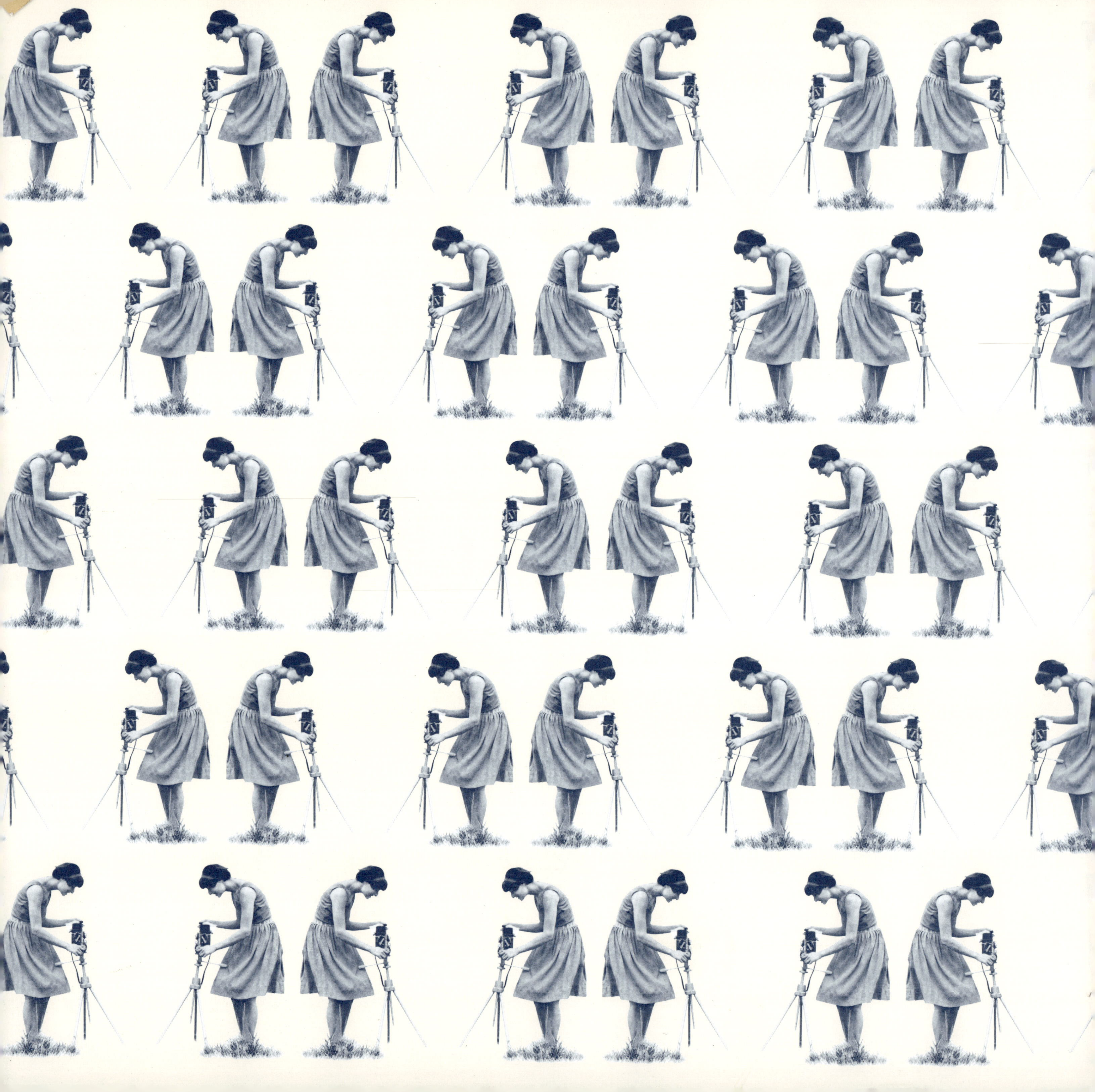